ISAAC ALBÉNIZ
Portrait of a Romantic

Albéniz entertaining friends in Nice

Isaac Albéniz
Portrait of a Romantic

Walter Aaron Clark

OXFORD
UNIVERSITY PRESS

OXFORD

UNIVERSITY PRESS

Oxford University Press, Great Clarendon Street, Oxford OX2 6DP

Oxford New York

Athens Auckland Bangkok Bogotá Buenos Aires Calcutta
Cape Town Chennai Dar es Salaam Delhi Florence Hong Kong Istanbul
Karachi Kuala Lumpur Madrid Melbourne Mexico City Mumbai
Nairobi Paris São Paulo Singapore Taipei Tokyo Toronto Warsaw

and associated companies in
Berlin Ibadan

Oxford is a trade mark of Oxford University Press

Published in the United States
by Oxford University Press Inc., New York

British Library Cataloguing in Publication Data

Data available

Library of Congress Cataloging in Publication Data
Clark, Walter Aaron.
Isaac Albéniz: portrait of romantic/Walter Araon Clark.
p. cm.
'List of works': p.
Includes bibliographical reference (p.) and indexes.
1. Albéniz, Isaac, 1860–1909.   2. Composers—Spain—Biography.
I. Title.
ML410.A3C53   1999   780'.92—dc21   [B]   97–32612

ISBN 0–19–816369–X

1 3 5 7 9 10 8 6 4 2

Typeset by Pure Tech India Ltd, Pondicherry
http://www.puretech.com
Printed in Great Britain
on acid-free paper by
Bookcraft Ltd, Midsomer Norton, Somerset

To Nancy and Robert

Acknowledgements

F OR over three decades, I have derived enormous pleasure and satisfaction from the music of Isaac Albéniz, as both a listener and a performer. For most of that time, however, the idea of writing a comprehensive study of his life and music was as distant and vague as the Magellanic Clouds. Now (suddenly, it seems to me) it is a reality. This project would never have reached fruition, however, without the generous assistance of so many people who shared their guidance and research. They have placed me under a debt that I cannot repay but that I gratefully acknowledge below and will never forget.

London: Barbara J. Peters, head of the Latymer Archive at the bank of Coutts & Co., and the 8th Lord Latymer, great-grandson of Francis Money-Coutts. Thanks also go to the British Library, the Westminster City Archives, and the Greater London Record Office and History Library. Clifford Bevan, the leading English authority on Albéniz, also deserves a sincere expression of thanks for sharing with me his excellent research on Albéniz's operas and English connections. I am also grateful to the Scottish musicologist Derek Watson, who graciously renounced the opportunity to write this biography for Oxford. I especially appreciate the interest and faith shown in this project by Bruce Phillips, senior music editor at Oxford University Press, and the excellent editorial work of his staff, in particular Jackie Pritchard, Helen Foster, and Janet Moth. *Brussels*: the library of the Conservatoire Royal, the Bibliothèque Royale Albert Ier, and the archive of the Théâtre de la Monnaie. *Leipzig*: the library of the Hochschule für Musik Felix Mendelssohn-Bartholdy, the music library of the city of Leipzig, and the Staatsarchiv and Stadtarchiv. *Prague*: the Municipal and National Libraries, and in particular Roman Lindauer, without whose timely assistance my work would have been much more difficult. *Budapest*: Maria Eckhardt of the Liszt Ferenc Memorial Museum and Research Centre, for her thorough investigations conducted on my behalf. *Paris*: Catherine Rochon of the Conservatoire National Supérieur de Musique et de Danse de Paris; the Bibliothèque Nationale and Archives Nationales for their patient assistance; and the firm of Max Eschig for its generosity. *Barcelona*: Ayuntamiento de Barcelona; Rosa Busquets of the library of the Museu Marítim; the Arxiu Municipal; Romà Escalas and his cordial assistants at the Museu de la Música, in particular Judit Bombardó; the Biblioteca de Catalunya; and the Arxiu Històric de la Ciutat. I am also indebted to Josefina Sastre of the Orfeó Català and the theatre museum of the Palau Güell for their help. I benefited from the assistance of the Arxiu Diocesa of the Arquebisbat de Barcelona, the Institut Universitari de Documentació i Investigació Musicològica Josep Ricart i Matas, María Luisa Beltrán Sábat of the Institut Municipal dels Serveis Funeraris de Barcelona, and Amparo Valera of the Teatre Romea. The musicologist Dr Monserrat Bergadà provided invaluable research support. Heartfelt thanks go to Albéniz's granddaughter Rosina

Moya Albéniz de Samsó for her hospitality and largess. *Granada*: María Isabel de
Falla and the Archivo Manuel de Falla for providing me access to Albéniz manuscripts
in their collection. I am also grateful to Dr Marta Falces Sierra for her assistance.
Madrid: Rafael Campos and the Secretaría of the Real Conservatorio; the Biblioteca
Nacional, Hemeroteca Nacional, the Hemeroteca Municipal, Archivo Histórico de la
Villa, Archivo del Palacio Real, Archivo General de la Administración, Archivo de la
Dirección General de Costes de Personal y Pensiones Públicas, and the Registro Civil;
Lola Higueras of the Museo Naval, and Antonio Gil of the Sociedad General de
Autores de España. I also wish to thank the Sociedad Española de Musicología and
the Fundación Isaac Albéniz for their assistance and generosity. I am extremely
grateful to the eminent musicologist Dr Jacinto Torres Mulas, the leading Spanish
authority on Albéniz, whose moral support and generous sharing of material were
essential to the completion of this book. *United States*: the libraries at the University
of California, Los Angeles, and the University of Kansas for their assistance. Thanks
go to the pianist and Albéniz scholar Dr Pola Baytelman Dobry for her research and
invitations to lecture. I also appreciate the expert proofreading of my late friend
Steven Gnagy and the assistance of Drs Alan Pasco and Kathleen Comfort in the
French department. My overseas research was made possible by funding from the Del
Amo Endowment (on two separate occasions) and the Program for Cultural Coop-
eration between Spain's Ministry of Culture and United States' Universities (also
twice awarded). In addition, these investigations were supported by University of
Kansas General Research allocation no. 3466. Additional research money was provided by the University of Kansas in the form of a New Faculty Reseach Grant. I wish
to thank my doctoral adviser, Dr Robert Murrell Stevenson, for his encouragement
and the invaluable example of his own work. I am also grateful to my friends Peter and
Mimi Farrell, Bill Jaynes, and my mother-in-law Grace Golden for their help and
interest in my work. Finally, thanks go to my wife Nancy and son Robert for their
patient understanding and support.

                                                                    W.A.C.

Lawrence
1997

Contents

List of Plates

List of Tables

Abbreviations

Ah Albéniz house, the current residence of Rosina Moya Albéniz de Samsó (the daughter of Albéniz's daughter Laura) in the Barcelona area

Bc Biblioteca de Catalunya, Barcelona. Albéniz's correspondence is located under signatura (sig.) M986, in alphabetical order according to author

Bn Biblioteca Nacional, Madrid

L Latymer Archive, Coutts & Co., London

Lc Library of Congress

LCM *La correspondencia musical*

Ls Staatsarchiv Leipzig

Mc Real Conservatorio, Madrid

MGG *Die Musik in Geschichte und Gegenwart* (new edn., Personenteil)

Mm Museu Municipal de la Música, Barcelona. 'Car.' stands for the *carpetas*, or boxes, in which the items are kept. Letters not in *carpetas* are organized by number, e.g. 10.031

Oc Biblioteca del Orfeó Català, Barcelona

Se Sociedad General de Autores de España, Madrid

List of Musical Examples

Sevilla, Triana, El Puerto—and your spirit and my spirit!—
The sonorous Guadalquivir,
Everything, in eternity, will sail in a calm
Of illusion and of gold!

(Juan Ramón Jiménez, 'To Isaac Albéniz')

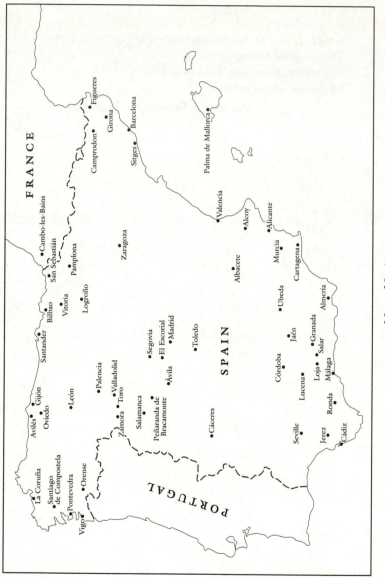

Map of Spain

Introduction

Step by Step

———

THE year 1909 represented a significant milestone in the passage from the Romantic period to the Modern. German expressionism was in full career as Wassily Kandinsky painted his first abstract *Compositions* and Arnold Schoenberg experimented with atonality in his monodrama *Erwartung* and the *Five Orchestral Pieces*, Op. 16. Igor Stravinsky began collaborating with Sergey Diaghilev on *The Firebird* ballet for its 1910 premiere in Paris, where Pablo Picasso was laying the foundation for cubism in his paintings *Harlequin* and *Ambroise Vollard*. Sigmund Freud lectured to American audiences on psychoanalysis, and Frank Lloyd Wright designed his innovative Robie House in Chicago. The king who gave his name to a decade of relative calm and prosperity, Edward VII, was in the last full year of his reign.

At 7.15 p.m. on 5 June of that eventful year, a train bearing a casket from the French Pyrenees pulled into the estació de França on the east side of Barcelona near the harbour. The station, serving as a funeral chapel for the occasion, was fragrant with the scent of numerous floral arrangements sent by the Orfeó Català, Acadèmia Granados, Real Conservatorio in Madrid, city councils of Camprodon and Tiana, Asociació Municipal de Barcelona, and many other organizations and individuals. Throughout the night, friends and admirers of the deceased maintained a vigil as the public filed by to view the corpse. The following day dawned partly cloudy, humid, and warm, moderated by a refreshing breeze that blew in from the Mediterranean.[1] At 9.15 a.m., a great multitude of people began to congregate in the patio of the station, mainly representatives of various organizations of writers, painters, sculptors, architects, scientists, and economists, as well as musicians and politicians bearing their various banners and standards. Gradually large numbers of onlookers formed around the nucleus of officialdom. Fifteen minutes later, mounted troops of the municipal guard arrived holding aloft the city flag, trimmed with the black crepe of mourning. At 9.45 other

[1] Humidity 90%, temp. 31.5 °C (89°F), wind at 20 km/hr. (12 miles/hr.).

dignitaries appeared, including the mayor, the governor, and members of the provincial administration. At 10.15, the crowd listened reverently as the municipal band performed Siegfried's funeral music from Wagner's *Die Götterdämmerung* while leading the procession bearing the coffin from the chapel to the hearse. As the pall bearers loaded the coffin into the hearse and covered it completely with flowers, the strains of Fauré's Requiem (performed by the Orfeó Català) floated over the sombre scene. Then the procession began moving slowly through the centre of the city toward the final resting place. Two horses drew the hearse, which was surrounded by six acolytes bearing torches and accompanied by police and members of the press. The rows of balconies above the streets were festooned in black crepe and Catalan flags, the sidewalks crowded with the public in their thousands watching in mournful silence as the cortège moved solemnly forward to the measured beat of Chopin's *Funeral March*. In the procession were represent-atives of the Gran Teatre del Liceu and the Asociació Wagneriana. Many students from the university and members of the various faculties joined in the procession bearing flowers to deposit on the tomb. The cortège paused for ten minutes in front of the Escola Municipal de Música so that its students could place flowers on the hearse. Further on it passed the barracks of an artillery detachment, and the soldiers lined up in formation to present a martial salute to the deceased celebrity. Roses, violets, and carnations of every colour rained down from the balconies above, offered by hundreds of ordinary citizens paying their final respects to one of the city's most famous figures. The cortège wended its way through various streets and plazas and then down the celebrated Rambla, stopping in front of the Gran Teatre del Liceu and its adjacent conservatory so that yet more music students could place their bouquets atop the hearse's burgeoning floral burden. The offices of the local newspapers, which had not always been the best friend of the departed when he was alive and productive, now exhibited façades respectfully draped in black.

Finally, at a quarter past one in the afternoon, the hearse's journey through Barcelona ended at the grave site in a cemetery on the eastern, seaward slope of historic Montjuïc.[2] Family members and government officials assumed places of prominence, and the casket, freshly adorned with yet more carnations and roses, was lowered into the grave. The two hundred or so persons present at the graveside consisted mostly of artists, writers, journalists, and friends. Finally, the mayor began to speak. He thanked all

---

[2] Now known as the Cementiri del Sud-Oest. The tomb lies near a monument dedicated to French soldiers fallen in battle. The precise address is Panteón número 20, via St. Jaume, Agrupació 8ª.

those who made the splendid memorial possible, and expressed gratitude to
the family for returning to native soil the mortal remains of one of its
most distinguished sons. 'The glorious labour of the illustrious composer
constitutes by itself a monument that will immortalize his name,' he
declared.[3] After a few other remarks and some emotional embraces between
the deceased's son Alfonso and the speakers, the ceremony came to an end at
precisely 2 p.m.[4]

Thus concluded the larger journey through life itself of the Spanish pianist
and composer Isaac Albéniz. Shortly after Albéniz's death on 18 May 1909,
his close friend Tomás Bretón wrote of him: 'If his life could have been
recorded step by step, the book would constitute one of the most curious
and pleasing of its genre.'[5] It has been this author's privilege (and, at times,
burden) to attempt to retrace Albéniz's steps through a remarkable career
that has assumed almost legendary proportions. The result of these labours is
a story that is indeed curious at times, and at the very least, one hopes,
pleasing.

Albéniz's death at the age of 49 was a great loss for Spanish music, but one
cannot escape the suspicion that in the twelve piano pieces of *Iberia* (completed a year before his death) Albéniz had given, as Debussy believed, the
best he had to offer. It is hard to imagine what he could have done to top it;
certainly the works he left unfinished at his death held no promise of doing
so. And it is even harder to imagine how he would have found his place in the
new world of abstraction and atonality. For Albéniz genuinely was a product
of the Romantic period now drawing to a close along with his own life. In his
persistent longing for a Spain that existed mostly in his imagination, in his
ceaseless flow of melodic inspiration, in his restless striving for public acclaim,
and especially in his mischievous penchant for reinventing his past, Albéniz
revealed himself a true romantic. He had staved off physical collapse just long
enough to say what he had come into the world to say. In *Iberia* he brought
forth a bona fide masterpiece, without doubt one of the greatest collections
of keyboard works ever written, and the foremost by a Spanish composer in
the modern era.

For good reason, then, Albéniz is best known to concert audiences today
for his piano works inspired by Spanish folk music, though he also essayed

[3] 'La labor gloriosa del ilustre compositor, constituye por si sola un monumento que inmortalizará su
nombre.'

[4] This entire account is a summary of a newspaper clipping without title or date found in the Albéniz
archive in the Mm, car. 3. A shorter report appeared on the front page of *La vanguardia*, 7 June 1909.

[5] 'En la muerte de Albéniz', *ABC* (21 May 1909), 4–5; repr. in Enrique Franco (ed.), *Albéniz y su tiempo*
(Madrid: Fundación Isaac Albéniz, 1990), 121. 'Si se pudiera escribir paso a paso su vida, constituiría el libro
uno de los más curiosos y amenos de esta índole.'

songs and musical theatre. His compositions have retained their popularity for well over a century, and his circle of admirers continues to grow due in no small measure to the dissemination of his works in guitar transcription. The majority of these piano pieces—such as 'Leyenda', 'Córdoba', 'Sevilla', and 'Granada'—owe this popularity to their highly accessible character. They derive their inspiration from appealingly exotic locales in Spain and are eminently lyrical, straightforward in structure, and full of the rhythmic verve so characteristic of Spanish folklore.

Musicologists, particularly those steeped in the Germanic tradition, are prone to dismiss these pre-*Iberia* nationalist creations as mere salon music.[6] After all, they are quasi-programmatic and depend on repetition and colour for their effect. Albéniz was not a symphonist and their structure is not developmental in nature. But this should not lead us to overlook them or the composer, for three reasons. First, though salon music was the popular music of the nineteenth-century bourgeoisie, there was no clear dividing line between it and 'high art' music, such as exists today between the works of, say, Karlheinz Stockhausen and the music of the Rolling Stones. Many composers worked successfully in both areas, and the same middle-class audiences patronized both types of music. Albéniz, for instance, also composed piano sonatas and concertos, a choral work, and several operas. *Iberia* has much in common with the earlier piano pieces mentioned above but crosses over into the realm of high art by virtue of its complexity and enormous technical difficulty. Second, for all their popular appeal, these pieces by Albéniz exhibit a certain refinement and sophistication. Their immediacy is deceptive and leads us to the mistaken conclusion that closer examination will yield few insights. If the goal of our analysis is to discover the encroachment of atonality or the presence of subtle narratological paradigms, then we may indeed come away empty-handed. But if we look at a wider range of possibilities, especially the idiomatic handling of the performing medium, sources of influence, the nature and origin of folkloric references, and the dynamic between public taste and personal musical vision, then even these earlier works by Albéniz have a great deal to offer the analyst. Finally, if the discipline of musicology has advanced to the point where it can treat seriously such icons of popular culture as Madonna and Heavy Metal groups, then certainly Albéniz and other composers of popular music in the last century merit no less scrutiny.

---

[6] For example, Carl Dahlhaus's *Nineteenth-Century Music*, trans. J. Bradford Robinson (Berkeley and Los Angeles: University of California Press, 1989) includes no discussion at all of Spain or Spanish composers. If we accept Dahlhaus's characterization of salon music as 'trivial', none of these works of Albéniz would fit under that rubric.

At all events, the indisputable fact remains that in his own time Albéniz was a prominent and celebrated musical figure in Europe. No study of the musical life of London, Paris, Barcelona, or Madrid from 1879 to 1909 could afford to overlook his conspicuous presence and important contributions as a piano virtuoso, chamber musician, teacher, patron, conductor, concert organizer, critic, and composer for both the piano and the stage. Musicologists, of course, tend to assess a composer's importance by the degree of influence he or she had on the overall evolution of musical style. In the history of Spanish music, at least, Albéniz clearly occupies a position of the greatest significance. He exerted a pronounced influence on his contemporaries Enric Granados, Manuel de Falla, and Joaquín Turina, providing them not only with a musical model but with moral and material support. And he cast a long shadow over succeeding generations, represented by Joaquín Rodrigo and Federico Moreno Torroba. Albéniz was the first Spanish composer of modern times to gain a secure niche in the pantheon of European composers, one who earned the admiration not only of eminent performers like David Popper, Artur Rubinstein, and Alfred Cortot, but of composers such as Claude Debussy, Gabriel Fauré, and, later, Olivier Messiaen and Pierre Boulez.

If this were not enough, Albéniz's biography would remain one of the most unusual in the annals of nineteenth-century music. His life story is full of travels and adventures, resounding triumphs and bitter failures, and associations with memorable individuals both famous and obscure. Indeed, it often reads like the script for a film, a fact that has inspired two movies about him.[7] Albéniz was bearded, short, rotund, outwardly sanguine, warm-hearted, generous, witty, and loquacious. As Georges Jean-Aubry remembered,

The kindness and the generosity of the man were unsurpassable. . . . He was sensitive without wishing it to appear, and the goodness of his heart was a thing of much charm. He was unstinting in his praise of others; his talk was always of friendship, affection, or joy. I never saw him otherwise.[8]

Marguerite Long praised his 'kindness and devotion',[9] while Paul Dukas simply summed him up as 'a Don Quixote with the manner of Sancho Panza'.[10]

---

[7] Both premiered in the 1940s, one in Argentina and the other in Spain, and both took enormous liberties with his life story. A third film project was in the works in Hollywood in the 1950s, but never got off the ground. More will be said of these films in Ch. 8.

[8] 'Isaac Albéniz', *Musical Times* (1 Dec. 1917), 536.

[9] *At the Piano with Gabriel Fauré*, trans. Olive Senior-Ellis (London: Kahn & Averill, 1980), 55.

[10] Edgar Istel, liner notes for *Iberia* performed by Alicia de Larrocha (Decca, SXL 6586–7). Cited in Jacqueline Kalfa, 'Isaac Albéniz à Paris', *Revue internationale de musique française*, 9/26 (June 1988), 30.

But his diaries and letters present an individual far more complex and multi-faceted than heretofore imagined, a personality tinged with melancholy, bitterness, resentment, and insecurity. Albéniz was a northerner, the son of a Basque father and Catalan mother, but one whose musical compass pointed ever towards his beloved Andalusia. Yet he, the quintessential Spanish nationalist composer, ultimately rejected Spanish politics, religion, society, and—most of all—critics, and chose to live as an expatriate, first in London and then in Paris, where he remained until the end of his life.

In spite of all this, the inverse proportion that often characterizes the relationship between a composer's popular appeal and the scholarly attention he or she receives has plagued the study of Albéniz's life and music. Scholars in Germany, Britain, and the United States have traditionally all but ignored Albéniz and his distinguished compatriots, including Granados (1867–1916). Only in Spain and France, the two countries with which he was most closely associated, has Albéniz received any consistent attention. In recent years, however, this situation has begun to change. A sudden surge of interest in Albéniz has taken place in academia, with the appearance of no less than six doctoral documents on his music since 1990. Before that time, only one had ever been written outside France,[11] though it was, to be sure, a notable contribution. Paul Buck Mast's 1974 dissertation 'Style and Structure in "Iberia" by Isaac Albéniz' was a landmark study in the field of twentieth-century Spanish music, as it was one of the first attempts to apply modern methods of theoretical analysis to Spanish music with a folkloric basis.[12] But over fifteen years passed before the appearance of Pola Baytelman's excellent study of the piano music of Albéniz,[13] which she has since revised and published under the title *Isaac Albéniz: Chronological List and Thematic Catalog of his Piano Works.*[14] Marta Falces Sierra's astute examination of Albéniz's songs to texts of the Englishman Francis Money-Coutts[15] and Clifford Bevan's well-researched treatise on Albéniz's London period and operatic collaboration with Money-Coutts[16] represented the first dissertations from Spain and England, respectively, in this field. The author's

---

[11] See Jacqueline Kalfa, 'Inspiration hispanique et écriture pianistique dans *Iberia* d'Isaac Albéniz' (thèse de 3e cycle de musicologie, Université de Paris-Sorbonne, 1980).

[12] The University of Rochester, Eastman School of Music. For an annotated bibliography on Albéniz, consult Walter Clark, *Isaac Albéniz: A Guide to Research* (New York: Garland Publishing, 1998). See also reviews by the present author of Baytelman, Torres, and Selleck–Harrison (as well as other books on Falla, Granados, and Bretón) in *Inter-American Music Review*, 16/1 (Summer-Fall 1997), 85–94.

[13] 'Albéniz: Chronological Listing and Thematic Catalogue of His Piano Works' (DMA thesis, University of Texas, Austin, 1990).

[14] Warren, Mich.: Harmonie Park Press, 1993.

[15] *El Pacto de Fausto: Estudio lingüístico-documental de los lieder ingleses de Albéniz sobre poemas de Francis Money-Coutts* (Granada: Universidad de Granada, 1993).

[16] 'Albéniz, Money-Coutts and "La Parenthèse londonienne"' (Ph.D. diss., University of London, 1994).

own study of Albéniz's opera *Pepita Jiménez*[17] and the long-awaited biography and thematic catalogue by Frances Barulich[18] are further contributions from the United States. Two others are John Robert Redford's study of folkloric influences in *Iberia*, and Maria Selleck-Harrison's doctoral essay on the theoretical and pedagogical aspects of four selections from the first *Suite española*, which provides practical insights into this portion of Albéniz's *œuvre*.[19] One must also mention the groundbreaking efforts of Jacinto Torres Mulas, the leading Spanish authority on Albéniz, who has compiled a systematic catalogue of all the composer's works and has published several articles dealing with his hitherto neglected theatrical and choral music.[20] Another Spanish scholar who has contributed much to our knowledge of Albéniz's music is Antonio Iglesias, whose two-volume survey of the piano music remains a valuable source of information.[21] Of necessity, all of these efforts touched to some extent on the issue of biography, though their main focus has been the music and its sources. In 1990 the Fundación Isaac Albéniz in Madrid[22] organized an important exhibition of the composer's life and work, which was accompanied by several publications (edited by Enrique Franco) shedding useful light on purely biographical issues.[23]

But until now there has been no up-to-date, comprehensive biography of Albéniz available to the general public in English. The most important efforts have emanated, as mentioned, from the pens of French and Spanish authors. Unfortunately, the results of these investigations—laudable in purpose though they were—leave a great deal to be desired. In fact, the existing biographical record in all secondary sources is shot through with errors and misconceptions. It is not possible simply to touch up this portrait. It must be painted anew, based on documentary evidence and not merely on hearsay, tradition, and a blithe indifference to glaring inconsistencies.

---

[17] ' "Spanish Music with a Universal Accent": Isaac Albéniz's Opera *Pepita Jiménez*' (Ph.D. diss., University of California, Los Angeles, 1992).

[18] 'Researches into the Life of Isaac Albéniz' (Ph.D. diss., New York University, in progress).

[19] 'The Application of Spanish Folk Music in the Piano Suite "Iberia" by Isaac Albéniz' (DMA document, University of Arizona, 1994); 'A Pedagogical and Analytical Study of "Granada" ("Serenata"), "Sevilla" ("Sevillanas"), "Asturias" ("Leyenda") and "Castilla" ("Seguidillas") from the *Suite española*, Opus 47 by Isaac Albéniz' (DMA essay, University of Miami, 1992). See also Paul Verona, 'The Iberia suite of Issac Albéniz . . .' (DMA thesis, Manhattan school of Music, 1991).

[20] Especially 'La producción escénica de Isaac Albéniz', *Revista de musicología*, 14/1–2 (1991), 167–212; and 'Un desconocido "Salmo de difuntos" de Isaac Albéniz', *Revista de musicología*, 13/1 (Jan.–June 1990), 279–93.

[21] *Isaac Albéniz (su obra para piano)*, 2 vols. (Madrid: Editorial Alpuerto, 1987).

[22] The Fundación was the brainchild of the Spanish pianist Paloma O'Shea, and its offices are now located at Juan Bravo, 20–6° Dcha., 28006 Madrid. There is also the French Association Internationale Isaac Albéniz, whose address is 52 rue La Fayette, F-75009 Paris. It is run by Dr Jacqueline Kalfa.

[23] The Fundación issued its first publication, *Imágenes de Isaac Albéniz*, in 1988.

In this introduction we will trace the history of Albéniz biography and present as clear a view as possible of the daunting difficulties that confront the would-be biographer. This is no mere exercise in scholastic protocol. It is rather a necessary, even intriguing, exploration of a crucial aspect of Albéniz as a man and an artist. For many of the problems the biographer encounters in relating Albéniz's life story derive from the fact that Albéniz, the great improviser at the piano, frequently improvised on the narrative themes of his early career. The differing accounts of his life that he dispensed to friends and journalists were accepted as gospel truth by his biographers. Their attempts somehow to reconcile these contradictions and simultaneously preserve Albéniz's credibility at times approached the comical. The situation reminds one of nothing so much as the strenuous exertions of late-medieval astronomers to accommodate their empirical study of planetary movements to the Ptolemaic system handed down from antiquity. Eventually, a different cosmological model became necessary. The present author does not pretend to Copernican status, but he has found it impossible to continue with the model handed down by those who have preceded him, or to ignore Albéniz's obvious prevarications. In *The Historical Figure of Jesus*, E. P. Sanders makes the following relevant statement: 'The historian who studies a great human being, and reports fully on his or her findings, will almost certainly write at least a few things that some admirers would rather not read.'[24] That Albéniz did not always tell the truth, and that many of the celebrated episodes of his career appear now to be distorted or even fictitious, need not dismay us; in fact, this makes his life story all the more engrossing. Certainly the reader will appreciate much better the tale that unfolds in the succeeding chapters after perusing the following historiographical exposition.

In 1886 Antonio Guerra y Alarcón published the first biography of Albéniz.[25] Albéniz's daughter Laura declared that information for the work was provided by the composer himself.[26] This simple fact seemingly made it the most reliable source for information about the first twenty-six years of his life, and thus it formed the basis for most of the biographical studies that followed. Biographical sketches by some of Albéniz's acquaintances appeared in the Spanish press after this date and particularly upon his death. The most important of these articles were by Felip Pedrell, Tomás

---

[24]   London: Penguin Press, 1993, 4.

[25]   *Isaac Albéniz: Notas crítico-biográficas de tan eminente pianista* (Madrid: Escuela Tipográfica del Hospicio). An extract appeared in G. Arteaga y Pereira (ed.), *Celebridades musicales* (Barcelona: Centro Editorial Artístico, 1886). A reprint of Guerra y Alarcón's biography is now available (Madrid: Fundación Isaac Albéniz, 1990).

[26]   According to Henri Collet, *Albéniz et Granados* (Paris: Éditions Le Bon Plaisir, 1948), 16.

Bretón, and Juan Pérez Guzmán. Pedrell presents intriguing (though sometimes dubious) reflections on Albéniz's brief apprenticeship with him as a
composition student in Barcelona in the early 1880s.[27] Bretón recounts his
first meeting with Albéniz in Madrid when the young pianist was only about
10 years old.[28] Guzmán, a friend of Albéniz's father Ángel, dwells on the
family's early years in Barcelona, as well as the suicide of Albéniz's sister
Blanca and Albéniz's supposed flight from home at the age of 10.[29] But no
systematic attempt was made to survey the whole of Albéniz's life and works
until the French musicologist Henri Collet published his landmark dual
biography of Albéniz and Granados in 1926.[30]

Collet was the first biographer to draw on sources other than personal
acquaintance with the composer, i.e. secondary sources (including Guerra y
Alarcón) and Albéniz's friends and family. He was also the first to attempt a
survey of Albéniz's works, offering not only some background on their
genesis and critical reception but a cursory analytical appraisal of them as
well. Thus, Collet's work became, along with Guerra y Alarcón, the chief
point of departure for later biographers. In fact, it remained the standard
work until after the Second World War. The year 1948 witnessed the publication of a brief biography by Albéniz's nephew (the son of his sister
Clementina) Víctor Ruiz Albéniz, a doctor who attended Albéniz on his
deathbed and who eventually gave up medicine to work as a music critic in
Madrid.[31] Though it is neither comprehensive nor entirely accurate, it presents some interesting glimpses into Albéniz's private life based on family
records as well as on the author's own relationship with the composer. In
1950 Michel Raux Deledicque spun an intriguing tale in the only attempt
ever at a novelistic treatment of Albéniz's life, in which Deledicque simply
invented large amounts of dialogue.[32] Unfortunately, though he made
admirable use of some primary source materials and included much useful

[27] *La vanguardia* (15 June 1909). The exact time frame is not stated in the article but must have been during that period. The article also appears in 'Albéniz: El hombre, el artista, la obra', in *Músicos contempor-áneos y de otros tiempos* (Paris: P. Ollendorf, 1910), 375–81; *Revista musical catalana*, 6 (1909), 180–4 (in Catalan); and Franco (ed.), *Imágenes*, 20–2.
[28] 'En la muerte', Franco (ed.), *Albéniz y su tiempo*, 121–4.
[29] 'Los Albéniz', *La época* (21 May 1909); repr. in Franco (ed.), *Albéniz y su tiempo*, 23–8.
[30] *Albéniz et Granados* (Paris: Librairie Félix Alcan, 1926; rev. edn. Paris: Éditions Le Bon Plaisir, 1948; repr. Paris: Éditions d'Aujourd'hui, 1982). A (poor) Spanish trans. by P. E. F. Labrousse also appeared in 1948 (Buenos Aires: Tor-SRL). All ensuing references are to the Paris, 1948 edition.
[31] *Isaac Albéniz* (Madrid: Comisaría General de Música, 1948).
[32] *Albéniz, su vida inquieta y ardorosa* (Buenos Aires: Ediciones Peuser, 1950). Deledicque was a French-man who moved to Argentina in 1914 and who had actually met Albéniz during the summer of 1908 when the two were in Bagnoles de l'Orne. His correspondence with the Albéniz family (Mm, car. 2) reveals an admirable desire to flesh out the true story of Albéniz's career. Though Vicente Moya (husband of Albéniz's daughter Laura) did send him some documents by mail, he could thereby get only a partial glimpse of the available documentation.

information in his book, the absence of rigorous scholarship (i.e. paucity of footnotes, no bibliography or index) makes it sometimes difficult to know where fact leaves off and fantasy begins, thus diminishing its value to the scholar.

The most noteworthy biographical efforts since Collet have come from two other Frenchmen, Gabriel Laplane[33] and André Gauthier.[34] Laplane's biography was the most thorough effort ever undertaken. Its three sections and nineteen chapters include not only a biographical discussion but an excellent treatment of Albéniz's musical style and a survey of his works. It concludes with a useful bibliography (a rarity in this field) as well as the customary discography and chronology of Albéniz's life. Twenty years separate Laplane's work from the appearance of Gauthier's biography. Although he clearly stands on the shoulders of those who went before him, Gauthier offers helpful synopses of Albéniz's stage works as well as a balanced discussion of *Iberia*. The discography and bibliography, however, are so cursory as to appear mere afterthoughts. Spanish biographers were not inactive during this period, but their efforts did not come up to the standards set by the Frenchmen. The accounts by Emilio Fornet,[35] Antonio de las Heras,[36] Ángel Sagardía,[37] Andrés Ruiz Tarazona,[38] and Xosé Aviñoa[39] are less ambitious in scope, short on musical detail, and rely heavily on secondary sources for their biographical data. The most recent Spanish biography is by José Montero Alonso,[40] but it offers nothing more than a rehash of previous accounts and little in the way of original research. None of these books includes an index, footnotes (except Aviñoa and Montero), or bibliography (except Montero).

None the less, it would seem that by some combination or permutation of the above sources one could establish a trustworthy summary of Albéniz's activities. This is certainly what all other biographers have attempted to do, and regarding the latter half of Albéniz's life, it may be, more or less, an acceptable method. But the first twenty-three years, the very period covered by Guerra y Alarcón's initial biography, remain problematic. We can illustrate

---

[33] *Albéniz, sa vie, son œuvre*, preface by Francis Poulenc (Geneva: Éditions du Milieu du Monde, 1956), and *Albéniz: Vida y obra de un músico genial*, trans. Bernabé Herrero and Alberto de Michelena (Paris: Editorial Noguer, 1958).

[34] *Albéniz*, trans. from French to Spanish by Felipe Ximénez de Sandoval (Madrid: Espasa-Calpe, 1978).

[35] *Isaac Albéniz*, Figuras de la Raza, 2/24 (Madrid: A. Marzo, 1927).

[36] *Vida de Albéniz* (Barcelona: Ediciones Patria, 1940).

[37] *Isaac Albéniz* (Plasencia, Cáceres: Editorial Sánchez Rodrigo, 1951). See also by Sagardia, *Albéniz*, Gent Nostra, 46 (Barcelona: Editions de Nou Art Thor, 1986).

[38] *Isaac Albéniz: España soñada* (Madrid: Real Musical, 1975).

[39] *Albéniz*, Conocer y Reconocer la Música de (Mexico City: Daimon, 1986).

[40] *Albéniz: España en 'suite'* (Barcelona: Silex, 1988).

this by taking a few episodes from this period as described in selected sources to highlight their incompatibility.[41]

According to Collet, who based his account on Guerra y Alarcón, Albéniz ran away from home at the age of 12 to tour Spain (his first escape from home was supposedly at the age of 10). He stowed away on a steamer leaving Cádiz for the New World in order to evade capture by the authorities in that city.[42] Guerra y Alarcón placed Albéniz on a course directly from Spain to the Greater Antilles and the United States before returning to Spain via Liverpool, London, and Leipzig. But Collet relied on other sources to place him first in Argentina, Uruguay, and Brazil.[43] Thereafter he toured Cuba, Puerto Rico, and the United States (as far as San Francisco!), before returning to Europe in 1874. In both accounts, he encountered his father, recently transferred to Cuba as a customs official. The father, impressed by his son's accumulation of lucre, allowed him to continue on his way to the United States. The 14-year-old pianist then concertized in Liverpool and London before taking up residence in Leipzig in the autumn of that year. He enrolled in the famous music conservatory there and studied with Carl Reinecke and Salomon Jadassohn. After nine months he returned to Madrid and was awarded a generous stipend by King Alfonso XII (through the agency of his secretary, Guillermo Morphy) for piano study with Franz Rummel and, later, Louis Brassin at the Conservatoire Royal in Brussels, where he remained for three years. Thereafter he became a disciple of Franz Liszt, following him to Budapest, Weimar, and Rome, presumably during the next two years (until 1880 and a return trip to the Americas). By an alternative account, found in both Laplane and Gauthier, Albéniz's first trip to the New World took him to Buenos Aires, Uruguay, and Brazil and lasted from 1872 to 1873, whereupon he returned to Spain after unendurable privations.[44] He set out for the New World again in 1875, reaching the Greater Antilles and the United States

[41] The author first presented much of the following material at the III. Congreso Nacional de la Sociedad Española de Musicología in Granada on 26 May 1990. See 'Albéniz en Leipzig y Bruselas: Nuevas luces sobre una vieja historia', *Revista de musicología*, 14/1–2 (1991), 213–18. It has appeared in English under the title 'Albéniz in Leipzig and Brussels: New Data from Conservatory Records', *Inter-American Music Review*, 11/1 (Fall–Winter, 1990), 113–16.

[42] Albéniz had Bretón, in 'En la muerte', Franco (ed.), *Albéniz y su tiempo*, 122, believing that he had left from the port of La Coruña, in Galicia, on the *Ciudad de Santander*. (The ship's name comes from an article by Juan de Gredos in *La voz*, c.1928 (clipping in the Mm, Arxiu carpeta premsa, Prov. M-987), who got his story from Bretón.)

[43] His source for this information was a friend of the composer, Carlos de Castéra (brother of René de Castéra, whose Édition Mutuelle published *Iberia*), who purportedly got his version of the story from Albéniz. Deledicque searched without success through the national library in Buenos Aires for any reference to Albéniz's putative sojourn in Argentina or the arrival of the *España*, the steamer on which he supposedly sailed.

[44] Francisco Agramonte Cortijo, 'Isaac Albéniz', *Diccionario biográfico cronológico*, 3rd edn. (Madrid: Aguilar, 1961), has Albéniz going as far as the Philippines!

before concertizing in Britain and spending the autumn, winter, and spring of 1876–7 studying in Leipzig. He returned to Spain in the summer of 1877 before commencing studies in Brussels, which lasted until 1879. An additional six months of study under Brassin in 1880 preceded a pilgrimage to Budapest and a brief encounter with Liszt. Both Laplane and Gauthier agree that he did not follow the celebrated Hungarian to Weimar or Rome.[45]

We can see from the above instance that the biographical waters are indeed murky. And they get murkier. In 1891, Albéniz was living in London, and in January of that year an article appeared in the *Pall Mall Gazette* entitled 'Señor Albéniz at Home: An Interview with the Spanish Pianist'.[46] In this interview, Albéniz gives a brief account of his life in which he declares that he first ran away from home at the age of 8½ . Later, after spending three years touring in South America, he received a stipend from the Spanish King with which to study in Leipzig, beginning in 1874. After studying for three years in that city, he spent a year in Italy with Liszt.[47] Here is an account of his life that conforms neither to the historical record nor to the version he provided to Guerra y Alarcón.

Albéniz's putative studies with Liszt pose additional problems for the biographer. According to Collet, he commenced his studies with Liszt in August of 1878. The account found in Albéniz's own diary,[48] in which he played for the Hungarian master only once, in Budapest on 18 August 1880, would seem more reliable, and this is the version that appears in works subsequent to Collet's. However, Liszt was not in Budapest at that time! Letters from Liszt on precisely that date (and on the days before and after) indicate that he was in Weimar (see Chapter 2 for more on this). Thus, we must admit to the realm of possibility the idea that Albéniz never even met Liszt, much less studied with him (at all events, one lesson would hardly have qualified him as a 'student').

Table 1 summarizes the various versions presented above and gives a clear picture of the startling discrepancies that until now have evaded reconciliation.[49] Given the peripatetic life Albéniz led as a youth, he may have found it

[45] Gauthier relies on Laplane in diverging from Collet. Laplane realized, after examining Albéniz's diaries and concert clippings, that Albéniz had been in Spain in 1873 and recorded only a single meeting with Liszt, in 1880. But Laplane still did not go far enough in his examination to ferret out the truth.

[46] 30 Jan. 1891, 1–2.

[47] Albéniz's studies with Liszt in Italy are also reported in the newspaper *Morning* (16 Jan. 1893). It also gives an incorrect birth year of 1861, as do the *Morning Post* (20 Feb. 1893) and the records of study at the Leipzig conservatory.

[48] Isaac Albéniz, *Impresiones y diarios de viaje*, ed. Enrique Franco (Madrid: Fundación Isaac Albéniz, 1990), 21. Also cited in D`edicque, *Albéniz*, 170–9.

[49] To his credit, Luis Villalba, 'Imagen distanciada de un compositor-pianista', *Gaceta de Mallorca* (1909), repr. in Franco (ed.), *Albéniz y su tiempo*, 56–7, does make reference to the numerous contradictions in the biographical record. But he makes no attempt to reconcile them.

TABLE 1. *Divergent accounts of major events in Albéniz's early career*

	GyA[a]	PMG[a]	C	L
First flight from home	unclear	1868/9	1870	1870
New World tour	1872–5 in Antilles, USA, Britain	3 yrs. in South America	1872–5 in Argentina, Brazil, Uruguay, Antilles, USA, Britain	1872–3 in Argentina; after a return to Spain, 2nd tour 1875–6 in Antilles, USA, Britain
Studies in Leipzig	9 mos.	3 yrs. 1874–7	9 mos. 1874–5	9 mos. 1876–7
Studies in Brussels	3 yrs.	no mention	1875–8	1877–9
Studies with Liszt	Weimar, Rome, Budapest	1 yr. in Italy	Weimar, Rome, Budapest, 1878–80[?]	18 Aug. 1880[a] in Budapest

[a] Account directly attributable to Albéniz himself.

Notes: GyA = Guerra y Alarcón (1886); *PMG = Pall Mall Gazette* (1891); C = Collet (1926); L = Laplane (1956).

difficult in later years to remember the precise sequence of events in every detail. But he clearly stretched the truth as well. Like any other struggling artist, he succumbed to the temptation to make himself appear more impressive to the public by improving details of his life story. Claiming nine months, or three years, of study in Germany with such illustrious teachers as Reinecke and Jadassohn compensated for what he feared was a lack of respectable formal training, especially in composition. He inflated the period of study in Leipzig for the London press because of the greater prestige a German musical education enjoyed in England. (In the event, he was in Leipzig for less than two months and worked only briefly with Jadassohn, and not at all with Reinecke.) The same holds true for his 'studies' with Liszt.

Our situation in surveying the secondary literature, then, is somewhat analogous to viewing an impressionist painting. If we stand very close to the record as it has been presented, we see little beyond a riotous clash of strokes and colours that do not coalesce into any coherent shape. By standing back, however, we perceive a discernible image. The contradictions outlined above provoke considerable confusion and frustration at first. But at some remove, certain large motifs emerge: extensive youthful concert tours (including concerts in the New World), royal patronage, studies in Leipzig and Brussels, and attempted studies with Liszt. These elements provide the raw material for our story, but we must reconstruct them on the basis of newly recovered data in primary sources.

The point to make here, then, is that until now there has been no one source a person could consult to get a reliable, thoroughly researched account of Albéniz's life. Attempts to write a biography based largely on secondary sources are doomed to founder on the shoals of contradiction. Even penetration to the level of primary sources often presents simply another layer of uncertainty, as the collection of *albeniziana* has been somewhat dispersed (though it remains largely in the Barcelona area) and is at times incomplete. To separate fact from fiction, it is necessary to go beyond the existing archive and mine information in conservatory, theatre, government, and cathedral archives. Records of admission, examination, performances, employment, birth, death, and marriage—in addition to a thorough sifting of letters, diaries, manuscripts, contracts, and contemporary periodical literature—provide the historian with the only firm foundation for reconstructing what actually happened. Though there are still gaps and unanswered questions, the results of this research paint a rather different picture from the one previously available. Of course, a biography is more than a compilation of facts. The purpose of any biography is to flesh out the inner person and to interpret the significance of that person's life and work in some larger context. But to wax eloquent, for instance, about the importance of Albéniz's studies with Liszt when in reality he probably never even met the man is ludicrous. Philosophical ruminations must have some grounding in fact.

We will have occasion to refer to numerous other discrepancies further on. It would have interrupted the narrative flow, however, to stop to explain these major inconsistencies later, and it has proven more efficient to summarize them here. What will emerge from this, one hopes, is a biographical portrait more true to life—and yet more fascinating—than the somewhat fictional one to which we have grown accustomed for over a century. The fictitious elements, however, remain a necessary part of the overall portrait's composition; in no way do they diminish the remarkable achievements of Albéniz's relatively brief but extraordinarily productive and eventful life.

This is not a life-and-times kind of biography. Whole libraries of books have been written on the late nineteenth century in England and France, and it is not the author's intention to remind the reader that Queen Victoria was sitting on the English throne during Albéniz's London tenure in the early 1890s or to place his lengthy residence in Paris in the context of French culture and history. It is true, however, that the history of Spain during Albéniz's life is unfamiliar to most readers, and an effort has been made to say something more about it for the sake of clarity. For example, the revolution of 1868 is one of the less celebrated in European history, though among its consequences was the Franco-Prussian War of 1870–1. It also had a direct bearing on Albéniz's early life. In a similar vein, dates and some background information are provided only for figures who are probably not familiar to the general reader, or perhaps even the specialist. Neither has the author made an attempt to present a complete and in-depth analysis of all of Albéniz's works. This would have gone well beyond the boundaries the publisher placed before him. In treating Albéniz's stylistic development, detailed discussion has been limited to the major works for piano, for voice, for orchestra, and for the stage. Because critical reaction to Albéniz's performances and compositions is crucial to understanding the course of his career, reviews have been amply quoted.

Unless otherwise noted, all translations are the author's own. Though modern Catalan spellings are utilized for persons, places, and institutions in that region, those of Albéniz and his immediate family appear in Castilian, per the composer's own usage. Basque regions and persons also receive Castilian spellings, as Basque, unlike Catalan, is not a Romance language. English spellings of common Spanish place names, such as Seville, Catalonia, and Andalusia, are the rule. Passages from letters, diaries, etc. retain their original spelling, punctuation, and orthography, unless they are taken from an edited source.

1

The Phenomenon
(1860–1875)

———

At the end of his life, Ulysses S. Grant penned the memorable phrase, 'I think I am a verb instead of a personal pronoun'.[1] Isaac Albéniz[2] was an adjective and a noun. The word *albéniz* comes from the Basque language[3] and means skinny, slender, or thread-like; it can also mean short or clever, in a devious sort of way. As a noun, it translates as a thread, strand, or even an abundance of hay.[4] By coincidence, all of the above adjectives applied to Albéniz in his early years, as he was thin, short, and exceedingly ingenious. Ironically, in adulthood he became rather corpulent and self-deprecatingly signed his letters 'Saco' ('Sack'), 'El Gordo' ('The Fat One'), or 'Saco gordo' ('Fat Sack'), a play on the second syllable of his first name. The mature Albéniz was anything but *albéniz*, at least in the principal sense of the word!

During his lifetime, however, there seems to have been some confusion as to the meaning of his patronym. An undated poem by the distinguished pianist Ricart Viñes (1875–1943) addressed to Albéniz begins with the following couplet:

---

[1] 'A verb is anything that signifies to be, to do, or to suffer. I signify all three.' Grant lay dying of cancer as he wrote these thoughts in an undated note to his doctor, probably from July 1885. Cited in William S. McFeely, *Grant* (New York: Norton, 1981), 516.

[2] There are variant spellings of this name. One often encounters 'Alvéniz' in 19th-cent. documents and publications, the v and b in Spanish receiving similar pronunciation. Albéniz himself was generally negligent in matters of orthography, and did not place an acute accent over the e in his surname as the rules of stress in Spanish require (the emphasis would otherwise be placed on the last syllable). In Catalan the accent is grave rather than acute (Albèniz). The 19th-cent Catalan rendering of his first name was also somewhat different, i.e. Isaach instead of Isaac. Nineteenth-century British editions of his music frequently spell the first name with a Y instead of an I; French and German editions sometimes use a J.

[3] Basque, or Euskera, is not an Indo-European language and, in fact, belongs to no known language group. The Basques may be descended from among the earliest inhabitants of western Europe. See Mary Vincent and R. A. Stradling, *Cultural Atlas of Spain and Portugal* (Abingdon: Andromeda Oxford, 1994), 21.

[4] See entry in *Diccionario Vasco-Castellano*, ed. Placido Mugica Berrondo (Bilbao: Mensajero, 1981), and Gorka Aulestia, *Basque-English Dictionary* (Reno and Las Vegas: University of Nevada Press, 1989).

Your name, in Arabic, architect means,
and well for the exquisiteness of your art.[5]

How Viñes got the idea that the name was Arabic and meant architect is unknown. It must have come from Albéniz himself, for no reference to the word appears in Spanish or Arabic dictionaries, or dictionaries listing Spanish names with Arabic etymologies. The seeming prefix 'al' and the z at the end certainly suggest an Arabic origin, but only Basque dictionaries contain the word.[6] A dedication inscribed by an admirer in his concert album from his early teens invokes the aid of the 'Great Architect' in guiding his footsteps 'on the path of honour and virtue'.[7] This, to be sure, is a Masonic reference, but it merely reinforces one's suspicion that Albéniz himself may have invented the 'architect' definition because it connected him with Moorish architecture in Spain, and because it was 'Masonic'. Freemasonry played an important role in his life, and though we cannot be sure of his own member-ship, his father and several of his friends and colleagues were lodge mem-bers.[8] All biographers have remarked that he often began his youthful concerts by giving the Masonic salute to the audience. Significantly, his paternal grandfather and great-grandfather had been bricklayers, and this may further have inspired the fantasy. In so far as Albéniz apparently also promulgated the notion that he was somehow Moorish ('soy un moro'),[9] the Arabic 'translation' would seem to be of a piece with that fiction.

The subject of this study was certainly not the first eminent musician to bear that name. Mateo Pérez de Albéniz, born in the Basque country around 1755, was a composer, music theorist, and *maestro de capilla* in San Sebast-ián, where he died in 1831. Though he composed primarily religious music, he also wrote some piano sonatas.[10] His son, the pianist Pedro Albéniz y Basanta, was born in the city of Logroño in 1795. After studies in Paris with Friedrich Kalkbrenner (1785–1849), he worked for a time in San Sebastián and Logroño before taking up a post as professor of piano at the newly

[5] This handwritten poem is now in the Mm, car. 4, tucked into the cover of the album he took with him on his concert journeys 1872–81. 'Tu nombre, en árabe, arquitecto reza, | Y bien por las de tu arte exquisiteces.'
[6] There persists in the family the notion that the name is Arabic for 'hijo de Al' (Son of Allah?) or even 'Son of Is' (Al-ben-Is).
[7] José Ramos de Anaya, Cáguas, Puerto Rico, 31 Aug. 1875: 'por la senda del honor y la virtud.'
[8] See Jacinto Torres Mulas, 'Isaac Albéniz en los infiernos', *Scherzo*, 80 (Dec. 1993), 150. This also appears as the prologue in Falces, *Pacto de Fausto*, 19–24. See also Edgar Istel, 'Isaac Albéniz', trans. Frederick H. Martens, *Musical Quarterly*, 15 (1929), 11. Albéniz's close friend Enrique Fernández Arbós, himself a lodge member, told Istel that Albéniz did not become a Mason.
[9] Gauthier, *Albéniz*, 61; Laplane, *Albéniz*, 96. To be sure, Albéniz meant this not so much in a racial sense as in terms of his personality, which was inwardly melancholy and prone to wistful reflection. In J. M. Corredor, *Conversations with Casals*, trans. André Mangeot (New York: E. P. Dutton, 1956), 163, Casals observed that 'it is curious to see how far a Catalan can become like a Moor'.
[10] *New Grove Dictionary of Music and Musicians* (1980 edn.), s.v. 'Albéniz, Mateo', by Robert Stevenson.

formed Madrid conservatory in 1830. A few years later he was appointed organist of the royal chapel.[11] Though a less impressive composer than his father, he authored the celebrated *Método completo para piano* (Madrid, 1840), which became the standard text at the Madrid conservatory, where the young Isaac Albéniz would later study.

Our pianist may have fancied himself a relative of Mateo and Pedro Albéniz. He was familiar with the latter's 'Method', perhaps even weaned on it, and his copy of the cover of this book survives.[12] In the *Pall Mall Gazette* article already cited, he makes a curious reference to a 'great uncle [who] was a musician of some eminence in his time'. He must have had Mateo or Pedro in mind, but he allows the reader to construct that association. In truth, he had no such great-uncle, and there was no connection whatever between the two families (see n. 13 below).

Isaac's father, Ángel Lucio Albéniz y Gauna, hailed from Vitoria, in the Basque country, where he entered the world on 2 March 1817. Thanks to the genealogical research of J. M. de Solà-Morales,[13] we can trace his family back several generations, to the late sixteenth century. The Álava region of the Basque country was the ancestral home of the Albéniz family. Both Ángel's father and grandfather worked as *mestres de cases*, or masons. The maternal side of Ángel's family, the Gaunas, had resided in the Álava region as far back as the early 1700s. Moreover, the connection of the Albéniz name with Álava has a geographic as well as demographic component, as there is a small farming village of the same name on the banks of the Araya River in the vicinity of San Millán. In 1960 it was a town of some 166 inhabitants; back in 1802, there were but 29.[14] The Albéniz family, however, seems never to have had any association with the place.

Ángel Albéniz was of short stature and walked with a slight limp. Intelligent, hard working, and of a liberal stripe politically, he admired the reformer Juan Prim who led the revolution of 1868.[15] At home he was a Don Juan, a tyrant, and at times verbally abusive of his son. Yet he was a dedicated Freemason[16] and even entertained political aspirations, running for elective

[11] *New Grove Dictionary of Music and Musicians* (1980 edn.), s.v. 'Albéniz y Basanta, Pedro', by Antonio Iglesias.
[12] Mm, car. 1.
[13] 'La sang gironina-gaditana d'Isaac Albèniz', *Annals de l'Institut d'Estudis Gironins*, 25/2 (1981), 233–53. Solà-Morales also traces the family tree of Pedro Albéniz back to the early 1600s and demonstrates that his ancestors came from Viana in Navarra. If there is any ultimate connection between the families of Isaac and Pedro, it is lost in the mists of the Middle Ages.
[14] *Enciclopedia general ilustrada del País Vasco* (San Sebastián: Editorial Auñamendi, 1970), s.v. 'Albéniz'.
[15] Solà-Morales, 'La sang', 235–6.
[16] One does not readily associate Freemasonry with Spain, but it played an important role there as elsewhere. See Jacinto Torres Mulas, 'Música y masonería en España', in J. A. Ferrer Benimeli (co-ord.), *La masonería española entre Europa y América: VI Symposium Internacional de Historia de la Masonería*

office as the congressional representative of Álava. A piece of his campaign literature survives and makes for interesting reading.[17] Ángel advocated equal and fair treatment for Álava and promised to defend its rights and interests. He was no separatist, however, and invoked Álava's 'ardent affection toward the new adoptive country' to which it had always made 'gigantic sacrifices in men and money'. In spite of this spirited campaign, he lost the election.[18] Although his loyalty to the central Castilian administration was constant, he obviously considered himself a son of the Basque country. Presumably he was fluent in that language, but Castilian appears to have been his only mode of written communication.

Ángel was also a poet, of sorts. Though his literary outpourings have not gained wide circulation, they were sufficient to earn him a place in modern Basque encyclopedias, alongside his more illustrious son.[19] He published just two works. The first, entitled *Glorias babazorras* (*babazorro* is a slightly derogatory name for a native of Álava), was published in 1855 under the pseudonym Peruchico as a paean to his heroic countrymen who defeated Napoleon's legions at the Battle of Vitoria on 21 June 1813. The fact that this poem went into a third edition, as late as 1890, indicates its enduring popularity in the Basque country.[20] Ángel was inspired to publish his poetry on only one other occasion, marking a far less felicitous chapter in Spanish history. In 1898 he penned a bitter and rueful reflection on Spain's humiliation in the war with the hated *Yanqui*, which resulted in the loss of his nation's last remaining overseas colonies (ouside of North Africa). Entitled *Chocheces que parecen verdades* ('Fantasies that appear verities'), it bears the attribution 'por A. Albéniz y Gauna, Bisabuelo de la Libertad [Great-Grandfather of Liberty], Noviembre 1898'.[21] One other literary effort, unpublished, deserves our attention here. Ángel composed his own epitaph (and

Española, 2 vols. (Zaragoza: Gobierno de Aragón, Dept°. de Educación y Cultura, 1995), ii. 769–813. Actually, it was established there as early as 1728, though there were periods of suppression, especially in 1814 during the restoration of Ferdinand VII. This did not prevent the spread of Freemasonry, especially among the officer corps in the army. There were lodges in Barcelona, Cádiz, San Sebastián, Vitoria, Santander, Salamanca, Seville, and Zaragoza, among others. Famous musicians included Ferran Sors (Fernando Sor), Ramón Carnicer, Enrique Arbós, Tomás Bretón, and Pau Casals. The authors Rafael Leopoldo Palomino de Guzmán and Eusebio Sierra, who would later collaborate with Albéniz on zarzuelas, were likewise Masons, as was his publisher Benito Zozaya.

[17] Mm, car. 4.

[18] '[A]rdiente cariño hácia la nueva pátria adoptiva', and 'gigantescos sacrificios de siempre, en hombres y dinero'. We do not yet know the year of the election, but one assumes it was prior to 1847, when he joined the civil service.

[19] *Enciclopedia general ilustrada del País Vasco*, s.v. 'Albéniz'.

[20] The 1855 edition consisted of two 'cantos'. Ángel composed a third canto in August of 1890, and this was included in the third edition published in Vitoria by Imprenta de la Ilustración in that same year. A copy of the third edition is located in the Mm, car. 4.

[21] Barcelona: Joaquín Collazos, 1898.

one for his wife), the longhand version of which shows clearly how he thought of himself.

> Here lies an Alavan
> A true Babazorro
> Lame of head and feet
> And poet of love[22]

Though Ángel could not gain elective office in the government, he made a fine career for himself as a customs official in the revenue department. In so doing, he departed from the vocation of his forefathers. This politician-cum-poet-cum-Freemason-cum-bureaucrat began his civil-service career in the city of Girona on 29 November 1847.[23] Here it was that he courted and married Dolors Pascual i Bardera (hereafter called Dolores), a native of the city of Figueres in the province of Girona. We know less about her than we would like, but she was 28 at the time of their nuptials, on 5 July 1849, putting her birth in the year 1821. Dolores's ancestors on the maternal side had lived in Girona since the early eighteenth century, where they worked as locksmiths and carpenters. Her father, however, José Pascual y Jiménez, hailed from the Andalusian city of San Fernando near the seaport of Cádiz.[24] While Ángel wrote inspired verse about martial glory, José actually achieved it. The records of his military service survive and give us a fascinating and detailed account of his exploits.[25] Born on 25 November 1783 to Catalans resettled in Andalusia, he entered military service in 1802 and was promoted to sergeant in 1808. He was stationed in Catalonia and fought the French in various actions starting in 1808–9, for which he was decorated. In December 1809 he was taken captive by the French but managed to escape a month later. He fought the French until the war's end, then resisted the French invasion of 1823. Once again taken prisoner, he languished eight months in captivity. He spent his entire military career in Catalonia, and remained in Girona after his retirement in 1843 at the rank of captain of infantry, with forty-one years of service.

---

[22] The epitaphs are in the Mm, car. 4. 'Aqui yace un Alaves | Babazorro sin ficcion | Cojo de cabeza y pies | Y poeta de aficion.'

[23] Ángel's employment records survive in his file in the archive of the Dirección General de Costes de Personal y Pensiones Públicas in Madrid, along with other documentation pertaining to the dispensation of his pension upon his death in 1903.

[24] To be sure, his own father had moved from Girona to Cádiz, for unknown reasons. His paternal grandfather was from Pals in Girona, where he worked as a farmhand. Therefore, the only genuinely Andalusian branch in Albéniz's family tree is on the side of his maternal great-grandmother, whose parents had lived in the region of Cádiz at least since the early 18th cent.

[25] Mm, car. 1. Also reproduced in Solà-Morales, 'La sang', 250.

Dolores gave birth to their first child, Enriqueta, in 1850, while she and Ángel were living in Girona. Ángel then received postings in Logroño (1852) and Pamplona (1853), where their second child, Clementina, was born on 23 November 1853. The small family then moved to Vitoria (1854), where a third daughter, Blanca, was born in 1855. Assignments in Salamanca (1856) and Figueres (1856) preceded Ángel's assuming the post of administrator of customs in the city of Camprodon in 1859.

Camprodon lies in a lush green valley in the Pyrenees, some 950 metres above sea level, at the confluence of the rivers Ter and Ritort. Its location only a few kilometres from the French border, in the province of Girona in northern Catalonia, has made it a bone of contention in territorial disputes between France and Spain, and invading French armies occupied it several times during the seventeenth and eighteenth centuries. In 1839, anti-government forces destroyed much of the city during the First Carlist War.[26] Though largely an agricultural community, it has been a centre for textile manufacture since the Middle Ages. It is most famous for its medieval architecture, especially the tenth-century church of the Benedictine abbey Sant Pere de Camprodon. The town's actual founding, however, dates back to 43 BCE, by the Roman Rotundo Cuestor, who gave it the eponymous designation Campus Rotundus ('round field'). The corruption of this name produced Camprodon. In 1860, it was a town of some 1,287 souls.[27]

On 29 May of that very year, Dolores Albéniz gave birth to her last child, a boy, who received the name Isaac Manuel Francisco Albéniz y Pascual. Although the city of Camprodon has honoured the memory of its most famous son by designating the supposed birthplace, that structure has been renovated so much over the decades that it no longer bears any resemblance to the building in which he was born.[28] The baby was baptized on 3 June in the parish church of Santa Maria by Father Francisco Pages (an annotation in the baptismal certificate confirms that he had been born five days earlier).[29] The child received the names of the saints whose feast days were celebrated on the third and fourth days of June, Isaac de Córdoba and Francisco de

---

[26] The Carlists were supporters of the pretender to the throne Don Carlos, brother of Ferdinand VII. They were opposed to the Infanta Isabel II and her mother María Cristina, the regent, who came to power in 1833 on the death of Ferdinand. The civil war between the government and the Carlists was an open wound that continued to bleed throughout the 19th cent.

[27] *Gran enciclopèdia catalana* (1986 edn.), s.v. 'Camprodon'. See also entries in *Gran Larousse català* (1987 edn.), and *Enciclopedia universal ilustrada europeo-americana* (1958 edn.).

[28] According to Albéniz's granddaughter, Rosina Moya Albéniz de Samsó, in a conversation with the author on 23 July 1995. Her family had considered purchasing the house, located on the Plaça d'Espanya in the city centre, and preserving it as a museum. But they soon realized that it could not have been the original house.

[29] A copy of this certificate is located in the Mm, car. 1.

Caracciolo.[30] Although the name of Isaac occasionally prompts questions as to Jewish ancestry, he was no more Jewish than he was Castilian or Moorish. The additional name of Manuel was given in honour of his godfather, who was present at the ceremony.[31]

The symbolism of Albéniz's birthplace, at the juncture of France and Spain, strikes one as significant in so far as his art would ultimately represent a blending of those two music cultures. But it is nothing more than symbolic. For though there seems to be some confusion about the length of the family's tenure in Camprodon, it was in any case short. All secondary sources state that the family departed the city for Barcelona only a few months after Albéniz's birth. But Ángel's employment records indicate that he, at least, remained there until May of 1863. A brief six-month stint in Sitges, just south of Barcelona on the coast, preceded his taking up a new post at Barcelona in December of that same year. It is possible that the family had moved to the Catalonian capital earlier without him, but in the absence of any proof, we must assume that they arrived together in Barcelona on the eve of 1864, when Albéniz was 3½ years old.[32]

According to family tradition, Isaac showed a proclivity for music in his earliest years, and his sister Clementina, also a talented musician, gave him his first lessons in piano. She claimed that he knew his scales and arpeggios by the age of 3 and his playing was 'full of expression'.[33] Indeed, his progress was so rapid that the two siblings made their first public appearance, at the Teatre Romea, when Isaac was but 4 years old. Clementina claimed that she could remember the event 'to the smallest details'.[34] The concert was a

---

[30] Isaac de Córdoba (d. 852) mastered Arabic and worked for the Moorish administration in that city. He was executed for denouncing Muhammad. Francisco de Caracciolo (1563–1608) was an Italian monk who founded the Minor Clerks Regular and established houses in Madrid, Valladolid, and Alcalá in the late 16th cent. See entries in Herbert Thurston, SJ, and Donald Attwater (eds.), *Butler's Lives of the Saints*, ii (New York: P. J. Kennedy & Sons, 1956).

[31] Deledicque, *Albéniz*, 15.

[32] Alejandro de Verastegui, 'Isaac Albéniz, oriundo Vitoriano', *Boletín de la Real Sociedad Vascongada de los Amigos del País*, 17/1 (San Sebastián: Museo de San Telmo, 1961), 44, states that the family lived on the carrer dels Escudellers, which is in Barcelona's Gothic quarter near the harbour. But he gives no evidence for this. Guerra y Alarcón places him 'in the neighborhood of San Francisco [Nou de S. Francesc]', which is the next street over from Escudellers; so, this area seems the probable location of the family's apartment during that period.

[33] Emilio Fornet interviewed Clementina in her later years for the Madrid periodical *Estampas*. The author has not yet been able to date the piece, but it must have been between 1931 (when the article states she received a silver medal for her teaching at the Asociación para la Enseñanza de la Mujer) and her death in 1933. A clipping of it is located in the Mm, car. 'Arxiu Premsa biogràfic 1872–1964'.

[34] One wants to believe her account but must bear in mind that her memory was not infallible. She states, for instance, that her father was posted to Cuba *before* the family moved to Camprodon, which was not true. She also states that she was only four years older than Isaac; in fact, she was seven years older than he. This concert may have taken place in other than Albéniz's fourth year, however, as sources differ on his age at the time. It definitely happened before Jan. 1868, when the family left the city. Amparo Valera, director of the

benefit for victims of a recent flood, and she and Isaac were two of several performers. Dolores dressed her son in what Clementina described as a Scottish-style outfit of velvet with a lace collar, in the manner of the sons of Prince Edward, a costume that became his customary concert attire.[35] They played, four hands, a piece entitled *Perlas y flores* ('Pearls and flowers').[36] So young were they that a 'small mountain' of pillows was placed on the piano bench so that they could reach the keyboard. After their performance, the public was 'delirious with enthusiasm' and threw toys on stage, mostly coloured balls, with which the young pianist became so fascinated that he started playing with them, utterly oblivious to the circumstances.

According to tradition, Albéniz also studied piano with Narciso Olivares, a local teacher in Barcelona.[37] But we have no independent record of those studies, and we do not know enough about Olivares to gauge the import-ance of Albéniz's contact with him. Neither do we have any evidence that Albéniz travelled to Paris in 1867, in the company of his mother and sister Clementina, to study privately with Marmontel[38] in preparation for an audition at the Conservatoire. The story of his Paris studies first emerged in Guerra y Alarcón's biography. According to Albéniz himself, he eventually passed the entrance audition but, in his youthful excitement, hurled a ball at a mirror and shattered it. The examiners declared he would have to mature for a couple of years before he could study there. Interestingly, in her inter-view (dealing exclusively with their early years) Clementina made no mention of this Parisian sojourn, which supposedly transpired over a period of nine months. In fact, she claimed that Albéniz did not read music until he was 6 or 7, and played until then by 'pure intuition'.[39] Juan Pérez Guzmán, who also focused on this period in the family's history, recalls that Dolores took her daughters Enriqueta and Blanca to Berlin, Brussels, and Paris for their education, while Clementina and Isaac stayed with their father in Barcelona

---

Teatre Romea's archive in Barcelona, could find no record of this concert, but this does not mean it never occurred.

[35] A picture of Albéniz in his outfit appears in Deledicque, *Albéniz*, 35, but he was 7 years old when it was taken.

[36] This seems to contradict what Albéniz told Guerra y Alarcón, i.e. that he played a fantasy on *The Sicilian Vespers*. This supposedly provoked a controversy in the local press as to whether he had merely been pretending to play while someone else performed the difficult piece for him offstage. Perhaps he played it later in the programme.

[37] First mentioned in Guerra y Alarcón. There is no entry on him in musical dictionaries and encyclopedias.

[38] Antoine-François Marmontel (1816–98) was among the greatest piano pedagogues of the 19th cent. and counted Bizet, d'Indy, and Debussy among his students at the Conservatoire, where he taught from 1848 to 1887.

[39] If we are also to believe Guzmán, that Albéniz could read music before he learned to read and write, then his education was sadly neglected, as he himself later acknowledged.

to study music.[40] In fact, Albéniz told Guerra y Alarcón that Enriqueta obtained a bachelor's degree in French from the University of Montpellier at the age of 17.[41] She evidently spoke several languages fluently, and Ángel even had plans for her to teach in the Barcelona area and establish an academy for young women. But this was not to be, as she died in Barcelona during a typhus epidemic in late 1867.[42] However, it is doubtful that Albéniz ever broke any mirrors at the Conservatoire. The minimum age for admission to that venerable institution in the 1860s was 9 years, though exceptions could be made for youngsters of extraordinary talent. Albéniz might have fitted into that category, but his name appears nowhere in the extant records of those who auditioned for admission during the years 1818–88.[43]

In 1868 occurred one of the many political upheavals that plagued Spain in the nineteenth century. General Juan Prim (1814–70) led a conspiracy to overthrow the regime of Isabel II, who had become 'notorious for her extravagance, sexual immorality, and favoritism'.[44] Prim's forces forged ahead against weak government resistance, and Isabel finally fled to France as the uprising spread throughout the country. Prim and his co-conspirators entered Madrid in triumph on 3 October, and Prim became premier in June of 1869. He was now at the pinnacle of political power but remained there only until 30 December 1870, when an assassin's bullet ended his life. Every account of Albéniz's life states that, as a result of this revolution, Ángel lost his job and sought to exploit his children by running them around the north of Spain, in the manner of Leopold Mozart, to give concerts. Eventually he moved the family to Madrid to seek the patronage of Prim. Once again, however, the employment records tell a slightly different story. Ángel was employed in Barcelona until January of 1868, at which time he took up a position in the customs office in Almería, on the Mediterranean coast in Andalusia. This position was terminated in August of that year, around the

[40] 'Los Albéniz' Franco (ed.), *Albéniz y su tiempo*, 23.

[41] *Albéniz*, 16.

[42] According to María Luisa Beltrán Sábat of the Institut Municipal dels Serveis Funeraris de Barcelona, Enriqueta was buried in the Poblenou cemetery in Barcelona on 8 Nov. 1867. She would have been less than 18 years old, as her parents married in July 1849 (assuming conception after marriage).

[43] The audition records are extensive and survive in the Archives Nationales in Paris under fonds A.137 in the materials connected with the Conservatoire. There is no entry for Albéniz in the alphabetic registry (A.137 328) of names of aspirants during these years. I am indebted to Catherine Rochon of the Conservatoire's Centre de Documentation et des Archives for information on admission regulations (from the years 1850 and 1878) and on the materials at the Archives Nationales, and to Dr Alan Pasco for checking the register for me. Not surprisingly, Albéniz is not listed in the register of Marmontel's students at the conservatory ('Tableaux des classes', 1866–70, A.137 157), but this does not rule out the possibility that he studied privately with him.

[44] Vincent and Stradling, *Cultural Atlas of Spain and Portugal*, 137.

time of the revolution. There followed a hiatus of almost a year before he was posted to Cáceres in the western province of Extremadura. Isaac was not, however, in Catalonia during this period of unemployment; he was studying in Madrid. Records of examinations given at the end of the 1868–9 school year at the Real Conservatorio in Madrid show that Albéniz was enrolled in first-year solfège there, under the tutelage of Feliciano Primo Ajero y Amatey (b. 1825).[45] He passed his solfège exam on 25 May 1869, with the noted composer Emilio Arrieta (1823–94) serving as president of the examining board. Albéniz does not reappear in the exam records until the year 1870–1, where he is listed as a piano student of José Mendizábal (d. 1896), who had been teaching there since 1854. He took the exam on 5 June 1871 and passed the first two years of piano.[46] His sister Blanca began voice studies in this year with Juan Gil. She passed her exam on 3 June, but an annotation in the record states that she is enrolled in voice 'under observation'. Her name appears again in the record for 10 June, once more stating she is a student *en observación*, but she was not examined on that date. Probably she had been admitted on a provisional status. She was clearly not as talented as her brother. Albéniz's schoolmates and lifelong friends Enrique Fernández Arbós (violin)[47] and Augustín Rubio (cello),[48] as well as future stage composers Tomás Bretón[49] and Ruperto Chapí, show up regularly in the records. But whereas they were sedulous in their studies, Albéniz's academic efforts were desultory.[50] He appears only once more, in the records for the year 1873–4 (p. 93), when he failed to show up for the exam in second-year solfège on 6 June 1874. We shall soon see that the young pianist had advanced from theory to practice, and that what his friends were preparing themselves to do, Albéniz was already doing.

[45] 'Actas de los exámenes de 1865–66 á 1871–72', 194. Though the archive of the Real Conservatorio in Madrid was closed for reorganization while the author was conducting his research, almost miraculously this manuscript volume just happened to be in the office of the Secretaría. A second volume covering the academic years 1872–3 to 1877–8 was also available. Had Albéniz been enrolled in the course but not appeared for classes, or for the exam, this would have been noted. The name of the Madrid conservatory has changed several times during its history. It was founded in 1830 as the Real Conservatorio de Música y Declamación de María Cristina. During Albéniz's studies there, however, it was called the Escuela Nacional de Música y Declamación. It is now the Real Conservatorio Superior de Música.

[46] *Actas 1865–72*, 317.

[47] Arbós (1863–1939) eventually became professor of violin at the Royal Conservatory of Music in London, which post he held from 1894 to 1915. He gained prominence as a conductor and composer as well.

[48] Rubio (b. 1856) studied chamber music with Joachim in Berlin. He, Albéniz, and Arbós formed the Trio Español, which performed throughout much of Europe. They were also the nucleus of the Quinteto Iberia, with the addition of viola and bass.

[49] 1850–1923. Celebrated conductor and a composer of some of the most successful zarzuelas, including *La verbena de la paloma* (1894).

[50] To be sure, Chapí (1851–1909) did fail to appear for several exams; however, he won first prize in harmony in 1869. He went on to compose over 100 zarzuelas, including the immensely popular *La revoltosa* (1897).

In 1869 Albéniz composed his first piece, for piano, which was published that year in Madrid by B. Eslava. The title, *Marcha militar*, appears on the cover in large bold type forming a crescent shape, with a musket and sabre crossing and intertwining with the words. The cover reveals the work to be 'by the 8-year-old boy Isaac Albéniz' ('por el niño de 8 años Isaac de Albéniz'). Though Albéniz was apparently inspired in infancy to keep time with the strains of a military band posted near the family's Barcelona apartment, the motivation for composing a military march probably lay closer to the realm of politics and favour-seeking. The cover bears the printed dedication 'Al Excelentísimo Señor Vizconde del Bruch'. An account of Albéniz's presentation of this simple but spirited piece as a gift to the Viscount appeared in a Barcelona newspaper shortly after the event. The *Correo de teatro* reported on 28 July 1869[51] that the 7-year-old (not 8 or 9!)[52] composer marched up to the front door of Prim's house, without any prearrangement, introduced himself, and requested a meeting with the Viscount, who was the general's son and all of 12 years of age. The young nobleman was thrilled with the composition Albéniz presented him and played at the piano, and afterwards he showed Albéniz his collection of weapons. The article's author states that he learned of this incident from a friend who had just arrived from Madrid, his place of residence. This 'friend' sounds suspiciously like Ángel. It stands to reason that Albéniz would present his composition in person to its dedicatee, but that the meeting was so impromptu seems a bit improbable (though not inconsistent with Albéniz's penchant for spontaneity), especially if Ángel had been behind the scheme. Interestingly, Ángel was appointed to his new position in Cáceres at this time, on 29 July 1869, and began his duties a month later, on 23 August. This raises the likelihood that the little composition's purpose was to win the favour of Prim, and that it succeeded. Or it may have been an expression of gratitude for a position already granted. We do not yet know.

Ángel remained in Cáceres until 16 November 1871, when his position there was terminated. We know that Albéniz was studying piano at the Madrid conservatory during the academic year 1870–1, so he clearly was not residing with his father. This is significant, because the first of Albéniz's supposed flights from home took place in November 1870. According to nearly every account, starting with Guerra y Alarcón, he was inspired by the

---

[51] This clipping is in his concert album, Mm, car. 4.

[52] Albéniz celebrated his ninth birthday on 29 May 1869. He may have composed this piece before that date, hence justifying the claim on the title page of its author's age. Shaving yet another year off his age was a publicity gesture, however. This was not the last time he or his father would dispense to acquaintances and the press an inaccurate age.

novels of Jules Verne to set out on his own adventures.[53] He also claimed that he wanted to earn money for the family (though by this time his father was again employed). He boarded a train on St Cecilia's Day (according to later, embellished accounts) and headed north-west towards El Escorial. On the train he encountered the mayor of that place, who was so impressed with the young man that he arranged a concert for him at the casino. This was a rousing success, and the mayor thereafter put him on a train back to Madrid. But the young runaway had no intention of returning home and changed trains at Villalba along the way, heading back north to give concerts in Ávila, Zamora, Peñaranda de Bracamonte, Valladolid, Palencia, León, Logroño, Zaragoza, Barcelona, and Valencia![54] Depending on which version one reads, he returned home voluntarily or was apprehended by authorities who had received urgent notification from Ángel of the youngster's absence.

It seems that Albéniz's own story-telling was as indebted to Jules Verne as his actual escapades. We cannot prove a negative and say that Albéniz never ran away from home or that he did not go on concert tours in this year of his life. Absence of proof is not proof of absence. And this account is repeated in every biography and in every autobiographical sketch Albéniz gave to journalists and friends, so there may well be some truth to it. But there are compelling reasons to doubt the above version of events. First, there is no mention in the examination records for that year that he was absent from classes, something that the examiners routinely noted in a student's test results. Second, a central motif in all accounts of this episode is an album that the youngster carried with him on his forays, in which he pasted reviews and admirers inscribed their encomiums. This album is extant, and its contents give a different chronology and sequence of events.

The album measures 23 cm. × 16 cm. and has a hard cover embossed with the word 'Album'. The poetic dedications written by his admirers do not appear in chronological order but were simply jotted down, some with considerable artistic flourish, wherever it was convenient. Newspaper clippings of reviews are also pasted inside. Occasional references to the 'Great Being', 'celestial harmonies', 'temples', and numerous comparisons to Mozart lead one to suspect that many of the concerts were for Masonic groups and that Ángel's Masonic connections may have been very useful in setting up these programmes. Performing the Masonic salute obviously helped to warm up such crowds.

---

[53] Guerra y Alarcón gives the impression that the flight from home occurred not long after the move to Madrid but does not specify the year. Clementina thought it occurred when he was 9.

[54] The exact course of his journeys varies from one version to the next, but this is the one in Guerra y Alarcón.

The first record of a concert is a clipping from the *Correspondencia teatral* in Valladolid, dated 15 February 1872, reviewing his performance in the Teatro Lope de Vega. It reports that he is giving concerts in northern Castile, and it is clear from the article that this was not his first concert but that he had been performing in January in Andalusia and Catalonia, and that the Barcelona papers were taking notice. But no records of those appearances surface in the archive. He was causing a sensation in Valladolid, however, where he was hailed as a 'little Mozart' and a 'genuine phenomenon'. 'Words fail us in praising such mastery, such feeling, such perfection . . . he will be one of the glories of Spanish art.'[55] Not bad for an 11-year-old. As was often the case in these performances, he was only part of the programme. Albéniz next appeared in Ubeda (17 March), Jaén (2 April), Córdoba (May), and Granada (June–July), where, on 16 July, two dedications on adjacent pages found their way into his album.[56] One praised the 'musical genius of the 9-year-old boy', while the succeeding one pegged his age at 10. Of course, he was already 12! He continued on to Lucena (July), Loja (31 July), Salar (1 August), Loja (2 August), and finally Málaga, on 29 August. He reappeared there in early November, bringing his season on the road to a close. This was a remarkable tour. There is no hint here, though, that Albéniz had run away from home or that these concerts were arranged at short notice after his arrival in town. Quite the opposite impression emerges, i.e. that these performances were arranged well in advance and that he was not out of touch with his family. For instance, how did he support himself between his appearance in Jaén on 2 April and his subsequent performance in Córdoba, over a month later, or between his two appearances in Málaga almost three months apart? His concert earnings could not have been sufficient. Albéniz probably gave more concerts than his album indicates (indeed, some of the entries are undated), and he must certainly have been the recipient of local generosity. But it is likely that he used his residence in Madrid as a base of operations and made arrangements from there. Some of his excursions were lengthier than others, but an inscription by Ángel himself casts doubt on his runaway status.

In the first half of 1873, only one inscription appears, dated 18 April in Madrid and containing a poem by one Fernando Martínez Pedrosa. On 30 September, Ángel (now working in Madrid) wrote a poem in Albéniz's album. Entitled 'Diálogo', it appears in its entirety below:

---

[55] 'Nos faltan frases para encomiar tanta maestría, tanto sentimiento, tanta perfección. . . . será una de las glorias del arte español.'

[56] The dates in parentheses are of the inscriptions, not necessarily the concerts.

Father, will you not place here
something of your inspiration?
am I nothing to you?
—nothing without application.
If God gives us genius,
He also gives us free will;
Nobody gets to the capitol
By the path of emptiness.
Son, you are no longer so young
That you know not how to meditate.
When I see you surrendered,
To art with lively faith,
In careless metre,
I will dedicate verses to you.[57]

Ángel casts the poem in the form of a conversation between himself and Isaac. Whether Isaac actually requested a dedication is impossible to know, but with or without invitation Ángel chides him, not for running away from home and scaring his family half to death but for neglecting his studies at the conservatory, to which the record shows he was less than devoted. This also puts the lie to any notion that, at this stage at least, Ángel was exploiting the child without regard to his artistic welfare. However, Ángel's employment records stimulate some speculation along those lines. His position in Cáceres ended in November 1871. This was shortly before Albéniz began the tour reported in the Valladolid newspaper. On 15 March 1873 Ángel assumed his new post in the federal office of Contabilidad e Intervención General (General Accounts and Auditing), and this is the period in which there is a dramatic attenuation of inscriptions in the album. It could well be that Ángel assisted his son in setting up these concerts and even accompanied him during the period he was evidently unemployed. Some parental guidance would have been in order, because the country was in the throes of civil war during this time, and it is clear from the album that the youngster performed in both federal and Carlist areas. (The northern regions of Navarre, Aragón, and the Basque country were hotbeds of Carlism, but revolts spread throughout the country after the abdication of Amadeo I in February of 1873.) Undoubtedly, these concerts would have provided welcome income. Once Ángel was settled in Madrid and working regularly, however, he expected his son to resume serious studies. But this Albéniz obviously did

---

[57] 'Padre, no pones aquí | algo de tu inspiración? | nada valgo para ti? |—nada sin aplicación. | Si Dios el genio nos dá, | tambien nos dá el albedrio; | nadie al Capitolio vá | por la senda del vacio. | Hijo, ya no eres tan niño, | que no sepas meditar. | Cuando te vea entregado, | al arte con viva fé, | en metro desaliñado, | versos te dedicaré.'

not want to do, and the inscriptions indicate that a spate of performances in the provinces ensued during the following academic year: El Escorial (28–30 November 1873), Ávila (2–9 December 1873), Toro (15 December 1873), Salamanca (30 December 1873 and 10 January 1874), Peñaranda de Braca-monte (21 January 1874), Valladolid (10 February 1874), Palencia (10 March 1874),[58] León (14 March 1874), Oviedo (29 March 1874), Avilés (5–9 April 1874), Gijón (18 April 1874), Orense (29 May 1874), Logroño (9 August 1874), and Barcelona (19 October 1874), where he played at the salon of the Bernareggi piano firm on the 18th.[59]

   Clearly, here is the string of concerts Albéniz referred to in the account he gave Guerra y Alarcón, though he was by this time a teenager and not a mere lad of 9 or 10. This certainly explains why he did not appear for his solfège exam on 6 June 1874. It is probable that father and son had a vehement disagreement over the studies-vs.-touring issue, and perhaps Albéniz did run away from home. Ángel must not have approved of this behaviour, but he could not have been trying very hard to curtail it, either. When Albéniz performed at the Escorial, for instance, the mayor was already acquainted with the family—far from being a stranger, he had recommended Ángel for the post he was currently holding![60] In his poem, Ángel acknowledged Isaac's genius and maturity, and he seems to have adopted a *laissez-faire* attitude. Ángel also encouraged the musical ambitions of his daughter Blanca, who aspired to sing zarzuela (Spanish operetta alternating spoken dialogue with set musical numbers). She was a chorister at the Teatro de la Zarzuela and substituted on one occasion for an ailing lead singer. She acquitted herself admirably but failed to secure a contract for the following season beginning in the autumn of 1874. Feeling rejected not only by the theatre but also by Ángel for this failure, she committed suicide in the Retiro (a large park near the Prado museum) at 1 p.m. on 16 October.[61] She was only 19 years old. This no doubt compelled Albéniz to bring his concert tour

[58] A dedication penned in Palencia on 10 Mar. 1874 salutes him as a 'son of the Vitorian poet Peruchico' and invokes the glory, fame, and pride of his native ground, in Vitoria. The critics in that region would always remain quick to claim him as one of their own.
   [59] Independent confirmation of this concert is to be found in the manuscript 'Concerts celebrats á Barcelona 1797–1901 de música simfónica i de camera', located in the Institut Univesitari de Documentació i Investigació Musicològica Josep Ricart i Matas, in Barcelona. The performance received a glowing review in *Diario de Barcelona*.
   [60] According to Ángel's employment records. In any event, rather than putting a runaway child alone on a train, does it not seem more likely that he would have held the boy until Ángel could come to pick him up?
   [61] Her death certificate is in the Registro Civil in Madrid, section 3 of volume 10-5, folio 233. It reveals that the family lived at San Onofre 4. Although the certificate does not state it was a suicide (she shot herself), this is what all sources report, including Laplane, *Albéniz*, 20 n. 2; Gauthier, *Albéniz*, 29; and in Guzmán, 'Los Albéniz', Franco (ed.), *Albéniz y su tiempo*, 24. The nature of the document itself substantiates this. Until now, however, the exact date has remained a mystery. The author thanks the Registro Civil for this information, and Jacinto Torres for helping to procure it.

to an abrupt close and return home. There are no more inscriptions in the album for the six months after his Barcelona appearance.

Events in the year 1875 provided the raw material for the most celebrated episode in Albéniz's youth: his stowing away on a steamer bound for the New World. Every biography places his wanderings in the Americas precisely during the period we have just surveyed, basing their chronology on Albéniz's assertion that he left on his transatlantic voyage at the age of 12. Of course, the album makes it abundantly clear that Albéniz was in Spain during the period 1872–5. But the following anecdote will illustrate just how far some writers would go to fit the proverbial square peg into a round hole. On 3 February 1947, Deledicque wrote from Buenos Aires to Albéniz's son-in-law Vicente Moya, the husband of his daughter Laura, asking about Albéniz's putative tenure in Argentina.[62] In pondering Collet's account, he could not comprehend why a steamer bound for Cuba would stop in Buenos Aires. (This would, after all, be the same as a steamer leaving Seattle bound for Tokyo and stopping first in Sydney.) The only steamers stopping in Buenos Aires were headed around Cape Horn for Peru. Moreover, he could find no evidence that that particular steamer, the *España*, had ever called at Buenos Aires.[63] None the less, if Albéniz said he toured in South America, then the city names that appear in his album must correspond to Ávila, *Ecuador*; Toro, *Colombia*; Valladolid, *Honduras*; and Palencia, *Guatemala*! He then reported his inability to find cities with the names of Avilés and Albacete on his map of Latin America. Deledicque eventually abandoned this convoluted and hopelessly improbable scheme and adopted a modified version of Collet's.

Albéniz's story of stowing away on a steamer in order to evade authorities in Cádiz is a fantasy based on fact. For he did concertize extensively in the Greater Antilles in the summer and autumn of 1875, and the album proves this beyond a doubt. He had performed in Albacete, Alicante, and Murcia in Spain during the period 3–17 April. His first known performance in the Americas took place on 21 May in San Juan, Puerto Rico.[64] On 12 June, he was in Mayagüez, Puerto Rico, and his next concerts took place at the end of August, in Cáguas, Puerto Rico. Here it was that José Ramos de Anaya wrote the Masonic dedication in his album, and even placed three dots in the shape

---

[62] Mm, car. 2.

[63] There was, however, such a vessel. According to Carlos Llorca, *La Compañia Trasatlantica en las campañas de ultramar* (Madrid, 1990), the steamer *España* belonged to the Trasatlantica Co. at least from 1876, and it transported troops and civilian passengers. The company's service to Cuba ran on the 15th and 30th of every month (according to advertisements in Madrid newspapers of the time). Unfortunately, most of the company's archives have been lost, and we cannot consult passenger manifests from this period to confirm Albéniz's voyage on that ship. I thank Lola Higueras of the Museo Naval in Madrid for this information.

[64] This is not mentioned in the album. See Emilio J. Pasarell, *Esculcando el siglo XIX en Puerto Rico* (Barcelona: Ediciones Rumbos, 1967), 96. He was merely part of the programme.

of a triangle (another Masonic symbol) inside his signature. Ángel's Masonic connections were still proving useful. The most extensive reviews come from newspapers in Havana, which covered his concerts there in the autumn. He performed in Santiago around 14 September, then made his way to Havana where he performed in late September and early October. These last two appearances merited reviews in the *Artísta de La Habana* on 23 September and 10 October. In September he had performed on the ship *Manzanillo* for some local luminaries, including the editors of *La bandera*, and executed selections from operas both facing and with his back to the piano. In October the paper reported that Albéniz brought together various distinguished people at his residence ('casa') at Amargura 14, including several writers, and again played both facing the piano and with his back to the piano. The report announced an upcoming appearance at the Casino Español (on the 12th) and later at the Teatro de Tacón. Revealingly, it also states that Albéniz is planning to go to Germany to complete his 'artistic education'. Later, on 6 November, *El espectador de La Habana* published a review of an Albéniz peformance that gives us a clearer idea of his 'act'. He performed with others in the salon of the restaurant El Louvre, executing a fantasy on motives from Donizetti's *The Daughter of the Regiment* and a 'Capricho de Concierto' of Weber, as well as a 'toy' ('juguete') on themes from Rossini's *The Barber of Seville*, which, to the audience's astonishment, he performed with his back to the piano.

This is the last clipping from 1875. Where he went after this date and until May of 1876 is unknown. It hardly seems possible that he could have gone to New York, toured the USA as far as San Francisco and back, crossed the Atlantic, and performed in Liverpool and London before commencing studies in Leipzig. Even if he did merely some part of this, why is there no indication of it whatsoever in the album? He continued to use his album into the early 1880s, yet not a single clipping or dedication places him anywhere in the Americas outside the Caribbean. For now, this six-month period remains shrouded in mystery. But it brings us back to a more important quandary, i.e. how did Albéniz arrive in the Greater Antilles in the first place? The stowaway story has always seemed suspect to this author. It is hard to imagine that even Albéniz's piano playing could have so charmed the ship's captain that he would neglect his duty, perhaps even international law, and not turn Albéniz over to the authorities at the first port of call (regardless of the passengers' having raised a collection for his passage); or that those authorities would have done anything but return the youth to Spain (especially when he was the son of an important government official). Again, Ángel's employment records suggest a more logical alternative. Ángel was appointed to the post of Interventor General (Inspector-General) in Havana in April of 1875, and he left the port of Cádiz on the 30th of that month to begin his new assignment. We now know from the following contemporary account that Albéniz performed in Cádiz on 29 April, the night before Ángel's departure:

In the function that took place on the evening of 29 April, a concert was given by the young pianist D[on] Isaac Albéniz, *in this city on his way to Cuba*, who at the tender age of thirteen has already succeeded in giving his name a profitable reputation. (Emphasis added.)[65]

As usual, Albéniz was a sensation; he thrilled the crowd with an arrangement of the Overture to Rossini's *Semiramide* performed with his back to the piano. As usual, he misrepresented his age; he was not 13 but only a month away from his fifteenth birthday. More to the point, this review makes it clear that his journey to the New World was no accident, no result of fleeing meddlesome authorities and stowing away on a ship. He knew his travel plans in advance and announced them to the press. He must have been travelling with his father, for how could they have been in the same city at the same time heading to the same destination overseas while having no inkling the other was about, especially when Albéniz was currently the toast of the town? Interestingly, Guzmán tells us that several of Ángel's friends were so impressed with young Albéniz's triumphs in Spain that they arranged a concert tour for him in the Americas, which they hoped would provide money for his education thereafter.[66] Thus we read in the Cuban newspapers that the 15-year-old had his own home and piano in Havana (something otherwise hard to imagine) and planned to continue his studies in Germany. All of this must have been in accord with Ángel's wishes to advance his son's career. Albéniz would soon attempt to fulfil those wishes, but the German gambit would merely provide him with another opportunity to overlay historical reality with a veneer of fantasy.

[65] José Rosetty, *Guía de Cádiz, el Puerto de Santa María, San Fernando y el Departamento 22* (Cadiz: Revista Médica, 1876), 153. 'En la función efectuada en la noche del 29 de Abril, dió un concierto el jóven pianista D. Isaac Albéniz, *artista que se hallaba en esta ciudad de paso para Cuba*, el cual á la tierna edad de trece años ha logrado ya unir á su nombre una ventajosa reputación.' The author is exceedingly grateful to Rosa Busquets of the library of the Museu Marítim in Barcelona for supplying this information. She received it from the Puerto de la Bahía de Cádiz, who also merit thanks.

[66] 'Los Albéniz', Franco (ed.), *Albéniz y su tiempo*, 28. It is worth mentioning that in Bretón's account of his first meeting with Albéniz, the young pianist announced to him his upcoming journey to the New World. Although Bretón's story in 'En la muerte', Franco (ed.), *Albéniz y su tiempo*, 122, of Albéniz's subsequent journey is inconsistent with the legend as usually presented (e.g. he was escaping from authorities in La Coruña), this is information he would have obtained directly from Albéniz. His personal experience of their first meeting is certainly more reliable. Though he described the youth as around 10 years old, many people inaccurately estimated his age, sometimes with Albéniz's assistance.

2

*With Distinction
(1876–1888)*

───────

ALBÉNIZ now entered a period of his life devoted to serious and persistent study. Ángel clearly understood that if the youth were to make the transition from child prodigy to mature artist, he would have to submit himself to a more disciplined path. The decision to study in Leipzig was logical, given the enormous prestige German music, musicians, and music schools enjoyed. How father and son imagined, though, that even so adaptable and clever a young man as he could survive in a country where he could not speak the local language, and few could speak his, is a mystery. But the famous conservatory held an irresistible lure, and it was in that direction Albéniz determined to go.

Despite the ravages of the Second World War, Albéniz's academic records survive in the library of the Hochschule für Musik Felix Mendelssohn-Bartholdy in Leipzig.[1] They reveal that he enrolled there on 2 May 1876, and terminated his studies a short time later, on 24 June (the Festival of St John) of the same year. During this brief tenure in Leipzig, Albéniz resided at the home of Dr Justus A. Bräutigam on Sebastian-Bach-Straße, 57 I.[2] Bräutigam was the director of the school for booksellers and the municipal vocational school for boys, a senior primary school teacher at St Thomas, and a member of the royal exam commissions for one-year volunteers and the regional post office.[3] Exactly what Albéniz's connection with him was is

[1] There are two documents: a record of Albéniz's admission (no. 2513), with personal information pertaining to his background, financial support, etc.; and a 'Lehrer Zeugniß' (also numbered 2513), which lists courses taken and provides comments of the respective professors. If we examine the records in Leipzig closely, we see that some familiar discrepancies appear. For instance, 1861 is stated as his birth year. It is also stated that he had been playing the piano since the age of 5 ('seit 5 Jahren', which could also mean for a period of five years); of course, we recall that, according to his sister Clementina, he knew his scales and arpeggios by the age of 3.

[2] This information was provided by the Stadtarchiv Leipzig in a letter to the author of 22 July 1991.

[3] Direktor der Lehranstalt für Buchhändler und der Städtische Fortbildungsschule für Knaben, Gymnasial-Oberlehrer an St Thomas, Mitgl. der Königliche Prüfungskommission für einjährig Freiwillige und der Prüfungskomm. b. d. kaiserl. Oberpost-Direktion.

uncertain. The records state that he was supporting Albéniz financially, and it is probable that he was serving as the boy's guardian, conveying to him funds sent from home. This would further support the view that Albéniz did not perfunctorily glide into Leipzig but rather that he and his family made arrangements for his study in advance.

According to the 'Lehrer Zeugniß' dated 9 November 1876, Albéniz studied theory and composition with Carl Piutti,[4] piano with Louis Maas[5] as well as Salomon Jadassohn,[6] and voice with Henry Schradieck.[7] He attended lectures by Oscar Paul[8] and participated in the chamber ensemble (under the supervision of Schradieck). With the exception of Jadassohn, none of these names appear in any biographical account. No studies with Carl Reinecke[9] are indicated in the records. His professors were almost unanimous in stating that he attended regularly at the beginning and was diligent,[10] which suggests he was enthusiastic. Jadassohn declared that he was not only diligent but that he 'started out making lovely progress'.[11] Why he withdrew so soon, then, is a matter of speculation. One possibility is that he was discouraged by difficulties with the language. According to Piutti, Albéniz remained absent from sessions in theory due to his insufficient command of German.[12] The explanation offered by Guerra y Alarcón was that, owing to his prodigality, he went through his savings (earned from his concerts in the Americas) in very short order, running out of money after only nine months. This explanation seems to hold a kernel of truth. Ángel's employment records indicate that he entered another hiatus in his work beginning on 9 July 1876 and that he did not resume his duties in Havana until February of 1877. His pay was suspended during this time, and he returned to Spain (embarking once again for Havana from Cádiz on 30

---

[4] Carl Piutti (1846–1902) was a composer and organist who began teaching at the conservatory in 1875. In 1880 he was appointed organist at the Thomaskirche. See Hugo Riemann, *Musik Lexikon*, 11th edn. (Berlin: M. Hesse, 1929), vol. ii.

[5] Louis Philipp Otto Maas (1852–89) was both a composer and piano virtuoso. He taught at the conservatory in Leipzig from 1875 to 1880, afterward moving to Boston, where he remained until his death. See *Grove's Dictionary of Music and Musicians, American Supplement (Revised)* (1935 edn.), 277.

[6] Jadassohn (1831–1902) was a teacher, conductor, and composer. A student of Liszt, he began teaching harmony, counterpoint, composition, and piano at the Leipzig conservatory in 1870. He was also the author of several theoretical treatises.

[7] Schradieck (1846–1918) was a violinist who had served as concertmaster of orchestras in Moscow, Hamburg, and the Gewandhaus in Leipzig. He took up a teaching post in Cincinnati in 1883 and later taught in Philadelphia and New York, where he died. See Riemann, *Musik Lexikon*, vol. ii.

[8] Paul (1836–98) was the author of numerous books on music theory, e.g. *Geschichte des Klaviers* (1868), *Handlexikon der Tonkunst* (1873), and *Lehrbuch der Harmonik* (1880). See Riemann, *Musik Lexikon*, vol. ii.

[9] Reinecke (1824–1910) was one of the outstanding piano teachers of the time, as well as a conductor and composer. He joined the faculty at Leipzig in 1860 and became director of the conservatory in 1897.

[10] 'Fleißig' was the adjective every professor except Piutti used to evaluate him.

[11] '[F]ing ansonst an hübsche Fortschritte zu machen.'

[12] '[W]egen mangelnder Kenntniß der deutschen Sprache.'

January of the following year). This imminent loss of income probably boded financial hardship and necessitated calling Albéniz home from Leipzig.

In the summer of 1876 it was obvious that if young Isaac were to continue his formal education abroad, he would require financial assistance. According to Guzmán, Albéniz was invited by several notables in Madrid to give a concert at the *Gaceta de Madrid* (located in the calle del Cid), of which the Baron of Cortes was the director. The audience of aristocrats, artists, and assorted literati was enchanted by his performance, and the Count of Romera evidently offered to introduce Albéniz to the royal family at La Granja to seek their assistance for his education.[13] Be this as it may, Albéniz did meet Guillermo Morphy y Ferriz, the secretary to King Alfonso XII, during the summer of 1876. Morphy (1836–99), of Irish ancestry, was himself a composer and musicologist[14] and had spent two years of his childhood in Germany (1844–6). After formal music training at Madrid, he studied for nine months in 1863 with Fétis[15] at Brussels, and he maintained connections with the musical establishment in that city. He entered royal service on 28 November 1863 and followed Isabel II into exile in 1868. He was responsible for Alfonso's education in Paris, and when the young man assumed the throne, Morphy became his secretary on 18 January 1875.[16] In 1885 he was made a count by Alfonso XII. Until 1891, he served as director of the Royal Concert Society in Madrid at the Teatro Real.

Morphy, then, was in a good position to judge musical talent, and he was suitably impressed by Albéniz's accomplishments and potential. He interceded with the king and secured a grant for the aspiring pianist so that he could study at the Conservatoire Royal in Brussels. Albéniz would not be the only representative from Spain, however. The talented young violinist Enrique Arbós, his former classmate at the Madrid conservatory, followed the next year to study with Henri Vieuxtemps in Brussels, on a grant from the Infanta Isabel, Princesa de Asturias. (Morphy also arranged this stipend and later served as patron of an aspiring young cellist from Catalonia by the name of Pau Casals.)

[13] 'Los Albéniz', Franco (ed.), *Albéniz y su tiempo*, 28.

[14] *LCM* 4/170 (3 Apr. 1884), 6, reported that his works included a *Zambra morisca* for piano four hands published in Berlin by Ries und Erler. His compositions also included, according to Collet, *Albéniz*, 24, a cantata, three operas, concert overtures, a sonata, piano pieces, and songs. As a scholar he made transcriptions of 16th-cent. vihuela music (*Les Luthistes espagnols du XVI siècle*, ed. Hugo Riemann and published in Leipzig in 1902) that were seminal in that field. While living in Paris, he came under the influence of the composer, conductor, and musicologist François Auguste Gevaert (1828–1908), at that time music director of the Opéra. Gevaert, himself an authority on Spanish music who had travelled in that country, stimulated Morphy's interest in Spanish 'lute' (meaning vihuela) music. See entry in Riemann, *Musik Lexikon*, vol. ii.

[15] An eminent musicologist, François Fétis (1784–1871) was director of the Brussels conservatory until his death. He was succeeded by Gevaert.

[16] This information is from the file on Morphy in the Archivo del Palacio Real in Madrid.

Albéniz was admitted to the Conservatoire Royal in Brussels on 17 October 1876.[17] According to the conservatory yearbook for 1876–7, on 27 July 1877 Albéniz performed the *Pastorale et scherzo* by Scarlatti (arr. by Tausig) in an 'audition des classes de moniteurs de piano', and he is listed as a student of Franz Rummel.[18] In the yearbook for the following academic year (1877–8) we learn that he and Arbós performed the *Rondo brillant* for piano and violin, Op. 70, by Schubert, on 14 February 1878.[19] He is now listed in Brassin's class, in which he was to remain. Louis Brassin (1846–84) was one of the great piano teachers of the era and had himself been a student of Ignaz Moscheles (1794–1870) at the Leipzig conservatory. In addition to piano, Albéniz studied harmony with Joseph Dupont[20] and solfège with Jan Lamperen. He also participated in the vocal ensemble. His initial address was rue Souveraine 71, but on the 'Demande' a line was at some point drawn through this and a new address inserted, at rue du Prince Albert 4. The former building still stands at that address, but the latter has since been demolished.

During these years of study, Albéniz also gave lessons to Rafael Merry del Val, son of the Spanish ambassador in Brussels and later a cardinal in Rome.[21] The ambassador evidently monitored the young pianist's activities and progress, but on at least one occasion Ángel himself travelled to Brussels to check up on his son (probably during 1878, when he was on leave from his post in Cuba). Arbós described him at this time as 'small, with white sideburns, impetuous and irascible, beside himself in hurling insults at his son', who understandably made himself scarce whenever his father was around.[22] Indeed, Albéniz may have travelled to the United States in the summer of that year as the accompanist for a Belgian lyric-theatre troupe, though there is as yet no evidence of it.[23] There are several amusing stories from this

---

[17] According to a 'Demande d'Admission' (no. 886) preserved in the records of the administration of the Conservatoire Royal.

[18] *Annuaire du Conservatoire Royal de Musique de Bruxelles*, vol. ii (Brussels: Librarie Europeénne C. Muquardt, 1878), 70. Franz Rummel (1853–1901) had been a student of Louis Brassin and also composed for the piano.

[19] *Annuaire*, vol. iii (1879), 62. The activities of Arbós and Albéniz were the subject of a piece in the *Diario de Cádiz* dated 23 Aug. 1878 (clipping in the Mm in Albéniz's album, car. 4). The critic effuses that 'under his able and agile fingers, the piano sighs, cries, and sings' ('bajo sus hábiles y ligeros dedos, el piano suspira, llora é canta').

[20] Dupont (1827–90) was a Belgian pianist and composer who began teaching at the conservatory in 1850.

[21] Collet, *Albéniz*, 26–7. There is a letter to Albéniz from Rafael Merry del Val (Bc, 'M') responding to the composer's question about a particular Gregorian chant. The musical authorities at the Vatican were unable to identify the melody Albéniz had sent, but it is not clear why he wanted this information. The letter is undated but came from Rome.

[22] Enrique Fernández Arbós, *Arbós* (Madrid: Ediciones Cid, 1963), 68–9: 'pequeño, con patillas blancas, impetuoso e irascible, deshaciéndose en denuestos contra el hijo.'

[23] This sojourn was first reported in Guerra y Alarcón, *Albéniz*, 26, and repeated in subsequent accounts.

period that Arbós related to Collet. They have the ring of authenticity and bear repetition here.[24]

Albéniz, Arbós, and fellow pensioner Eusebio Daniel (an organ student) enjoyed playing with lead soldiers, amassing thousands of them in mock battles inspired by those taking place in the war between Russia and Turkey (1877–8). Albéniz evidently spent much of his stipend on these toys, something the other two could not afford to do. On one occasion the 'canonades' became so loud that the concierge summoned the police to see what was going on.

Albéniz also had a great love of practical jokes. Daniel was enrolled in François Gevaert's composition class, and Gevaert instructed Albéniz to tell Daniel that he should procure a viola because the class would be learning how to write for strings. Albéniz instead told him that he was to get a bassoon because they would be studying winds. Daniel went to some trouble to do this, only to report to class with the wrong instrument! Gevaert was at first annoyed, but soon forgave the credulous organ student upon hearing his explanation for the error.

The most sensational episode from these years concerns a suicide pact that Albéniz entered into with a fellow student from Latin America (Arbós could not remember his name). How serious Albéniz was about this is hard to tell. It may have been a youthful whim, or perhaps he was genuinely depressed. Whatever the case, his friend decided to let Albéniz live and went ahead with the plan on his own. This tragedy jolted Albéniz out of his complacency, and he redoubled his efforts to prepare for the coming examinations.

Albéniz tied with Louvain native Arthur de Greef[25] for first place, *avec distinction*, in the 1879 piano competition in Brassin's class (they were evenly matched, and the jury could not decide).[26] There were four contestants on this occasion. These competitions examined more than mere digital dexterity, and Albéniz's victory gives us ample reason to admire his overall musicianship at this stage in his career. In addition to playing works of their own choice, contestants were required to perform a work announced by the examiners only fifteen days in advance of the competition. They also had to read a work at sight; transpose at sight to a given pitch the accompaniment of

---

[24] These accounts appear in Collet, *Albéniz*, 28–31. The author debated whether to use them. Though Arbós was not always a reliable source of information (he was relating the events several decades after they took place), he was not prone to fabrication. And they seem consistent with what we know about Albéniz, especially during his teens.

[25] De Greef (1862–1940) went on to study with Liszt in Weimar, then joined the faculty at Brussels. He was also a composer. De Greef said that the competition resulted in a tie in a conversation with Ramón Reig, 'Isaac Albéniz', *Revista de Gerona*, 5/6 (Primer Trimestre de 1959), 55–6.

[26] The certificate of First Prize in Piano with Distinction is in his correspondence (Bc, 'V' (Varia)).

a vocal or instrumental work; read at sight an orchestral score; and realize a figured-bass accompaniment. Albéniz performed a 'capriccioso' of Scarlatti and the *Variations brillantes* of Chopin as works of his own choice.[27] The required piece on this occasion was the Allegro from Mozart's C major Piano Concerto. Arbós also won first prize, *avec grande distinction*, in violin, and completed a *diplôme de capacité*. Three years later, Daniel won in organ.[28] According to Arbós, Gevaert was inspired to exclaim to the jury, 'Send us more Spaniards!'

Albéniz terminated his studies at the conservatory in September of 1879. He returned to Barcelona a local hero and gave a concert on 12 September 1879 at the Teatre Espanyol that had the critics singing his praises.[29] Shortly thereafter he made an appearance at the Teatre de Novetats, which was reported in *Publicidad de Barcelona* on 16 September.[30] His programme consisted of Liszt's *Rigoletto* paraphrase, Brassin's transcriptions of excerpts from Wagner's *Ring*, an impromptu by Schubert, capriccios by Scarlatti, a movement from a Mendelssohn concerto (unspecified, but probably the D minor), and études and variations by Chopin. The reviewer noted his excellent hand position, clarity and cleanness of execution, admirable contrasts in tone colour, and equality in repeated notes, tremolo, and arpeggios. This reminds us of Casals's observation that Albéniz's hands were small but had an 'astonishing strength and suppleness'.[31] On the 28th of that month his appearance at the salon of the piano makers Raynard y Maseras again received favourable attention from *Publicidad de Barcelona*. Finally, on 30 September the *Diario de Barcelona* gave notice of Albéniz's departure for Madrid.

All sources state that, after this triumphal appearance in Barcelona, he returned to Brussels for additional studies with Brassin. In the event, Brassin retired from the Conservatoire at the end of the 1878–9 academic year and moved to Russia, where he took up a post as professor of piano at the conservatory in St Petersburg. This does not altogether preclude the possibility that Albéniz studied with him further, but we cannot confirm or deny

[27] *Annuaire*, vol. iv (1880), 66. The rules for the competition appear in this volume on pages 32–7 and indicate that the jury consisted of from five to seven members. There is no corroborating evidence to support the claim in *Diario de Barcelona* (20 Sept. 1879) that the jury included Hans von Bülow and Anton Rubinstein. If the paper got that information from Albéniz, there would be good reason to doubt it.

[28] Daniel's success was reported in *LCM* 2/90 (20 Sept. 1882), 6.

[29] Reference to this is made in 'Concerts Celebrats á Barcelona'.

[30] This clipping is found in his album. Other clippings in the album, from the *Gaceta de Cataluña* and *Diario de Barcelona* (both dated 24 Aug. 1879), indicate that he also performed in the salon of the Navas piano factory in late August in Barcelona. The *Crónica de Barcelona* (30 Sept. 1879) placed him in the 'escuela clássica' of pianists.

[31] See Corredor, *Conversations with Casals*, 162.

this on the basis of existing records.[32] We do know that he performed in
Vitoria, his father's home town, on 30 April 1880, exactly seven months after
he had left Barcelona for Madrid.[33] Here he was hailed as a hero of whom all
Vitorians could be proud, the son of their very own Peruchico! The casino of
Vitoria even made him an honorary member and presented him with a set of
golden buttons. To make sure there was no doubt as to his Basqueness, the
local paper explained that the reason he was born in Catalonia was simply
that his mother was called there on family business a few days before his
birth.[34] This in no way prevented the locals from claiming him as a 'son of
the White Virgin'. Three months after this triumph, Albéniz set out to
realize his dream of studying with Liszt, and on his journey he kept a diary,
three pocket-size notebooks filled with observations jotted down in pencil.[35]
What ensues is a perplexing blend of fact and fiction.

   According to this journal, Albéniz leaves Brussels by train on 12 August
1880 in search of Liszt. His immediate destination is Prague, passing through
Cologne, Magdeburg, and Dresden on the way. He is enchanted by the
beauties of the Bohemian capital, but has little money to live on. He finds
that, with their scarves, shawls, and large black eyes, the women of the city
resemble Spaniards; in fact, all the people are attractive, and he spots not a
single one he could describe as ugly. His astonishing explanation for this is
that the Bohemians are a 'pure race', unlike the bastardized folk of Belgium!
Finding that Liszt is not in Prague, he determines to set out for Budapest,
selling his watch to secure rail passage. The reader wonders why Albéniz
would ever have thought he might find Liszt in Prague. At this time in his life,
Liszt made an annual circuit between Weimar, Rome, and Budapest. Prague

[32] In spite of the report in the London newspaper *Lady* (6 Nov. 1890) several years later, it is not likely
that he followed Liszt to Italy and in his spare time played for Brassin while the latter pursued his hobby
of painting. This account improbably places Brassin in Italy in 1880, and further declares that Brassin 'used to
say that he could never use the brush so well as when Albéniz was playing to him!' Where this fiction
originated is unknown. Secondary sources do not all agree on the year of Brassin's retirement. The *New
Grove Dictionary of Music and Musicians* (1980 edn.) gives 1878 as the year, while Nicolas Slonimsky, *Baker's
Biographical Dictionary* (8th edn.), provides the correct year of 1879. Brassin's retirement in that year is
corroborated by a biographical summary contained in an obituary that appeared in *LCM* 4/179 (5 June
1884), 7, upon Brassin's death. The *Annuaire*, vol. iv (1880) informs us that Brassin's replacement, Jules de
Zarembski, assumed his position on 30 Jan. 1880. Albéniz's participation in the 1879 competition in Brassin's
class, as reported in the *Annuaire*, proves that Brassin's vacated post was filled only six months after his
departure.
[33] As reported in the *Anunciador de Vitoria*, 4 May 1880. Clipping in the Mm, car. 4.
[34] Evidently, it was important that his conception and gestation had transpired in the Basque country, but
whether this was Albéniz's or the journalist's invention we do not know.
[35] These are in the Mm. The third notebook is in car. 4, while the first two are kept on display in the
Albéniz exhibit in the museum. A typewritten copy of this document was later executed by his daughter Laura
(Mm, car. 1), and it is on the basis of this that Enrique Franco edited the printed version now available,
Impresiones y diarios de viaje, which also contains entries from diaries Albéniz kept later in his life. Regrettably,
Franco did not consult the original notebooks and diaries, and Laura's expurgation of potentially offensive or
embarrassing remarks persists. (She also cleaned up his punctuation and orthography.)

was not one of his regular haunts. The potential for sheer waste of time, energy, and money tracking down Liszt in this unmethodical way must have occurred to him, or at least to his friends and elders. (Would not Brassin have offered useful advice? Brassin had encouraged de Greef to study with Liszt, and the young Belgian proceeded directly to Weimar in 1880 to do so. Certainly Albéniz must have been aware of this.) Normally, one would have telegraphed or written to Liszt to arrange a meeting. But Albéniz had a propensity for spontaneity and improvisation, and one must simply accept most of this account, incredible to us though it may seem. On his way to Budapest he stops in Vienna, but not without first losing some money in a card game on the train. From Vienna he takes a boat to Buda on the Danube—a river he considers to be more muddy than 'blue'—leaving at 7 a.m. and arriving at 7 p.m. After a change of craft, though he only purchased a second-class ticket, he makes himself comfortable in first class 'with the utter shamelessness that is characteristic of me', he exults.[36] Albéniz is enraptured by the beauty of the scenery along the river. His roving eye takes in a Turkish girl near him whom he finds very attractive but who remains indifferent to his advances. (He later discovers that she is not a Turk but an Assyrian Jewess.) Finally, on 15 August, three days after leaving Brussels, he disembarks in Budapest, taking rooms at the Hotel Kaizerin Elisabeth. Albéniz is evidently not without connections, as he refers to having supper at the house of a 'friend', where he promptly gets drunk. He wakes up the next morning with a hangover and resorts to magnesia and tea to relieve his symptoms.

He finally leaves his hotel around 11 a.m. to visit his friend, who lives nearby on the same street. He finds Budapest 'a thousand times' better than Vienna, and notices again the similar appearance of the people he sees to Spaniards. After commenting favourably on a statue of Christopher Columbus, he briefly mentions seeing Liszt: 'I have seen Liszt; I will study; he receives me tomorrow.'[37] He then launches into a description of the museum of natural history, which contains a 'rich collection of birds', and his admiration of the city's museums occupies the next several paragraphs. Since his ostensible reason for making this trip was to study with Liszt, his offhand reference seems oddly like an afterthought. Moreover, he does not see Liszt on the following day, which is instead given over to more sightseeing, in spite of the fact that he is still feeling in poor health and considers calling a doctor (intestinal problems would plague him the rest of his life and eventually kill him). The following day, the 18th, is cited in every post-Collet biography as the one on which the all-important meeting with the Hungarian master takes

---

[36] *Impresiones*, ed. Franco, 11. '[C]on la poquísima vergüenza que me caracteriza.'
[37] Ibid, 14. 'He visto a Liszt; voy a estudiar; mañana me recibe.'

place. But in the diary, Albéniz reveals that other activities are competing for his attention. He starts his day early, around 7 a.m., by viewing a military parade in honour of the Emperor (Albéniz's youthful love of things martial ever to the fore). He is enchanted by the precision of the soldiers' movements on the parade ground, to the strains of the 'Austrian March' of Haydn. He rejoices also in the return of his appetite, which has been absent for five days. But he restrains these carnal longings and instead nourishes his soul on the *objets d'art* in the museums of sculpture and painting, whose holdings he contemplates with remarkable attention to detail for someone who shortly will be playing for the greatest pianist of the nineteenth century. Suddenly, without any lead-in, he inserts the famous single paragraph describing his encounter with Liszt, which follows:[38]

I went to see Liszt; he greeted me in a most friendly manner; I played two of his études and a Hungarian rhapsody; this appeared to please him greatly, above all when I improvised an entire dance on a Hungarian theme he gave me; he requested details about Spain, about my parents, about my ideas on religious matters, and, finally, on music in general. I responded frankly and categorically what I thought about all of that, and he appeared to be enchanted. The day after tomorrow I am supposed to return to see him.

In the next paragraph, he states that he must buy works by Zola and Tourgueneff [*sic*]. Whether these were Liszt's instructions or not is unclear. His narrative then veers back to his health problems and a sudden interest in homeopathy. The entries for the next two days make no mention of Liszt or any further meetings with him. Instead, he meditates on more sightseeing, money problems, and the need for patience in 'conquering' a lovely young girl he has met (all his normal 'methods' of conquest have proven useless). He is waiting for money to arrive from his father, but in the meantime he relies on the generosity of a restaurateur by the name of Holzwart (possibly the 'friend' he has referred to). All of this strongly suggests that Albéniz and/or his father had made some arrangements in advance and that this trip was not undertaken in a completely perfunctory manner; or perhaps he made this person's acquaintance during his journey. But his plans are thrown into confusion when he discovers that Liszt is leaving immediately for Rome. He himself departs on the afternoon of the 22nd, only a week after his arrival, and threads his way back to Madrid through Vienna and Paris.

[38] This entry is contained in the second of the three notebooks. The following excerpt is taken from the Franco edition, 21. 'He ido a ver a Liszt; me ha acogido de la manera más amable; he tocado dos de sus estudios y una rapsodia húngara; le ha gustado mucho, al parecer, sobre todo cuando sobre un tema húngaro que él me ha dado he improvisado toda una danza; me ha pedido detalles sobre España, sobre mis padres, sobre mis ideas en materia de religión y, en fin, sobre la música en general. He respondido franca y categoricamente lo que pensaba de todo eso y ha parecido quedar encantado; pasado mañana debo volver a ir a verle.'

There is only one major problem with Albéniz's diary entries concerning his meetings with Liszt in Budapest: the encounters did not take place. We know for certain that Liszt was not in Budapest in August 1880, as his extant correspondence includes a letter he wrote to the Ödenburger 'Liederkranz' dated '18ten August, 80. Weimar'.[39] On the previous day Liszt had written from Weimar to Ferenc Erkel informing him that he would not return to Budapest until the middle of January of the following year. Why Albéniz fabricated the encounters is uncertain. If his father were funding this central European safari in search of Liszt, then Albéniz would indeed have been well advised to return with some evidence that he had bagged, or at least got a piece of, his quarry. In the event, the only trophy he could offer was bogus diary entries. Though at first glance they seem detailed, in fact they are remarkably cryptic compared to the lengthy accounts of local attractions, both cultural and sexual, he carefully inscribes. One would at least expect some description of Liszt's appearance and residence, how and where he contacted him, and so on. We notice, too, that in his brief lesson with the master, the young Spaniard did all the talking! Liszt was simply feeding him questions, and apparently had nothing specific to say about Albéniz's playing or about his own extensive perambulations of the Iberian peninsula in 1845. Albéniz obviously inserted these fictional meetings with Liszt in order to justify to his family—and perhaps to posterity, of which he was keenly aware even early in life—what turned out to be little more than a sightseeing excursion.[40]

In their fixation on the Liszt episode, biographers have neglected other passages in his diary that tell us much more important things about the young man. For instance, at an outdoor religious ceremony in Budapest on the 20th, Albéniz notes a 'high degree of religious intolerance' among the locals when a man is beaten by the mob for neglecting to doff his hat as the sacrament passes. This behaviour he finds simply 'stupid'.[41] The behaviour of

[39] See Margit Prahács (ed.), *Franz Liszt: Briefe aus ungarischen Sammlungen 1835–1886* (Kassel: Bären-reiter, 1966), 232.

[40] In another diary that Albéniz started during a stay in Nice in 1898 (Mm, car. 4), his introductory entry, dated 1 Apr., states that he is 'leaving to posterity an undying memory of my important passage through this enchanting world' (see Ch. 6 for more on this diary). He had wanted to do this since the age of 10. There is no reason to think that his earlier journals were not likewise intended for more than merely personal perusal. Though it may seem too cynical, one cannot exclude the possibility that studying with Liszt was no more than the excuse he offered for going on a vacation. As to the possibility that the dates in the diary are incorrect and that all this happened at some other time, according to Maria Eckhardt of the Liszt Ferenc Memorial Museum and Research Centre (in a letter to this author of 27 Dec.1991), no reference to Albéniz is to be found in the archive, either as a student or in correspondence. Neither was Liszt in Budapest in the summer of 1878, when Collet placed Albéniz there.

[41] During his earlier encounter with the Jewish family on the boat to Budapest, he had written that their religion was 'all the same' to him. Throughout his life he would resist anti-Semitism, even in the privacy of his thoughts. See Ch. 6 for his response to the Dreyfus affair.

his father earns as much opprobrium. The money Ángel was supposed to send is very late in arriving, putting Albéniz in a precarious financial position. To make matters worse, Ángel had apparently travelled to Brussels and was discrediting his son to some important friends, including Edmond Picard (1836–1924), one of the founders of the modernist organization Libre-Esthétique. We do not know the exact details of this intrigue, but the stakes were evidently high, as Albéniz wrote on the 23rd that if his 'secret' were disclosed by Ángel to Picard, he himself would be 'lost'. In any event, he finds his father's machinations indefensible for a man his age. But his confidence in himself remains unshaken, and he crows that 'I was born for extraordinary things'. His money having finally arrived, Albéniz sets course for Vienna on the 22nd in order to become better acquainted with that city. He soon realizes that during his first stop he had seen the worst quarter of Vienna. Now he is overwhelmed by the splendour of the place. Although Albéniz dutifully records the exact amount he pays for his lodging and other purchases, he is not altogether thrifty and is unable to resist occasional luxuries, such as riding in a private coach to the Prater park (we recall his earlier loss of money in a card game). He tours an exposition of mechanical inventions there that merits his close attention, then finds refreshment at an outdoor café. His observation of his waiter leads him to philosophical ruminations on life itself. He notes that though his waiter is a fine-looking young man, he seemed resentful that Albéniz did not tip his hat when he requested service. No one is really happy with his lot in this life, Albéniz reflects. He has never encountered anyone who was satisfied with the world, and he himself feels a discontent that even riches could not ameliorate. But he does not remain in this mental rut for long. He is proud of the fact that he successfully posed as a foreign journalist in order to gain access to some areas of the exposition closed to tourists. Albéniz's deceptions, secrets, and manipulations (e.g. 'methods of conquest') suggest a well-developed capacity for dishonesty. One suspects that this and his acute powers of observation were the essential survival skills he acquired in his turbulent home life. At some point, however, they became habits he could not always control, as we noted in the introduction. Yet, on the 25th he virtuously claims that he has tried hard not to take advantage of the 'easy' Austrian women, who were showing great interest in him. Overall, however, his lack of artistic success on this trip is a disappointment to him, and once back in Madrid on 16 September, he reveals that he was close to taking his own life a few days earlier in Paris. In Albéniz, depression and exuberance always existed side by side.

Most accounts relate that during the autumn of 1880 Albéniz 'got religion', at least for a brief spell. Under its influence, and perhaps that of Abbé

Liszt, he spent some time in a Benedictine monastery in Salamanca and considered becoming a monk. But it soon became clear that he was not cut out for the life, and he resumed his concert touring.[42] Though we have, in fact, no evidence of his religious 'calling' during 1880, we know that he did enter the army reserves, enlisting in the Buena Vista district.[43] His fascination with military trappings may have got the best of him, or perhaps the service was obligatory. But it in no way slowed down his concert career.

December of 1880 found Albéniz back in Havana giving concerts. The *Diario de La Habana* reported in that month that he performed at El Louvre, half of the concert's proceeds going to the Real Casa de Beneficia y Maternidad. He entertained his audience with the *Rhapsodie espagnole* of Liszt as well as the E flat Polonaise of Chopin, capriccios by Scarlatti, and a waltz by Joachim Raff (1822–82). He also performed in a Beethoven trio that had to be repeated at the insistence of the audience. A later concert at the Círculo Español, reported in *El bien público* on 10 February, gives our first notice of Albéniz's talents as a conductor, leading the local orchestra in selections from *Le Pré aux clercs* by Hérold.[44] He then played the G minor Concerto of Mendelssohn, followed by the solo numbers mentioned above. The critic enthused that Albéniz delivered an 'interpretation that makes us think that music as a subjective art penetrates the head in the very region of the psychology and manifests the feelings, ideas, intentions, and the fabric that constitutes human nature'.[45] In Santiago a few days later he performed in the Teatro de la Reina, rendering Chopin's C minor Polonaise, a *Fantasia on a Theme of Halévy* (composer unnamed; perhaps an improvisation by Albéniz), a solo arrangement of the Mendelssohn D minor Concerto, and Boccherini's famous Minuet, as well as *Rigadon de Dardanus* by Rameau and an étude by Liszt, which left the reviewer praising the perfection, taste, and feeling of a 'delicate soul'.[46]

Our information about Albéniz's activities during the rest of 1881 is more limited, but it was an eventful year for him and his family. Ángel retired as Interventor en la Ordenación de Pagos de la Isla de Cuba (Inspector of

---

[42] Collet, *Albéniz*, 40. Albéniz evidently related this episode to Carlos de Castéra, who then told it to Collet, in whose account it first appears. Deledicque, *Albéniz*, 184–7, greatly elaborates on it, but without any substantiation.

[43] His military papers are in the Mm, car. 1, but they do not provide the exact date of his enlistment.

[44] Louis Joseph Ferdinand Hérold (1791–1833). His three-act *opéra comique Le Pré aux clercs* premiered in Dec. 1832, weeks before the composer's death. The review does not specify what numbers appeared on this programme.

[45] '[I]nterpretación que... nos hizo pensar que la música como arte subjectivo penetra al cabo en el terreno propio de la psicología y manifesta los sentimientos, las ideas, los propósitos y en fin el tejido que constituye la humana naturaleza.'

[46] This notice appeared in *Santiago de Cuba* (15 Feb. 1881). Press notices of these Cuban concerts are found in the album.

Payment Arrangements for the Island of Cuba) on 7 January, probably due to ill health, which had necessitated his returning to Spain for a respite some years earlier (from April to July in 1878). Among Ángel's records of employment and retirement one finds other papers detailing a seamy side of his character that placed a huge emotional and financial burden on the family. When Ángel died in 1903, a woman by the name of María Romero Cebrian applied, unsuccessfully, to receive his pension.[47] Ángel had married this woman in 1901, after the death of Dolores, but she had been his mistress for many years. According to Albéniz's granddaughter Rosina Moya Albéniz de Samsó,[48] María was the family cook. She and Ángel had five children during the period 1877–89, and they lived together for many years after his retirement.[49] Ángel and Dolores were obviously not happily married, and Ángel's long absences from the family during his career must have contributed greatly to their eventual separation. This entire situation was a source of continuing bitterness to Albéniz, who eventually wound up partially supporting his mother as well as Ángel and his illegitimate children.

A photograph of a certain Quintin Garreta[50] raises the intriguing possibility of a trip to New York on the way back from Cuba. It is signed on the back and dated New York, 18 March 1881 (the photograph itself was taken on 1 November 1880). Its inscription reads: 'Here you have, oh great pianist, the humble proof of your sincere friend's appreciation.' But substantive evidence of Albéniz's New York concerts has yet to surface.[51]

We do know a great deal about his trip to Granada in July of that year.[52] He had performed there nine years earlier, as a boy of 12. Now, he was a grown man and an artist of impressive stature. Albéniz had a great love of

---

[47] It went to Albéniz's elder sister Clementina. María appealed again in 1933 on the death of Clementina, but was turned down because she and Ángel had married too late in life for her to qualify.

[48] In a conversation with the author, 23 July 1995.

[49] It is unclear if she accompanied him to Cuba. This would seem improbable, as it would have been scandalous for a man in his position to be living openly with such a woman. It seems unclear how the first child, Antonia, born 13 June 1877, could have been conceived, until we recall that Ángel returned to Spain in the last six months of 1876, during a period of unemployment.

[50] In the photograph collection of the Albéniz archive in the Mm. '¡Aquí tenéis oh gran pianista! la humilde prueba de aprecio de vuestro sincero amigo.'

[51] An account in *LCM* 1/14 (6 Apr. 1881), 5, reports on his Santiago concerts of 10 Feb. 1881, stating that the young pianist had toured Germany and the USA *before* his arrival there. A search of the index to the *New York Times* for the 1870s and 1880s, however, reveals no mention of Albéniz. His obituary notice on page 9, column 4, of the 20 May 1909 edition is extremely brief and makes no mention of any New York connections. An extensive obituary in the Mexican *Correo musical*, 1/4 (Aug. 1909), 1–3, likewise makes no mention of any Albéniz concerts in that country.

[52] The following is based on Luis Seco Lucena, 'En la Alhambra', in Franco (ed.) *Albéniz y su tiempo*, 105–9 (reprint of an article that appeared in *Cuadernos de la Alhambra* (Granada, 1982)). Lucena's father was present at Albéniz's 11 July concert. Ten years later, during his triumphal concerts in London, Albéniz sent the elder Lucena clippings from the English press to demonstrate the efforts he was making to promote Spanish music and musicians there, asking that the reports be published in the Granada newspaper *El defensor*.

Granada, which he expressed in some of his most popular piano pieces, e.g. *Zambra granadina*, 'En la Alhambra', 'Granada (Serenata)', 'Torre Bermeja', and 'El Albaicín'. Granada—with its dramatic setting at the foot of the snow-clad Sierra Nevada mountains, its whitewashed buildings with red-tile roofs, Renaissance cathedral, and famous Moorish fortress-palace, the Alhambra, last stronghold of the Muslims in Spain—was a mecca for artists, writers, and musicians seeking the heart and soul of Andalusia.[53] Albéniz gave private performances in the homes of Granada's leading citizens, who were lovers of music already familiar with the spreading aureole of his fame. Albéniz spent his days not in solitary practice but enjoying the splendours of the Alhambra and the adjacent gardens of the Generalife. He made the acquaintance of the archaeologist in charge of conservation there, Rafael Contreras, who answered his many questions about the history and art of the famous complex of buildings. As repayment for this generous tutelage, Albéniz proposed to give a concert in Sr. Contreras's own home for his friends and family on the evening of 11 July. Among those present was the host's daughter, whom Albéniz had noticed with interest during his tours of the Alhambra. (Lacking a formal introduction, he had been unable to make her acquaintance earlier.) Albéniz poured forth his emotions in works from the Romantic repertoire, and concluded with improvisations that might well have contained the thematic seeds that later sprouted into his Granada-inspired compositions. On this occasion, he solemnly vowed to his audience that the themes upon which he had improvised would form the basis of an opera dealing with the fabled past of Granada, if he could prevail upon a writer-friend of his to craft the libretto. Nothing ever eventuated in regard to this laudable intention, or his latest romantic infatuation.

Albéniz next travelled north to Santander, where a critic exulted that under his hands 'the instrument reveals all of the divine mysteries of music; it thunders, sings, shouts, laughs, cries, moans, sobs, and sighs, mimicking as only art knows how to do, the agitations, the anguish, the sorrows, and the jubilation of the soul'.[54] 'Frenetic applause' greeted Albéniz in Zaragoza that

---

[53] Washington Irving is one of the more celebrated writers to live in and write about Granada (*The Alhambra*, 1832). According to Lucena, 'En la Alhambra', 109, Anton Rubinstein (1829–94), to whom Albéniz was later often compared by the press, visited Granada in Mar. of 1881, four months before Albéniz's arrival. The violinist Pablo de Sarasate (1844–1908) performed there in 1887, and the Catalan guitarist Francisco Tárrega (1854–1909) resided there for several weeks in 1899. His famous tremolo study *Recuerdos de la Alhambra* is one of the most popular compositions inspired by Granada, which was later the home of Manuel de Falla (1876–1946) and is currently the location of the Archivo Manuel de Falla.

[54] *LCM* 1/31 (3 Aug. 1881), 6. This item was based on a review that had appeared in the local newspaper *La montaña*: 'el instrumento revela todos los divinos misterios de la música; truena, canta, grita, ríe, llora, gime, solloza y suspira, remedando, como sólo el arte sabe hacerlo, las agitaciones, las angustias, los dolores y el júbilo del alma.'

autumn,[55] and a later appearance on 3 December in Pamplona was 'listened to until the final note amidst the most religious silence'.[56]

January of 1882 found Albéniz still in the north country. He performed in Bilbao between Acts I and II of a production of Joaquín Gaztambide's zarzuela *El juramento* ('The judgement'), which was a benefit for the Santa Casa de Misericordia. Shortly after this performance, Albéniz entered into a new musical arena, composing for the stage. That he fancied his future to be in writing musical theatre was abundantly clear already in Granada the previous year. Now he actually began to realize that ambition. It is one of the curiosities of Albéniz's career as a composer that, though he is best known for his piano works, his first important compositions were zarzuelas. In fact, Albéniz's greatest aspiration was to compose for the stage. *Iberia* was written only after he had exhausted himself attempting to gain acceptance, particularly in Spain, as a composer of musical theatre.

Albéniz told Guerra y Alarcón in 1886 that he had composed three zarzuelas. But he gave no specific dates for them, and evidence of their existence has been lacking until recently. Guerra y Alarcón states that in early 1882 Albéniz took up residence in Madrid and there became the director of a zarzuela company. He gives no specifics concerning any performances except to say that the project soon foundered on the shoals of insolvency, and Albéniz resumed his career as a travelling virtuoso in order to recoup his loses. Today nothing remains of these early works except their titles,[57] though we have a more accurate picture of their genesis and production than that available to earlier commentators. *Cuanto más viejo*, composed to a one-act libretto by one Sr. Zapino, 'colonel of the military administration', premiered in Bilbao in 1882.[58] Notice of the impending completion of this zarzuela appeared in the press in early February.[59] Two weeks later the following report emanated from Bilbao:

[55] *LCM* 1/46 (3 Aug. 1881), 7.

[56] *LCM* 1/49 (7 Dec. 1881), 7. Based on a review in *El navarro*: 'escuchada hasta la última nota en medio del más religioso silencio.' *LCM* does not provide the exact date of the concert, but Albéniz's album contains a dedication from Ricardo Monasterio y Poyó dated 3 Dec. 1881. In the album is also a printed sheet containing a poem commemorating this event and bearing the dedication 'Al Fénix de los Pianistas Isaac Alvéniz'. The 'Fénix' would appear to be a Masonic reference. A letter bearing eleven signatures (dated 5 Dec. 1881, Bc, 'C') from the Casino Militar de Navarra expresses 'admiration and enthusiasm' for his performance.

[57] According to Gauthier, *Albéniz*, 45, Albéniz did not preserve these works because they were 'errors of youth'.

[58] Ibid. 45. Gauthier probably got this information from an article by J. Roca y Roca, 'La semana en Barcelona', *La vanguardia* (12 May 1895), 4, which accompanied the premiere of *Henry Clifford* at the Liceu. Roca y Roca further stated that the little zarzuela 'died' on opening night in Bilbao, but there is nothing in the critics' comments to suggest this.

[59] *LCM* 2/58 (8 Feb. 1882), 8.

The little zarzuela entitled ¡Cuanto más viejo...! was produced by the zarzuela company that performs at the Coliseo in said city.... with a libretto by Sr. Zapino and music by the distinguished pianist Isaac Albéniz. The performance has been good and the success gratifying for its authors, especially for the composer Sr. Albéniz.[60]

But we still have no indication as to the story or the character of the music.

We know only a little more about a second zarzuela, *Catalanes de gracia*, also in one act, with a libretto by Rafael Leopoldo Palomino de Guzmán. Guzmán, a Freemason, was active as an author in the 1870s and 1880s and worked as an editor for several papers in Madrid, Cádiz, and Barcelona, in which city he died in 1900.[61] A short notice appears in the press on 22 March[62] declaring that the following Saturday *Catalanes de gracia* would be premiered in the Teatro Salón Eslava, with music by the 'distinguished' concert artist Don Isaac Albéniz, who had just returned from his most recent 'artistic expedition'. The reviewer reports in the next weekly issue that the 'little work' accomplished its objective, characterizing the music as 'pleasant' and the drama as 'amusing'.[63] The execution on the part of the lead singers, Sres. Ruiz and Rosell, was enthusiastically applauded, and they received many curtain calls, along with the authors. A final reference in April states that the zarzuela is continuing to draw large audiences at the Eslava.[64] None of the reviews in the local papers gives much information about the music itself. The most extensive review, consisting of only a few sentences, appeared in *El liberal* (29 March 1882, 4). It simply describes the work as a comic-lyric 'skit' and concludes with the following intriguing observations:

Mesejo cleans boots and sings *seguidillas* against the ministers. Señoritas Latorre and Campini talk awhile in vernacular and then in verse. Rosell and Ruiz wear sheepskin and Catalan caps and are guilty of attempted carousing; at the last minute they declare themselves the victims of a swindle to the tune of 400 reales. The audience laughs.[65]

---

[60] *LCM* 2/60 (21 Feb. 1882), 6. 'Por la compañia de zarzuela que actúa en el Coliseo de dicha villa se ha estrenado la zarzuelita titulada ¡Cuanto más viejo...!, libro del Sr. Zapino y música del distinguido pianista Isaac Albéniz. El desempeño ha sido bueno y el éxito lisongero para sus autores, muy particularmente para el de la música Sr. Albéniz.'

[61] See entry in *Enciclopedia universal ilustrada europeo-americana*, 1958 edn. (under 'Palomino de Guzmán, Rafael Leopoldo'). According to Arbós, 'Santander 1883', in Franco (ed.), *Albéniz y su tiempo*, 117, he also served as Albéniz's 'secretary' (*secretario*).

[62] *LCM* 2/64 (22 Mar. 1882), 7.

[63] *LCM* 2/65 (29 Mar. 1882), 7.

[64] *LCM* 2/67 (12 Apr. 1882), 7.

[65] 'Mesejo limpia botas y canta seguidillas contra los ministros. Las señoritas Latorre y Campini, hablan un ratito en chulo y en esdrujulos otro rato. Rosell y Ruiz llevan zamarra y gorro catalán, se hacen culpables de una tentativa de juerga, y se declaran á última hora víctimas de un timo por valor de cuatrocientos reales. El público se ríe.'

An examination of the remaining issues of *La correspondencia musical* for that year reveals that by May Albéniz was back on the concert trail—in this instance, at the Gran Teatro in Córdoba[66]—where he remained at least until November. No mention has yet surfaced of the third zarzuela (keep in mind that we have no idea of the chronology of their composition), *El canto de salvación*, in two acts (author unknown). Collet assures us that Albéniz's company performed in Málaga, Alcoy, Murcia, and Cartagena.[67] It remains open to speculation why no mention is made of this in the periodical. It seems unlikely that such a tour took place in so short a time as two months (between April and June). Did Albéniz resume concertizing while continuing to act as director of the company? If so, why did his activities as impresario attract no attention while his concert appearances continued to arouse the greatest excitement wherever he went? Why is he never mentioned as the director of any company? We do not yet know, but we may reasonably assume some embellishment of actual historical fact by Albéniz himself, as he later fed the London press even more extravagent claims than these. In 1890 he provided biographical details to *Lady*,[68] claiming that after six months with Liszt in Rome and twelve months of concertizing in the United States, in 1881 he returned to Spain and conducted at opera houses in Valencia, Cádiz, Granada, Seville, and Barcelona! Spreading it on even thicker, he went on to boast that he held appointments as 'Professor to the Philharmonic Institute of Madrid' and to the conservatories of Cádiz, Málaga, Valencia, and Barcelona. The following year, readers of *Queen* learned that after studying eight months with Liszt in Rome and spending an entire year in America, he returned to Spain to conduct 'an Italian Opera Company'.[69] All of this was presumably done in addition to his directing the zarzuela company. As we will see, in London Albéniz was active as a conductor and composer of operetta, so these prevarications served a useful public-relations purpose by adding lustre to his credentials.

After his Córdoba success he moved on to the Cádiz area, where he performed at the casino in San Fernando (the birthplace of his war-hero maternal grandfather) in early June.[70] Here he delighted his audience by improvising on three themes given him by a local composer, a certain Sr. Juarranz. A short time later he organized a concert in Cádiz itself at the

---

[66] *LCM* 2/73 (24 May 1882), 6.

[67] Collet, *Albéniz*, 40.

[68] 30 Oct. This clipping is in the bound volumes of press notices in the Bc, M987, vol. i. It also states that he was born in 1861 and fled home at the age of 11 and toured Spain and the Americas for two and a half years. His subsequent studies in Leipzig lasted eighteen months!

[69] 11 Apr. 1891. Bc, M987, vol. i.

[70] *LCM* 2/76 (14 June 1882), 7. Based on a review in *La palma*.

Academia de Santa Cecilia, where his performance of both solo and chamber music was 'warmly applauded'.[71] Albéniz then performed in Seville, at the Jardines de Eslava,[72] before returning to Cádiz to give more concerts.[73] On 7 August he performed on the other side of the country, in Valencia, in a concert that featured a variety of artists. His programme included an *Estudio* and a *Pavana* from his own pen that the critics singled out for praise.[74] Clippings in the Albéniz archive[75] document concerts in Málaga (19 April 1882) as well as in Pontevedra and Vigo, where he performed with a sextet including his friends Arbós and Augustín Rubio. In addition to the sextet's interpretation of works by Boccherini, Suppé, David Popper, and Ruperto Chapí, Albéniz also performed his own *Pavana-capricho* and *Serenata napolitana*. A reviewer in Alicante in this year exclaimed, 'I salute you, Albéniz, artist without rival, possessor of the mysterious amulet that steals the will and enraptures the heart.'[76] The last entry in Albéniz's album recalls a concert in Alcoy in September (dated the 10th of that month), for which he was made an honorary member of the Sociedad 'El Iris'. According to the local paper, *El Serpis*, the ovation given to Albéniz was 'extremely noisy'. After the concert, a crowd of admirers accompanied him to his room at the Fonda de Rigal, where they were all serenaded by a local orchestra![77] On 29 September 1882 Albéniz wrote to the newspaper to express his appreciation to the music organization La Novísima for its assistance in making the first series of subscription concerts a success, humbly acknowledging his own inexperience as a conductor.

Not one to rest on his laurels for very long, Albéniz continued on to Cartagena to give several concerts, one of which, on 10 November, featured 'very difficult pieces' rendered with 'delicate taste'.[78] It was perhaps this appearance that inspired *El eco de Cartagena* to declare that Albéniz was 'una gloria nacional'.[79] The end of the year found him once again in the capital city, performing at the home of Sra. Duquesa de Medinaceli.[80] His last known performance that year took place in Madrid in the elegant salon of the Círculo Vasco-Navarro, where he played his well-rehearsed repertoire of Chopin, Scarlatti, Boccherini, Beethoven, Raff, and Mendelssohn.[81]

---

[71] *LCM* 2/77 (21 June 1882), 6.

[72] *LCM* 2/80 (12 July 1882), 8.

[73] *LCM* 2/81 (19 July 1882), 6.

[74] *LCM* 2/85 (16 Aug. 1882), 6, based on a review in *La nueva alianza*.

[75] Mm, Prov. M-987a.

[76] 'Yo te saludo, Albéniz, artista sin rival, poseedor del misterioso amuleto que roba las voluntades y enagena los corazones!'

[77] *LCM* 2/90 (20 Sept. 1882), 6.

[78] *LCM* 2/97 (8 Nov. 1882), 6; and 2/98 (15 Nov. 1882), 6–7.   [79] Mm, Prov. M-987a.

[80] *LCM* 2/101 (6 Dec. 1882), 6.   [81] *LCM* 2/103 (20 Dec. 1882), 5.

The following year Albéniz moved to Barcelona and continued his concertizing from there. In April he gave another concert at the piano firm of
Raynard y Maseras that the local critics declared gave the audience 'truly
delicious moments'.[82] A short time later a caricature of Albéniz appeared in
the press, showing a dapper, moustached, and already paunchy young man
with the caption 'as a man, a boy; as a pianist, a giant'.[83] Around this time the
young pianist met, briefly courted, and married Rosina Jordana Lagarriga—
one of his students and the daughter of a prominent family in the Catalonian
capital—and adopted a more settled lifestyle. *La correspondencia musical*
stated in its 7 June 1883 issue (3/127, 4) that Albéniz was engaged to a
'beautiful and rich' señorita from Barcelona. The marriage occurred on 23
June and was reported a week later in the same periodical (3/130, 7). It
describes his bride as 'pretty and discreet' and the daughter of the 'industri-
ous and honourable businessman D. Simon Jordana'. Rosina Moya Albéniz
de Samsó related to this author the meeting of the two young people.[84]
Rosina Jordana had gone to a local music store on the Rambla to look for
sheet music by the sensational young pianist Isaac Albéniz. She approached a
young man in the store and asked if he could direct her to any of Albéniz's
music. He replied that he had something better, and gave her an autographed picture of himself. They were married three months later at the
church of Mare de Déu de la Mercè, in the Gothic quarter of Barcelona near
the harbour.[85] With the intercession of Ángel, Albéniz was able to free
himself of his military obligations, receiving his discharge from the reserves
on 7 June. Fortunately for him, Spain's state of nearly continuous civil
war had experienced a respite during his period of service, and he was
never called up.

Albéniz did not, however, allow matrimony to keep him off the concert
trail. In September he joined Arbós's sextet in Santander, where it began a
concert tour of the north coast. Arbós and the others, including Rubio,
could not believe the news that the confirmed bachelor Albéniz had
got married.[86] The sextet played the 'Capricho cubano' from Albéniz's
Concert Suite (now lost; probably strongly resembled the later *Suite*

---

[82] *La ilustración musical*, 1/2 (14 Apr. 1883), 4.

[83] *La ilustración musical*, 1/3 (21 Apr. 1883), 4. 'Como hombre, un niño; como pianista, un gigante.'

[84] In an interview on 23 July 1995. She further stated that Albéniz got on well with his mother-in-law, but
not his father-in-law. This could explain why he does not seem to have benefited much from marrying into a
wealthy family, though during a lean period in the 1890s he did borrow a sum of money from her family. But
he was quick to pay it back. See Ruiz Albéniz, *Albéniz*, 37.

[85] The Arxiu Diocesal of the Arquebisbat de Barcelona states that the marriage certificate was destroyed
during the Spanish Civil War (1936–9).

[86] An account of this tour is in Arbós, 'Santander 1883', in Franco (ed.), *Albéniz y su tiempo*, 117–19,
which in turn is taken from Arbós's autobiography.

característica for orchestra), and Albéniz rendered some solo numbers. On the 20th in La Coruña, for instance, Albéniz performed the *Rigoletto* paraphrase of Liszt in their programme.[87] From La Coruña the group moved on to Vigo, Santiago de Compostela,[88] and Orense, but according to Arbós, after La Coruña the tour was a failure and drew small audiences. Albéniz parted company with them and passed through Madrid on his way back to Barcelona.[89] A concert in Cartagena in this year featured Albéniz's own *Fantasía sobre motivos de la jota*, as well as his *Pavana-capricho*.

It was most likely during this Barcelona period that he made the acquaintance of Felip Pedrell and studied composition with him. Albéniz had studied composition only briefly in Leipzig, as we have seen, and though some authorities claim he studied with Gevaert in Brussels, the existing records at the conservatory there indicate nothing to that effect. Albéniz possessed a very facile intelligence and keen musical instincts. His zarzuelas were most likely a product of imitation rather than innovation, which may explain why one, at least, was so well received.[90] But he knew that he had yet to acquire any real technique as a composer and that he would have to grapple with the complexities of form, counterpoint, and orchestration before he could aspire to anything higher than the charming little entertainments he was already capable of writing.

By 1883, the Catalan Felip Pedrell (1841–1922) had already established a reputation as an opera composer and musical nationalist. He had composed several zarzuelas and four operas (some of which had been produced in Barcelona), though in the early 1880s he was occupied chiefly with musicology and would not resume composing operas until 1887 (with the three-act comic opera *Eda*). It was during this period that Albéniz sought him out for instruction.[91] After Albéniz's death in 1909, Pedrell wrote a eulogy to his compatriot, student, and friend that sheds some light on Albéniz's studies, however brief, with him. Pedrell avers that these studies took the form more of 'conversations' between friends than of formal lessons. He elaborates on Albéniz's musical temperament as having been one that could not be taught but only guided, and then only to the extent that it would not 'restrict or muddy the crystal-clear rivulet of his native intuition'.[92] He states that Albéniz

---

[87] *LCM* 3/143 (27 Sep. 1883), 6.

[88] *LCM* 3/144 (4 Oct. 1883), 6.   [89] *LCM* 3/147 (25 Oct. 1883), 6.

[90] That is, given the aversion of the critics to anything that broke the established mould, especially in the *género chico*, or light zarzuela. As we shall see, Albéniz would not be so fortunate when next he appeared in Madrid as a composer of musical theatre.

[91] Tradition holds that these lessons took place during the year 1883, but no documentary evidence of this has yet surfaced.

[92] Pedrell, *Músicos*, 377: 'á fin de no contener ni enturbiar jamás el hilito de agua cristalina de su intuición nativa.'

became somewhat discouraged when certain errors in notation or orchestration were pointed out to him and that the young virtuoso and aspiring composer had no stomach for the rules and regulations of composition:

I noticed that when we spoke of these things or of other, more intricate technical problems, he became extraordinarily concerned and preoccupied; and as I observed that the dry, cold rule made no impression on his intelligence, I determined to speak no more of rules, neither of chords nor of resolutions.[93]

This passage should not be construed to suggest, as it sometimes has, that Albéniz was little more than a guileless wunderkind who, in the final analysis, depended upon improvisation and had only a tenuous command of the science of composition.[94] We must bear in mind that at this time Albéniz was only 23 years old. His greatest works were written over ten years later, after he had gained considerable knowledge and experience. Anyone who takes the trouble to examine his 1904 revision of *Pepita Jiménez* or his score for *Merlin* will soon realize that Albéniz had by that time gained a sophisticated understanding both of theoretical language and of instrumentation.

And there is some reason to hold Pedrell's testimony suspect. In this same article,[95] he declares that after renouncing the rules of composition, the young composer wondered aloud how he would refer to musical phenomena without knowing their precise technical designations. In an oft cited passage, Pedrell advises him to make up his own terms, proposing that Albéniz name dominant-seventh chords after 'Hertz waves', and scales after 'X-rays'. This is very amusing, but undoubtedly spurious. Pedrell could not have referred to X-rays during the early 1880s because Wilhelm Röntgen did not discover them until 1895, at which time he coined the term. Though it may have been unintentional, Pedrell was clearly embellishing his recollections. Further corroboration of our doubts is offered by William S. Newman, who describes the 'craftsmanship in harmony, scoring, and voice-leading' of Albéniz's piano sonatas of 1886–7 as 'beyond reproach'.[96] Since these sonatas were written only a few years after his sessions with Pedrell, Albéniz must have learned his lessons well and quickly. Or perhaps he was not as

[93] Ibid. 378. 'Notaba yo que cuando se hablaba de estas cosas ó de otros problemas técnicos más intrincados, se preocupaba y ensimismaba extraordinariamente; y como observase que la regla seca y fría no penetraba en su inteligencia, determiné no hablarle jamás de reglas, ni de acordes, ni de resoluciones.'

[94] For a particularly condescending estimation of Albéniz's compositional skills, see P. Luis Villalba Muñoz, *Últimos músicos españoles del siglo XIX*, i (Madrid: Ildefonso Alier, 1914), 182. He states that Albéniz did not possess the technique of the 'art of composition': 'to write music and to know counterpoint were the two venerable summits of art that he adoringly revered, but which were inaccessible to his character as a free artist.' ('No poseía la técnica del arte del componer... escribir de música y saber contrapunto, eran para él las dos cumbres venerandas del arte que reverenciaba adorante, por lo inaccesibles á su carácter de artista libre.')

[95] Pedrell, *Músicos*, 378.

[96] *The Sonata since Beethoven* (Chapel Hill: University of North Carolina Press, 1969), 653.

untutored and helpless as Pedrell suggests. Certainly his studies at Brussels and successful navigation of the final exams there, as well as his subsequent activities as conductor, composer, and improviser, indicate that Pedrell was overstating the case for Albéniz's *naïveté* in theory and composition. But the essence of his remarks is correct: Albéniz was a learner, and he did feel a certain sense of inadequacy in composition, particularly orchestration. He sought out assistance in this area throughout his life.

Albéniz himself certainly was unstinting in his praise of Pedrell as a teacher. In 1902, after the premiere in Barcelona at the Liceu of Pedrell's operatic trilogy *Els Pirineus*, Albéniz wrote a review of the work and shed further light on their relationship.[97] He identified himself as a student of Pedrell and said he owed to him the 'first initiation in the difficult art of transcendental composition'. More specifically, he had learned from Pedrell the 'difficult handling of orchestral colours [and] the elements of culture and aesthetics that time, experience, and study have been developing in my mind'.[98] Most of all, though, he learned the 'potent and moral example of *high artistic integrity* with which he has illustrated his life, sustaining with matchless strength the furious attacks directed at him, the general indifference, the supine ignorance, and the rabid envy!'[99] He credited Pedrell with having composed 'the cornerstone of the edifice of *our future lyric nationality*' ('la piedra angular del edificio de *nuestra futura nacionalidad lírica*'). Then Albéniz's prose sprouted wings and took etheric flight in addressing his readers:

you are going to hear the song of your land, the tender voice of your mothers, the ancient and sweet melodies that have lulled our sorrowful soul during the terrible combat that we have borne throughout our existence; you will recall and renew sorrow and longings that have passed, leaving a profound imprint on your heart; and after such sweet sufferings, a gigantic wave of enthusiastic hope will invade your being...![100]

In his letters to Pedrell, Albéniz addressed him as 'Dear Master' ('Querido Maestro') and signed himself 'your eternally affectionate disciple' ('tu siempre cariñoso discípulo').[101]

---

[97] In *Las noticias*, 2 Jan. 1902.

[98] '[D]ificil manejo de los colores orquestales, le debo así mismo, los elementos de cultura y estética que el tiempo, la experiencia y el estudio han ido desarrollando en mi cerebro.'

[99] '[P]otente y moral ejemplo de *alta probidad artística* con que constantemente ha ilustrado su vida, sosteniendo con sin igual valor, los furiosos embates de que le han hecho objeto, la general indiferencia, la supina ignorancia, y la rabiosa envidia!'

[100] '[V]áis á oír el canto de vuestra tierra, la tierna voz de vuestras madres, las atávicas y dulces melodías que adormecieron vuestra alma dolorida en el terrible combate que durante nuestra existencia sustentamos, váis á recordar y á renovar penas y añoranzas que pasaron dejando profunda huella en vuestro corazón, y despúes de tan dulces sufrimientos, una gigantesca ola de entusiástica esperanza invadirá vuestro ser...!'

[101] See four letters in the Bc, M964, dated 20 Apr. 1891, 23 Nov. 1901, 24 Jan. 1902, and 29 June [no year, but during his London period]. It is this last one that bears the affectionate signature.

Aside from the adulation his apprenticeship aroused, the most important point usually made about Albéniz's studies with Pedrell is that they stimulated his determination to use the musical folklore of his own country as the basis for composition. Pedrell was an advocate of musical nationalism who believed that folk song formed the legitimate foundation for national music. To be sure, Pedrell was not a Catalan nationalist but rather pan-Spanish in his outlook, and it was this aesthetic to which Albéniz also adhered.[102] However, once again we must temper our estimation of Pedrell's influence with the realization that Albéniz was probably inspired as much by Liszt's example, and that he had already begun to write pieces in a Spanish style (e.g. the *seguidillas* referred to by the reviewer of *Catalanes de gracia*) by the time he met Pedrell.

Whatever the origin of his muse, the 1880s witnessed Albéniz's increasing output of charming and distinctive Spanish-style pieces for the piano, which received an enthusiastic reception by the concert-going public in Spain and elsewhere. Many of these works (to be discussed later in this and ensuing chapters) have found a permanent place in the piano repertoire, though they are most frequently heard in transcriptions for the guitar. They are so convincing that it is indeed easy to take their originality completely for granted. These works represent Albéniz's characteristic blend of indigenous and non-Spanish elements: lively rhythms, modality, elementary formal structure, and haunting melodic arabesques couched in poignant, chromatic harmonies reminiscent of Chopin. Though he continued to write polkas, minuets, mazurkas, waltzes, and other light pieces in the salon style so popular at that time, Albéniz's 'Spanish' pieces represent the first flowering of his unique creative genius.

Albéniz signed a lucrative contract to entertain at the popular Café Colón in Barcelona. Here he was persuaded by acquaintances to speculate on the stock market, and he lost a considerable amount of money. But he simply gave more concerts to make good his losses. He toured southern France and northern Spain, appearing in Marseilles, Toulon, Biarritz, Cauterets, and Arcachón.[103] Concerts in the Catalonian capital during 1883 included appearances at the Teatre Espanyol in January, at the Tívoli on 2 February, and at the Liceu on 15 May, where he performed works by Chopin (Berceuse, Mazurka, Impromptu, E flat Polonaise), Scarlatti (Scherzo,

---

[102] Pedrell's *Por nuestra música* (Barcelona: Juan Bta. Pujol, 1891) was a virtual manifesto of Spanish musical nationalism in opera and exerted considerable influence on Albéniz and his compatriots. Pedrell based his philosophy in part on Wagner, and in part on the writings of the 18th-cent. Spanish theorist Padre Antonio Eximeno.

[103] See Guerra y Alarcón, *Albéniz*, 30–1. For a photograph of the Café Colón, see Antonio Iglesias, 'Isaac Albéniz', in *Enciclopedia Salvat de los grandes compositores*, iv (Pamplona: Salvat SA de Ediciones, 1982), 240.

sonatas), and Wagner–Liszt (*Forest Murmurs*).[104] It was probably during one of these appearances that Rosina first heard him perform. Unfortunately, we know little about his activities in 1884 in Barcelona. A press clipping[105] does refer to two concerts at the Ateneu, during the second of which choral works by Pedrell were also performed. In fact, records in the Matas archive confirm a total of three concerts at the Ateneu during March to May of this year. His programme again included *Forest Murmurs*, as well as an étude by Charles Mayer (1799–1862) and the Sonata No. 17 in D minor, Op. 32, No. 2, by Beethoven. The death of Brassin on 17 May 1884 no doubt saddened him,[106] but the birth of his first child, Blanca, in the late summer of that year was a cause for rejoicing. Albéniz's final appearance in Barcelona took place on 22 March 1885, in a benefit at the Liceu. On 8 August 1885 he gave a recital at the Casino Luchón, part of whose proceeds went to aid the poor.[107]

Albéniz's second child was born during the summer of 1885 in Tiana, a hamlet outside Barcelona. The boy was named Alfonso, after the king who had made possible Albéniz's studies in Brussels. Soon thereafter, Albéniz moved his family to Madrid. Why he did so is unclear, though it was probably due to his habitual wanderlust, a seeking after new fields to conquer, and a desire to be closer to his family. In October the press reported on his two appearances before the royal family at the Palacio Real, describing him, intriguingly but without explanation, as the 'spoiled child' ('*enfant gaté*') of Madrid society.[108] The 4th of November found him again entertaining the royal family, at the request of the Infanta Doña Isabel, who specifically requested he play his latest compositions.[109] It is no coincidence that Edición Zozaya, the publisher of the journal in which the Infanta's approbation was reported,[110] was also the publisher of Albéniz's music. It was also at Zozaya's offices that Albéniz began offering piano classes for those who could not afford private instruction. Albéniz was now a fixture in the world of musical mercantilism in Madrid, and this relationship with Benito Zozaya, who was a Mason, was providing the new family man with needed income. In the 17 December 1885 issue of *La correspondencia musical* (5/259, 6), we learn that Albéniz is offering

[104] According to 'Concerts celebrats á Barcelona'.

[105] Mm, Prov. M-987a.

[106] Reported in *LCM* 4/179 (5 June 1884), 7.

[107] A programme of this concert is in the Bc, M987, vol. ii.

[108] *LCM* 5/249 (8 Oct. 1885), 5.

[109] Bevan, 'Albéniz', 18, reports that he became court pianist to Queen Cristina at an annual salary of £80. Many sources state that he was court pianist, but this was a bit of an exaggeration on Albéniz's part. At all events, Bevan does not provide the source for the exact salary amount.

[110] *LCM* 5/253 (5 Nov. 1885), 5.

private instruction for those needing help preparing for exams at the conservatory, and that he is teaching at his home in the Plaza de Antón Martin 52, 54, and 56. This building, located in the Atocha district not far from the Real Conservatorio, still stands today.

One of the most important concerts Albéniz ever gave took place at the elegant and fashionable salon of his publisher Antonio Romero on Sunday, 24 January 1886, when he was still 25 years old. It was in conjunction with this appearance that the first biography of Albéniz appeared in print.[111] Its author, Antonio Guerra y Alarcón, was a critic who published articles on music in *Heraldo de Madrid* and other periodicals. He was also the author of the *Curso completo de declamación* (1885). His booklet on Albéniz was the first in a proposed series of biographies entitled *La galería de la juventud artístico-literaria*, dedicated to highlighting the artistic accomplishments of young Spaniards. Most of the information for this booklet was provided to the author by Albéniz himself, and critics reviewing the concert borrowed from it extensively. Guerra y Alarcón included in his biography a copy of Albéniz's extremely ambitious three-part programme at the Salón Romero, a list of his already vast repertoire, and an inventory of his compositions to that time. All three are of interest to us and are reproduced in Tables 2–4.

Torres believes that Albéniz was probably exaggerating his compositional output,[112] but the young artist's repertoire was unusually broad and well developed for one of his years, and it revealed a marked predilection for music of the eighteenth century. Many of the works he himself had composed by this time are no longer extant, such as the *Suite morisca* and the *Marcha nupcial*. Moreover, the list appears to be incomplete, as it lacks a number listed on his programme, i.e. his own arrangement of part of the Prelude to Boito's *Mefistofele*. Earlier works, such as the *Serenata napolitana* performed in Vigo in 1882, and the *Fantasía sobre motivos de la jota*, which he had performed in Cartagena in 1883, are also absent (and now lost), though this latter work was probably an improvisation. Also, it lists a second *Pavana-capricho* but does not mention the celebrated first one! To the best of our knowledge, Albéniz composed only a single *Pavana-capricho*.

---

[111] This biography also provided Felip Pedrell with information for the entry on Albéniz in his *Diccionario biográfico y bibliográfico de música y escritores de música*, vol. i (Barcelona: V. Berdós y Feliu, 1894).

[112] Jacinto Torres, 'La inspiración "Clásica" de Isaac Albéniz', liner notes for *Isaac Albéniz: Sonatas para piano no 3, 4, 5/L'Automne* (Harmonia Mundi CD HMI 987007, 1994). For instance, *Capricho cubano* and *Serenata morisca* were actually movements from the Concert Suite. Much valuable information on the piano works of this period is found in Torres's liner notes 'La metamorfosis de Isaac Albéniz: De intérprete a creador', for *Albéniz: Klavierwerke* (Koch-Schwann CD 3-1513-2, 1996).

TABLE 2. *Albéniz's programme at the Salón Romero in Madrid, 24 January 1886*

Part One	
Italian Concerto	Bach
Gavotte with Variations	Handel
Pastoral	Scarlatti
Sonata	
Toccata	
Capriccio	
Sonata, Op. 14	Beethoven
Part Two	
Impromptu in E flat	Schubert
Lieder ohne Worte in A flat and C	Mendelssohn
Minuet	Weber
Polonaise in A flat	Chopin
Impromptu	
Berceuse	
Waltz	
Étude No. 12	
Sonata in B flat minor	
Part Three	
Barcarolle No. 3	Rubinstein
Concert Étude	
Suite espagnole	Albéniz
'Serenata'	
'Sevillana'	
'Pavana-capricho'	
Tarantela	Heller
Concert Étude	Mayer
Forest Murmurs	Wagner–Liszt
Excerpt from the Prelude to *Mefistofele*	Boito–Albéniz

Of the extraordinary success of the Romero concert, one reviewer wrote: 'Albéniz dominates the piano with surpassing ease, and in his hands, the keys reproduce in a marvellous manner the thoughts of the musician and of the poet.'[113] According to this source, the Mayer étude was repeated at the audience's insistence. Another critic wrote simply that this work 'set off an explosion of thunderous applause' ('arrancó una explosión de atronadores aplausos'). He further declared that Albéniz was 'the passionate and ardent interpreter, who sometimes poeticizes and at others nearly mistreats the piano, and who, in short, carries away and moves his listener'.[114] Tomás Bretón wrote in his diary that Albéniz 'obtained the hoped-for success,

[113] *LCM* 6/265 (28 Jan. 1886), 1–3. 'Albéniz domina el piano con pasmosa facilidad, y en sus manos, las teclas reproducen de maravilloso modo los pensamientos del músico y del poeta.'
[114] *La ilustración española y americana* (8 Feb. 1886). Reprinted in Franco (ed.), *Albéniz y su tiempo*, 69–71: 'el intérprete apasionado y ardiente, que poetiza unas veces, y otras hasta maltrata el piano, y que, en suma, arrastra y conmueve a su auditorio.'

TABLE 3. *Albéniz's repertoire in 1886 (according to Guerra y Alarcón)*

Bach	*Chromatic Fantasy, Italian Concerto, English Suite*, ten diverse pieces
Handel	Two suites, prelude and fugue, gavotte, and allemande
Scarlatti	Twelve works, including sonatas, toccatas, capriccios, pastorales
Rameau	Two suites for harpsichord
Couperin	Ten pieces for harpsichord
Haydn	Four sonatas and a prelude and fugue
Mozart	Three concertos, a fantasy, five sonatas, and three minuets
Beethoven	Two concertos, six sonatas, a fantasy, two collections of bagatelles
Weber	A sonata, minuet, two concertos, and two pieces [unspecified]
Mendelssohn	Two concertos, a fantasy, *Rondo capriccioso, Variations sérieuses*, prelude and fugue, six *Lieder ohne Worte*
Chopin	Fourteen études, five polonaises, eight waltzes, six mazurkas, four nocturnes, five preludes, *Krakowiak*, a fantasy, two impromptus, a sonata, a concert allegro, a scherzo, a barcarolle, and a concerto
Moscheles	Two concertos
Ries	A concerto
Dussek	Three pieces
Schumann	Concerto in A minor, *Konzertstück, Les Papillons, Carnaval, Noveletten*, and transcriptions of his *Romances*
Rubinstein	A concerto, two études, two barcarolles, and two dances
Heller	Two tarantelles, four preludes
Mayer	A concerto, two études
Liszt	A fantasy, two concertos, a tarantella, three études, *Gondoliera*, two transcriptions, a 'Grand Hungarian Fantasy'
Brassin	A barcarolle, two caprices, three Wagner transcriptions
Morphy	Two caprices
Bretón	Funeral March, transcribed by Albéniz
Grieg	Concerto in A minor

immense, frank, and deserved.... If he cultivates well his marvellous aptitudes, he could become within five years the premier pianist of his epoch.'[115]

Word of his great triumph at the Romero spread throughout the country, and Albéniz received numerous invitations from various cities in Spain to perform.[116] One such appearance took place in May in Málaga, where money and applause greeted him in abundance and the audience insisted he repeat five or six numbers during his programme of twenty-six pieces.[117] On 11 March he played at the Teatro de la Zarzuela in Madrid in a concert featuring the renowned soprano Adelina Patti,[118] and in late March he again appeared at the Romero.[119] But triumph soon blended with tragedy. On 4 April 1886, Albéniz's twenty-month-old daughter Blanca died.

[115] Tomás Bretón, *Diario 1881–1888*, 2 vols., ed. Jacinto Torres Mulas (Madrid: Acento Editorial, 1994), ii. 483. 'Obtuvo el éxito que era de esperar, inmenso, franco y merecido.... Si cultiva bien sus maravillosas aptitudes, puede ser dentro de cinco años el primer pianista de su época'.
[116] *LCM* 6/266 (4 Feb. 1886), 6.   [117] *LCM* 6/280 (13 May 1886), 5.
[118] *LCM* 6/271 (11 Mar. 1886), 3.   [119] *LCM* 6/274 (1 Apr. 1886), 5.

TABLE 4. *Albéniz's works list in 1886 (according to Guerra y Alarcón)*

For voice:
    Cuanto más viejo, zarzuela in one act
    Catalanes de gracia, zarzuela in one act
    El canto de salvación, zarzuela in two acts
    Four romances for mezzo-soprano with French text
    Three romances with Catalan text
For orchestra [or chamber ensemble]
    Concert Suite
    Scherzo
    Serenata morisca
    Capricho cubano, for sextet
    Trio No. 1, in F
For piano
    Six mazurkas
    Two caprices
    Suite morisca
        'Marcha de la caravana'
        'La noche'
        'Danza de las esclavas'
        'Zambra'
    Pavana No. 2 (Capricho)
    Six études
    Two *Caprichos andaluces*
    Gavotte
    Two *Grand Concert Études*
    Minuet
    Barcarolle No. 1
    Grand Sonata No. 1, in four movements
    First movement of the First Concerto
    Six waltzes
    Marcha nupcial
    Three mazurkas
    Suite espagnole [*sic*]

This was an especially bitter loss, as the child had been named after his sister who had committed suicide. One index of the emotional devastation this must have caused is the fact that no biographical account, family diary, or letter makes reference to her. Mention of the death appears in *La correspondencia musical*, which expressed its condolences to the composer.[120]

    In spite of this heartbreak, on 17 and 19 July he was back on stage in San Sebastián appearing with a sextet (not Arbós's group) and in a final recital for two pianos, with a local pianist accompanying him.[121] In 1886 Albéniz also performed in Zaragoza, where his programme featured not only the

---

[120] *LCM* 6/275 (8 Apr. 1886), 6. Reference to it also appears in Bretón's *Diario*, ii. 515.
[121] *LCM* 6/290 (22 July 1886), 5. Reported in *El eco de San Sebastián*.

Schumann Concerto but also his own *Escenas sinfónicas* and *Suite caracter-*
ística ('Scherzo', 'Rapsodia cubana', and 'En la Alhambra') for orchestra.[122]
On 21 March 1887 he again appeared at the Salón Romero performing
many of his own works; several of his students also appeared performing
his music.[123] On 20 September 1887 he ventured across the waters of
the Mediterranean to perform in Palma de Mallorca, where the local
press declared that Albéniz was 'yesterday a hope for art; today he is a
reality'.[124]

For the rest of Albéniz's tenure in Madrid until 1889 we have as yet little
data. We can safely assume that life settled into a routine of concerts, teaching, and dealing with family matters. He also spent many evenings at Count
Morphy's, in the company of Bretón, Arbós, and others, his wife often with
him. An important new source of information on this period is Bréton's
diary. Among other things, we learn that it was Bretón who orchestrated
Albéniz's Piano Concerto and the *Rapsodia española* for piano and orchestra
in early 1887, at the composer's request.[125] Despite Pedrell's tutelage,
Albéniz was still a diffident orchestrator. But he was composing more
piano music than ever before, and the profusion of works from these years
constitutes what Albéniz and his biographers have referred to as his first style
period. The piano pieces of this period represent most of the genres of salon
music: mazurkas, waltzes, barcarolles, pavanes, minuets, romances, polkas,
polonaises, serenades, études, and caprices. We know these figured promi-
nently in his concerts during the 1880s and 1890s, and nearly all of them
bear dedications to students, friends, and family. The majority of these pieces
were suitable for amateur use and served the dual pupose of bringing in
income and spreading his name. Along with Zozaya, Romero in Madrid
and Juan Ayné in Barcelona published most of them. The influence of
Chopin in them is strong; for example, No. 6 of the *Seis pequeños valses*
(Barcelona: R. Guardia, 1884) bears a striking resemblance to Chopin's

[122] From newspaper clippings in the Mm, Prov. M- 987a. There is some confusion as to the exact date of
the suite, but the clipping in this file contains the earliest known reference to it. The orchestral score is now
lost. The *Rapsodia cubana* was composed for solo piano already in 1881, and Romero published this version
of it in Madrid in 1886.

[123] Laplane, *Albéniz*, 191, gives 20 Mar. as the date, but Bretón, *Diario*, ii, 600, confirms 21 Mar.

[124] Mm, Prov. M-987a. 'Albéniz era ayer una esperanza para el arte, hoy es una realidad.' A letter from
Palma de Mallorca dated 17 Nov. 1887, written by Vicente Llorens and bearing thirteen other signatures (Bc,
'L'), thanks him for his performance and makes him an honorary president of their association, Parnasillo.

[125] Entry for 23 Jan. 1887. Bretón, *Diario*, ii. 586–90. He finished the *Rapsodia* three days later and the
concerto on 6 Feb. He sent the scores to Albéniz on the following day. But the work was premiered in a two-
piano arrangement by the composer and the orchestration was not published. Georges Enesco and Cristóbal
Halffter both made their own orchestrations of the second piano part many years later. Jacinto Torres has
reconstructed the original orchestration using diverse manuscript sources, and this 'new' version was premiered 26 Aug. 1994 in La Coruña by the Orquesta Sinfónica de Galicia, with Antonio Ruíz-Pipó as soloist
(pub. Madrid: Instituto de Bibliografía Musical, 1997).

Waltz in A flat major, Op. 64, No. 3, in its key, formal plan, and melodic contour.[126] Some are intended only for advanced performers, e.g. *Deseo: Estudio de concierto* (Romero, 1886), which rivals the études of Liszt in virtuosity, while others clearly serve a pedagogical function, e.g. *Pavana fácil para manos pequeñas* ('Easy pavane for small hands', Romero, 1887). Albéniz's love of the eighteenth century reveals itself in his *Suites anciennes* 1–3 (Romero, 1886–7), consisting of two gavottes, two minuets, a chaconne, and a sarabande. In addition, Albéniz wrote all of his seven sonatas during this time, though only Nos. 3–5 are complete. Nothing remains of 2 and 6, while only single movements of 1 and 7 (a scherzo and minuetto, respectively) are extant. These three complete sonatas were published in Madrid by Romero in 1887. No. 3 bears a dedication to the pianist Manuel Guervós, who premiered it at the concert in the Salón Romero on 21 March 1887. No. 4 is dedicated to his 'beloved Maestro' Count Morphy and was premiered by Luisa Chevalier at this same concert. The sonata-form opening movement of the Fourth Sonata (in which he writes out the repeat of the exposition) is noteworthy for its rhythmic propulsion and lyric sweep, while the succeeding Scherzino begins with a playful fugato that once again shows his love of the eighteenth century. Like the Scherzino, the Minuetto third movement is laid out in ABA form and is the musical equivalent of a fine porcelain figurine in its graceful melodic contours and tasteful harmonic setting. The bravura Rondo reminds one of Chopin's études in its parallel-octave melodies and vaulting arpeggios. This beautiful work alone would cement Albéniz's reputation as the greatest Spanish composer of keyboard sonatas since Antonio Soler (1729–83), but the others are every bit its equal in craftsmanship and elegance.

These works demonstrate that there was a strong classical streak in Albéniz's musical personality, as he was usually not given to empty virtuosic display or harmonic ambiguities. His preference is for a 'two-handed' style in which there is a clear delineation between melody and accompaniment. There is no attempt to simulate an orchestra contained within the piano, and he avoids extremes of register. The sonatas in particular reveal a firm grasp of formal organization, though development is accomplished principally through modulation, sometimes to remote areas. But they contain scarcely a hint of the nationalism he was consciously cultivating in other pieces of the time.

The most enduring and popular of his compositions from this period are, of course, precisely these Spanish-style pieces. Albéniz freely adapts from Spanish folk music certain generic rhythmic and melodic elements that give

---

[126] According to Baytelman, *Catalog*, 10.

the works their flavour. In a sense they are idealized vignettes for popular consumption, and they form a musical parallel to *costumbrismo* (literally, 'customs and manners'), a literary style of the time that sought to capture the vistas and language of everyday life, with a strong regional flavour. Albéniz felt a special attraction to flamenco,[127] the exotic folk music of Andalusia (where he toured extensively during his youth and returned later as a tourist). In the nineteenth century flamenco emerged as a public rather than purely private art form, in taverns known as *cafés cantantes*. One of the most famous of these was the Venta Eritaña in Seville, which inspired the final number in the *Iberia* collection. These gave birth to commercial flamenco as we know it today and were no doubt where he gained his exposure to it.[128] Certain genres of flamenco in particular recur again and again in his music, especially the *malagueña*, a regional variant of the *fandango*. But they are sometimes stylized to such an extent that they bear only a faint resemblance to the real thing.

Albéniz frequently evokes the *punteado* (plucking) and *rasgueado* (strumming) of the guitar, and his pieces often begin with the suggestion of a guitar accompaniment before the entrance of the actual melody. The influence of folk music is also perceptible in his penchant for symmetrical phrasing in four-bar units. Modality is common, especially the Phrygian mode, though his harmonies are otherwise conservative by the standards of the time (*Tristan und Isolde* premiered twenty years earlier).[129] Triple metre or compound duple, sometimes alternating to produce hemiola, predominates in his nationalist music, just as it does in Spanish folk music. Another aspect to note is the alternation between sections that clearly denote dancing in their rhythmic vivacity, and more lyrical sections expressive of the *copla*, meaning a song or the verse of a song (alternating with the *estribillo*, or refrain). Here very often one perceives the influence of the *jota*, an essentially northern song and dance from Aragón that exists, like the *fandango*, in many regional variations, even in Andalusia. *Jota coplas* have distinct characteristics that we often find in Albéniz's melodies. They possess a smooth melodic contour (stepwise motion prevails) and conclude with a rhythmic flourish, usually a triplet. Moreover, their rhythm reflects the octosyllabic lines so typical of Spanish poetry and song verse in general. A typical line, 'Tie-nes la

[127] The precise meaning of this word is obscure, and theories abound concerning its etymology. Whatever the case, it is traditionally the music of lower-class groups in Andalusia, especially Gypsies. See Donn E. Pohren, *The Art of Flamenco* (Shaftesbury: Musical New Services Ltd., 1984), 41–2, for a discussion of the origins of flamenco.
[128] See ibid. 90.
[129] His love of flat keys and double-flat accidentals may derive in part from the use of modes like Phrygian, Aeolian, and Mixolydian that already contain 'lowered' pitches. See Mast, 'Iberia', 129.

ca-ra ma-ñí-ca', could easily be fitted to many of his *copla* melodies.[130] At other times, however, Albéniz evokes the *cante jondo* ('deep song') of pure flamenco, with its characteristic rhythmic freedom, melismas, and vocalizations on the syllable 'ay'. This very oriental-sounding style of singing has its origins in the earliest history of flamenco and in particular the folk and liturgical song of the Jews, Muslims, and Christian fugitives who mingled with their fellow outcasts the Gypsies. Its lyrics are often fatalistic and tragic, something to which the melancholy side of Albéniz's personality readily responded. But Albéniz does not feel obliged to match the dance and *copla* sections in terms of genre, and a work's title or programme may not correspond to the folkloric character of the actual music.

'Granada' (Zozaya, 1886), the opening number in his first *Suite española*,[131] illustrates many of these features very well. It is subtitled 'Serenata', and thus a song-like character predominates, as opposed to the dance rhythms of most of the other pieces. Albéniz wrote this charming composition during a stay in Granada in 1886. In a letter to his friend Enrique Moragas he describes his feelings about the city and his latest creation, making clear his enchantment with Granada's Moorish past:

I live and write a *Serenata*, romantic to the point of paroxysm and sad to the point of despair, among the aroma of the flowers, the shade of the cypresses, and the snow of the Sierra. I will not compose the intoxication of a collective *juerga* [flamenco party]. I seek now the tradition, which is a gold mine ... the guzla [Arabic string instrument], the lazy dragging of fingers over the strings. And above all, a heartbreaking lament out of tune. ... I want the Arabic Granada, that which is all art, which is all that seems to me beauty and emotion, and that which can say to Catalonia: *Be my sister in art and my equal in beauty*.[132]

---

[130] 'You have the plump face of a little Zaragozan peasant girl.' From a *jota* in Antonio Ramírez Ángel, (ed.), *Mil canciones españolas* (Madrid: Editorial Almena, n.d.). Cited in Redford, 'Iberia', 61. Albéniz rarely quoted folk songs verbatim, but he was familiar with serveral collections, and they can serve us as useful points of reference. Other such compendia include José Inzenga, *Cantos y bailes populares de España* (Madrid, 1888); Federico de Onís and Emilio de Torre, *Canciones españoles* (New York: Instituto de Las Españas en Los Estados Unidos, 1931); P. Lacome and J. Puig, *Échos d'Espagne: Chansons et danses populaires* (Paris: Durand, n.d.); Felipe Pedrell, *Cancionero musical popular español*, 3rd edn. (Barcelona: Casa Editorial Boileau, 1958); and Juan del Aguila, *Las canciones del pueblo español* (Madrid: Unión Musical Española, 1960). See also Hipolito Rossy, *Teoría del cante jondo* (Barcelona: Credsa, n.d.).

[131] See Selleck-Harrison, '*Suite española*', for analyses of selections from this suite, including 'Granada'. The analysis here, however, is this author's own.

[132] Rafael Moragas, 'Epistolario inédito de Isaac Albéniz', *Música* 1/5 (1938), 38–44. Cited in José María Llorens Cisteró, 'Notas inéditas sobre el virtuosismo de Isaac Albéniz y su producción pianística', *Anuario musical*, 14 (1959), 99. 'Vivo y escribo una *Serenata* romántica hasta el paroxismo y triste hasta el desespero, entre el aroma de las flores, la penumbra de los cipreses y la nieve de la Sierra. No voy a componer la embriaguez de la juerga colectiva: busco ahora la tradición, que es una mina de oro ... la guzla, arrastrando perezosamente los dedos sobre las cuerdas. Y por encima de todo un lamento desentonado y desgarrador. ... Quiero la Granada árabe, la que toda es arte, la que toda me parece belleza y emoción y la que puede decir a Cataluna: *Sé mi hermana en arte y mi igual en belleza*.'

Despite this rhapsodizing, the piece bears little relation to Moorish music. Albéniz places the opening melody in the tenor voice, and its arabesque contour and concluding triplet flourish mark it as Spanish, most resembling a *jota copla* (compare it with the *copla* of 'Aragón') (Ex. 1).

Ex. 1. *Suite española* No. 1, 'Granada', A theme, bars 1–12 (repeats not in the original edition)

The four-bar antecedent phrase is repeated and dutifully followed by a conseqeunt phrase of identical length, which is restated with only a slight embellishment of the second bar (an intensification through elevation to a' on the anacrusis of beat two). The thematic structure could not be simpler, *aabb*, with the *a* phrase in the tonic, and the *b* phrase in the dominant. All the while the incessant 'strummed' chords in the right hand are perhaps meant to suggest the guzla, but remind us of the guitar (the guzla was not a chordal instrument, and the whole notion is alien to Middle Eastern music). For this reason, the piece sounds very natural on the guitar and is usually heard in transcription for that instrument. To avoid an exact repetition of this theme, the restatement of the *a* phrase is suddenly transposed to A♭ (by means of the common tone C), adding a refreshing twist. This aberration is only temporary, however, and the *b* phrase commences a series of fifth-related movements (V^7–I–V^7/ii–ii–V^7) leading to an authentic cadence in F major. A repeated four-bar extension of the tonic harmony (coloured with a tonic augmented chord) brings us to the B section. Here again the music is song-like, but the melody removes to the soprano register in the right hand. The theme is once again divided into two phrases, *a* and *b*.

We see now that the brief excursion to A♭ in the A section was a premonition of the key of four flats in the B section, except that we are now in the parallel minor (Ex. 2).

Ex. 2. *Suite española* No. 1, 'Granada', B theme, bars 45–52

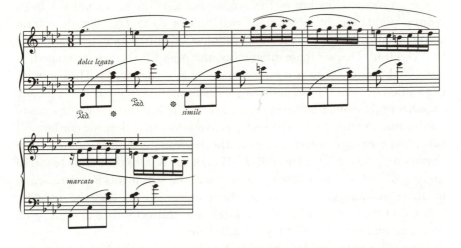

Here is the Moorish lament Albéniz sought to capture. His reference to its being 'out of tune' has nothing to do with a poor performance. It is his way of referring to the modality and intonation of Middle Eastern singing, which sounds strange to western ears. He approximates this through the F harmonic-minor scale, which contains the characteristically oriental-sounding interval of the augmented second (between E♮ and D♭). The strong upward thrust of the opening three bars of the B theme (*a* phrase) is counterbalanced by a sinuous stepwise descent (reminiscent of the melismatic character of Moorish song) over the next five bars of the theme (*b* phrase). This theme is immediately transposed into the parallel major, then directly to D♭ major with a lowered seventh and sixth degree, a seeming mixture of Mixolydian and Aeolian.[133] The theme from the A section makes an unexpected appearance in D♭ major and gradually returns us to the B theme, stated again first in F minor then major. The conclusion of the B section cleverly superimposes the codetta of the A section on the left-hand accompaniment of the B theme to ease into the retransition and a verbatim da capo. A simple four-bar arpeggiation of the tonic chord serves as a coda.

---

[133] This scale reappears in *Iberia* as the basis of the *copla* theme in 'Jerez' (bars 67–94), in 'El polo' (bars 111–42), and in the fourth phrase of the *copla* in 'Almería' (bars 113–16). See Mast, 'Iberia', 133.

The B section of 'Granada' presents us with some intriguing features. It has the character of a development in its tonal instability, which contrasts with the static tonic–dominant relationships of the A section. Interesting, too, is how the B theme is less symmetrical in its phrasing, divided as it is into two phrases of three and five bars each. There is also a suggestion of hemiola, as the syncopated rhythm of the accompaniment in the second bar helps create a single bar of 3/4 out of two bars of 3/8. This slightly offbeat accompaniment contrasts with the relentless downbeat-oriented pattern of the A section. Despite these differences, the A and B themes are related, as bar 4 of the latter is a mirror inversion of bar 2 of the former. Their motivic connection becomes apparent during the presentation of the B and A themes together in the same tonality in the middle of the B section. Albéniz's use of double bars to separate the various transpositions of the B theme cordons off this middle passage, which is clearly the keystone in a kind of arch form (dashes represent double bars): B–B′–B″A–B–B′–retransition. This union of 'northern' and 'southern' themes may reflect the sentiments he expressed in his letter to Moragas. In any event, the work reveals not only the unfailing lyric gift of the composer but also an interest in abstract formal designs based on modal and melodic types rooted in folklore.

The suite contains the ever-popular 'Sevilla (Sevillana)', which employs the spirited rhythms of the *sevillanas* (a light-hearted song and dance performed during the summer *feria* in Seville) in the A section as well as a stirringly lyrical and animated *copla* in the B section, interspersed with motivic reminiscences of the A section. The other original numbers from this suite are: 'Cataluña (Curranda)', one of the few pieces he wrote inspired by his native province and which appropriately bears a dedication to his 'dear mother', who was Catalan. The subtitle refers to a traditional Catalonian dance related to the French courante and the Italian corrente; and 'Cuba (Capricho or Nocturno)', another da capo-form piece that is based on the rhythm of the *habanera*, so popular in Spain at that time. 'Cádiz (subtitled variously as Saeta, Canción, or Serenata)',[134] 'Asturias (Leyenda)', 'Aragón (Fantasía [in the style of a *jota*])', and 'Castilla (Seguidillas)' were added to this collection later on. According to Baytelman, on 21 March 1887 Albéniz assembled this suite to honour the Spanish queen, who was an ardent fan of his. However, though he listed the above eight titles, he included scores for only the four original numbers. The other pieces appear first in later collections, under other titles, and were inserted into this suite by the publishers Hofmeister (in 1911) and Unión Musical Española (in 1913), with their titles adjusted

---

[134] The 'Saeta' subtitle of 'Cádiz' is a complete misnomer, as the piece has nothing to do with that genre at all (see Ch. 7 for a discussion of the *saeta* in 'Fête-Dieu à Séville' from *Iberia*).

to reflect Albéniz's original list.[135] Thus, the designations are not always relevant to the actual musical character of the piece. This is especially true of 'Asturias (Leyenda)', which has absolutely nothing to do with that region (see discussion in the following chapter).

Publishers' misapplication of titles is not the only source of confusion regarding the works of this period. The opus numbers of Albéniz's compositions are nearly meaningless, as he did not keep good track of his own works, and his several publishers, of course, never consulted about the correct sequence of composition and publication. Even the same publisher of two different Albéniz works could make an error. For instance, the *Seis mazurkas de salón*, published in Madrid by Romero in 1886, bear the opus number 66, as does the *Rapsodia cubana* published the same year by the same publisher![136] Baytelman's study of the plates reveals that the six mazurkas were, in fact, published in between the *Siete estudios en los tonos naturales mayores*, Op. 65 (Romero, 1886), and the *Rapsodia cubana*. This was either the publisher's error or Albéniz's.[137] The actual opus numbers themselves seem to be taken from thin air, as no conceivable inventory of his works to that time could yield sixty-five separate *opera*. Even more amusing is the London publisher Chappell & Co.'s 1892 designation of Albéniz's *Album of Miniatures* (composed in 1892) as opus 1. His *Mallorca (Barcarola)* composed about this same time in London (1890; first published London: Stanley Lucas, Weber & Co., 1891) bears the opus number 202![138] For these reasons, recent editions and works lists do not rely on opus numbers but rather on a chronological organization determined from manuscripts, contracts, plates, correspondence, and references to these pieces in contemporary periodical literature.

Of the numbers from *Recuerdos de viaje* ('Souvenirs of a journey', Romero, 1886–7), the best known is 'Rumores de la caleta ['Murmurs of the cove'] (Malagueña)', a reference to a well-known cove on the coast near Málaga.

---

[135] Baytelman, *Catalog*, 43. See also Laplane, *Albéniz*, 150–1. According to Antonio Gallego, 'Isaac Albéniz y el editor Zozaya', *Notas de música* (Boletín de la Fundación Isaac Albéniz), 2–3 (Apr.–June 1989), 11, the manuscripts for 'Cataluña' and 'Cuba' are in the Real Conservatorio in Madrid and are dated 24 Mar. 1886 and 25 May 1886, respectively. We learn in Laplane, *Albéniz*, 193, that Albéniz himself premiered 'Sevilla' on 24 Jan. 1886 and dedicated it to the wife of Count Morphy. According to Torres, *MGG*, s.v. 'Albéniz' (works list), 'Cádiz' is identical to the later *Serenata española* (Barcelona: Pujol, 1890). 'Asturias' appears first in *Chants d'Espagne* in the early 1890s under the less specific title 'Prélude'. 'Aragón (Fantasía)' is identical to the first of the *Deux Morceaux caractéristiques* (London: Stanley Lucas, Weber & Co., 1889), entitled 'Jota aragonesa'. 'Castilla (Seguidillas)' first appeared in *Chants d'Espagne* simply as 'Seguidillas'. Zozaya published the four original pieces separately in 1886 ('Granada' and 'Sevilla') and 1892 ('Cataluña' and 'Cuba').

[136] According to Torres, *MGG*, this work was possibly composed as early as 1881.

[137] Baytelman, *Catalog*, 50.

[138] Ibid. 70.

The opening of the A section imitates the *falsetas* (melodic passages) and *rasgueado* of the guitar. The animated *estribillo* theme features brief syncopations creating the sensation of 3/4 in the right hand against 6/8 (two bars of 3/8) in the left, a characteristic pattern. The B section presents a *copla* whose sinuous runs are, in typical fashion, punctuated by guitar-like interjections. The lengthy concluding melisma before the da capo is a forceful evocation of *jondo* singing. The modern *malagueña* is metrically free and does not sound much like this piece. But there were more varieties of *malagueña* then than now, and even this stylized version possesses much of the intense emotion of the real thing. The *malagueña* was popularized in Spain during the late 1800s by the celebrated singer Juan Breva (1844–1918) of Málaga. Albéniz was no doubt inspired by this trend, and he often returned to this paradigm of the *malagueña* through the years, experimenting with it in many ways.

However, Albéniz did not confine himself to works for piano in the 1880s. Vocal works from this decade included the *Tres romanzas catalanas* and *Cuatro romanzas para mezzo-soprano* (both lost), and the five melodies of *Rimas de Bécquer* (Zozaya, 1892), for voice and piano, on poems of the celebrated Sevillan poet Gustavo Adolfo Bécquer (1836–70).[140] The *Seis baladas* to Italian texts of Marquesa de Bolaños were composed in 1887 (Romero, *c.*1889). In both these collections Albéniz pays close attention to the natural rhythms of the poetry and highlights them through a syllabic, often declamatory, vocal line. Unlike his later song collections, however, the piano plays a supportive role and does not compete with the voice. Some of these songs, such as 'La lontananza' from the *Seis baladas* and '¿De donde vengo?' from *Rimas de Bécquer*, are among his finest efforts in this genre. Two choral works also flowed from his pen during the Madrid years: the oratorio *El Cristo* (lost),[141] and *Salmo VI: Oficio de difuntos* (1885), for SATB chorus, composed upon the death of Albéniz's patron Alfonso XII.[142] This piece, recently brought to light by Jacinto Torres, is written in the style of the Cecilian movement that exerted such a strong influence on Bruckner and Liszt as well.

[139] See Pohren, *Flamenco*, 125–6, for more on the *malagueña*. That author's *Lives and Legends of Flamenco* (Madrid: Society of Spanish Studies, 1988), 50–4, contains a biography of Juan Breva (né Antonio Ortega). Other notable interpreters included Antonio Chacón (1869–1929) and Enrique el Mellizo (1848–1906).

[140] Bécquer's nearly 100 *Rimas* deal with love, loneliness, and disillusionment. He also wrote prose works entitled *Leyendas* ('Legends'), and one wonders if they inspired Albéniz's use of that word in the titles of some of his piano pieces.

[141] According to Torres, *MGG*, this oratorio probably remained unfinished.

[142] The King died 5 Nov. 1885 of consumption. The manuscript came to light at the Madrid conservatory, and the piece is dated 24 Dec. 1885. A reproduction of the MS appears in Torres, 'Un desconocido "Salmo de difuntos"', 285–93. A modern edition of it (pub. 1994) is available from the Instituto de Bibliografía Musical in Madrid.

Though vocal music, in the form of opera, would dominate Albéniz's output in the following decade, instrumental music remained king in the 1880s and included a Trio in F for piano, violin, and cello (*c*.1885, now lost). A number of orchestral works mentioned in the press were published in piano reduction during this period, including the *Rapsodia española* for piano and orchestra (composed 1886–7 and published for two pianos by Romero in 1887) and Piano Concerto No. 1 (composed 1886–7 and published for two pianos by Unión Musical Española, *c*.1890 (orchestral version 1975)).[143] Not only was Albéniz reviving the sonata in Spain, but he was establishing a tradition of concerto writing that would blossom in the next century. He was also helping foster Spanish symphonic music, though the *Escenas sinfónicas Catalanas* of 1889 remained unpublished and his most important contribution, *Catalonia*, would not appear for another decade.[144] According to Torres, Albéniz also published some works for piano under the pseudonym Príncipe Weisse Vogel ('Prince White Bird'). These include *Balbina Valverde (Polka brillante)*, and *Diva sin par*, a mazurka-capricho dedicated to Adelina Patti (1843–1919), the internationally acclaimed Italian soprano with whom Albéniz concertized in 1886.[145]

As a result of these many accomplishments, on 30 March 1886 the Queen Regent appointed Albéniz to the position of assistant professor of piano at the Real Conservatorio. Several months later, on 11 November 1886, the Dirección General de Bellas Artes made Albéniz a member of the Royal Order of Isabel the Catholic, and the actual ceremony took place on the 22nd at the Royal Palace. On this occasion he received the designation 'Ordinary Knight Commander' (*Comendador Ordinario*). Two years later, on 9 July 1888, he was given the same honour again, now with the designation as 'Full Knight Commander' (*Comendador de Número*).[146] In the summer and autumn of 1888 he made several highly successful appearances

[143] Also known as the *Concierto fantástico*, it has very little about it suggestive of fantasy. See Ch. 3 for a discussion of the music.

[144] Torres, *MGG*, states that the first number of the *Escenas sinfónicas catalanas*, 'Fête villageoise catalane', is identical to *La fiesta de aldea* ('Village festival') of 1888 (a piano reduction pub. Madrid: Unión Musical Española, 1973). The other numbers of this suite are entitled 'Idilio', 'Serenata', and 'Finale: Baile campestre'. See Ch. 3 for a treatment of the music.

[145] Torres, *MGG*. Both were published by Romero in 1886. Albéniz's tenuous grasp of German grammar is apparent in his pseudonym, in which the ending of the adjective should reflect the gender of the noun it modifies, i.e. Weisser Vogel. If the adjective were preceded by the definite article, 'der', of course, Weisse would be correct. Difficulties with German persisted throughout his life. For an excellent study of Patti's life, see John Frederick Cone, *Adelina Patti: Queen of Hearts* (Portland, Ore.: Amadeus Press, 1993).

[146] The two letters informing him of these honours are in the Bc, 'D'. The actual notices of appointment are in the same collection, under 'V' (Varia). Like most other sources, Laplane, *Albéniz*, 35, states that he was also made a Knight of the Order of Carlos III, but the author has as yet found no documentation to support this. He was awarded the Cruz del Cristo de Portugal by King Luis of Portugal, according to a letter Albéniz received from Fernando G. Souza of the Portuguese consulate in Barcelona (dated 10 July 1885 (Bc, 'S')).

at the Exposición Universal in Barcelona, and these served as a springboard
for the next phase of his career. The piano manufacturer Erard & Co. invited
Albéniz to give a series of concerts in the French section of the Exposition,
and he gave no fewer than twenty recitals between 20 August and 11
October. In works for two pianos, including his own concerto, he was
assisted by José María Arteaga y Pereira, professor of piano at the Liceu.
His friend and mentor Felip Pedrell wrote an extensive review of these
appearances,[147] which were causing a sensation in the Catalonian capital.
In it he hails Albéniz's Piano Concerto No. 1 as 'without precedent' in
Spanish music history, lavishes praise on the 'poetic calm and inspiration'
of his sonatas, and applauds his use of folkloric references in the *Rapsodia
española*. In conclusion, Pedrell predicted that 'the name of Albéniz is
destined to represent a grand personality in the European musical world'.
Albéniz was ready to fulfil that prophecy, and he soon sought a wider stage
on which to do so.

---

[147] His review appeared in *La ilustración musical española*, 1/14 (15 Aug. 1888); repr. in Franco (ed.),
Albéniz y su tiempo, 63–7.

3

Veni, Vidi, Vici
(1889–1893)

ALBÉNIZ appeared in a concert on 7 March 1889 at the Teatro de la
Comedia in Madrid with the orchestra of the Sociedad de Conciertos conducted by Tomás Bretón. The programme included his *Suite característica*
for orchestra, made up of arrangements of three piano works: the Scherzo
from his Sonata No. 1, 'En la Alhambra' ('inspired by Arab legends'), and
'Rapsodia cubana' ('an exact transcription of the rhythm and melodic design
of Cuban songs').[1] Albéniz also performed his Piano Concerto No. 1, or
Concierto fantástico. Despite its title, the work is conservative and straightforward in nature. The lengthy Allegro first movement is in sonata form with
a principal theme in A minor and a secondary theme in E major. Much of the
melodic inspiration, in addition to the tonality, seems indebted to Schumann. The second movement supposedly expresses 'the vagueness of a
dream' ('la vaguedad de un ensueño'), and it is probably this 'fantasy'
element that inspired the concerto's title. It is divided into two sections:
the Andante's principal theme is clearly derived from the opening theme of
the Allegro, while the second section, marked 'presto', is a scherzo in the
style of Mendelssohn. The final movement, Allegro, is dominated by the
piano and is once again based on themes related to those of the first movement. Albéniz's *Escenas sinfónicas catalanas* ('Symphonic Catalan scenes')
also appeared on the programme. This work depicts a country fiesta in the
mountains of Catalonia and consists of four sections. The first is in sonata
form and includes a third theme of a popular character that recurs as a
leitmotif in the third and fourth sections of the work. The 'Idilio' ('Idyll')
paints a picture of two lovers. The 'Serenata' features a quartet of strings with
violin solo. The final movement presents two separate themes of a popular
character, and the work concludes with reminiscences of the leitmotif and the

[1] The translated descriptions in this paragraph are from a programme in the Bc, M987, vol. ii: 'una
transcripción exacta en el ritmo y diseño melódico' of Cuban songs.

'Idyll'. Albéniz's interest in formal unity through thematic interrelationship and recurrence is something he clearly derived from the symphonic works of Beethoven, Schumann, and Liszt. The illustrious zarzuela composer Francisco Barbieri congratulated Albéniz on the success of the concert, hailing him in a letter as 'a true musical genius'.[2]

Sometime during the first half of 1889 Albéniz appeared in Vitoria, and once again they claimed him as 'our countryman': 'Enthusiastic Álaves and good patriot, [Albéniz] informed us of his intention to write a musical composition and dedicate it to the erection of the Moraza monument.'[3] Oddly, though Albéniz seems to have played up his Basque heritage for all it was worth when he concertized in that region, he rarely did so elsewhere. Culturally, he was situated closer to Catalonia. His only pieces inspired by Basque folklore seem to have been two *zortzicos* for piano. The first appears in *España: Six Feuilles d'album* (*España: Seis hojas de album* in Spanish), composed in 1890 (London: Pitts and Hatzfield, 1890), and it exhibits the

Ex. 3. *España: Six Feuilles d'album*, 'Zortzico', bars 1–6

characteristic 5/8 metre and distinctive rhythm of this dance (Ex. 3). However, this 'album leaf' was dedicated not to Moraza but rather to Albéniz's dear friend the Basque painter Ignacio Zuloaga (1870–1945), who like Albéniz chose to live in Paris. Albéniz composed the other one about a year later, but it is in E minor rather than major and bears no dedication.

---

[2] Dated 8 Mar. 1889 (Bc, 'B'). Barbieri (1823–94) was a central figure in the revival of the zarzuela and contributed several masterpieces to the genre, including *Jugar con fuego* (1851) and *Pan y toros* (1864).

[3] Clipping from a Vitoria newspaper in the Mm, Prov. M-987a. Mateo Benigno de Moraza (1817–78) was a Vitorian politician and jurist of great renown. 'Entusiasta alavés y buen patriota [Albéniz] nos manifestó su propósito de escribir una composición musical, y dedicar su producto á la erección del Monumento á Moraza.'

Albéniz as a composer and soloist was already beginning to outgrow the peninsula and seek a larger arena for his talents. Erard invited him to perform in their hall in Paris on 25 April 1889. The concert was devoted exclusively to his own works, and he was accompanied by the orchestra of Édouard Colonne in his *Concierto fantástico*. The orchestra also rendered his *Escenas sinfónicas catalanas* (retitled *Scènes villageoises catalanes* for the occasion). *La Patrie* reported favourably on his performance, stating that he added 'charm to his mechanical prodigiousness; grace to his strength'.[4] *La Ménestrel* found in his works 'notable rhythmic qualities'.[5] Those in attendance at the performance included Debussy, Ravel, Fauré, and Dukas. Albéniz's piano playing and his style of writing, especially in 'Torre Bermeja (Serenata)' from *Douze Pièces caractéristiques* (Romero, 1888–9), were a revelation to them in the way he was able to evoke from the piano the characteristic sounds of the Spanish guitar (e.g. *rasgueado*).[6] Charles-Marie Widor wrote to Albéniz and congratulated him on his performance: 'The concert was very interesting and your execution superb!'[7]

In Madrid on 23 July 1889, Rosina gave birth to another daughter, this one named after the other of Albéniz's deceased sisters, Enriqueta. But Albéniz was concertizing in Britain, where he established his reputation with assistance from a letter of introduction to the British royal family written by the Infanta Isabel de Bourbon herself.[8] He made his first known appearance in London at Prince's Hall in Piccadilly (seating for 716 persons) on 13 June 1889.[9] *Trade & Finance* (19 June 1889)[10] enthused about his 'delicate taste, refined reading, dainty execution', remarking that his 'strength lies in the rendering of light, graceful compositions'. A short time later *Vanity Fair* (25 June 1889) admired his 'velvety touch'. Reporting on a performance at St James's Hall, a critic for the *Pall Mall Gazette* (25 June 1889) was reminded of Anton Rubinstein 'in [Albéniz's] refined and delicate passages, and of Hans von Bülow in his vigour'. *Dramatic Review* (28 June 1890) confirmed that Albéniz 'moves his audience not by astonishing them but by charming them', and that 'the same exquisite delicacy that marks the playing of Sarasate [who was also active in London at this time] distinguishes also that of Albéniz'. These observations sum up what nearly all reviewers would

---

[4] '[E]ncanto a los prodigios del mecanismo; la gracia, al rigor.' Cited in Laplane, *Albéniz*, 34–5.

[5] Cited in Gauthier, *Albéniz*, 62.

[6] Kalfa, 'Albéniz à Paris', 19.

[7] In a letter dated 26 Apr. 1889 (Bc, 'W'). 'La concert était très intéressant et votre exécution superbe!' Widor especially enjoyed the *jota* that Albéniz played.

[8] 19 Sept. 1890 (Bc, 'I').

[9] According to Bevan, 'Albéniz', 18.

[10] Unless otherwise noted, all the reviews cited in this chapter come from the two volumes of clippings in the Bc, M987.

say about Albéniz's execution, and give us some real insight into what type of pianist he was. In July, Albéniz performed at 19 Harley St., including in his programme works by himself and his friends Arbós, Chapí, and Bretón. With characteristic generosity, Albéniz had already determined to serve as a pathfinder for Spanish composers and performers in the concerts he gave and organized during his tenure in London. Bevan informs us that Albéniz 'deputized for the eminent Russian pianist Vladimir de Pachman in a promenade concert at Her Majesty's Theatre, and appeared again at the same venue on 2 September'.[11] Other performances during this year took place in Derby Drill Hall (14 October), in Leeds at one of Edgar Haddock's Musical Evenings, at a Royal Amateur Orchestral Society concert (with Arbós and Sarasate), at the Lyric Club,[12] and at the Crystal Palace.[13] He played once again at St James's Hall in October, where he presented his own compositions in addition to works by Bach, Scarlatti, and Chopin. This concert prompted the *Daily Telegraph* (24 October 1889) to comment on the 'charming fashion in which he executes works by Scarlatti and other masters of refinement'. The following day this same newspaper reported that 'Mr Albéniz has received permission from the Spanish Government to copy, for the purpose of [an upcoming] concert, several important manuscripts in the library of the Escorial'. This seems a first taste of the public-relations poppycock Albéniz would shamelessly dispense to a fawning and credulous press in London. Perhaps the highlight of his concerts in London in 1889 was a December performance at a *conversazione* of the Wagner Society, held in the Institute over Prince's Hall. No less formidable a critic than George Bernard Shaw himself reported the following:

and Señor Albéniz, after playing Brassin's transcriptions of the rainbow scene from Das Rheingold and the fire charm from Die Walküre, had a final tremendous wrestle with the Walkürenritt. The dead silence produced by his playing, particularly during the second piece, was the highest compliment he could have desired.[14]

In early 1890 Albéniz set out on a tour of the provinces with a group of performers, serving as both soloist and accompanist (e.g. he accompanied the cellist in the Andante and Finale of the Second Sonata of Rubinstein). Their travels took them to many locales, including Brighton, Lancaster, Leeds, Bradford, Halifax, Huddersfield, Sheffield, Chatham, Rochester,

---

[11] 'Albéniz', 18.
[12] Ibid. 19.
[13] According to a report in the *Sunday Times* of 24 Oct. 1889.
[14] From 'A Talk with Dr Heuffer', *Star* (6 Dec. 1889); repr. in Bernard Shaw, *Shaw's Music: The Complete Musical Criticism in Three Volumes*, ed. Dan H. Laurence, i: *1876–1890* (New York: Dodd, Mead & Co., 1981), 868.

Stourbridge, Manchester, Birmingham, Bristol, and Glasgow. The *Rochdale Observer* (22 January 1890) found his rendition of the Chopin Berceuse the 'gem' of the concert: 'The velvety softness of touch—the cadences dying to almost a whisper, yet audible all over the room—must have been the wonder and the admiration—and also the despair—of the amateur pianists present.' The *Bristol Times & Mirror* (6 February 1890) declared his scales 'perfect' and his tone shading 'remarkable', while the *Strand Journal* (14 February 1890) expressed awe at his 'lightning-like feats, varied by interludes of sweet, dreamy melody, which none but a past master of his art could hope to rival'. The *Huddersfield Daily Examiner* (10 January 1890) found Albéniz's own pieces 'light but remarkably beautiful, thoroughly distinctive, yet all full of the colour of the composer's nationality, and of that graceful individuality which is so strongly characteristic of his playing'.

Albéniz may have returned to Paris briefly after this tour,[15] and he was probably present when his third daughter and last child, Laura, was born on 20 April 1890 in Barcelona. But June found him once again in London, now resolved to settle in the city that had received him so favourably. He inspired *The Times* (10 June 1890) to remark of his concert two days before at Steinway Hall[16] that he had 'the rare power of producing the full tone of his instrument without having recourse to violence of any kind, or ever exceeding the limits of acoustic beauty'. The *Musical Standard* (14 June 1890) simply commented on his 'soft and sympathetic touch'. Shaw wrote that Albéniz was 'so far this season, the most distinguished and original of the pianists who confine themselves to the rose-gathering department of music', presumably alluding to his penchant for playing popular and accessible pieces.[17]

Later this same month, Albéniz signed a contract with a London business-man that would have repercussions throughout the rest of his life and eventually inaugurate a relationship referred to by most biographers as the 'pact of Faust'. Henry Lowenfeld was a successful businessman of Polish descent[18] who had founded the Universal Stock Exchange in 1865 and whose association with Kops' Ale, a non-alcoholic beer, made him a fortune. He had even authored several popular books on finance, and was now taking

---

[15] According to Bevan, 'Albéniz', 19, he returned to Paris in 1890 to study with Dukas and d'Indy, but the present author has found nothing to substantiate this.

[16] Bevan, 'Albéniz', 19, reveals that Steinway Hall, located in Lower Seymour Street and seating 400 people, 'was associated with the debuts of young pianists and singers'.

[17] G. B. Shaw, *Music in London 1890–94*, rev. edn., i (London, 1932), 15. Cited in Bevan, 'Albéniz', 19 n. 20.

[18] The *Mirror* reported on 5 Jan. 1890 that Lowenfeld had returned for a visit to 'Galicia, the home of his birth'.

a keen interest in concert and theatrical management.[19] W. MacQueen-Pope described him as 'in his seventh heaven in business deals.... He would always beat you and still keep within the bond.'[20] On 26 June 1890, only eighteen days after his Steinway Hall appearance, Albéniz signed a contract with Lowenfeld placing his 'entire work and services as a composer and musician under the control of Lowenfeld ... in consideration of Lowenfeld agreeing to advance money for his personal expenses and the promotion of his interests'.[21] Whether 'the clever pianist [was] being exploited by an enthusiastic capitalist [referring to Lowenfeld]' remains in the realm of speculation, but that was the opinion of *Modern Society* (15 November 1890). In any case, Albéniz did not enter into this agreement lightly or suddenly, and Bevan surmises with good reason that it was not directly a result of Albéniz's recent concert triumph but 'had been under negotiation for some time beforehand'.[22] This arrangement also provided Albéniz with a spacious house at 16 Michael's Grove, Brompton, a district traditionally populated by accomplished musicians and actors, including Muzio Clementi and Jenny Lind.[23] Arbós, a frequent visitor to the Albéniz home, described this residence as 'una casa magnífica',[24] and it would provide ample room for Albéniz's wife and three children, who now moved to London to join him.

Lowenfeld probably provided financial backing for our pianist/composer's ensuing ambitious concert ventures. Albéniz organized two orchestral concerts at St James's Hall in November. The first programme, on the 7th, attracted but few auditors, probably due to the large venue and competition from Hans Richter's concert series there.[25] Another reason was inclement weather (according to the *Standard* of 22 November 1890). The programme featured orchestral works by Bretón and Chapí, with Bretón directing a pick-up group composed of members from the Crystal Palace and Richter orchestras. The offerings included Bretón's four-movement Symphony No. 2 in E♭, the Prelude to his opera *Guzmán el Bueno*, and a serenade

[19] Bevan, 'Albéniz', 22. See also the review of *The Magic Opal* in *Hearth & Home*, 9 Feb. 1893. According to Diana Howard, *London Theatres and Music Halls 1850–1950* (London: Library Association Publishing, Ltd., 1970), 184, he was Lord Chamberlain of the Prince of Wales's Theatre from 1893 to 1898.
[20] W. MacQueen-Pope, *Carriages at Eleven* (London, 1947), 189–90, cited in Bevan, 'Albéniz', 22.
[21] From a subsequent contract, to be discussed later, now in the Latymer Archive at the banking firm of Coutts & Co. in London. Interestingly, in a contract of 1 May 1890 with the publisher Pujol in Barcelona, Albéniz ceded rights to all his compositions from that date forward, except in Great Britain. This would seem to violate the spirit of his contract with Lowenfeld, if not the letter.
[22] 'Albéniz', 22.
[23] F. H. W. Sheppard (ed), *Survey of London*, xxix: *The Parish of St. James Westminster*, part 1: *South of Piccadilly* (London, 1960), 97. Cited in Bevan, 'Albéniz', 25. Bevan explains that this area was renamed Egerton Terrace in 1898, but that the houses still bear their previous numbers.
[24] Arbós, *Arbós*, 217.
[25] According to Bevan, 'Albéniz', 20, the hall held 2,127 people and was London's principal concert venue until it was torn down in 1905.

entitled *En la Alhambra*. Bretón also conducted Chapí's 'Moorish fantasy' *La corte de Granada*, consisting of four movements entitled 'Grenade (March to the Tournament)', 'Rêverie', 'Sérénade', and 'Finale'. The concert featured a number of Albéniz's works, including the enchantingly lyrical *Mallorca* (*Barcarola*).[26] In addition, Albéniz performed the Schumann Concerto, the Mozart D major Concerto, and the *Hungarian Fantasy* for piano and orchestra by Liszt.

Not suprisingly, one of the chief complaints about the concert was its duration, which exceeded three hours. *Footlights* (15 November 1890) protested that such length 'savours of wanton cruelty to tax long suffering [*sic*] humanity so heavily'. Shaw himself railed at the 'insanely long' programme and at the 'procrustean torturings' of the 'ingeniously horrible' symphony of Bretón (*World*, 12 November 1890). By Shaw's account, Albéniz did not deliver his bravura pieces until much of the audience had left the hall. *Figaro* (8 November 1890) gave Bretón credit for conducting well, but also dismissed his symphony, an early work, as a 'bold imitation of Beethoven'. Chapí's offerings fared much worse, being characterized as 'barbaric, long-drawn-out, and flimsy' (*Figaro*, 8 November 1890), 'cheap, trashy noise' (*Pall Mall Gazette*, 8 November 1890), 'sheer tea-garden blatancy' (*Daily Graphic*, 10 November 1890), and 'circus music' (*Referee*, 9 November 1890). *Queen* (15 November 1890), on the other hand, reported that the audience received the work favourably, and that the serenade movement was repeated at their insistence. The reaction to Albéniz's own performance was uncharacteristically mixed. Shaw assessed his execution of the Schumann as 'monotonously pretty' and lacking 'fire and breadth'. The *Pall Mall Gazette* accused him of 'lacking, especially in the left hand, wrist power. There is too little contrast and he would be a much greater pianist if he would consent to let himself go.'[27]

No one had ever before suggested Albéniz had difficulty letting himself go! But this gives us pause to reflect on what was expected of him and his countrymen as Spaniards. The reviewer for the *Daily Graphic* (cited above) described Bretón's conducting as lacking 'the animation and impetuosity one associates with a Southerner'. However, in a review of the

---

[26] Baytelman, *Catalog*, 78, places the composition of this popular work *c*.1891 and its publication *c*.1895 (Pujol, Barcelona). However, Torres, *MGG*, posits its composition much earlier, *c*.1883, and publication already in 1891 in London. Copies of the programme in the Bc, M987, constitute the first mention of this piece the author has encountered in the press; and it found no place in Guerra y Alarcón's works list of 1886. Thus, a composition date of 1890 seems most likely. In terms of style, it appears too mature for so early a date as 1883.

[27] *Mistress & Maid* (4 Mar. 1891) did agree that Albéniz's playing 'lacks strength … not delicacy', a sentiment echoed in *Woman* (5 Mar. 1891), which said he was 'more charming in the delicate and fanciful music than in the more severe school'.

next concert, the *Country Gentleman* (29 November 1890) found nothing incongruous about his manner and placed Bretón in possession of 'all
the proverbial solemnity of his race'. The *Pall Mall Gazette* (27 February
1891) did not view Spaniards as at all solemn: 'there is always something emotional about a Spanish musician which is more serious than Italian
and more wild than French passion ... [Spaniards are] a people implacable
alike in love and war, and ready to languish at one moment and stab
the next.'

Albéniz found himself navigating his way, Odysseus-like, between this
Scylla and Charybdis of ethnic stereotyping. He succeeded in London by
offering his audiences a variety of Spanish works and traditional Germanic
fare, by blending salon-style pieces with more serious compositions. But he
would not pander to those who expected him alternately to languish and to
stab. In fact, his stage presence was pleasant but somewhat reserved, the *Pall
Mall Gazette* (22 November 1890) describing him as 'an undemonstrative
pianist, with but few mannerisms, but much technical ability'. The *Daily
Telegraph* (27 February 1891) simply noted his 'subdued neatness and
delicacy'. This avoidance of romantic posturing reminds us that there was a
strong streak of classical objectivity and restraint in Albéniz's artistic temperament, a point that we will make again in discussing his music. But we
may jump ahead of our story a bit to relate an incident that occurred several
years later in Paris.

In his prologue to Laplane's biography, Francis Poulenc remarked that
whenever a Spanish pianist performed in Paris, there would always be someone who would accuse him (as the *Daily Graphic* accused Bretón) of being
'cold' and his interpretation 'lifeless'. The expectation was, of course, that he
should be very animated and demonstrative—'romantic'. To show how
misinformed such stereotypes were, Poulenc repeated a story told to him
by the conductor André Messager. One afternoon at the house of Vincent
d'Indy, Emmanuel Chabrier performed his *España* for Albéniz in a two-
piano arrangement. He played with a great display of exuberance and emotion, but when he was done, Albéniz appeared unimpressed. The Spaniard
then took his place at the keyboard and proceeded to play his own compositions very calmly, even austerely. Thus he refuted Chabrier's notions of
Spanish passion.[28]

---

[28] Laplane, *Albéniz*, 10. Those who witnessed the performances of Andrés Segovia will recall that he, too,
made no extraneous gestures or facial expressions to impress those who were not fully concentrated on the
actual sounds he was producing. The same is true of Alicia de Larrocha. The author's personal experience is
that Spanish passion is indeed intense but often belied by an impassive exterior, which only serves to intensify
the emotion. The very essence of flamenco is intense *duende* (profound emotion) expressed through a precise
and highly disciplined technique.

If there were a valid generalization we could make about Spaniards like Albéniz, then, it would be their intense dislike of crude foreign stereotypes of Spanish people, culture, and especially music. However, Albéniz bore himself with friendliness and dignity; he never expressed any resentment about his reception in London, largely because he was doing so well there. And his programmes of Spanish music were having their intended effect. Before the November concerts, a newspaper like the *Pictorial World* (2 November 1890) could print the following sentiments, which probably enjoyed some currency in Britain: 'there is no distinctive school of musical art belonging to [Spain] and . . . its music is but a pale reflection of French or German thought. It has gone out of use—if it ever was to the fore—with Cordovan leather and liquorice, or Baracco juice.' But as a result of these November concerts, the *Daily Chronicle* (22 November 1890) came to see things in this light:

For several generations Spain is supposed to have been in the background in the matter of high-class music, but after what we have heard of late at St James's Hall . . . we begin to be doubtful . . . of the imputation. It is quite possible that other nations have been wilfully blind as well as deaf to the labours of Spanish musicians.

'Argus', writing for *Land & Water* (15 November 1890), praised Albéniz's 'little Spanish dissertations' and intended to 'offer a silent prayer for a repetition of these pleasing trifles at his next concert'. His prayers were answered on the 21st of the month, once again at St James's Hall.

This concert featured *Love and Fate*, a Wagnerian-style dramatic overture by Arthur Hervey (1855–1922), conducted by the composer, as well as several of Albéniz's solo works, his piano concerto, and his *Scènes symphoniques catalanes* (another retitling of the *Escenas sinfónicas catalanas*). This suite reminded one reviewer not at all of Spain but of French ballet music.[29] Albéniz also delivered solo works by Scarlatti, Weber, and the Grand Polonaise in E flat for piano and orchestra by Chopin. Bretón reappeared for this concert, conducting the Prelude to his own opera *Los amantes de Teruel*, as well as a *zapateado* and a scherzo in C sharp minor, both from his own pen. In spite of the mixed reviews that greeted the previous concert, the public had evidently been satisfied enough and this time Albéniz and his associates played to a much fuller house. The *Standard* (22 November 1890) deemed Bretón's pieces 'clever' and 'excellently scored', and *Country Gentleman* (29 November 1890) declared that Bretón 'may now be considered an established favourite, both as a conductor and composer'. But it was Albéniz who

[29] The *Standard* (22 Nov. 1890) found that his orchestral works 'scarcely suggest a Spanish origin, resembling . . . the ballet music of Massenet [and] Delibes'. The *Musical Standard* (29 Nov. 1890) sniffed that 'the Cuban Rhapsody in G failed to satisfy strict *connoisseurs*'. The critic carelessly neglected to note, however, the precise number of Cuban-rhapsody connoisseurs in attendance.

again stole the show, the *Daily Telegraph* (22 November 1890) averring that his salon pieces (*Champagne vals, Pavana-capricho*, and Scherzino) were 'the greatest success of the evening . . . so much applauded that the pianist-composer returned to throw in another piece'. To sum up, *Vanity Fair* (29 November 1890) marvelled at the remarkably short time in which Albéniz had won over the public: 'Señor Albéniz may well inscribe upon his escutcheon the words, "Veni, vidi, vici".' It further announced that he had 'elected to make London his home', as indeed he had. But Spain did not lose touch with him, and these concerts were enthusiastically reported in *La época* and *El resumen* in Madrid.

Buoyed by this success and enjoying the financial backing of Lowenfeld, Albéniz set about organizing a series of ten concerts in St James's Hall the following year.[30] They took place on 27 January, 12 and 26 February, 14 March, 9 and 24 April, 8 and 21 May, and 14 and 18 June.[31] These programmes featured not only Albéniz but many of his friends, including Arbós and the Hungarian violinist Tividar Nachez (1859–1930). Albéniz's playing won the now customary plaudits, prompting comparisons with Ignacy Paderewski and Sigismond Thalberg. Consistently, Albéniz was seen as representing 'a reaction against the slap-bang-and-hack school which the genius of Liszt invented'.[32] This reaffirms our conviction that, even if he did at some point play for Liszt, the impact of that pianist's style on Albéniz was negligible. A review in *Bazaar* (16 February 1891) is worth quoting to give us a fuller picture of his pianism:

His great excellence lies in the power to play softly. . . . He can preserve a special shade of tone for a very long period without the slightest fluctuation or variety. The pianoforte under Señor Albéniz's hands utters tones which are more like those of a flute than a piano. This skilful executant has entirely subdued the hard metallic ring which is almost inseparable from the pianoforte, and by his wonderful art produces tones which resemble the ripple of water, and which charm the ear by their delicate softness.

Regarding his use of the pedals, *Vanity Fair* (21 February 1891) proclaimed that 'Beethoven's intentions were realised' when Albéniz played the first movement of the 'Moonlight' Sonata 'without making use of the pedals', which resulted in an appropriate absence of 'blurred sound'.

---

[30] In Jan. of 1891, Albéniz journeyed north once again to perform in Leeds. His concert received lavish praise in both the *Yorkshire Post* (14 Jan. 1891) and the *Leeds Mercury* (14 Jan. 1891). In addition to the usual adjectives—charming, brilliant, dainty, polished, singing, masterly (in his use of the pedals)—the latter periodical said that his command of the music was so thorough, he appeared 'to be virtually improvising'.

[31] I am indebted to Bevan, 'Albéniz', 21, for this tidy summary of dates.

[32] *Pall Mall Gazette* (27 Feb. 1891), already cited.

Perhaps as impressive as his playing was his performance as impresario. Albéniz seems to have learned from his mistakes of the previous year, avoiding inordinate length in the programmes and including a few welcome innovations. The *Daily Telegraph* (27 February 1891) admired the maximum length of one and a half hours, the inexpensive tickets, free cloakroom and programmes, and the fact that subscription could begin with any concert in the series.

During the course of these ten concerts, the press reported on his intention to write an opera. *Dramatic Review* (14 February 1891) stated simply that he was writing a light patriotic opera. The action was to take place in Spain at the beginning of the War of Independence against Napoleon, the hero to be a reformed brigand converted into a guerrilla chief. *Gentlewoman* (28 March 1891) specified the locale as Salamanca in 1808, while *Queen* (28 February 1891) reported the librettist to be H. Sutherland Edwards. Though nothing seems to have come of this project, Albéniz's destiny in London did indeed lie in writing musical theatre, and that destiny was soon to become manifest.

But Albéniz did not stop concertizing, nor did he confine his appearances to England during these years. In early February 1892, he and the Belgian violinist Eugène Ysaÿe (1858–1931) appeared in a programme as part of the Valleria concerts at the Philharmonie in Berlin. Nearly a month later, on 1 March, Albéniz presented a solo concert at the Singakademie in Berlin, to which the critics had decidedly ambivalent reactions. Albéniz played the Prelude and Fugue in A Minor of Bach (arr. Liszt) as well as the 'Moonlight' Sonata of Beethoven and the famous B flat minor Sonata of Chopin. He included some of his own pieces, which the critics sniffed at as 'Salonstücke' ('salon pieces'), and closed with Tausig's arrangement of Weber's *Aufforderung zum Tanze*.[33] This was just the kind of programme that had proven so successful in London. However, though the German critics praised his technical command and tone production, they found his playing too pretty, too polished—in fact, too French. Some compared him to his friend Francis Planté (1839–1934) and the 'new French virtuosos' (e.g. *Berliner Courier*, 2 March 1892; *Berliner Börsen-Zeitung*, 4 March 1892). The *Berliner Tageblatt* (3 March 1892) went so far as to recommend that he abandon Bach and Beethoven, as his elegant style and fast tempos revealed much practice but only a superficial rapport with the music. Another criticized his inexact rhythm and lack of dynamic contrasts (*Norddeutschen Allgemeinen Zeitung*, 4 March 1892). Inevitably, at least one critic found that his music lacked the

---

[33] These Berlin press clippings are in the Mm, Prov. M-987d.

'fiery blood' typical of the 'Southerner' (*Volks-Zeitung*, 4 March 1892). The turnout was small, but at least the audience received him with enthusiasm. In this same year he performed with Arbós in Brussels and made another tour in England with Arbós and the Czech cellist David Popper (1843–1913).

The year 1892 represented the apex of his career as a concert pianist, and after this time he gave himself over more and more to serious composition. In a letter of 12 January 1893, Bretón advised him never to abandon the piano, but otherwise encouraged him to pursue his *nuevo camino* ('new road').[34] Albéniz's commitment to devote more of his time and energy to composition may have had something to do with declining health, brought on by his expanding girth.[35] He did continue to concertize over the next few years, but far less actively than had been his custom. The main reason for this was his growing occupation with musical theatre in London. His initial foray into this arena came in the form of incidental music to poems by Paul-Armand Sylvestre (1837–1901), read by the celebrated actress Sarah Bernhardt (1845–1923). Collet recalled these as twelve numbers for Sylvestre's *Légendes bibliques*, but no record whatsoever of such a work by Albéniz has come down to us. What we do retain are a manuscript and press notices for his incidental music to Sylvestre's *Poèmes d'amour*, arranged as a series of twelve *tableaux vivants* by Cyprien Godebski and premiered on Monday afternoon, 20 June 1892, at the Lyric Club, Barnes. Albéniz had begun composing the work only a week earlier, on 14 June, and finished the manuscript but a day before the concert, on the 19th.[36] The unusual scoring was for flute, oboe, horn, harmonium, piano, and strings. In terms of style, these pieces are not memorable, and the work seems never to have been done again. The poetry deals with spiritual love, and treats of such biblical characters as David and Bathsheba, Adam and Eve, Christ and Mary Magdalen. This is probably what caused the confusion in Collet's mind. Albéniz relies greatly on the repetition of large blocks of material, and on ostinato and pedal notes, features also characteristic of his Spanish style but handled here with far less charm.

[34] Bc, 'B'. 'Pero no abandones nunca el piano.' Albéniz clearly did not intend to do anything quite so drastic. He began work on a second piano concerto at this time, but only got as far as the secondary theme group in the first movement. The MS is a two-piano reduction dated 'Broadstairs August 1892' and is now in the Bc, M985.

[35] This, at least, was the opinion of his friend Herman Klein, a London music critic, who confidently stated that 'it was only after he had grown too stout, that the pianist succumbed and the composer took his place'. This appears in the *Musical Times* (1 Mar. 1918), 116–17, and is cited in Bevan, 'Albéniz', 46 n. 40.

[36] Now in the Bc, M985. The MS consists of fifty-eight pages and is a conflation of fair copy and sketch pages, revealing the haste of their assembly. The poems are written directly into the score. The individual parts are in the Mm, Lligall 12. Torres, 'La producción escénica', 184–5 and 199–200, was the first to surmise correctly the true nature of these pieces, but Bevan, 'Albéniz', 25–7, must be credited with actually ferreting out information about the performance.

Early in his London tenure, Albéniz had established contact with Horace Sedger,[37] manager of the Lyric Theatre, and now became involved in his production of the operetta *Incognita*, an English adaptation of Charles Lecocq's *Le Cœur et la main*, which opened on 6 October 1892 and ran for 101 performances.[38] For this production the work was expanded from two acts to three, and Albéniz was called upon to compose a finale for Act II, entitled 'Oh! Horror! Horror!'[39] This, however, was an arrangement by Albéniz based on fragments of the original score, and thus cannot be said to constitute an original composition by him. This project was shortly followed by the premiere of a work that definitely bears Albéniz's imprimatur and constitutes the first musico-theatrical production by him about which we know anything substantial.

In the summer of 1892 Albéniz began work on an operetta in two acts entitled *The Magic Opal*, on a text by Arthur Law, a popular English librettist of the day.[40] According to Ángel Sagardía,[41] Arbós, who was then also residing in London, agreed to share the work of writing the operetta. Unfortunately, a family crisis required him to leave London after only a little of the music had been composed, and Albéniz was left saddled with the entire project.[42] None the less, he acquitted himself admirably, and the work premiered on 19 January 1893, at the Lyric Theatre (cast in Table 5).

The Magic Opal is scored for two each of flutes, oboes, B♭ clarinets, bassoons, F horns, B♭ trumpets, as well as trombone, timpani, snare drum, and strings. Winds and strings are segregated, frequently playing the melody

---

[37] Sedger is a slightly less obscure figure than Lowenfeld. According to Howard, *London Theatres*, he was Lord Chamberlain of the Prince of Wales's Theatre from 1887 to 1892 (184), and of the Lyric Theatre from 1890 to 1896 (146). During the run of *The Magic Opal*, he was not only manager but was responsible for the staging as well. For W. S. Gilbert's difficult relations with him, see Andrew Goodman, *Gilbert and Sullivan's London* (Tunbridge Wells: Spellmount Ltd., 1988), 65–6. In a letter to Albéniz dated 9 July 1900 (Mm, 10.272), Albéniz's friend Francis Money-Coutts states the following regarding Sedger: 'Some other people and myself are trying to arrange to get him out of the country (as you said). I am afraid, however, that do what we may, he will never be anything but a *worthless creature* [emphasis in original]. He knows really nothing, except how to spend other people's money; which is a form of embezzlement.'

[38] The original premiered in Paris at the Nouveautés on 19 Oct. 1882.

[39] On a text by Harry Greenbank. The overall book was written by Sir Francis Cowley Burnand (1836–1917). This number was published separately by Hopwood & Crew, London, 1892. Additional numbers were contributed by Hamilton Clarke (1840–1912), a prolific composer and accomplished musician who toured with the D'Oyly Carte Company, and Herbert Bunning (1863–1937), music director at the Lyric Theatre (1892–3) and at the Prince of Wales's Theatre (1894–6). See Bevan, 'Albéniz', 48.

[40] According to Bevan, 'Albéniz', 49 n. 55, Law (1844–1913) had served in the Royal Scots Fusiliers before becoming 'an actor and author of some 67 plays, most famously adapting for the stage Fergus Hume's novel, *Mystery of a Hansom Cab*'.

[41] *Albéniz*, 51.

[42] This is corroborated by a letter Albéniz wrote to his sister Clementina, dated 19 Dec. 1892, in which he states that Arbós was never enthusiastic about the project and, 'to his great shame', left Albéniz 'on the horns of the bull' after writing only two of the numbers. Nothing is said of any emergency. This letter is cited in Torres, 'La producción escénica', 188.

TABLE 5. *Cast of the* The Magic Opal, *premiere,*
London, Lyric Theatre, 19 January 1893

Telemachus Ulysses Carambollas	Harry Monkhouse
Alzaga	John Child
Aristippus	Fred Kaye
Pekito	Tom Shale
Trabucos	Wallace Brownlow
Curro	George Tate
Martina	Mary Yohe
Olympia	Susan Vaughan
Zoe	Emmeline Orford
Christina	Dora Thorne
Irene	Elena Monmouth
Thelka	Rose Hamilton
Alethia	Cissy Cranford
Leila	Dolly Webb
Lolika	Alda Jenoure
Conductor	Herbert Bunning

in alternation, and doublings are kept to a minimum. At first glance, there appears to be some justification here for Pedrell's remark that Albéniz treated the orchestra like a big piano,[43] with the violins carrying the melody and the winds and lower strings providing 'left-hand' accompaniment.

The plot is complex, perhaps overly so, and is full of the misguided love interests common to English operetta. Although the manuscripts are extant and the piano–vocal score was published, these do not contain any of the spoken dialogue.[44] Because Law's libretto has apparently not survived, we are dependent on press accounts for the story. The following narrative is based on a piece in the *Stage* (26 January 1893, 12).

The work opens in the marketplace of Karakatol, Greece. It is not yet day, and stealing through the streets comes a band of brigands, anxious to escape before the inhabitants awaken. They sing the opening chorus, 'Lightly tread and softly creep', in hushed pianissimo tones. Their chief, Trabucos, stops underneath the window of the girl he loves, Lolika, the niece of the wealthy merchant Aristippus, and softly serenades her in 'Star of my Life'. This number displays some of the Spanish rhythms that reviewers noted throughout the opera (Ex. 4).

---

[43] Pedrell, *Músicos*, 380.

[44] The MSS for the *The Magic Opal* and *The Magic Ring* are in the Bc, M975 and M974, respectively. The Mm retains a bound copy of the proofs for *The Magic Opal* (BM3) and *The Magic Ring* (BM10). In the latter, Albéniz made markings in red pencil indicating changes in Spanish, possibly for the Madrid production of *La sortija* (like *The Magic Ring*, a revision of *The Magic Opal*).

Ex. 4. *The Magic Opal*, Act I, No. 1: 'Star of my Life', bars 129–32

But the girl is in love with another, Alzaga, the son of the mayor, to whom she is to be married that day. When she discovers Trabucos, she quickly closes her window, at which moment her beloved Alzaga appears. Trabucos and Alzaga now express their competing claims to Lolika's affections in the duet 'She is mine'. Alzaga is suddenly apprehended on the orders of the brigand chief and carried away to the mountains, while the brigands resume their chorus. Trabucos, not discouraged by Lolika's disdain, declares that if he possessed the magic-opal ring she would be his. This ring has the property of making everyone of the opposite sex fall in love upon touching its wearer. It had been stolen from the late chief of the brigands, and for years has been in the mayor's private museum without its power being suspected. Next, a choral number ('The sun is up, the morn is bright, The mists have roll'd away') celebrates the arrival of a new day as the marketplace fills with people in anticipation of Lolika's wedding. Carambollas, the pompous mayor, enters and gives to Lolika as a wedding present the magic ring, which immediately exercises its influence, as both Carambollas and Aristippus fall in love with Lolika upon touching her. This leads to the amusing duet and chorus 'From boyhood I was noted', which could have come straight out of a Gilbert and Sullivan operetta[45] with its rapid patter and incessant rhyme: 'From boyhood I was noted for my wonderful sagacity! | The neighbours were astounded at his youthful perspicacity, | I swallow'd information with remarkable avidity | And so his head expanded with a marvellous rapidity', etc. (Ex. 5).

Lolika sings a charming solo, 'Love sprang from his couch', the kind of air one might expect in a work by Lecocq or Offenbach (Ex. 6). She is then joined by her two newly acquired admirers. At this point Trabucos and his sister Martina arrive on the scene disguised as pedlars. They plan to steal the ring and replace it with a counterfeit. They sing a duet, followed by a crowd scene in which Trabucos sings parlato in alternation with the chorus as the

[45] Albéniz's own music library, preserved in the Mm, included scores for *The Mikado*, *Patience*, and *The Yeomen of the Guard*.

Ex. 5. *The Magic Opal*, Act I, No. 6: 'From boyhood I was noted', bars 12–14

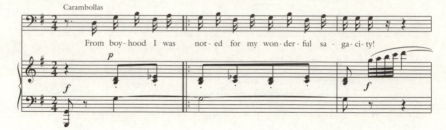

Ex. 6. *The Magic Opal*, Act I, No. 7: 'Love sprang from his couch', bars 10–14

two 'merchants' sell their wares amidst general commotion. While Trabucos stealthily borrows the ring from Lolika and passes it on to his sister, he gives in return the false one. Martina attempts to elicit the crowd's sympathy by singing of the hardships they endure in their ceaseless travels. The mayor, impatient to begin the wedding ceremony, is mightily annoyed at Alzaga's failure to appear and orders the pedlars to leave town. But while so doing he places his hand on Martina's shoulder. Of course, he falls in love with her, and to the astonishment of everyone he proposes marriage! A messenger now arrives to say that he has seen the brigand kidnappers taking the bridegroom to the mountains. During the ensuing confusion, Trabucos and Martina escape, followed by the lovesick mayor who is now irresistibly drawn to her. The first act concludes with everyone singing 'Unlucky chance, unlucky chance, To say the very least, Alas! alas!'

    The second act opens in a ruined monastery in the mountains. This has been adopted by the brigands as their hideout, and they are safe within its walls because the country people think it is haunted. The brigands sing a spirited drinking chorus whose undulating chromatic melody suggests their inebriation. This *brindisi* is the only one Albéniz ever composed (Ex. 7). Olympia, an elderly spinster, enters and anxiously enquires about the opal, thinking that, once in her possession, it will enable her to win the handsome

Ex. 7. *The Magic Opal*, Act II, No. 16: 'Chorus and Drinking Song', bars 10–11

chief, Trabucos. The latter, accompanied by Martina, soon afterwards enters, and everyone rejoices at their return because with the opal ring they hope to ensnare more wealthy prisoners. Trabucos sings of the 'Legend of the Monastery', with its creaking doors, wailing night winds, wolves, and grave-yard. This is another singular number in Albéniz's output and delightfully evokes the scene through its wraithlike descending chromatic line and rustling rhythmic ostinato (Ex. 8).

Jarring dissonances and syncopations help to create a things-that-go-bump-in-the-night effect. Alzaga now confronts Trabucos, who informs

Ex. 8. *The Magic Opal*, Act II, No. 17: 'Legend of the Monastery', bars 9–15

him of his intention to marry Lolika himself, and the four characters (Olympia, Alzaga, Trabucos, and Martina) sing a quartet before Alzaga is confined once again to his cell. Olympia soon sees her chance, and under the pretence of taking care of the ring, she obtains it from Trabucos. She then devises a plan to win the love of the chief. At this point the fat old mayor, travel-stained and almost in rags, enters, dragging his feet feebly. He has been forced to follow Martina all the way and is exhausted. Seeing Olympia, he touches her arm to gain her attention, and at once falls passionately in love with her. She, knowing him to be the mayor, sees a large ransom in the future if she can make him her prisoner, and accordingly she flirts with him and eventually induces him to accompany her outside the ruins. This flirtation is done to the amusing duet 'Little Bird, Little Bird', which contains some birdsong-like ornaments and birdbrain-like text: 'Ducky-darling, sweety-meaty, kissy-missy me, Nicey-picey, Periwinkle, tickley-ickle-ee, Lovey-dovey, rosy-posy Oh! kernoodle do, Popsy-wopsy, kicksy-wicksy, winky-pinky-poo!' (This number was 'rapturously encored', according to the *Sunday Chronicle* of 13 March 1893.) Presently Aristippus, Lolika, and her companions enter with the idea of finding the mayor and persuading him to give up Martina and return home with them. They separate to search the building, and Lolika is left behind. In the solo and chorus 'Here we are at last', Lolika and her companions express their urgent desire to find Alzaga. Meanwhile, Martina sings of her desire to find a husband. This number, 'Where, Oh! Where', features a *zambra*-like syncopated ostinato figure throughout (Ex. 9*a*). The next number, 'The hours creep on', also displays distinctively Spanish rhythms, as Lolika hears Alzaga singing in his cell (Ex. 9*b*). Like those at the opening of 'Little Bird, Little Bird' (Ex. 9*c*), they seem derived from the *malagueña*. She manages to release him, and is on the point of escaping with him when Olympia re-enters. At once Olympia devises a scheme to secure the love of Trabucos. Sending Alzaga away to keep watch, she explains to Lolika all about the ring, and how it was changed. She asks Lolika to give her the false ring that she may hand it to Trabucos, who will think it the real one. Thus, Trabucos will say it is true love when he is attracted to her (Olympia's) side. To aid her, Lolika promises to feign love when Trabucos touches her, but on condition that Alzaga shall be set free.

In the ensuing finale, Trabucos and Carambollas now appear, followed by the townsfolk, and immediately afterwards by the brigands. Trabucos is overjoyed at seeing Lolika, and at once obtains the false ring from Olympia. Faithful to her word, Lolika pretends to fall in love with him when he takes her hand, and for her lover's sake lets him embrace her. Of course, the embrace is witnessed by Alzaga, who then believes Lolika false. Olympia

Ex. 9. *The Magic Opal*, Act II, Spanish rhythms in (*a*) No. 21, 'Where, Oh! Where',
bars 1–4 (*b*) No. 23, 'The hours creep on', bars 3–6 (*c*) No. 19, 'Little Bird, Little Bird',
bars 1–2

congratulates the chief, and gives him her hand, with the result that he is
instantly smitten. He abandons Lolika and promises to marry Olympia,
which clears the way for Lolika and Alzaga to patch up their differences.
Trabucos, by command of Olympia, releases all the prisoners, and the
operetta is brought to a rousing conclusion.

As noted, though the story takes place in Greece, the music is often at
home in Andalusia. Several numbers exhibit the rhythmic flourishes, syncopated ostinato figures, and modality characteristic of Spanish music. In fact, a
certain Mlle Candida was engaged from Madrid to appear in Act II, snapping
her fingers in the manner of castanets and undulating in flamenco fashion.
This prompted some critics to wonder why the opera could not just as easily
have been set in Spain, for consistency's sake. Evidently the presence of
Gypsies in the story served as sufficient reason for such allusions. A revealing
description of her dance appeared in *Sketch* (8 February 1893):

Candida's dance in the second act of the new comic opera has a strange flavour of
mystery. One sees a tall woman, with dark-brown hair streaming down her back, clad in
a rather barbaric dress, which consists of a fawn-coloured silk jersey, closely moulding
the figure, surmounted by some heavy spangled gold and brown cloth, cut so as to

show a finely-sculptured neck and bust; below it a sash of similar material, and then long, dark electric-blue silk gauze skirts. She steals on to the stage and moves about in rhythm with the music, holding her arms above her head and clicking her fingers and thumbs with a sound suggesting castanets. Hardly does she raise her feet, save in a few steps where she beats time sharply in a staccato way. In every movement there is a fine supple beauty; each muscle seems called into play without effort, and to be obedient to the music. One thinks of some mystic enchantress making mute incantations. The end is characteristic: the almost snake-like movements grow slower and slower, the music becomes fainter and fainter, till she sinks back into the arms of a man, her hands still raised heavenwards. Grace of movement is hers to absolute perfection.

A Spanish dancer was not the only dash of local colour added to the production. A white donkey and four sheep also made cameo appearances!

Looking back on this work many years later, Edgar Istel[46] dismissed the music as 'impersonal', that is, in its obedience to convention and dissimilarity to Albéniz's own style. Actually, as already noted, Albéniz's musical personality shines through in many places in the score and imparted a charm to the operetta that was almost solely responsible for whatever success it enjoyed. The reviewer for *Lady* (9 February 1893), however, was somewhat sceptical about Albéniz's eclectic approach:

It is called, with equal justness, either light opera or comic opera. As a matter of fact, the composer has chosen to attempt a compromise between both styles, and, moreover, has made several departures into the field of grand opera. Whether such a course is exactly a wise one is doubtful. The plain and simple methods of Offenbach, Lecocq, and other composers of the palmy days of comic opera, have been discarded of late by most composers.

George Bernard Shaw reviewed the production in the *World* (25 January 1893) and found the music objectionable for rather different reasons:

The Magic Opal, at the Lyric, is a copious example of that excessive fluency in composition of which Señor Albéniz has already given us sufficient proofs. His music is pretty, shapely, unstinted, lively, goodnatured, and far too romantic and refined for the stuff which Mr Arthur Law has given him to set. But Albéniz has the faults as well as the qualities of his happy and uncritical disposition; and the grace and spirit of his strains are of rather too obvious a kind to make a very deep impression. And he does not write well for the singers. It is not that the phrases are unvocal, or that the notes lie badly for the voice, but that he does not set the words from the comedian's point of view, his double disability as a pianist and a foreigner handicapping him in this department.[47]

---

[46] 'Isaac Albéniz', 136.

[47] Shaw's article was entitled 'Miss Smyth's Decorative Instinct'. This passage appears in Shaw, *Music*, ii. 796.

Shaw was the only London critic who accused Albéniz of 'excessive fluency', but that criticism presaged the nearly unanimous opinion of Madrid journalists who would review the operetta there in the following year.

Others thought differently. A critic writing in the *Theatre* (1 March 1893, 154–5) praised Albéniz's music as 'distinguished by a melody, a force, and an eloquence rare indeed in compositions for the comic opera stage'. He even had praise for the libretto—a rare occurrence with Albéniz's operas—which he described as 'full of happy humour, dramatic vigour, and pretty sentiment'. An anonymous reviewer writing in the *Athenaeum* (28 January 1893, 131) put it this way: 'The melodies are for the most part fresh and piquant, and there is no sense of incongruity in the Spanish rhythms which are conspicuous at times. . . . The part-writing for the voices is excellent, and the orchestration is at once refined and picturesque.' The writer further characterized it as 'the most artistic of the many pieces of the same nature upon which theatrical managers have pinned their faith—unwisely, as it would seem, for the most part—during the current season'. Finally, *The Times* (20 January 1893, 6) lauded the music as 'bright, tuneful, and original', and went on to say that 'No inexperience is to be traced . . . in the construction of the many effective numbers, or in the vocal and instrumental writing. The orchestral scoring is, indeed, remarkably interesting and refined, and the ideas throughout original and most characteristic.'

The operetta initially proved so successful that Sedger formed a touring company only three weeks after the premiere to perform *The Magic Opal* in other cities, opening at the Royalty Theatre in Glasgow and continuing on to Edinburgh, Manchester, Brighton, Hull, Liverpool, Newcastle, Sheffield, and Leeds, finally closing at the Bolton Theatre Royal on 20 May. In spite of all this, the London run ended ignominiously on 27 February. This was due in part to the mediocre libretto, but financial difficulties lay at the heart of the matter. In an article entitled 'The Decline of Comic Opera', *Truth* (23 February 1893) speculated that competition from music halls had cut into the operetta market. Concurring with this view, *Figaro* (23 February 1893) ascribed the failure to 'the popular leaning towards the "Ta-ra-ra" and "The Man who broke the Bank at Monte Carlo" style of melodies'. This, combined with high ticket prices and excessive production costs, sounded the death knell for many an operetta. The expenses of *The Magic Opal* alone were £720 a week. In addition, the Lyric Theatre, which opened in 1888 and held 1,306 persons, cost £6,500 per year to rent, an enormous sum at the time.[48] Even if only half full, the theatre could still have brought in £1,800 weekly,

---

[48] See Bevan, 'Albéniz', 48. His source for this information on rent was F. H. W. Sheppard, *Survey of London*, xxxi: *The Parish of St James Westminster*, part 2: *North of Piccadilly* (London, 1963), which gives a

but the production lost money none the less and closed after only seven weeks. These pecuniary embarrassments did not escape the attention of the *Sunday Chronicle* (previously cited), which was inspired to publish the following bit of doggerel:

> Dear O-pal, costly O-pal,
> Dear O-pal, costly O-pal.
>   Making for Sedger,
>   A hole in the ledger:
> Give us one better than dear Opal.

In an attempt to do just that, Albéniz and company undertook a revision renamed *The Magic Ring*, which reduced the number of characters, simplified the plot, and cut some numbers and added others (see Table 6). An element of superstition was perhaps involved in the name change. The opal is a gem associated with bad luck, and just in case that fact had anything to do with the operetta's early demise, the word was deleted from its title the second time around. Of course, the new title served the more rational purpose of indicating to the public a reworking of the operetta. It premiered at the Prince of Wales's Theatre on 11 April 1893, conducted by the composer. Lowenfeld, Albéniz's manager, served as impresario and would soon become manager of the Prince of Wales's Theatre.[49] This venue was somewhat

TABLE 6. *Cast of* The Magic Ring, *premiere, London, Prince of Wales's Theatre, 11 April 1893*

Telemachus	Harry Monkhouse
Alzaga	Edwin Wareham
Aristippus	Fred Kaye
Pekito	Frank Walsh
Curro	Arthur Watts
Trabucos	Norman Salmond
Martina	Susie Vaughan
Zoe	Lilian Stanley
Christina	Anita Courtenay
Irene	Annie Laurie
Lolika	Marie Halton
Conductor	Isaac Albéniz

plan in fig. 9.75, and lists Sedger as licensee, manager, and sole lessee. Capacity information is found in Howard, *London Theatres*, 146.

[49] According to Bevan, 'Albéniz', 29, this was probably Lowenfeld's first 'direct involvement in theatrical promotion, although he may have been associated with Sedger in financing the two Lyric productions involving Albéniz'. This is strongly suggested by the title page of the published piano–vocal score of *The Magic Opal*, which bears a dedication to Lowenfeld's wife.

smaller than the Lyric, holding a maximum audience of 960.[50] The *Theatre* (1 May 1893, 294) did not view the new version as an improvement over the old. In spite of revisions in the text and restructuring of the cast,[51] the libretto remained 'lamentably weak'. Albéniz's score, however, was 'really excellent throughout ... being musicianly and artistic in the extreme'. But this alone, the reviewer states, could not make a success of the operetta. Shaw concurred in this, describing the new production as an 'attempt ... to rescue Señor Albéniz's score of The Magic Opal from sinking under the weight of its libretto'. He concedes, however, that 'the revised version of the opera leaves [Albéniz] easily ahead of the best of his rivals'.[52] *The Times* (13 April 1893, 13) states unequivocally that it was 'far superior, musically speaking, to the average comic opera of the day'. Taking quite a different view from both Shaw and the *Theatre*, though it describes the comic interest of the first version as 'meagre', it extols the 'distinct improvements' that have been made in the second, especially the addition of an 'extremely effective duet for Lolika and Trabucos'. We learn from these reviews the high regard in which Albéniz was now held by critics not only as a pianist but as a serious composer, a remarkable accomplishment considering his unfamiliarity, just four years earlier, with England, English, and native musical theatre.

One measure of the operetta's popularity is the number of arrangements of it that were published at the time. The piano–vocal score was published by J. Williams in 1893, in two versions (the second slightly abridged), both under the title of *The Magic Opal*. In addition, Williams also published *The 'Magic Opal' Valse*, by Conrad Huber, for piano solo; *'The Magic Opal' Quadrille*, also by Huber, for piano; *Fantasia on 'The Magic Ring'* by F. Robinson, for violin and piano; selections from *The Magic Ring*, arranged by Charles Tourville, for piano; a piano transcription of the abridged piano–vocal score, also by Tourville; and finally, selections from the operetta, for piano and voice (excerpted from the complete score). All of these appeared in the year 1893.

How unfortunate it is, then, that Albéniz's work, which premiered so auspiciously, should so soon have been relegated to utter obscurity. The reviewer for *The Times* expressed the hope that 'in its revived form the piece will achieve popularity, for it appeals both to the lovers of good music and to the larger public [who presumably loved not-so-good

[50] See Howard, *London Theatres*, 184.
[51] Particularly a reduction in the number of characters, from fifteen to eleven, including the elimination of Olympia. The restructuring of the libretto was executed by Brandon Thomas, who, according to Bevan, 'Albéniz', 29, was 'the author of the phenomenally successful *Charley's Aunt*, which ran from 1892–1896 in its first production and enjoyed numerous revivals'.
[52] This review appeared in the *World* on 19 Apr. 1893. It is taken from Shaw, *Music*, ii. 859.

music]'. Alas, this was not to be, either in England or in Spain. The *Sportsman* (3 March 1893) went further and wondered,

What a strange, inexplicable, incomprehensible people [Albéniz] must by now think that we English are. There is not much need to pity him, however. He has the capacity to do something which must win him fame far exceeding any that even the phenomenal success of 'The Magic Opal' would have brought in its train.

This was prophetic, but Albéniz would have to endure many a bitter disappointment on the stage before he awakened to his true calling.

Albéniz's activities on the London stage did not cease with *The Magic Ring*, however. He was soon involved in the production of the two-act musical comedy *Poor Jonathan*, an English-language adaptation (translated by C. H. E. Brookfield) of Karl Millöcker's *Der arme Jonathan*. *Poor Jonathan* premiered at the Prince of Wales's Theatre on 15 June 1893.[53] Albéniz not only conducted the production but contributed sixteen musical numbers in addition to those by Millöcker, with lyrics written by Harry Greenbank, who had also collaborated with him on 'Oh! Horror! Horror!'[54] The story is of the prince-and-the-pauper variety, with a wealthy man trading places with a poor one to demonstrate his sincerity to and win the hand of the woman he loves. In the end he wins her heart, resumes his station, and provides for the poor man so that he, too, can marry the one he loves. Albéniz's music was hailed by the *Era* (17 June 1893) as 'charming in style and admirably scored for the orchestra'. The *Daily Graphic* (19 June 1893) went so far as to declare that 'the additions to the score for which the Spanish composer is responsible are in nearly every instance superior in construction, charm, and elegance to the work of the original composer', who had produced 'a thoroughly third-rate German opera'.

Despite the production's failure, Albéniz's stock was higher than ever, and in the summer of 1893 the London press was astir with speculation that William S. Gilbert was going to collaborate with him on a new stage work (unnamed), to be premiered in October at the Prince of Wales's Theatre. (Other names bandied about included Dr Hubert Parry.) Though some papers reported it as a certainty, Gilbert finally decided upon Dr F. Osmond Carr (1858–1916), composer of the operetta *Morocco Bound* (1893), who went on to compose *His Excellency* (1894) on a book by Gilbert. However, Albéniz did secure exclusive rights to compose an opera based on the three-

[53] The original work, on a text by H. Wittmann and J. Bauer, premiered 4 Jan. 1890, in Vienna.

[54] The dishevelled state of the manuscript does not confirm sixteen numbers. This is according to Albéniz in a letter to Clementina of 6 June 1893. See Torres, 'La producción escénica', 200–1. The MS of this work is in the Bc, M975, though it is bound with *The Magic Opal* and the pages of the two are frustratingly, perhaps hopelessly, conflated.

act romantic tragedy *Mar i cel* (1888) by Àngel Guimerà (1849–1924), the famous contemporary Catalan playwright. Although Albéniz was greatly intrigued by the idea of writing musical theatre based on Spanish or Catalan texts, his acquaintance with an English gentleman, who was to play an important role in the drama of his own life, soon caused him to set aside this laudable project, which he never finished and of which only a fragment survives.[55]

Albéniz did not cease to compose piano music during his London tenure, and several of his best-loved works were clearly written for his concerts in Britain, including the lovely *Zambra granadina* (London: Carlo Ducci, *c.*1891) with its haunting modality and characteristic syncopated ostinato in the left hand. In addition to the 'Zortzico', *España: Six Feuilles d'album* contains the ever-popular 'Tango', whose rhythm and mood more strongly resemble the Cuban *habanera* than the Argentinian tango (though the tango sprang in part from the *habanera*, the two are quite distinct).[56] It bears no relation, of course, to the eponymous flamenco genre. *Chants d'Espagne* (*Cantos de España* in Spanish)[57] contains some of the most celebrated and widely performed of his works, especially the 'Prélude' (or 'Preludio'), a warhorse in the guitar repertoire. Although this piece was later inserted by publishers into the *Suite española* No. 1 under the title 'Asturias (Leyenda)', it is important to understand that this work is pure Andalusian flamenco and has absolutely nothing to do with folk music of the Asturias region in the north.

'Prélude' is laid out in Albéniz's wonted da capo form. The incessant monorhythm of the A section acquires an unusual degree of intensity through repetition (Ex. 10). This theme mimics the guitaristic technique of alternating the thumb and fingers of the right hand, playing a pedal-note open string with the index finger and a bass melody with the thumb. It naturally lends itself to interpretation on that instrument. However, guitarists have changed the rhythm to make it more idiomatic. The resulting triplet

---

[55] In the Bc, M984, dated 28 Jan. 1897 and consisting of twelve pages of full score. The original Catalan title of the drama was *Mar i cel* ('Sea and sky'), but Albéniz used the Castilian conjunction (*Mar y cel*). As is the case in many of his scores, the piano part below was completed first, then the orchestration rendered above. The forces are large and include bass clarinet, contrabassoon, cor anglais, and tuba. Albéniz begins with a sustained tonic pedal in E minor. Then he abruptly ends. The vocal writing is recitative-like, and the scoring dense. These two traits, reflecting Wagnerian influence, would prove his undoing as an opera composer. In May of 1895, Roca y Roca wrote in *La vanguardia* that Albéniz was still planning to complete the work. Guimerà wrote to Albéniz on 12 Feb. 1897 (Bc, 'G') requesting news about the work's progress and when it might come to Barcelona. But Albéniz by this time was absorbed in other tasks.

[56] In the 1890s, the tango was still a low-class song and dance in the slums of Buenos Aires; it would not become popular in Europe until the early 20th cent. Indeed, in Felip Pedrell's *Diccionario técnico de la música* (Barcelona: Víctor Berdós, 1894), the entry on the tango does not even mention Argentina. It describes it only as a genre of folk music in Spain, Mexico, and Cuba. Albéniz had the Cuban 'tango' in mind.

[57] According to Torres, *MGG*, the suite was composed 1891–4 and published in two stages by Juan Bautista Pujol in Barcelona. Nos. 1–3 appeared in 1892, while 4–5 came out in 1897.

Ex. 10. *Chants d'Espagne*, 'Prélude', A theme, bars 1–4

arpeggiations and tremolo require a slight pause after each chord is struck, thus breaking up the continuous rhythmic stream Albéniz clearly intended. Although the piece is still very effective, it is curious that few enterprising guitarists have gone back to the piano score and tried to transcribe it with the original rhythm. In any event, the frequent evocation of the guitar in his piano music was no coincidence, and he knew that instrument well. According to Octave Maus, Albéniz played the guitar to accompany his own singing of Andalusian folk songs: 'Leaning on a table or on the arm of a chair, his eyes wrinkled with laughter, his fingers nimbly plucked the chords.'[58]

The opening theme strongly suggests the rhythm of the *bulerías* (or perhaps the slower *soleá por bulerías*). This genre of flamenco has a lively tempo (though it is faster now than in Albéniz's day) and is based on a twelve-beat *compás*, or metre. In contrast to the *alegrías* and *soleares*, the *bulerías compás* begins on twelve, not one, i.e. *12* 1 2 3 4 5 *6 7* 8 9 *10* 11. Thus, this *compás* can be imagined as a bar of 6/4 followed by one of 3/2, or hemiola. Albéniz has spelled this out by placing accents under the bass notes corresponding to the principal accented beats of the *bulerías compás*, i.e. twelve, three, and six. The 'marcato'/'staccato' indications suggest not only the guitarist's *punteado* but also the footwork of the dancer, called *taconeo*. The piece begins piano within a tight melodic compass of a perfect fifth. Though we are in G minor and G is initially iterated in the bass, in bar 8 the bass quickly moves through a descending tetrachord to D, which is 'tonicized' not only through its prominence in the bass for the rest of the A section but through the D pedal in the right hand. This, of course, produces the Phrygian mode so characteristic of the *bulerías*. Still, there is an inherent ambiguity about its function as 'final' or as 'dominant', because it is harmonized as a major chord, another trait of flamenco modality. The chordal interjections that begin in bar 25 evoke the technique of percussively striking

---

[58] Cited in Frederic V. Grunfeld, *The Art and Times of the Guitar* (New York: Macmillan, 1974), 288. Regrettably, Grunfeld neglects to provide the source of the quote. This is also true of the ejaculation he attributes to Albéniz after hearing Francisco Tárrega perform a transcription of one of his works: 'This is precisely as I had conceived it!' But all of this is consistent with what we infer from other sources about Albéniz's relationship to the guitar.

Ex. 11. *Chants d'Espagne*, 'Prélude', B theme (copla), bars 63–6

the strings called *rasgueado*. Curiously, most guitarists refrain from doing precisely this, perhaps because it seems too blatant. These punctuations could also be viewed as evocative of *jaleo*, the participation of onlookers through shouts of *olé*, clapping (*palmas*), and finger-snapping (*pitos*). The height of tension is reached at the section's midpoint as the dynamic level increases to fortissimo and the register of the chords is extended upwards to *g‴*. There follows a denouement, and the section concludes on a D major chord. The ensuing B section in D Phrygian opens with a languid yet passionate evocation of *cante jondo*, full of unfulfilled longing (Ex. 11).

This *copla* is marked 'espressivo e rubato' and is presented monophonically but doubled at the fifteenth for more fullness of sound.[59] This is a favourite device of Albéniz's and creates a refreshing contrast to the disciplined hammer blows of the preceding texture. The 'singer' delivers short, three-bar phrases that are separated by the gentle chordal punctuations in the 'guitar'. This kind of alternation of solo and accompaniment is typical of flamenco. The final two phrases of the *copla* exhibit some modal colouring in their use of an augmented second between C♯ and B♭ within the melodic outline of a descending tetrachord from D to A (Bizet resorted to similar means in Carmen's 'fate' motive). The 'Phrygian cadence' that closes out this *copla* is spiced up with a French augmented-sixth chord substituting for the iv⁶ chord one might have expected to precede the dominant in G minor. There shortly ensues a dance-like middle section in the style of the *malagueña*. Though in livelier, stricter rhythm than the preceding material, it grows motivically out of the two quavers of the *copla*. This dance reaches a height of tension in bar 105 and is soon followed by a reminiscence of the A theme. This also serves as an anticipation of the da capo, which is preceded by an abbreviated restatement of the *copla*. The poignant coda presents a hymn-like chordal passage that expresses an almost fatalistic resignation to sorrow. It is very symmetrically phrased in four-bar segments, like all the melodies in this piece, and progresses

---

[59] See the discussion of 'El Albaicín' in Ch. 7 for another interpretation of Albéniz's use of doubling at the fifteenth. Certainly the modaltity and chromatic inflections of this *copla* have a Middle Eastern quality.

first to the tonic (G) and then to the dominant. The A theme makes a final brief appearance to finish the piece with a defiant flourish in G minor.

The four remaining pieces in the suite are entitled 'Orientale', 'Sous le palmier (Danse espagnole)', 'Córdoba', and 'Seguidillas'. 'Orientale' is remarkable for its intense melancholy and opens with a dissonant clash between a pedal on A and a dominant-seventh chord on E. The Phrygian colouring and subdued dynamics contribute to a mood of wistful reflection. Despite its title, it is thoroughly rooted in Spanish folk music, and its principal theme (bars 8–9) is a model of the octosyllabic *copla* rhythm. 'Sous le palmier (Danse espagnole)' utilizes the rhythms of the *habanera*, a song and dance whose name is derived from the capital city of Cuba, La Habana (Havana). It commences with a theme of languorous good spirits, but the introspective mood of the 'Orientale' persists, and Albéniz's chromatic exploration of the parallel minor key in bar 17 expresses a sadness that we can fully understand only if we recall the depression that underlay his outward sanguinity. 'Córdoba' is one of the finest numbers Albéniz ever composed, and in it he evokes two Spains, one Christian and one Moorish. The introduction begins with an open-fifth pedal between F and C in the left hand that suggests the tolling of church bells in the distance. Above this soon floats an enchanting hymn in G Dorian (the series of first-inversion chords resembles *fauxbourdon*). Ties over the bar line group two measures of 3/4 into one of 6/4 creating a slight sensation of metric ambiguity and rhythmic freedom appropriate to liturgical singing (Ex. 12). The juxtaposition of modes between left and right hands creates a wonderfully spatial effect. But the basic tonal movement is from F major, emphasized in the 'bells', towards the D minor key of the A section. The A theme is completely contrasting in character and takes us on the magic carpet of imagination to a legendary Moorish past, with an impassioned serenade accompanied by the lusty strumming of guzlas (Ex. 13).

This is followed by the B section at bar 101, in the parallel major, that mounts to a stirring climax before a sudden, abbreviated restatement of the introduction and the principal thematic material, ending with a brief coda. The ostinatos of the accompaniment throughout 'Córdoba' reinforce the

Ex. 12. *Chants d'Espagne*, 'Córdoba', introduction, bars 5–12

Ex. 13. *Chants d'Espagne*, 'Córdoba', A theme, bars 57–64

impression of folk music. But in truth, the work is animated by rhythms thoroughly Spanish in character and bears no similarity to Moorish music. So strongly did Albéniz feel about the Moorish ambience of this piece, however, that he provided a programme at the beginning: 'In the silence of the night, interrupted by the whispering of the jasmine-scented breezes, guzlas are heard accompanying serenades and radiating into the air ardent melodies and notes so sweet, like the wavering of the palms high in the heavens.'[60] Albéniz's intensely romantic attraction to Córdoba may have been partly inspired by his ninth-century namesake St Isaac of Córdoba, who died there defending his faith, and by the Great Mosque that still stands there today.

The suite closes with the lively 'Seguidillas'[61] in which dance rhythms alternate with brief *coplas*. *Chants d'Espagne* represents the furthest advance in Albéniz's Spanish style to date in its seriousness, harmonic richness, and formal variety. Aside from the 'Prélude', none of the movements exhibits the routine, verbatim repetition of his earlier da capo procedure. The 'Orientale' is laid out as ABA'B', framed by a brief introductory phrase in triplets that appears only at the beginning and the end. The A section of 'Sous le palmier' is repeated before the B section, and when it returns after the B section the parallel-minor area is replaced by new material that meanders lazily to the conclusion (AABA'). The formal layout of 'Córdoba', Introd.AB(Introd.') A'coda, is unlike anything he had composed before. The frenzied

---

[60] 'En el silencio de la noche, que interrumpe el susurro de las brisas aromadas por los jazmines, suenan las guzlas acompañando las Serenatas y difundiendo en el aire melodías ardientes y notas tan dulces como los balanceos de las palmas en los altos cielos.'

[61] The *seguidillas* is a lively couple dance in triple metre. There are regional variations, but it is largely associated with Castile and hence is not considered flamenco. The exception to this is the *seguidillas* of Seville, the *sevillanas. Siguiriyas*, a Gypsy corruption of the word, is a genre altogether different in style and mood.

leapfrogging of the two principal ideas in 'Seguidillas' passes through several key areas, giving the middle of the work the feeling of a development section. The maturation of Albéniz's style so apparent in these pieces would be accelerated by his deepening involvement with musical theatre, an involvement prompted by the arrival on stage of one of the principal characters in the drama of his career.

Sometime during the year 1893, Albéniz entered into a revised agreement with Lowenfeld that now included a third party. This man was Francis Money-Coutts,[62] a London solicitor, poet, librettist, and wealthy heir to the fortune of the Coutts banking family. Through his involvement with the finances of both the Lyric and Prince of Wales's Theatres, Coutts became an avid admirer of Albéniz and his music. Over time he became an intimate friend and generous benefactor as well. But the essential nature of their association was a collaboration in which Coutts supplied Albéniz with a large income in exchange for Albéniz's setting his poetry to music and bringing him what he craved most: fame as a librettist and vindication of his *déclassé* literary ambitions. With the advent of Coutts, we come to a dimension of greatest significance in Albéniz's life story, one that has been grossly misunderstood and misrepresented.

All biographers have railed at Coutts as a kind of Mephistopheles who seduced Albéniz into a 'Faustian pact' in which the hapless Spaniard was compelled to expend his precious creative energies on projects, such as an Arthurian trilogy, that were alien to his fundamental nature as a composer. The remaining chapters of this biography will make it clear that this view is distorted and fails to take into account the highly remunerative and benign aspects of their friendship. While not ignoring the agreement's negative effects, we must refute the outright falsehoods and slanders concerning Coutts that have persisted in the literature with demonic tenacity. The clarification of their collaboration also adds to music history one of the most intriguing and unusual examples of patronage in an era when that venerable institution and the society that made it possible were about to breathe their last in the cataclysm of world war.[63]

[Albéniz's] connection with the Prince of Wales's Theatre brought him an acquaintance who, while very useful to him financially, was to do him incalculable damage

---

[62] His surnames are usually, but not always, hyphenated. In this book he will hereafter simply be referred to as Coutts (pronounced 'coots'), the name under which he published many of his writings.

[63] This material first appeared in the author's 'Isaac Albéniz's Faustian Pact: A Study in Patronage', *Musical Quarterly*, 76/4 (Dec. 1992), 465–87. See also Falces, *Pacto de Fausto*, 29–85, for an excellent treatment of the true relations between Coutts and Albéniz. Falces has also contributed to our understanding of Albéniz's London years in 'Albéniz en Inglaterra: Una etapa oscura', *Revista de musicología*, 14/1–2 (1991), 214–19.

humanly and artistically, and, perhaps, was responsible—in so far as inner reasons come into question—for Albéniz's untimely end. A very wealthy banker, Francis Money-Coutts, was financially interested in the aforementioned theatre, and this man had the weakness, not only of writing dramatic verse in his leisure hours, but also of using every means to get it performed. So he got in touch with Albéniz and persuaded him to sign a contract to receive an annual stipend of $5,000 ... on the sole condition that he set to music only librettos written by the banker under the pseudonym 'Mountjoy'. The wretched Albéniz was unable to resist the temptations of Mammon although he soon enough revised his opinion and—at first merely in jest—called his agreement 'the pact of Faust'. Now Albéniz was obliged to inter all plans for operas in the Spanish style for which he was specifically adapted ... in order to prostitute his art as the splenetic Englishman's slave. Even worse is what Arbós told me: that Albéniz, against the counsel of his wife, who advised him to break his diabolic pact with the English banker, thought—so blind was he—that his real gift was for serious opera composition, and clung to this fallacy almost to the end of his days.

Thus spake Edgar Istel in the *Musical Quarterly* in 1929,[64] twenty years after Albéniz's death and only six years after the demise of Coutts, the intended victim of this poison-pen attack. Istel was not alone in his condemnation. The eminent Spanish musicologist Federico Sopeña reiterated Istel's sentiments thus:

The banker Coutts played Mephistopheles. Like many bankers, he capriciously played the part of Maecenas, but in the service of his vanity, and his vanity consisted in writing opera librettos. Here you have the Mephistophelean pact with Albéniz: in exchange for a pension, truly large considering the value of the money at the time— £200 monthly—Albéniz had to compose music for operas whose texts in no way corresponded to his nature.[65]

As to the exact amount of remuneration, there seems to have been considerable disagreement. Michel Raux Deledicque stated unequivocally that it was £1,000 a year, and that it was conditional upon Albéniz's not working for any other librettist: 'A contract of this kind really tied his hands, as it obliged him to set to music anything that Money-Coutts fancied to give him, though the subject matter did not resonate with his own sensibilities.'[66] By this

[64] 'Isaac Albéniz', 136.

[65] 'Gracia y drama en la vida de Isaac Albéniz', *Historia y vida*, 2/12 (Mar. 1969), 127. 'El banquero Coutts ha hecho de Mefistófeles. Como tantos banqueros, tenía el capricho de aparecer como Mecenas, pero al servicio de su vanidad y su vanidad consistía en hacer libretos de ópera. He aquí el pacto mefistofélico con Albéniz: en pago de una pensión, en verdad crecida para el valor de la moneda de aquellos—200 libras mensuales—Albéniz tenía que componer la música para óperas cuyo texto en nada casaba con la manera de ser de Albéniz.'

[66] *Albéniz*, 226. 'Un contrato de esta índole le ataba en realidad las manos, a la vez que lo ponía en la obligación de escribir música para cualquier cosa que le pluguiera a Money-Coutts encomendarle, aunque el tema no respondiera a su propia sensibilidad.'

account, Albéniz was hypnotized by the prospect of a steady income and did not reflect sufficiently on its consequences. Gabriel Laplane summed up the situation in the following terms: 'The pact of Faust produced its tragic effect. A union against nature could produce nothing but abortions.'[67]

Strong language, indeed! But who was Coutts, really? None of Albéniz's biographers condescended to find out anything about him independent of word-of-mouth and second-hand accounts, in spite of the fact that over 100 letters from him to Albéniz are extant.[68] And there persists a conspicuous lacuna about him in English biographical reference sources. This absence of substantiation has provided an irresistible opportunity for those who wished to create their own portrait of him, usually in stygian hues, for the purpose of sensationalizing Albéniz's life. Fact would have proven more sensational than fiction. What follows is a brief biography of Coutts.

Francis Burdett Thomas Nevill Money-Coutts, the 5th Lord Latymer,[69] who adopted the pen name of 'Mountjoy' (he signed his letters to Albéniz simply 'Frank'), was born 18 September 1852 and died 8 June 1923. His mother Clara (d. 1899) was the daughter of Sir Francis Burdett (1770–1844), a prominent politician, and Sophia Coutts (d. 1844), daughter of the eminent banker Thomas Coutts. Francis's father was the Revd James Drummond Money (d. 1875). When Francis's aunt Angela, by marrying a foreigner (and an American at that), violated the condition upon which she had inherited the Coutts fortune, the money was divided between her and Francis's mother Clara until their deaths, at which time it devolved upon Francis in its entirety (Clara and Francis therefore began to use the Coutts name in 1881). In 1875 he married Edith Ellen Churchill (he called her 'Nellie'; she signed her letters 'Helen'), who survived him by nineteen years. Though Francis is always described as a banker, he seems to have had too artistic a bent to be interested in banking. A booklet detailing the history of the London firm of Coutts & Co. (founded in 1692),[70] mentions Francis only in connection with his inheritance of the family fortune. His contributions to the company's success were not sufficient to warrant any further mention in its annals. According to Barbara Peters, head of the Latymer Archive at Coutts & Co., Francis was at one point being considered for a

---

[67] *Albéniz*, 104, 'El pacto de Fausto producía su efecto nefasto. Una unión contra naturaleza no podía dar mas que abortos.'

[68] All of the correspondence from Coutts to Albéniz is located in the Bc ('C') and the Mm. The Mm has catalogued and numbered most of Coutts's letters; however, letters written by him to Albéniz's wife Rosina and daughter Laura remain uncatalogued and are to be found in car. 2. Coutts was very fond of underlining words, and unless otherwise indicated, all such emphasis (as well as his idiosyncratic punctuation) is original.

[69] He was not born with this title but assumed it in 1912.

[70] M. Veronica Stokes, *A Bank in Four Centuries* (Derby: Bemrose Security Printing, 1982). See also Edna Healy, *Coutts & Co. 1692–1992: The Portrait of a Bank* (London: Hodder & Stoughton, 1992).

partnership in the firm, but the idea was scotched because he possessed too unstable a temperament to occupy such a position. The fact that Coutts arrived late in his parents' lives and was an only child would probably give psychologists sufficient grist to explain this state of affairs. For his part, Coutts wanted the partnership but not the work it entailed. That he felt his calling to be in the arts and not in banking is suggested by the fact that in all his letters to Albéniz one finds almost no mention of the world of finance. His chief preoccupations were with writing and with the vicissitudes of married life.

Coutts was educated at Eton and later took advanced degrees at Cambridge (MA; LL M., 1878). He became a barrister-at-law in 1879, worked as a solicitor in Surrey, and eventually became a prolific author, his preferred vocation.[71] According to *Who Was Who in Literature—1906–1934*,[72] he was the author of *Poems* (1896), *The Revelation of St. Love the Divine* (1898), *The Alhambra* (1898), *The Mystery of Godliness* (1900), *The Poet's Charter* (1902), *Musa Verticordia* (1904), *The Song of Songs* (1906), *Book of Job* (1907), *Romance of King Arthur* (1907), *Psyche* (1911), and *Ventures in Thought* (1914). The British Library catalogue lists in addition *The Nutbrown Maid* (1901), *Egypt and Other Poems* (1912), *The Royal Marines* (1915), *The Spacious Times, and Others* (poems) (1920), *Well* (a guidebook to the village of Well, Yorkshire) (1922), and *Selected Poems* (1923). He also did a considerable amount of editorial work for his publisher John Lane in London, writing prefaces for and editing collections of poems by other authors (e.g. twenty-seven volumes of poems entitled *Flowers of Parnassus* between 1900 and 1906). Alfred, Lord Tennyson he may not have been, but on the basis of all this, Coutts cannot be dismissed as a dilettante or a mere amateur.[73]

Documents in the Latymer Archive at Coutts & Co. indicate that Coutts was a financier of sorts, making loans and investing in securities. And he seems to have regarded his activities at the Lyric and Prince of Wales's Theatres as a kind of speculation. One document (L1449, dated 10 April 1888) is an agreement by which Coutts purchased the rights to a 'dramatic

---

[71] See entries under 'Latymer' in *Dod's Peerage, Baronetage, Knightage, Etc.* (London: Dod's Peerage, 1923); and *Burke's Peerage* (London: Burke's Peerage, 1970).

[72] Detroit: Gale Research Co., 1979, s.v. 'Latymer'.

[73] Writing talent seems to have run in his family. His aunt, Baroness Angela Georgina Burdett-Coutts (1814–1906), was the editor of a volume of writings on the philanthropic work of women. Coutts's son, Hugh Burdett (1876–1949), took up the pen, under his title Lord Latymer, in an autobiography entitled *Chances and Changes* (Edinburgh: William Blackwood & Sons, Ltd., 1935), which, regrettably, contains little information about his father. See William Archer, *Poets of the Younger Generation* (London, 1902), for a twelve-page assessment of Coutts's poetry. Archer states that 'he is a serious and strenuous craftsman who places a fine and individual faculty at the service of a lofty ideal'. (This is cited in Bevan, 'Albéniz', 97.)

piece' entitled *Christina*, by Mark Ambient and Percy Lynwood, which premiered at the Prince of Wales's Theatre on 22 April 1887. On another occasion (L1450, dated 10 September 1892) Horace Sedger, who was the principal shareholder of both the Prince of Wales's and Lyric Theatres, promised to give Coutts the profits from the production of *The Wedding Eve* at the Trafalgar Square Theatre to pay off a mortgage of £1,320 Coutts had made to the Lyric Theatre. Coutts's initial interest in Albéniz seems to have been in the form of a similar sort of business speculation. Below are the true origins of the notorious 'pact'.

Document L1453, which is dated simply 1893 (the spaces for day and month are blank), is an agreement between Lowenfeld, Coutts, and Albéniz in which Coutts buys into Lowenfeld's original contract with Albéniz of 26 June 1890, thus becoming joint manager with Lowenfeld. The stipulations of this contract make a nonsense of claims that Coutts arrived at some arrangement with the Spaniard that was diabolical. Moreover, they provide useful insights into the relationship between artist and manager in the last century.

The amount Lowenfeld had disbursed under the 1890 arrangement by the date of the new agreement was put at 'about five-thousand pounds'. The new agreement annulled the old and released Albéniz from any liability to Lowenfeld for the expenses previously incurred.[74] Coutts now purchased a piece of the action, at a price of £6,000. The conditions of the new contract were declared to be similar to those of the previous contract and were as follows (punctuation and spelling unedited):

Albéniz hereby absolutely assigns and makes over to Lowenfeld and Money-Coutts ...all music compositions and work as a musical composer of every kind to be written or produced by him during the period of ten years [from the date of the contract] and the copyright performing rights and every other property right and interest in the same and also all fees payments moneys and considerations which shall be earned or received by him as a composer musician or performer during the said term.

Albéniz places his entire work and services as a musical composer and performer exclusively at the service and under the control of Lowenfeld and Money-Coutts for the said period of ten years. He will perform in public or private at all such reasonable times and places and on such terms as they may direct. He will reside in London or such other place as they may reasonably require but shall be entitled to not less than two months vacation in every year. He will produce work as a composer to the best of

---

[74] Some legal wrangling concerning the house in Michael's Grove went on in 1895, and marginalia in the document from that year suggest that the contract's legality was being questioned. Coutts declared to Albéniz, in a letter of 10 Jan. 1895 (Bc, 'C'), that Lowenfeld was trying to make him (Coutts) pay for the house but that he would assume no responsibility for it.

his ability and in all respects act in such a way as to give effect to the intention of this agreement and enable it to be carried out to the greatest possible advantage of all the parties.

Albéniz will not during the said term do any work or render any services as a composer or performer or in any other capacity as a musician for any person or persons or association other than Lowenfeld and Money-Coutts without the previous express consent of both of them.

Other stipulations provide for the promotion and publication of Albéniz's works by Lowenfeld and Coutts. Of course, the heart of the matter was money.

The proceeds to and from the sale publication or other dealing with the works rights and property which are the subject of this agreement and the moneys to be earned or received by Albéniz after allowing for all payments and expenses shall be divided in the following shares. Albéniz three eighth parts Lowenfeld three eighth parts Money-Coutts two eighth parts.

This agreement shall be binding on Albéniz only so long as a sum of Eight hundred pounds per annum shall be provided by Lowenfeld and Coutts for his personal support and expenditure. This sum shall be drawn out of the proceeds to be derived from Albéniz works and his earnings and if the same shall be insufficient shall as between Lowenfeld and Coutts be contributed by them in the proportions of three fifths by Lowenfeld and two fifths by Money-Coutts.

This agreement shall continue after the expiration of the term of ten years [in superscript: 'or its earlier termination'] sofar as concerns works created (whether completed or incompleted) during the ten years [in superscript: 'or before the earlier termination'] and the property rights and interest therein and the proceeds to arise from them.

As severe as some of these conditions may seem to us, they were probably not unusual at the time. It bears repetition that this was a pre-existing agreement to which Coutts became a partner, not one that he initiated or defined. This contract demonstrates, moreover, that Albéniz was hardly in a 'wretched' state at the time he signed it and that he was not driven to it by 'the temptations of Mammon'. Indeed, he was already quite well provided for.

On the last page of the document, which was left blank in 1893, is written a memo to Coutts from Lowenfeld dated 23 June 1894. It states that he is selling to Coutts his interest in the agreement of the previous year as of 31 June 1894 (he forgot that June has no 31st day). Now the agreement concerned Coutts and Albéniz alone, and what happened next gives us a true picture of the relations between the slightly eccentric Englishman and his Spanish protégé.

According to the contract of 1893, Albéniz was obliged to confine his professional collaboration to Lowenfeld and Coutts. When Lowenfeld dropped out of the deal, presumably Albéniz would have been committed to working only for Coutts,[75] and this is the sticking point for many commentators, who have echoed Istel's assertion that Albéniz became the 'splenetic Englishman's slave', working simply for the money. With the exception of one opera on a Spanish subject, *Pepita Jiménez*, the librettos Coutts 'forced' on Albéniz were, it is maintained, completely out of sympathy with Albéniz's instincts and inclinations and condemned him to a life of drudgery from which he was increasingly powerless to escape, legally and financially. But we will see that Albéniz never felt himself constrained to work only for Coutts and that he set librettos by other writers or at least left several such projects in various stages of completion. One such completed work was a zarzuela to be premiered in Madrid in 1894 on which he began serious work in late 1893. This coincided with his decision to leave London for a trip to Spain before moving permanently to Paris.

Exactly when he left London and how long he remained in Spain before taking up residence in Paris remain unknown. But Albéniz clearly did not intend to build on the substantial foundation of success he enjoyed in London. What would have become of him as a composer had he remained in London we can never know, but his decision to move to France was of the greatest importance in his development. It is also certain that without the financial backing of Coutts, Albéniz would have had great difficulty making this move, especially as he now intended to devote himself to serious composition and to perform much less often, thus greatly reducing what had been his principal source of income. 'Faust' now set his sights on France, and he never turned back.

---

[75] There were apparently no later contracts, and most of what we know of the relationship comes from their correspondence.

4

Prophet without Honour
(1894–1895)

———

ALBÉNIZ'S first assignment from Coutts was to set the libretto for an opera whose action takes place in fifteenth-century England, during the Wars of the Roses, eventually entitled *Henry Clifford*. Albéniz began work on this new opera about the time he decided to leave London, for reasons of health, in the autumn of 1893.[1] Another motivation for the change of locale was that his wife Rosina did not care for the climate and ambience of London.[2] She much preferred Paris, which she found more congenial to her temperament and where she could speak French, in which she was more fluent than English (though born in Catalonia, she was of French extraction[3]). He was no doubt also attracted to Paris as the artistic and intellectual mecca of Europe.

Exactly when Albéniz settled in Paris is uncertain, but it was sometime before August 1894. We know he was in Barcelona on 22 October 1893 to perform the Schumann Piano Concerto in a programme of the Societat Catalana de Concerts at the Teatre Líric under the baton of Antoni Nicolau. Several more concerts followed early the following year. He performed the Schumann Quintet in E flat, Op. 44, with Rubio's group on 18 February 1894 at the same place and for the same organization. Eleven more such appearances took place between 18 February and 1 April, and included chamber music by Beethoven, Schubert, Mendelssohn, and Brahms, as well as works by Enric Morera and Arbós.[4] It bears pointing out that Albéniz was

---

[1] According to Torres, 'La producción escénica', 180, the Prelude to Act I was finished already by Oct. of 1893.

[2] A letter from Coutts dated 9 Feb. 1894 (Bc. 'C') expresses concern for her welfare and confirms that Rosina was enduring poor health at that time.

[3] According to Collet, *Albéniz*, 37. Istel, 'Isaac Albéniz', 125, stated she was the 'offspring of a musical family in the French Pyrenees'. Both authors knew her personally.

[4] From the manuscript 'Concerts celebrats á Barcelona'. Their repertoire included the Schubert B flat Trio, Op. 99, the Mendelssohn D minor Trio, Op. 49, the Brahms Quartet in G minor, Op. 25, and the Beethoven A major Violin Sonata, Op. 47 ('Kreutzer').

not only a brilliant soloist but a sensitive and knowledgeable interpreter of chamber music. In fact, Mathieu Crickboom hailed him as the best chamber-music pianist he knew, an assessment shared by the others in his group.[5] Yet he did not remain in Barcelona more than a few months, at most. He had indicated already in London that he had no desire to resettle in Spain. He declared in a letter to his sister Clementina that 'I am very disheartened with our country, and you must believe that it will be exceedingly difficult for me to return to her unless it is to leave my bones.'[6]

An interview with Albéniz appeared in *Heraldo de Madrid* on 26 August 1894 in which the author, Luis Bonafoux, describes him as a resident of Paris and offers in a sardonic way the reason for his expatriate status:

Albéniz is more Spanish than Pelayo, but for Albéniz Spanishness does not consist in writing pages of music at five francs a page, nor in resigning himself, as a consequence, to eating cold food in a garret. Albéniz lives in Paris and in London because there he can eat and sleep. He is not a bullfighter, and therefore he cannot live well in Spain.[7]

Bonafoux makes no mention of the fact that Albéniz had found an English 'sugar daddy' who was making his comfortable life in Paris and London possible. But this establishes beyond doubt that Albéniz was living in Paris already in August 1894. Other proof comes in a letter from Coutts to Albéniz dated 30 August in which he complains of the 'trouble and bother' of settling the matter of Albéniz's Michael's Grove residence. Evidently Rosina had gone to straighten things out and was returning to Paris the next day.[8] And he may have been there as early as May. A small notebook of Albéniz's survives in which he was apparently taking notes during lectures on medieval music.[9] Written in Spanish, the material moves through tetrachords and neumatic notation, with Albéniz's own tentative renderings of the virga, punctum, podatus, and clivis. Heighted neumes, staff notation, clefs and their evolution, and the development of rests are covered as well. On page 14 appears the date '1 Mayo 1894' and a note to himself, 'Received the shipment from the Schola Cantorum except for the last volume (after the *Pope*

[5] See Llorens Cisteró, 'Inéditas', 94–6. Crickboom (b. 1871) was a noted violinist, conductor, and composer. His letter from Barcelona is dated 4 July 1898 (Bc, 'C').

[6] Dated 14 Feb. 1893, cited in Ruiz Albéniz, *Albéniz*, 33. 'Estoy muy descorazonado con nuestra tierra, y cree que me será dificultosísimo el volver a ella si no es a dejar los huesos.'

[7] A clipping of this article is located in the Bc, M987, vol. ii. 'Albéniz es mas español que Pelayo; pero para Albéniz no consiste el españolismo en escribir páginas musicales á cinco francos la página, ni en resignarse, por consecuencia, á comer cocido frío en un piso cuarto. . . . Albéniz vive en París y en Londres, porque en París y en Londres come y duerme. No es torero, *luego* no puede vivir bien en España.'

[8] Coutts had written already on 10 Jan. 1895 (Bc, 'C') complaining, 'Don't you see that Lowenfeld is simply trying to see what he can get out of me? I must leave it to you and him to settle. I never contemplated having to pay anything for it & I must refuse to do so.'

[9] This notebook measures 13 cm. × 8.3 cm. and is located in Mm, car. 4.

Marcellus Mass from pages 48 to 97)'. Evidently he was immersing himself in the works of Palestrina. The following page again gives the date of 1 May and proceeds with the subject of melodic structure. What leads one to suspect these are lecture notes is Albéniz's reference to 'Hugo Riman', the famous German music theorist Hugo Riemann whose name he spelled phonetically in Spanish. The Schola Cantorum was established on 6 June 1894[10] with the aim of promoting plainchant and Palestrina-style religious music, but classes were not actually offered there until 1896. For now this remains a mystery. All the notebook tells us for certain is that he was embarking on a new phase of serious music study, and that he had already established some connection with the newly forming Schola Cantorum in Paris.

Albéniz's successful performances in 1889 were a living memory, and now, five years later, many influential people welcomed him back with open arms. Among these were Ernest Chausson and his wife Jeanne, who helped introduce him to Parisian musical society through soirées at their home, which attracted the city's brightest musical luminaries. The Chaussons also had an extensive collection of paintings by such moderns as Degas, Renoir, and Puvis de Chavanne, which no doubt appealed to the art lover Albéniz. He attended salons at the home of the Princesse de Polignac, where the third book of his *Iberia* received its premiere in 1908. At the Palais de l'Art he made the acquaintance of literary figures such as Camille Mauclair and Pierre Louÿs, in addition to Debussy, Ravel, Massenet, and other famous musicians. At these functions Albéniz often improvised at the piano, charming the guests with his distinctive style. His own home became a mecca for Spanish writers, artists, and musicians, including Sarasate, Arbós, Granados, Casals, Miguel Llobet, Santiago Rusiñol, Ramón Casas, Josep-Marià Sert, and Zuloaga, to name but a few. Laura Albéniz described this epoch in her journal: 'What tranquillity was ours in those days... leaning with all our trust on that immense column that my father represented, certain that it would always exist.'[11]

But his growing popularity was due not simply to his creative gifts, but to his own humanity, warmth, and vivacity. He was a genuine *raconteur*, and the French loved him for it. His friend Paul Gilson, for example, declared that Albéniz enjoyed expatiating on a wide range of subjects, from the brand of his socks to the prowess of certain bullfighters, to the best hotels in Europe.[12]

---

[10] According to Danièle Pistone, 'Paris et la musique, 1890–1900', *Revue internationale de musique française*, 10/28 (Feb. 1989), 39.

[11] This unpublished journal is in the possession of Jacqueline Kalfa, who received it from one of the composer's descendants. Cited in Kalfa, 'Albéniz à Paris', 30. 'Quelle tranquillité était la nôtre alors... nous appuyant avec toute notre confiance sur cette colonne immense que représentait mon père, certaine qu'il existerait toujours.'

Artur Rubinstein also remarked on his wonderful sense of humour and ability to make others laugh. He described Albéniz as a 'fat little man with a round face, black beard, and upcurled, abundant mustachios. . . . a jovial fellow, whose eyes had a charming, smiling twinkle. We loved his stories, which made us scream with laughter.'[13] Georges Jean-Aubry recalled that

He who met Albéniz, were it but once, would remember it to his dying day. At first his effusiveness could surprise, yes even displease, but soon one felt that a living fire inspired all his gestures, and the great soul of the man dominated his outward frame; and to astonishment would succeed an affection which nothing could alter.[14]

Thus he endeared himself to the Parisians very quickly. He aided himself by participating in concerts given by the Société Nationale de Musique and by eventually enrolling in the Schola Cantorum, where he studied counterpoint with Vincent d'Indy starting in October 1896[15] and made the acquaintance of Charles Bordes (1863–1909), director of the Schola Cantorum and a pupil of César Franck. Bordes devoted much study to Basque music and composed several pieces inspired by it (*Suite basque* (1888) and *Rapsodie basque* (1890)).[16] Albéniz became acquainted with Erik Satie, Albert Roussel, and Déodat de Séverac. He attended the 1894 premiere of Debussy's *Prélude à l'après-midi d'un faune*, as well as the opera *Pelléas et Mélisande* in 1902, and cultivated an admiration for that composer's music. Albéniz's rapport with Paris and French culture became second in importance only to that with his homeland. And the affection was reciprocal. For nowhere else, not even in Spain, were the general public and the musical intelligentsia so receptive to his particular brand of musical nationalism. In Paris he entered a new stage in his career as a composer, one marked by increased sophistication and technical ability. Of course, these traits in and of themselves would not have endeared his compositions to anyone. It was because his inner artistic compass remained pointed towards Spain that he was able to integrate these new influences into his style, weaving them into a coherent and convincing musical pattern.

By January of 1894 Albéniz had completed work in Barcelona on the piano–vocal score for the second act of the new opera, but the title of the work was as yet uncertain.[17] It was then known as 'The Shepherd Lord',

[12] See Paul Gilson, 'Albéniz à Bruxelles', in *Notes de musique et souvenirs* (Brussels: Collection Voilà, 1924), 11–19; repr. in Franco (ed.) *Albéniz y su tiempo*, 29–32 (in Spanish translation).
[13] Arthur Rubinstein, *My Young Years* (New York: Alfred A. Knopf, 1973), 140 (paperback edition).
[14] 'Isaac Albéniz', 536.
[15] According to Gauthier, *Albéniz*, 89–90.
[16] Istel, 'Isaac Albéniz', 139.
[17] The other two acts were finished in Paris. Act I is dated 'Paris 1894–95', and Act III, 'Paris 7bre 1894'. Earlier working titles included 'The Two Roses' and 'Pastore e Cavaliere'. Other MSS, including the

which title appears on a piano–vocal autograph in Barcelona, but other possibilities were bandied about. In a letter to Albéniz dated 29 January 1894,[18] Coutts struggles with the title. 'The Shepherd Prince' is one idea, 'The Nut-Brown Maid' another.[19] Perhaps in anticipation of a production of the opera at the Liceu in Barcelona, where it would have to be done in Italian, he devotes much thought to the title's translation into that language. 'Does not "La Donzella Bruna" sound somewhat common?' he asks. ' "The Brown (or brunette) Maid" sounds to me unpoetic! The "Nut" gets left out altogether!' A year later, on 4 January 1895, he was still turning over the question in his mind. He preferred 'The Nut-Brown Maid' or 'The Shepherd Lord' if a 'proper equivalent' in Italian could be found. Finally, 'Henry Clifford', translatable as 'Enrico Clifford', appeared to be the best alternative. Albéniz and Coutts remained in frequent contact, and sometimes the Englishman would visit his Spanish friend in Paris to discuss details of the work.[20]

While progress continued on *Henry Clifford*, Albéniz was busy with other projects. On 13 September he performed for the family of the Grand Duke of Wladimiro and other notables at the Miramar Palace in San Sebastián. The reviewer wrote rapturously of his mastery, describing him as 'the emulator of Rubinstein'.[21] But his chief occupation during the summer of 1894, in Paris, was finishing work on a one-act zarzuela entitled *San Antonio de la Florida*,[22] on a text by his friend Eusebio Sierra, for performance in Madrid that autumn. Born in Santander in 1850, Sierra started out studying law but went into journalism and literature, eventually becoming editor at two Madrid newspapers, *El solfeo* and *El liberal*. He was also a Freemason. Beginning in 1878 he wrote for the theatre, including zarzuela librettos for such celebrated composers as Federico Chueca (*La caza del oso*, 1891) and Ruperto Chapí (*Blasones y talegas*, 1901).[23] When his friendship with

completed orchestral score in a copyist's hand, are in the Mm, Lligall 6. Incomplete piano–vocal and orchestral scores for *Henry Clifford* are also in the Bc, M978 (2 volumes). The Oc retains a manuscript copy of the piano–vocal score of the first act of *Henry Clifford*.

[18] Bc, 'C'.

[19] Though this idea was rejected, Coutts did publish a poem by that title (London: John Lane, 1901). In a letter to Albéniz of 4 Jan. 1895 (Bc, 'C'), Coutts explained that nut-brown meant brunette to peasants of the 15th cent.

[20] Bevan, 'Albéniz', 63, states that 'The Nut-Brown Maid' was originally a 15th-cent. border ballad 'of some significance'. He also points out the 'The Shepherd Lord' idea's debt to Metastasio's *Il rè pastore* (1751), which was set by Gluck and Mozart.

[21] This clipping from *La correspondencia de España*, 17 Sept. 1894, is in Bc, M987, vol. ii. The reviewer was 'Aguilar'.

[22] According to Torres, 'La producción escénica', 174–5, the work was originally entitled *En San Antonio de la Florida*. The preposition was dropped before the premiere and in the publication of the libretto. MSS are in the Mm, Lligall 12 (autograph, signed, and dated Paris, Sept. 1894), and Bc, M985.

[23] See entry in *Enciclopedia universal ilustrada europeo-americana* (1958 edn), s.v. 'Sierra'.

Albéniz began we cannot say, but the first evidence of their collaboration is found in a letter from Sierra to Albéniz dated 21 January 1893. In it Sierra refers to their three-act zarzuela, of which he will be sending him the third act. This work was never completed, and we do not even know its title.[24] At all events, there is a hiatus in their correspondence until November of the following year, after the premiere of *San Antonio de la Florida*, by which time Albéniz was living in Paris.

Zarzuelas are distinguished from operas by the fact that they contain an abundance of spoken dialogue, usually in verse, interspersed with musical numbers. At that time, there were two basic kinds of zarzuela, the *género chico* ('small genre') and *género grande* ('large genre'). The work by Albéniz and Sierra belongs to the former category in that it consists of a single act, divided into two scenes. Its total duration was, according to the critic 'A', writing in *El imparcial*, 'seven quarters of an hour'.[25] Moreover, its content is characteristically comic and frivolous. The published piano–vocal score (Barcelona: Juan Bta. Pujol, n.d.) lists seven numbers in all, two of which are subdivided into two distinct sections.[26] The printed version bears the dedication 'A la Exma. Sra. Condesa de Morphy', the wife of Albéniz's dear friend and benefactor Count Morphy. The text represented a departure from the norm in its eschewal of verse in favour of prose.[27] The story itself deals, predictably, with love and is set during a period of political instability under the reign of Ferdinand VII, in 1823.[28]

Scene i takes place at night on a street in Madrid. The drama commences with a brief orchestral prelude, followed by an offstage chorus of majos and majas singing their charming 'Venimos de la orilla del Manzanares' ('We come from the banks of the Manzanares') (Ex. 14). This is an obvious reference to a famous painting by Goya depicting young people dancing and singing on the banks of that river. As the curtain goes up we see Don Enrique Cifuentes, a young liberal who is sought by the authorities, talking to a girl named Rosa. She soon perceives the approach of Enrique's conservative nemesis, Don Lesmes Calasparra, and urges Enrique to flee. Lesmes now appears and calls to Rosa to learn if Irene and her mother Doña

[24] By 30 Apr. 1895, Sierra was expressing frustration at getting no response from Albéniz about the project; the idea was eventually dropped. Their correspondence is in the Bc, 'S'.

[25] 27 Oct. 1894, 3, 'durante los siete cuartos de hora que duró la representación'. This was rather longer than the typical comic zarzuela, a fact that contributed to the negative press notices.

[26] No. 1 consists of parts A and B, the first part containing a prelude, recitative, and chorus, and the second part presenting chorus with soloist, concluding with a piece for solo voice. The third number is likewise divided into two parts, the first consisting of a 'canción y escenas' and the second, a duet.

[27] Libretto published Madrid: R. Velasco, 1894.

[28] The exact year is not given in either the score or libretto from the original production. The year 1823 is stated in the French libretto published for the 1905 staging in Brussels.

Ex. 14. *San Antonio de la Florida*, No. 1*a*: 'Venimos de la orilla del Manzanares', bars 14–17

Ascensión have returned. Rosa responds that they have not yet come back from the church of San Andrés, and Lesmes bids her farewell. Rosa retreats into her house. Gabriel, who will marry Rosa in the morning at the church of San Antonio de la Florida,[29] now appears in the company of assorted majas and majos. These continue to sing their song about the Manzanares where their burdens and worries remain behind, where they love to watch the waters flow. The majo/as leave, and Gabriel sings to his beloved to show herself. She greets him from her balcony and then descends to discuss their plans. Gabriel reveals that Enrique intends to meet his beloved Irene at their wedding (Irene is to be Rosa's bridesmaid), by disguising himself as a Franciscan monk. Gabriel further discloses that Enrique's only hope for redemption is that the current Minister of Justice, Lozano de Torres, may soon die and be replaced by a friend of Enrique's father. Gabriel coaxes an embrace out of his betrothed, at which moment Lesmes steps out of the shadows where he had been concealed (eavesdropping, unbeknownst to them, on their conversation) and chides them for their public display of affection.

Lesmes and his henchman Pascual now plot Enrique's arrest. We learn that Enrique's chief offence has been to state that the King has a big nose. For this the Minister of Justice has ordered his detention, but Lesmes is determined to go further and kill Enrique. His reasons for this are not only to defend 'society, religion, and the throne', but to eliminate him as a rival for the hand of Irene. The *alguaciles* (police) and royal volunteers will assist in Enrique's seizure, and they now appear on their nightly rounds, singing of their duty to catch conspirators against the regime. They move in parade-ground fashion to the orders their officer barks out, and finally leave satisfied that all is tranquil. The four-square, downbeat rhythms of their chorus possess none of the folkloric charm of the earlier majo number. They do,

[29] On the outskirts of Madrid, famous for its frescos by Francisco Goya (1746–1828), who is buried there.

Ex. 15. _San Antonio de la Florida_, No. 2: Alguaciles motive, bars 12–14

however, have a motive associated with them that recurs whenever they are on stage (Ex. 15).

Irene and Doña Ascensión, on their way home from church, greet Lesmes and Pascual. Lesmes informs them that Enrique is to be punished for plotting with three others to kill all the royalists in Spain! He compounds his deceit by saying that all the conspirators are now in prison. Irene, who loves Enrique, seems distressed by this news, but her mother states that their family will have nothing to do with traitors. As Irene walks away, Lesmes confides in Doña Ascensión that, in fact, Enrique is still at large. He warns her that Enrique is planning to disguise himself as a Franciscan monk at the wedding so that he can abscond with Irene. He advises her to be watchful and assures her that he himself will also be present, though incognito. Irene sings her delightful 'Canción del Pajarito': 'Little bird who is in the tree, giving to the wind your songs of love' (Ex. 16).

Ex. 16. _San Antonio de la Florida_, No. 3a: 'Canción del Pajarito', bars 9–13

Her voice attracts Enrique and Gabriel, who now join her. They dance and sing together until the night patrol nears. Rosa warns her friends to hide, and while concealing themselves Irene and Enrique sing of their love and anticipation of the nuptials soon to take place. But the patrol finds nothing and leaves. After Irene's departure Doña Ascensión catches a glimpse of the fugitive Enrique, and Lesmes, Pascual, and the soldiers set off in pursuit, bringing scene i to a close. An orchestral _intermedio_, 'Salida de los algua-

Ex. 17. *San Antonio de la Florida*, No. 4: 'Intermedio', bars 37–40

ciles', separates the two scenes. The first part of this *intermedio* is dominated
by the motive associated with the soldiers. The second part is a lovely *jota
copla*, whose lilting melody and simple accompaniment create a welcome lull
in the excitement before the next scene and the climax of the drama (Ex. 17).

Scene ii takes place outside San Antonio de la Florida. On one side of the
stage is the church, and opposite it is a restaurant where the wedding guests
will refresh themselves. The proprietor, Joaquín, is Gabriel's godfather and is
being assisted in his preparations by a young boy. Lesmes now appears,
disguised as a Franciscan. While he chats with Joaquín, Enrique enters. He
was unable to find a Franciscan's outfit, as he had planned, and has had to
don the robe of a different order ('de la Merced'). As a result, Lesmes does
not recognize him, nor he, Lesmes. They exchange pious greetings, each
believing the other to be the genuine article. Lesmes happens to know all the
brothers at Enrique's monastery, and his questions about them threaten to
compromise Enrique's impersonation. Enrique makes a hasty and contrived
exit, and is replaced by Gabriel, who mistakes Lesmes for Enrique. Lesmes
brushes him off as the wedding party approaches.

Gabriel joins Irene, Rosa, and the majo/as in singing of the forthcoming
festivities. The music is dominated by the lively strains of the *sevillanas* as the
chorus sings 'Long live the bride and bridegroom'. Lesmes thereafter con-
verses with Irene, who, thinking he is Enrique, makes insulting remarks
about his (Lesmes's) pretensions to winning her hand. Lesmes controls
himself, however, and simply requests an embrace, which she gives him.
Doña Ascensión now denounces the Franciscan who is hugging her daughter, suspecting him of being none other than Enrique. A quintet ensues
during which Lesmes reveals his identity to Doña Ascensión, and Enrique his
to Irene and Rosa. Doña Ascensión feels remorse at having reproached a man
of the cloth, even if it was merely Lesmes, and confesses her situation to a
reluctant Enrique, in his guise as a 'Brother of Mercy'. Enrique thus learns of
the plot to arrest him and of the real identity of the other 'monk'. He
informs Doña Ascensión that only a few days earlier Lesmes had confided
to some of his (Enrique's) fellow monks that Irene was poorly educated and

that her mother had no sense. Doña Ascensión is naturally incensed at this disclosure and heeds Enrique's counsel to go home and do penance by reciting her rosary.

The march-tempo finale commences as the police come on the scene to arrest Lesmes (their motive makes one last appearance), mistaking him in his Franciscan garb for Enrique. Gabriel, Irene, and Enrique reflect on the fact that their good fortune will probably last only until Lesmes establishes his real identity with the police. However, Doña Ascensión now returns with the news that Lozano de Torres has died and that Sr. Ceballos, the friend of Enrique's father, has assumed the position of Minister of Justice. Not only is Enrique now free, but he has been granted an important position, and both his father and the King himself desire his marriage to Irene. The zarzuela closes with the lovers rejoicing that 'through such burdens and such suffering, we have triumphed in the end'.

The zarzuela premiered 26 October 1894, at the Teatro de Apolo, one of the main theatres in Madrid then as now (casting not available). It ran until 11 November of the same year, receiving a total of fifteen performances (according to the theatre listings in *La correspondencia de España*). It was briefly revived before Christmas, receiving five more performances (17–21 December) before closing for good. Sierra ascribed the prompt termination of this second run to the fact that Arbós had conducted, and the public compared him unfavourably to Albéniz, the original conductor.[30] All in all it was an average run; respectable, but not a big hit. Running concurrently with it at that theatre was Bretón's immensely popular zarzuela *La verbena de la paloma*.[31]

The music is altogether folkloric in character and possesses a charming simplicity that almost conceals to our modern eyes and ears the subtlety and refinement of the score for its day and venue of performance. The critics evidently perceived Albéniz's novel chromaticism and attempt to unify the entire score through a cyclic recurrence of certain themes as a threat to tradition. But their hostile reaction can scarcely be comprehended today. One of the zarzuela's critics, 'Zeda',[32] could hardly contain his invective and

[30] In a letter to Albéniz dated 26 Dec. 1894 (Bc, 'S'). The audiences were not large, but they were enthusiastic.

[31] In a letter to Sierra and Albéniz, dated 10 Nov. 1894 (Bc, 'A'), Enrique Arregui, director of the theatre, explains his reasons for dropping the show from their repertoire. He states that after a 'noisy' premiere, the attendance slacked off. By contrast, Bretón's work was still going strong. He suggests that they try Barcelona, as the public there has a much better appreciation of 'this class of production'. In the absence of subsidies (which theatres elsewhere in Europe enjoyed), he continues, bad press and poor turnout spelled doom.

[32] Francisco Fernández Villegas (1856–1916). All ensuing references to the identities of critics using pseudonyms are taken from P. P. Rogers and F. A. Lapuente, *Diccionario de seudónimos literarios españoles* (Madrid: Editorial Gredos, SA, 1977).

cited in his review (*La época*, 27 October 1894, 2) a fellow critic ('intelligent and distinguished') who had posed the following explanation for Sierra's choice of prose instead of poetry: 'He has generously renounced, on the altar of musical clarity, the beauties of versification, the complications of the story, and everything that could distract attention from the principal element of the new zarzuela.' To this 'Zeda' acidly remarked: 'There is nothing in the text that could distract the attention of the public.'[33] 'Zeda' persisted in this unflattering vein:

The lyrical comedy premiered last night at the Teatro de Apolo belongs to the *boring* genre.... The text is made up of a series of drab scenes, without interest, without grace, without types, with neither customs, nor comic situations, nor jokes, nor originality, nor anything.[34]

Though he offered praise for the introduction and the finale of the first scene, his conclusion was that 'Sr. Albéniz has incurred the defect of the character in *Los pavos reales*, who wanted to put truffles in everything.... He has abused the truffles.'[35]

These sentiments were echoed by 'A' in his review (cited above), in which he states that the zarzuela presented 'nothing or almost nothing capable of exciting the interest or hilarity of the public'.[36] In his view, Albéniz

has taken the work as a pretext for demonstrating that he is a musician of great talents. Has he demonstrated that? To excess, in my judgement, insofar as the enormous quantity of music, though of the highest quality, is too great for so diminutive a book.[37]

The emerging consensus was, then, that the music was good—too good, in fact, for such a libretto and for the particular theatre and its clientele. Nonetheless, this same reviewer observed that 'the public received Albéniz with genuine affection ... and requested the repetition of three or four truly beautiful numbers, at the end calling Isaac Albéniz and the author of the text, D. Eusebio Sierra, to the stage.'[38] The observations of an anonymous

---

[33] 'Nada hay en el libro ... que pueda distraer la atención del público.'

[34] 'El sainete lírico estrenado anoche en el teatro de Apolo pertenece al género *ennuyeux*.... El libro está formado por una serie de escenas deslavazadas, sin interés, sin gracia, sin tipos, ni costumbres, ni situaciones cómicas, ni chistes, ni originalidad, ni nada.'

[35] 'El Sr. Albéniz ha incurrido en el defecto del personaje de "Los pavos reales", que quería poner trufas en todo.... Ha abusado de las trufas.'

[36] '[N]ada ó casi nada capaz de exitar el interés ó la hilaridad del público.'

[37] '[H]a tomado la obra como pretexto para demostrar que es un músico de grandes alientos. ¿Lo ha demostrado? Con exceso, á mi juicio, puesto que la enorme cantidad de ella que hay allí, con ser de primera calidad, es demasiado grande para tan poco libro.'

[38] 'El público acogió con verdadero cariño a Albéniz ... y pidió la repetición de tres o cuatro numeros verdaderamente hermosos, llamando á escena al final a Isaac Albéniz y al autor de la letra, D. Eusebio Sierra.'

reviewer writing in *La correspondencia de España* (27 October 1894, 3) provide further evidence that the public enjoyed the performance:

the public of the Apolo, despite being accustomed to popular music—inspired and playful—applauded extraordinarily last night the [music] of Sr. Albéniz, demanding a repetition of the introductory chorus, the duet in the first scene, and the prelude of the second.[39]

Concerning the make-up of the audience, we have the reviewer of *El correo español* (27 October 1894, 3), 'Pipí',[40] to thank for this account: 'The hall was completely full, the intelligent element predominating, who applauded all the numbers with enthusiasm, especially the prelude, the serenade, and some of the choruses.'[41] As for the music itself, the critics who found it so unsuited to its venue provided few descriptions. The following, by 'J. A.' (real name unknown), writing in *El liberal* (27 October 1894, 3), is an exception to that rule: 'It abounds in melody, and the instrumental parts are handled admirably.'[42] But here, too, the Final Judgement is inescapable:

The composer sometimes ascends in flight to altitudes in which the exigencies of the genre are lost from view, lacking the sobriety necessary in order to contain himself in the limits the poet has set for him in the poem he has placed at his service.[43]

That the work was pleasantly melodious was reiterated by 'Don Cualquiera'[44] in *La justicia* (27 October 1894, 3): 'From the first note to the last there dominates a taste and an elegance in the composition, and [in] the entr'acte between the first and second scenes a brilliant melody is developed with enchanting simplicity.'[45] In his opinion, however, 'When the public goes to see a little piece of a popular kind, it does not request excellence of composition or lofty harmonic effects; it is content with something light that

---

[39] '[E]l público de Apolo, á pesar de venir acostumbrado a música popular, inspirada y juguetona, aplaudió anoche extraordinariamente la del señor Albéniz, haciendo repetir el coro de introducción, el dúo del primer cuadro y el preludio del segundo.' A letter from Count Morphy of 19 Dec. 1894, which he signed using his paternal pseudonym 'Abraham', confirms that the public liked the work and implies that the venture was somewhat lucrative, in so far as the money was good for the 'soul and the body' ('el alma y el cuerpo').

[40] Antonio Fernández Grillo (1845–1906).

[41] 'La sala estaba completamente llena, predominando el elemento inteligente, que aplaudió con entusiasmo todos los números, muy especialmente el preludio, la serenata y algunos coros.'

[42] 'Abunda en ella el elemento melódico, y la parte instrumental está admirablemente tratada.' Unfortunately, the orchestral score for the zarzuela is lost.

[43] 'El compositor remonta á veces al vuelo á alturas en las que llegan á perderse de vista las exigencias del género, falto de la sobriedad necesaria para contenerse en los límites que el poeta le ha trazado en el poema que ha puesto á su servicio.'

[44] Possibly Federico Balart (1831–1905).

[45] 'Desde la primera á la última nota domina un gusto y una elegancia exquisita en la composición, y el intermedio del primero al secundo cuadro, una melodía brillante se desarrolla con una sencillez que encanta.'

the ear can enjoy.'[46] His view of the libretto was shared by nearly all the critics: 'the text of *San Antonio de la Florida* is poor, and what is more than poor, insubstantial and lacking in verisimilitude.'[47]

As bitter a draught as these reviews were for both Albéniz and Sierra, the two had yet to drink the dregs from the cask of press hostility in Madrid. For they had hoped to score a double knockout in the capital by staging, in rapid-fire succession, *San Antonio de la Florida* followed by a Spanish adaptation of *The Magic Opal*, now to be called *La sortija* ('The ring'). It is difficult to tell exactly to what extent the work was modified for performance in Madrid, but most of the operetta seems to have remained in its original version. Of course, the text was translated into Spanish, by Sierra. Yet this change was evidently made in the parts, for only cues and other admonitions to the conductor appear in Spanish in the score itself. To accommodate the tastes of the new audience, Albéniz added some more Spanish numbers, e.g. Act II, No. 3, 'Recitado y Baile' (Nos. 4 and 10 also appear to have been written for the Madrid production). Regrettably, the condition of the manuscript does not allow for anything more than educated guesses.[48]

The operetta premiered on 23 November 1894, at the Teatro de la Zarzuela (casting not available). The production was actually delayed a day because the costumes were not yet ready. One of Madrid's most notorious critics, 'El Abate Pirracas',[49] renowned for his caustic commentary, characterized the composer Albéniz as 'one of those eternal talkers...who spout words and words and words without pause and without saying anything'.[50] He further insisted that

the music of *La sortija* DOES NOT SOUND. And I will add that it is *hollow* and lacks colour, sonority, grace, freshness, and the *stamp* of that which is inspired and spontaneous.... Therefore, the music of Sr. Albéniz is opaque and cold. The notes fall on the ear and remain in the ear, accumulating to form an offensive noise.[51]

[46] 'El público, cuando va á ver una piececilla de las que se usan, no pide primores de composición ni efectos armónicos de altos vuelos; le basta con que el oído se recree con algo ligero.'

[47] '[L]a letra de "San Antonio de la Florida" es pobre, y además de pobre, insubstancial, inverosímil.'

[48] The manuscripts now in the Bc (M974/5) were apparently used in all performances of this work, with additions and emendations added directly to the score.

[49] Matias de Padilla y Clara (1851–99) was from Cuba and worked for both *La correspondencia de España* and *El heraldo* in Madrid.

[50] In *La correspondencia de España*, 24 Nov. 1894, 1, entitled 'Telones y bambalinas' ('Curtains and scenes'). 'Albéniz, como compositor, es uno de esos habladores sempiternos...que echan por la boca palabras y palabras y palabras, sin darse vagar ni punto de reposo, pero ningún concepto.'

[51] '[L]a música de *La Sortija* NO SUENA. Y agregaré que es *hueca*, le falta color, sonoridad, gracia, frescura, el *sello* de lo que es inspirado y espontáneo.... Por eso la música de Sr. Albéniz es opaca, y fría. Las notas caen en el oído y en el oído se quedan, y se amontonan formando un ruído ensordecedor.'

The libretto fared no better, and he described it as 'without novelty or interest', with 'scenes badly united which form two eternal acts'.[52]

'Don Cualquiera' (*La jusificia*, 24 November 1894, 2) gave Albéniz credit for wanting to restore Spanish music to its ancient glory, and was sure that the composer did not want to 'torment our ears with modern music'.[53] He praised Albéniz's perfect knowledge of the rules of harmony but deplored the lack of 'inspiration' in the work: 'Perhaps, within the melodic mania that obsesses him, the cognoscenti will find no musical defect in the whole score. But the public, the anonymous masses, are extremely bored.'[54] Albéniz's musical prodigality was further decried in a review by E. Contreras y Camargo in *El resumen* (24 November 1894, 2):

The numbers follow one another without interruption, without allowing time for the ear to rest. Moreover, the numbers are so long that they constitute an invasion of oppressive notes. Twenty-odd numbers in two acts! . . . Choruses and more choruses, romances, duets, trios . . .[55]

A certain 'J. de L.', writing in *El imparcial* (24 November 1894, 2–3), was anything but impartial when he declared that Albéniz 'has nothing to learn; on the contrary, he has much to forget'.[56] Along this same line, 'Z' (alias 'Zeda', previously encountered) wrote in *La época* on the same date that he had never experienced such boredom:

Intelligent people say that the music is very *learned*. But logarithmic tables are also learned, and I do not believe there is a spectator capable of enduring a recital of them for two and a half hours. The public, despite giving evidence of the patience of Job, manifested, at various times, its disgust.[57]

Another cause for the public's disgust, according to an anonymous reviewer in *El heraldo* (24 November 1894), was the meagre novelty of the libretto: 'Those scenes of bandits, those falsified Andalusians, that amulet ring, and those mishandled love interests could not interest anybody or inspire a musician [of Albéniz's stature].'[58] The critic 'J. A.' (*El liberal*, 24

---

[52] '[E]scenas mal unidas que forman dos actos eternos.'

[53] '[N]o quiere atormentar a nuestros oídos con la música moderna.'

[54] 'Acaso, dentro de la manía melódica que le obsesiona, los más entendidos no hallarán un defecto musical en toda la partitura, pero el público, la masa anónima, se aburre soberanamente.'

[55] 'Los números se suceden sin interrupción, sin dejar tiempo á que el oído descanse, y son los números tan largos además, que constituyen una invasión de notas abrumadoras. ¡Veintitantos números en dos actos! . . . Coros y más coros, romanzas, duos, tercetos!. . .'

[56] '[N]o tiene nada que aperender; al contrario, tiene mucho que olvidar.'

[57] 'Dicen los inteligentes que la música es muy *sabia*; pero también son sabias las tablas de logaritmos y no creo que hubiera espectador capaz de sufrir una lectura de ellas durante dos horas y media. El público, a pesar de que dió pruebas de paciencia dignas de Job, manifestó varias veces su disgusto.'

[58] 'Aquellas escenas de bandidos, aquellos andaluces falsificados, aquella sortija amuleto, y aquellos amores tan mal traídos como llevados, no podían interesar á nadie, ni inspirar a un músico.'

November 1894, 3) confirmed the audience's reaction as 'cold and reserved'. But it was 'Pipí' (*El correo español*, 24 November 1894, 2) who came closest to ferreting out the real cause of the hostility: 'Albéniz and Sierra are too *foreignized*.'[59] Here was the heart of the matter. It was as if to say, 'How dare they introduce to our stage and in our theatres something that breaks the established mould! Two and a half hours of music, indeed. And in a style that is alien to our tastes, that is *foreign*.' It was Albéniz's cosmopolitanism, his seriousness and musical erudition that they resented, and perhaps feared. In short, he was now an outsider who posed a threat to the local zarzuela establishment. This xenophobic response to Albéniz's music helps to explain the composer's increasing ambivalence towards his homeland. Count Morphy wrote to him a year later castigating the provinciality of the local critics (describing them collectively as a 'wild beast'). As an example, he cited their recent disapproval of a singer's French style—in a performance of Meyerbeer's *L'Africaine*![60]

Long-suffering Albéniz. What a tortuous road he had travelled, from being the supposedly unlettered, intuitive prodigy labouring under Pedrell's tutelage ten years earlier, to the now overly sophisticated and erudite composer, the local boy who had made good and was 'putting on airs'. This would be his enduring curse: in Spain, he was foreignized, a traitor; elsewhere, he was an exotic provincial.[61] *La sortija* was a fiasco and folded after only three nights. Several reviews reported that he was present for the premiere and that he appeared on stage at the end of the performance to accept the audience's tepid applause.[62] But it appears he left for Paris, disillusioned and disheartened, before the bitter end of its run. On 30 November 1894 Sierra wrote to him to explain that the theatre had been contractually bound to run it for at least three nights but dropped it immediately thereafter.[63] In fact, Sierra's poor adaptation of the text had been

[59] 'Albéniz y Sierra están demasiado *extranjerizados*' (emphasis in text).

[60] Letter of 19 Oct. 1895, signed 'Abraham' (Bc, 'A'). His surrogate paternal role is further expressed by referring often in the letters to 'Dear son Isaac' ('Querido hijo Isaac'). In some letters, he signs his name Papa Guillermo (Bc, 'P'). When dispensing medical advice, he signs his letters 'Doktor Jacob', or just 'Doctor'. The majority are signed using his actual name (Bc, 'M'). In all cases, however, he addresses Albéniz using the formal 'usted', never 'tu'.

[61] In *La música contemporánea en España* (Madrid: Ediciones La Nave, 1930), 117–53, Adolfo Salazar explains that Albéniz was rejected not only because of the foreign influence in his work but also because of his expatriate status.

[62] *La epoca, El liberal*, and *La publicidad* all report this. Sierra evidently did not appear with Albéniz on stage. There is no indication that Albéniz conducted the performance, or that part of the way through he put down his baton, called the audience 'barbarians', and stalked out of the theatre. This dramatic scenario appears in Laplane, *Albéniz*, 53.

[63] Bc, 'S'. This raises the question as to whether Albéniz was even present for the production. According to most sources, he conducted the first night but was so disgusted with the audience's hostility that he left for Paris after the premiere. The manuscript of the score bears many cues in Spanish, but not in his hand.

partly responsible for the calamity. He did not understand English very well, and his translation made little sense to the audience. The orchestra was reduced in size and not well prepared. The style of music was not familar to them, and that only made matters worse.

Albéniz had many detractors in the Spanish capital, but he also had some valuable friends. Count Morphy, for one, was not going to look the other way while the press mercilessly savaged his protégé. He published an article that appeared on the front page of *La correspondencia de España* on 30 December 1894, in which he came to the defence of Albéniz, averring that, with all their shortcomings, *San Antonio de la Florida* and *La sortija* were better than many works successfully presented in theatres in Madrid. Though the critics accused Albéniz of breaking established moulds and of being 'dangerously innovative', the public reacted well enough to his music's freshness. In response to a critic who had accused Albéniz of 'using a frigate to cross a river', he replied that a 'simple raft' could only appear like a frigate to someone accustomed to crossing rivers, like the Africans, 'on an inflated hide'. He let fly another shaft in the direction of the notorious 'Zeda', who had accused Albéniz of abusing truffles by putting them in everything: 'Could it not be closer to the truth to affirm that in the *género chico* the garlic and the onion have been so abused that the tired palate does not know how to distinguish the potato from the truffle?'[64] He lamented the lack of true 'lyric drama' in Spain and encouraged the public and critics to support young composers like Albéniz and Arbós (whose *El centro de la tierra* had also appeared that autumn at the Apolo) who were attempting to write stage works with more musical substance. All to little avail. The Madrid stage would wait sixty years for another production of a musico-theatrical work by Albéniz.[65]

The sour taste this experience left in the mouths of Albéniz and Sierra can be gauged by some letters in his correspondence in the Bc. Sierra wrote to Albéniz from Madrid on 21 May 1895 expressing his 'indignation' over the treatment the two of them had received at the pens of the journalists in Madrid, and the resulting failure of the productions. In his view, the unrelenting negativity of the press was completely unfair. In a letter to Albéniz dated 7 December 1894 (Bc, 'S'), the writer Francisco Serrano de la Pedrosa (d. 1926)[66] offered this insight: 'The Madrid public does not go to the

---

[64] '¿No pudiera estar más cerca de la verdad afirmando que en el género chico se ha abusado tanto del ajo y de la cebolla que el paladar estragado no sabe distinguir la patata de la trufa?'

[65] *San Antonio de la Florida* was revived 18 Nov. 1954, at the Teatro Fuencarral in Madrid (see Ch. 8).

[66] A copy of Serrano's *El derecho del pataleo* (pub. Madrid, 1893) is in Albéniz's personal library and bears a dedication to 'the eminent composer I. Albéniz [from] his admirer, friend, and collaborator'. In what sense they were collaborators is unclear.

theatre to hear music...it goes to enjoy itself, in accordance with its culture....This uncouthness consequently rejects the more psychological element in modern music.'[67] Albéniz's friend the composer Enric Morera (1865–1942) wrote from Barcelona in response to feelings of disappointment Albéniz had evidently expressed to him in a previous letter. Morera consoled him by remarking on the 'very great artistic ignorance that reigns there [Madrid]' and advising him to come to Barcelona, 'where they will recognize your great talent'.[68] Albéniz heeded this advice and moved forward toward his next theatrical venture.

Albéniz focused his efforts on finishing the score for *Henry Clifford* in time for its premiere in Barcelona in the spring of 1895. Coutts explained to Albéniz the literary sources he drew upon for this tale.[69] They included Wordsworth's *Song on the Feast of Brougham Castle* ('Glad were the vales and every cottage hearth, | The Shepherd Lord was honoured more and more, | And ages after he was laid in earth, | The Good Lord Clifford was the name he bore'); *The White Doe of Rylstone*, also by Wordsworth; Shakespeare's *King Henry VI*; and 'The Ballad of the Nut-Brown Maid', from Percy's *Reliques*.

The work is labelled an 'Opera Romantica' and was Albéniz's first attempt at a serious, large-scale work with the full assortment of arias, duos, trios, dance numbers, and choruses. The orchestral forces were also much larger than anything he had commanded before: piccolo, two flutes, two oboes, cor anglais, two B♭ clarinets, bass clarinet, two bassoons, contrabassoon, four F horns, two B♭ trumpets, trombones, tuba, timpani (in E♭ and B♭), triangle, xylophone, tam-tam, tambourine, cymbals, harp, and strings. His handling of the orchestra exhibits a great deal more aplomb than was heretofore evident. The dynamic range has been extended to extremes, including quadruple pianissimo (such extremes became a hallmark of his style and are especially evident in *Iberia*). Whereas the orchestration of *The Magic Opal* could best be described as functional, at times witty, here it reveals an attempt at greater subtlety and skill, especially in Albéniz's choice of doublings (e.g. clarinets and violins; bassoons and cellos; clarinet, horn, and violins). The singers face difficulties of Wagnerian dimensions, since they are often made to compete with full- or nearly full-orchestra accompaniments.

[67] 'El público madrileño no va al teatro á oír música...el público va al teatro a divertirse con arreglo á su cultura....Esta incultura rechaza por consiguiente el elemento más psicológico de la música moderna.'

[68] Morera's letter is dated 19 Nov. 1894 (Bc, 'M'): 'la grandísima ignorancia artística que allí impera... donde reconocéran tu gran talento.'

[69] In a typewritten 'argument', now located with his other correspondence in the Bc, 'C'.

As already mentioned, the story is set in fifteenth-century England during the Wars of the Roses, between the rival houses of Lancaster and York.[70] The cast consists of young Henry Clifford, of the House of Lancaster, his mother Lady Clifford, and Nicholas, an archer in Lord Clifford's army; the House of York is represented by Sir John Saint-John and his wife, Lady Saint-John, a sorceress. Their daughter, Annette Saint-John (the 'Nut-Brown Maid'), supplies the love interest in the story. Essentially, this is a 'Romeo and Juliet' situation, except that in this case love triumphs over the rivalry of the opposing families. Act I begins with a prelude whose solemn, hymn-like opening is succeeded by a spirited Allegro, which concludes with an abbreviated return of the opening material. This is followed by a children's chorus, whose 'innocent air', as Bevan has remarked, provides 'an ironic introduction to a work concerned with factional and personal strife'.[71] This chorus paves the way for the entrance of Lady Clifford and her son Henry, who now sing a

Ex. 18. *Henry Clifford*, Act I, scene vi: funeral chorus, bars 77–84

[70] Despite the opera's setting, Albéniz made no attempt to create atmosphere by using historical or folk melodies of England. The avoidance of such quotation seems to have been an article of faith with him, as will be seen in *Pepita Jiménez*. This differentiates him markedly him from Pedrell, who was very fond of quotation in his operas.
[71] 'Albéniz', 106.

duet. Lord Clifford has fought in a decisive battle at Towton, and they anxiously await its outcome. Young Henry, of course, wishes to participate in the struggle, but his mother restrains him. Lady Saint-John enters and sings a duet with Lady Clifford, who is her friend in spite of the present conflict. Lady Saint-John has had a vision that Henry will be the future king, but this revelation causes confusion and distrust among the Cliffords. A messenger now appears bearing the bad news that Lord Clifford has fallen and their faction has lost the battle. Nicholas arrives with the body of Lord Clifford and relates the circumstances of his demise. A funereal choral passage ensues that is one of the most memorable moments in the opera (Ex. 18).

Enraged, Henry now issues a call to arms and vows revenge, but Lady Saint-John has other ideas. She advises him to flee into the wilderness and promises him that after three years he may return and marry her daughter Annette, whose betrothal to Henry she has also foreseen. At first Henry scornfully spurns this advice, but Annette enters and exercises her powers of persuasion. The issue is decided when Sir John Saint-John arrives to confiscate the Clifford family's estates on behalf of the new king, Edward of York, and to arrest Henry, who escapes with his friend Nicholas. The act concludes with a lengthy and impressive ensemble number.

Three years elapse between the events of Acts I and II, the time allotted by Lady Saint-John for Henry's exile, during which he has assumed the disguise of a shepherd (thus 'The Shepherd Lord' or 'Il rè pastore') and lived in an enchanted mountain vale. After a lengthy instrumental introduction replete with musical references to the presence of fairies, Henry sings a 'Romance' about his sufferings in the forest and his hoped-for reunion with Annette. An actual fairy dance ensues that develops the thematic intimations heard thus far (Ex. 19). Gnomes join in entertaining the enchanted Henry before both fairies and gnomes exit, leaving him alone. Annette appears before Henry as if in a vision, while the fairies sing a chorus offstage. In fact, it *is* Annette, and the following scene presents the two lovers singing a duet full of rapturous longing (Ex. 20).

The sounding of horns announces the arrival of Ladies Clifford and Saint-John, accompanied by Nicholas and some foresters, and a double chorus hails Henry's impending release from exile. Dancing peasants join in the celebration, and out of their ballet grows another chorus. The festivities are interrupted, however, by the appearance of Sir John Saint-John and his soldiers, who have come to arrest Henry in the name of King Richard III. Annette intervenes, declaring her love for Henry, but to no avail as the curtain comes down on Act II with all the characters reacting to these events in a final ensemble.

Ex. 19. *Henry Clifford*, Act II, scene i: Dance of the Fairies, bars 168–73

Ex. 20. *Henry Clifford*, Act II, scene ii: Henry and Anne's duet, bars 91–4

The action in Act III takes place only a few days later. Henry is now held captive, and after a brooding soliloquy by Sir John Saint-John, Lady Saint-John pleads for mercy on Henry's behalf. Annette and Henry thereafter sing a duet in which Henry proposes escaping together. Sir John comes upon them and declares that Henry will be spared death and allowed to marry Annette only if he renounces his faction and proclaims for Richard and the House of York. Henry must now choose between family loyalty and his love for Annette. He is leaning strongly toward the latter course when his mother appears and exhorts him to 'remember Towton!' Henry is now defiant, and Sir John calls the guards to lead him away. At precisely this moment, however, news arrives of the death of Richard III at the Battle of Bosworth.

Henry succeeds to the throne, and Sir John presents him with his sword as a token of fealty. The opera ends in grand style with a celebratory chorus.

The opera reflects the influence of Verdi not only in its historical subject matter but in the emotional directness of the music and the largely accompanimental role of the orchestra. Recurring themes lend coherence to the work, as do ostinatos and pedal notes, which facilitate transitions from scene to scene. Albéniz's inveterate Hispanism does not go completely on holiday. There are subtle modal and melismatic touches in some of the vocal writing, and very obvious references to the *zambra* in certain syncopated ostinato patterns. The minor descending tetrachord ending on a Phrygian cadence in major also figures on occasion, another cliché of Spanish music.[72]

Whatever the music's merits, the subject matter and libretto have been roundly criticized from that day to this. Gauthier described it as 'too nordic' for Albéniz's temperament and lamented its 'heaviness'.[73] Edgar Istel characterized the text (and the music) as 'tiresome', and went on to assert that the theme was 'entirely removed from Albéniz's sympathies' and that his relationship to it was 'exclusively financial'.[74] None of these assaults was aimed directly at Albéniz himself but rather at Coutts, who by these critics' lights had locked the impecunious Spaniard in a gilded cage. The untruth of this point of view is already clear, and at any rate, Albéniz was fully capable of writing effective music in styles other than the Spanish manner he usually cultivated. And Albéniz was hardly passive in the whole process of the libretto's genesis, as Coutts consulted with him regularly concerning it. The following admission by Coutts was characteristic of their collaboration, which was not one of master and slave but rather between friends:

My whole desire is, & always has been to do everything you want. I feel sure now that you are *perfectly right* about Act III. I have come to this opinion, in thinking over your suggestion. I am now sorry I did not see it in that light, *at once.* How you chaff me, when you say I have more experience of the theatre! No, my dear friend, you have more experience, & what is better, *more taste.*[75]

At all events, the above criticisms form an interesting counterpoint to the opinions of the critics and the general public who actually attended the performance.

---

[72] See Bevan, 'Albéniz', 204–7.

[73] *Albéniz*, 72.

[74] 'Isaac Albéniz', 137.

[75] Dated 9 Feb. 1894 (Bc, 'C'), in regard to *Henry Clifford*. Bevan, 'Albéniz', 105, is of the opinion that, in terms of the variety of numbers Coutts provides and the quality of the versification, the libretto of this opera is the best of the three that he and Albéniz produced.

The premiere took place under the composer's baton at the Gran Teatre del Liceu in Barcelona on 8 May 1895, and ran for five performances, to 12 May (cast in Table 7).[76] Though Coutts's libretto was in English, Italian reigned at the Liceu; thus, the production, the only one ever mounted, was sung in Italian under the title *Enrico Clifford*.[77] An anonymous critic, writing in *La vanguardia* (9 May 1895, 5–6), cited the 'applause, acclamations, and shouts of enthusiasm that still sound in our ears, mixed and confused with the capital themes [of the opera]'.[78] In particular, he praised the funeral chorus in the first act (sung for Lord Clifford), saying that it was received amidst bravos and clapping and had to be repeated. The second act, which all critics agreed was the best, received a 'genuine ovation' from the public at its conclusion, with Albéniz, Coutts (in Barcelona for the premiere), and the singers appearing on stage to receive the applause. The third act was a disappointment, a fact ascribed to an inferior performance, especially by the singer in the role of Annette. He also commented on the 'elevated tessitura' of the vocal parts (a point of criticism in other reviews), which was, for the most part, successfully negotiated by the singers and chorus.[79]

TABLE 7. *Cast of* Enrico Clifford *(Henry Clifford), premiere, Barcelona, Gran Teatre del Liceu, 8 May 1895*

Enrico Clifford	Emanuel Suagnes
Sir Giovanni Saint-John	Andrea Perellò
Annetta Saint-John	Adele Marra-Mirò
Lady Clifford	Angelica Nava
Lady Saint-John	Concetta Mas
Nicòla	Francesco Puyggener
Conductor	Isaac Albéniz

Predictably, Albéniz's orchestration has its detractors. Collet, for one, reiterates Pedrell's observation that he treats the orchestra in pianistic fashion.[80] This criticism was common in the nineteenth century and was ancillary to the debate over whether one should compose at or away from the piano. In so far as Albéniz was an inspired improviser who composed at the

[76] This original cast appeared on the title page of the piano–vocal score, published Barcelona: Juan Bta. Pujol, 1895. Bevan, 'Albéniz', 74, also reveals that Coutts claimed to have done the 'whole work of staging' himself.

[77] Translated by Giuseppe M. Arteaga Pereira. The libretto was published in both English and Italian (Barcelona: Imprenta Gutenberg, 1895).

[78] '[L]os aplausos, aclamaciones, gritos de entusiasmo que suenan todavía en nuestros oídos mezclados y confundidos con los temas capitales [de la ópera].'

[79] The authors themselves seem to have acknowledged shortcomings in the third act and later made some revisions, to which Coutts alludes in a letter to Albéniz of 26 Aug. 1897 (Bc, 'C').

[80] Collet, *Albéniz*, 124.

piano, he made a conspicuous target for those on the opposite end of this argument. Armando de la Florida (*Lo teatro català*, 11 May 1895, 4) accused Albéniz of giving preference to the orchestra over the voices. Laplane echoed this criticism when he wrote that 'the orchestra continually oppresses the voices under an excessive weight'.[81] Albéniz attempted to mitigate the force of the orchestra *vis–à–vis* the singers through dynamics. Many reviewers referred to deficiencies in the actual performance, and it is possible that the orchestra itself, and not Albéniz's instrumentation, was responsible for any imbalance (though Albéniz, as the conductor, would have to bear some responsibility for this).

J. Roca y Roca, a prominent critic in Barcelona, commented on the difficulties Albéniz faced in getting the opera produced. Here his problems were not with critics or the public, as in Madrid, but with the house management:

Never has a work been produced under worse conditions, at the end of the season and with obviously deficient elements, as if the management had tried to dismiss from above a contractual agreement; and this notwithstanding, seldom has an author emerged more vindicated from so rude a trial.[82]

He expands on this theme later in the article:

Albéniz triumphed over everything: over the distrust of certain unimaginative spirits ill-disposed to recognize the superior merits of a composer who has excelled as an outstanding concert pianist; he has triumphed over the suspicions and fears of the theatre management, which gives every aid to works like *L'amico Fritz* and *I pagliacci*, for no other reason than the nationality of a powerful Italian publisher,[83] then sits back when the work of a compatriot is tried; Albéniz, finally, has succeeded in becoming a prophet in his own country.[84]

A prophet perhaps, but still without honour. For apparently Barcelona, too, was afflicted with parochialism, but of a different kind. In Madrid Albéniz was criticized for being too 'foreign'; in Barcelona, he was evidently not foreign enough, as far as the management of the Liceu was concerned.

---

[81] *Albéniz*, 104.

[82] *La vanguardia*, 12 May 1895, 4. 'Nunca una obra se ha puesto en escena en peores condiciones, al final de la temporada y con elementos á todas luces deficientes, cual si la empresa hubiese tratado sólo de sacudirse de encima un compromiso contraído; y no obstante, pocas veces, un autor ha salido mejor librado de una prueba tan ruda.'

[83] This was a clear reference to Ricordi, which held a large financial stake in opera houses in Barcelona and Madrid and controlled to a great extent what was produced there.

[84] 'Albéniz ha triunfado de todo: de la desconfianza de ciertos espíritus rutinarios mal dispuestos á reconocer en quien ha sobresalido como aventajado concertista de piano los méritos superiores de compositor; ha triunfado de los recelos y temores de la empresa, que mientras da todas las facilidades á obras como por ejemplo, el *Amico Fritz* y *Pagliacci*, sin otro mérito positivo que el patrocinio de una poderosa casa editorial italiana, se echa atrás cuando se trata de la producción de un compatricio; Albéniz, en fin, ha logrado ser profeta en su patria.'

Such were the obstacles that not only Albéniz but also Pedrell and Bretón faced in gaining acceptance as opera composers in their native land and that hampered the development of Spanish national opera. Albéniz bore the additional burden of having been known as a pianist. This evidently caused the management of the Liceu to doubt his capacity as a composer of opera. F. Suárez Bravo (*Diario de Barcelona*, 10 May 1895, 5561–3) expresses his indignation at such prejudices by citing luminaries like Mozart and Beethoven, Liszt and Brahms as examples of successful pianist-composers. He admires the 'mastery demonstrated in the instrumentation—full, picturesque, and . . . of an extreme fineness'.[85] And he avers that the high tessitura in which Albéniz placed the voices was not the result of incompetence but rather of his desire for that particular sonority, and of his expectation of eventually finding singers equal to the task. He also delineates Albéniz's employment of leitmotif thus: 'Albéniz does not subject himself to the rigorous theory of leitmotif . . . but neither does he absolutely scorn it. There are a few characteristic themes that, handled with skill, underline situations and characters.'[86] There is thematic recurrence and some development of themes, but these cannot be considered leading motives. Bevan has identified seven themes that function in this way, but such means merely reflect an ongoing interest in formal unity evident already in the piano and orchestral works of the previous decade.[87]

As to other Wagnerisms apparent in the score, Suárez Bravo points to a 'predilection for semitones' in the melody and the music's tendency to 'modulate with extraordinary richness'. But these, he insists, are not solely characteristics of Wagner, or of any other composer, but rather of the 'artistic epoch' in which they were living. Finally, he declares Albéniz's major triumph to have been 'to write a seriously composed opera while preserving intact his personality; it bears the stamp of his style in all its scenes and this style is as individual, exclusive, and original' as that of other composers, like Grieg.[88] Other critics detected this originality in the score as well. An anonymous reviewer in *El correo catalán* (9 May 1895, 3) observed that '*Henry Clifford* . . . , in reality, does not belong to any school: it bears the stamp of originality of all the works of its author.'[89] The one aspect of the

---

[85] '[D]ominio que demuestra de la instrumentación llena, pintoresca, y . . . de una finura estremada.'

[86] 'Albéniz no se sujeta á la rigurosa teoría del *leit-motive* . . . pero tampoco la desprecia en absoluto, y hay un corto número de temas característicos que manejados con habilidad subrayan las situaciones y los caracteres.'

[87] 'Albéniz', 176–7.

[88] '[E]scribir una ópera sériamente trabajada conservando íntegra su personalidad; lleva el sello de su estilo en todas sus escenas, y este estilo es tan propio, tan exclusivo, tan original.'

[89] 'Henry Clifford . . . no pertinece en realidad a ninguna escuela: lleva el sello de originalidad de todas las obras de su autor.'

work that failed to win general approval was the libretto. The critic 'Fray Veritas' writing in *El diluvio* opined thus: 'The day that Albéniz works with a libretto that is fashioned to his manner of being and feeling, Albéniz the composer will rival Albéniz the pianist.'[90]

Though Albéniz's experience in Barcelona was not nearly as disappointing as in Madrid, it was tinged with some regret—and some resentment. A couple of years later, Albéniz wrote in his journal of the 'puerile and ignorant intransigence of which the Barcelona public is possessed (it is understood I refer to those who wish to pass for connoisseurs)'.[91] Still, being a savvy publicist, Albéniz wrote to *La vanguardia* on 23 May 1895 expressing his gratitude and affection to the press, public, Liceu management, and his colleagues for their warm reception of the work. But Coutts threw interesting light on their real experience at the Liceu when he wrote this a decade later: 'But indeed I [am] quite sympathetic with you about the terrible business of producing a work on the stage. What I saw of it at Barcelona gave me the horrors! and after I came home I was quite ill for some time!'[92]

Albéniz's zarzuela *San Antonio de la Florida* was performed at the Tívoli in Barcelona on 6 November[93] of that same year at a benefit concert for the soprano Ángeles Montilla.[94] The reaction seems to have been mixed, if the reviews are any guide. *La Renaixensa: Diari de Catalunya* (8 November 1895, 6267) stated that:

Sr. Albéniz has attempted to perform the miracle of imparting interest with his inspired music to a libretto that possesses absolutely nothing to recommend it . . . but as it is impossible to raise the dead, so here all the charming melody the music breathes is lost in futility. It is a genuine pity that the composer finds himself in a labour that under other circumstances would reward him with glory and profit.[95]

The critic 'V', writing in *La vanguardia* (7 November 1895, 3), praised the music, particularly the 'Preludio', but found that the libretto produced

[90] 12 May 1895, 11–12, entitled 'Una oleada de música' ('A surge of music'). 'El día que Albéniz dé con un libro que se amolde á su manera de ser y de sentir, Albéniz compositor será digno rival de Albéniz pianista.'

[91] *Impresiones*, ed. Franco, 41: 'pueril e ignorante intransigencia de que está poseído el público barcelonés (refiérome a los que quieren pasar por sabios, se entiende).' This entry was made in Prague on 31 Mar. 1897.

[92] Letter dated 17 Apr. 1905 (Bc, 'C').

[93] According to a letter of 9 Jan. 1895 from Sierra (Bc, 'S'), Arregui postponed a Jan. premiere of *San Antonio* in Barcelona until Albéniz himself could conduct it in Feb. But on 2 Mar. 1895 he again writes of the suspension of rehearsals, though he gives no reason.

[94] Angeles Montilla had sung the role of Lolika in the Madrid production of *La sortija* and was credited by some critics with saving the performance from being a complete disaster.

[95] 'Lo senyor Albéniz ha pretingut fer lo miracle de donar interés ab sa inspirada música á una lletra que no 's recomana gens ni mica . . . pero com es impossible ressucitar á un mort, d' aquí que tot aquell ambent melódich que respira la música se perdi inútilment, essent una verdadera llástima que 'l compositor se trobi tan sol en un travall que en altras circunstancias hauria poguit proporcionarlo gloria y profit.'

fatigue and heaviness, the result of 'repetition of situations', 'lack of popular atmosphere', 'dimensions disproportionate to a few scenes', and 'lack of novelty and interest in the plot and the text'.[96] None the less, he credited it with 'initiating a new current in this genre of works'.[97]

A well-known critic of the time, Armando de la Florida, editor of *Lo teatro català* (9 November 1895, 2), found much less to applaud: 'The work of Sr. Sierra is a disgrace. . . . The music is . . . a calamity.'[98] In his estimation, the work did not come up to the standard set by *Henry Clifford* and was, therefore, a disappointment. One reason for this lacklustre reception was that the zarzuela did not begin until after midnight. It followed a production of Bretón's opera *La Dolores*, and it was almost two in the morning before the audience could finally go home.[99]

Albéniz was not easily daunted. He determined to heed the counsel offered by friends and critics and set a libretto more in harmony with his own inclinations. In 1895 Albéniz requested and received authorization from Joaquín Dicenta (1863–1917) to use that author's drama *Juan José* (1895) as the basis for an opera. Dicenta was an anticlerical socialist whose politics must have appealed to the liberal Albéniz as much as they did to the public. A letter from Dicenta of 15 December 1895 (Bc, 'D') expressed pleasure that so 'eminent' a musician as Albéniz was converting his play into a lyric drama. But nothing came of this.[100] Sierra continued to importune him for information about a further collaboration they were evidently planning. On 18 February 1895 (Bc, 'S') he states that he will be sending Albéniz the libretto for a zarzuela in three acts. But he gets little response from Albéniz, and on 30 April asks if Albéniz is dead! He has put the new work entirely in verse (avoiding his miscalculation in *San Antonio de la Florida*), but on 11 May he asks openly if Albéniz still desires to collaborate. The next letter from Sierra in the archive dates from the end of 1900. He apparently got his answer.

In March 1895 Albéniz helped organize a series of five symphony concerts in Barcelona conducted by his friend d'Indy. These progressed chronologically from Bach onwards and concluded with a programme dedicated to modern French composers. Albéniz also helped organize a concert of contemporary Catalan music, with works by Granados, Lluís Millet, Morera, and

[96] In the original: 'repetición de situaciones', 'falta de ambiente popular', 'dimensiones desproporcionados de algunas escenas', and 'la falta de novedad é interés en el asunto y la letra'.

[97] '[I]niciada una corriente nueva en este género de obras.'

[98] 'Lo treball de 'l Sr. Sierra és una desgracia. . . . La música és . . . una calamitat.'

[99] From an unmarked clipping, Mm, Prov. M-987a.

[100] Albéniz makes reference to this ambition in a letter to Moragas, cited in Llorens Cisteró, 'Inéditas', 100.

including his own *Rapsodia española.*[101] But by now Albéniz was chiefly absorbed in his next stage work, based on another text by Coutts. This was to be his most successful opera, due in large measure to the fact that he prevailed on Coutts to craft a libretto based on a Spanish work, the celebrated novel *Pepita Jiménez* by Juan Valera. At last he had the vehicle he believed would bring him the 'glory and profit' the critics had predicted for him.

[101] See Gauthier, *Albéniz*, 88.

5

A Man of Some Importance (1896–1897)

——

JUAN VALERA Y ALCALÁ GALIANO (1824–1905) was one of the best writers Spain produced in the nineteenth century. Born to a prosperous family in Córdoba, he studied Latin, law, and philosophy as a youth and was fluent in several languages. In 1847 he was appointed ambassador to Naples, where in his spare time he studied classical and modern Greek. Later diplomatic assignments took him to Lisbon, Rio de Janeiro, Dresden, Paris, Berlin, St Petersburg, and Washington, DC. Valera was, like Albéniz, a man of cosmopolitan tastes and refinement. He was also a member of the liberal faction in Spain, and much of his writing was political in nature. All of this has a direct bearing on his first novel and most famous literary achievement, *Pepita Jiménez* (published 1874).[1]

Pepita Jiménez is an epistolary novel in which the story unfolds in a series of letters narrated after the events have taken place. It deals with the conflict between human and divine love, with the distinction between genuine religious devotional ardour on the one hand, and spiritual vanity and egoism on the other. Valera presents this conflict in minute psychological detail before resolving it in the union of the religious aspirant Don Luis de Vargas and the woman whom he falls in love with and marries, Pepita Jiménez. Unlike Mérimée's *Carmen*, this story has a happy ending. It was hardly a secret to literary critics or Valera himself, however, that the dramatic stuff of the book is meagre. Indeed, this is a plausible plot for a cheap novel: young priest-to-be seduced by village temptress, etc. What makes *Pepita Jiménez* a sublime literary achievement instead is the message that lies behind the plot, and the exquisite language Valera uses to convey that message.

Albéniz was apparently very keen to use this novel as the basis for an opera, but his precise reasons must remain in the realm of speculation, for no

---

[1] For a detailed study of the opera, its genesis, literary and musical dimensions, and performance history, see Clark, 'Spanish Music with a Universal Accent'. See also Bevan, 'Albéniz'.

correspondence or other documents have yet surfaced to confirm them. None the less, we can make some valid deductions based on existing data. The most obvious of these is that Valera's novel dealt with a region of Spain to which Albéniz was always attracted, i.e. Andalusia.[2] In this respect it was an example of *costumbrismo*, a literary style in nineteenth-century Spain that found musical expression in Albéniz's piano pieces. The setting of the novel, at least on the surface, seemed to lend itself perfectly to Albéniz's kind of musical nationalism and use of local colour. Just as Valera idealizes Pepita and the natural world around her, so Albéniz's evocations of various locales in Spain present idealized musical portraits distanced from their subjects by the admixture of non-Spanish elements. Thus, Albéniz's brand of musical nationalism was compatible with Valera's brand of literary idealism. Such an operatic subject, moreover, was consonant with public taste in the 1890s, given the phenomenal success of the veristic operas of Pietro Mascagni and Ruggero Leoncavallo. The fact that the action in *Pepita Jiménez* takes place in a rural setting on a single day during a religious festival clearly parallels the plot of *Cavalleria rusticana* (1890). Whatever the similarities to contemporary verismo, however, the novel and opera are essentially idealistic and comic in their orientation and contain no low-life characters or murders. Indeed, the idyllic tone and atmosphere of *Pepita Jiménez* more strongly resemble Mascagni's *L'amico Fritz* (1891), which is similarly labelled a 'lyric comedy' and also based on a regionalist novel (by Erckmann-Chatrian). Albéniz no doubt hoped to benefit from the popularity of the novel and the renown of its author. Of course, this posed the danger that the opera would suffer from comparison with the original and not live up to expectations. But the optimistic Albéniz was clearly unconcerned about that possibility.

There can be little doubt that Albéniz also felt a certain sympathy with Valera's philosophical orientation. We know that Albéniz was a political liberal and a free thinker in matters of religion. A letter to him from Coutts, dated 17 March 1905 (Bc, 'C'), reflects something of the composer's views:

Dearest friend: Your letter is *too good*! Very often both in conversation and in writing you travel over such a tremendous extent of ground that it would take a month to follow you! You know that I cannot agree with you in your *conclusions*. I refuse to deny a Mystery in the Universe; & why not call that mystery God, just as well as any other name? Is there any advantage in calling it x or y or z? Nor do I accept Socialism as a *practical* solution of life. The abolition of capital is an unattainable dream. But of course in the sense of love (that is, of true brotherhood) I agree; though I don't believe it will ever come to pass.

---

[2] Specifically, near Córdoba, where Valera grew up, an area that aroused Albéniz's romantic imagination.

Although Albéniz's letter to Coutts has been lost, he recorded corroborating sentiments in his diary, and the entries make for fascinating reading. On 21 February 1901, he made the following assertion:

Those who search for God, those who discuss him, seem to me like those who wish to find a three-legged cat; they forget that it has four, and that God does not exist except in the here and now, that is to say while we live, think, and express ourselves; thus we are God, and everything else is songs!!![3]

Another entry on this same date states the matter unequivocally: 'Man has invented God solely and exclusively out of fear of death.'[4]

In a letter of 17 March 1905 (Bc, 'C'), Coutts's rebuttal again points towards Albéniz's religious scepticism:

But as to the Old Testament and the Christ—it always seems to me that you somewhat fail in imaginative power, when you speak of them. Imagine the awful state of the world when the Hebrews first seized the idea of One God. That idea is stale to us, but to their countrymen it was a revelation. So in regard to Jesus—imagine what a fearful social condition of things he strove to break down. Remember also that it is only from imperfect chronicles that we know anything either of the Hebrews or of the Christ. You must not judge either as if everything was told correctly.

Though Albéniz's doubts about religion far exceeded those of Valera, the two shared in common a basically optimistic outlook, a benign view of humanity, and a passionate love of life.

A more mundane but equally intriguing possibility has to do with Albéniz's—and Coutts's—attitude towards women. There might have been some element of attraction to the character of Pepita, something about her that inspired his imagination. She is far more prominent in the opera than in the novel, as virtually all of Don Luis's 'dark night of the soul', which he expresses in his letters, is expunged from the libretto and we no longer apprehend the story through him. She becomes the central dramatic and musical presence. In a letter to Albéniz dated 6 February 1901,[5] Coutts poses this question:

What you say amounts to this:—that women have a violent egotism of the body; men (?some men) have the same of the mind. Which is best? Which ought to prevail? Where did you learn your theory of women. That they are mere children; and that we are fools to treat them otherwise?

---

[3] Mm, car. 4. As stated in the Introduction, all quotations from his diary and letters are unedited, unless taken from an edited source. 'Los que buscan á Dios, los que le discuten, me hacen al efecto de los que quieren encontrar tres pies al gato; olvidan que tiene cuatro, y que Dios no existe sino actualmente, es decir mientras vivimos, pensamos, y nos expresamos; entonces *somos* Dios, todo lo demas son canciones!!!'

[4] Ibid. 'El hombre ha inventado á Dios, única y esclusivamente por miedo á la muerte.'

[5] Mm, 10.275.

This view of gender exhibits a striking resonance with the psychology and imagery of *Pepita Jiménez*. Don Luis has a powerful 'egotism of the mind'. In fact, the essence of his problem is intellectual and spiritual vanity. Pepita is the ideal of feminine beauty who is always immaculately attired and groomed. Her physical radiance and inner, childlike purity (which is *not* to say *naïveté*), as well as her passion for Don Luis, make her irresistible to him and ultimately 'prevail' over his egotism. Perhaps here was the answer to Coutts's question. In this sense, of course, Pepita possesses power over Don Luis and is able to influence him accordingly. She is not a child, and neither is Don Luis able to get away with treating her like one. Far from contradicting his view of women, however, this probably made her all the more intriguing a character to Albéniz. Bevan astutely observes, moreover, that in all three of the Coutts–Albéniz operas a central theme emerges relative to women, whether it is Annette, Pepita, or Elaine: 'The power of a woman's will to vanquish a man's dedication to duty.'[6] Although this may run counter to Coutts's philosophy as expressed in his writings, e.g. *The Marriage Ring* and *The Training of the Instinct of Love*, it fits hand-in-glove with his daily experience of living with Nellie, of whose interference with his ability to work he frequently complained in his letters to Albéniz (more on this in Chapters 6 and 7).

Even as he was attracted to the character of Pepita, Albéniz may have actually identified personally with Don Luis. If he had indeed spent a short time in a Benedictine monastery in Salamanca when he was 20, and even contemplated becoming a monk, he may have seen something of his own past in the story of Don Luis. (Even if he did not actually do this, that he spun the yarn says something about his aspirations and state of mind at that time in his life.) Of course, in Albéniz's case marriage followed three years later, to someone he did not know at the time he 'renounced' his 'vocation'. Coutts, too, may have seen something of himself in this story. Pepita inherits a fortune upon the death of her wealthy but elderly moneylender husband, just as Coutts had inherited the banking fortune of his family.[7]

After gaining Coutts's approval of the project, Albéniz got in touch with Juan Valera. Their correspondence has survived and sheds a good deal of light on the genesis of the work.[8] Valera's initial response was highly

---

[6] 'Albéniz', 73.

[7] Bevan, ibid. 68, makes this point about Coutts.

[8] Mm, 10.315–21. The correspondence has been transcribed and discussed in Pilar Aparicia, ' "Pepita Jiménez", correspondencia Valera–Albéniz', in Franco (ed.), *Albéniz y su tiempo*, 80–100 (reprint of an article in the *Boletín de la Real Academia Española*, 1975). Count Morphy served as the go-between and actually initiated the contact. At the same time, he expressed his doubts about this project, complaining that Albéniz would not 'listen to the voice of experience and affection' (Bc, 'A', undated).

negative. In a letter from Vienna of 12 June 1895 to Albéniz's friend Count Morphy, Valera considers the composer's proposal as follows:

I understand that in the libretto everything would have to be altered to create something dramatic, and so it might as well be called *Ramona González* as *Pepita Jiménez*. My book is psychological, ascetic, and mystical, though in order to make fun of false asceticism and misguided mysticism; my book is hardly a novel, and suited neither to comedy, drama, zarzuela, nor to opera. Such is my frank opinion and my firm conviction. If Mozart were to set *Pepita Jiménez* to music, Mozart would create a fiasco.[9]

Valera goes on to make an interesting comparison of the project with Bizet's opera:

Carmen, it cannot be denied, is a pretty novel by Mérimée; and as an opera I am unable to tolerate it, influencing me as it does so perversely in spirit that the novel repulses me and I can never read it again. And in *Carmen* there is ten times more dramatic action than in *Pepita Jiménez*.[10]

In one of his more colourful passages, he describes the project thus: 'For me, proposing an opera on *Pepita Jiménez* is like proposing to prepare me a partridge with custard. . . . Albéniz, I feel, would ruin his custard, and I my partridge.'[11]

The prospect that Valera would deny Albéniz permission to use his novel was distressing news to Coutts (Albéniz conveyed to him the letter Valera sent to Morphy), who wrote the following, fourteen days after Valera's missive:

My dear Albéniz: I return the wire and letter. As to the latter, if Valera really refuses to allow us the use of his book, it is a very serious matter for us, and you should, by all means, do everything possible to secure his consent; going, as you say, to Vienna, yourself, if necessary. I shall be very anxious until this is settled. He ought to know that you are not likely to accept a poor libretto (even from me, I hope!) and how curiously ignorant he is of the poetry of his own creation. I have conceived the idea from reading *Doña Luz* that *Pepita* is his greatest work and that he will never write one to equal it. He does not seem to know the power of it, himself.

---

[9] '[Y]o entiendo que en el libretto sería menester desnaturalizarlo todo para que tuviese algo de dramático, y entonces lo mismo de llamarla *Ramona González* que *Pepita Jiménez*. Tal como es mi libro, psicológico, ascético y místico aunque sea para burlarse algo del falso ascetismo y del misticismo mal fundado, mi libro apenas es novela, y mucho menos vale para comedia, para drama, para zarzuela ni para ópera. Tal es mi franca opinión y mi firme convencimiento. Si Mozart pusiese en música *Pepita Jiménez*, Mozart haría fiasco.'

[10] 'Carmen, ¿cómo negarlo?, es una linda novela de Mérimée; y en ópera yo no la puedo aguantar, influyendo asimismo tan perversamente en mi espíritu que ya me repugna la novela y no he de volver jamás a leerla. Y eso que en *Carmen* hay diez veces más acción dramática que en *Pepita Jiménez*.'

[11] 'Para mi, proponerme una ópera de *Pepita Jiménez* es como si me propusiera guisarme una perdiz con natillas. . . . Albéniz, en mi sentir, estragaría sus *natillas* y yo mi perdiz.'

He says even if Mozart wrote an opera on it, it would be a fiasco! Is this modesty or insensibility?[12]

The correspondence between Valera and Albéniz continued throughout the summer of 1895. The author wrote to the composer on 30 July and expressed his doubts about the opera:

Pepita Jiménez is a nice novel . . . but its plot is neither dramatic nor comic, nor suited for setting to music. The libretto, by its able and ingenious author, will either lose all its grace or distort the mother work. Of course, despite what I said, if you compose, as I hope, excellent and inspired music for the libretto of *Pepita Jiménez*, the work will be applauded; but it will be in spite of my work and that of the librettist, who, without the defence of the beautiful music, would merit a hiss.[13]

He concedes that the story, dealing as it does with things Andalusian, might find an audience in London; but in Spain, deprived as the opera would have to be of its 'mystic, ascetic, and psychological discourses', the tale of a seminarian abandoning his vocation and marrying would descend to vulgarity. The strength of his novel, he avers, lies in its style and its theological subtleties, in imitation of 'our beautiful books of devotion, etc.', which would be lost in translation to the operatic medium. Even Count Morphy got in on the act, warning Albéniz against the idea of using *Pepita Jiménez* for an opera.[14] Their objections would prove remarkably prophetic.

None the less, Valera had faith in Albéniz's talent and expressed the desire to provide him with a libretto. In almost all of his letters to Albéniz, he presents an alternative that is clearly dear to his heart. Some years before, he had written a zarzuela libretto for Emilio Arrieta, who, though he demanded many changes in the text, never set it to music. It was entitled *Lo mejor del tesoro* ('The best of the treasure') and was based on one of the tales from *A Thousand and One Nights*. With the indefatigability of a Cato, Valera kept pressing this argument home. Albéniz seems never to have warmed to the idea, however. Instead, he became interested in another of Valera's works, *El maestro Raimundico*. According to Pilar Aparicia, this work contains no more dramatic interest than *Pepita Jiménez* and could hardly have been an attractive prospect to Valera.[15] Later, in the penultimate letter in their correspondence, written on 15 March 1898, Valera politely parried this

[12] Mm, 10.270.

[13] '*Pepita Jiménez* será bonita novela . . . pero no es su asunto ni dramático, ni cómico, ni para puesto en música. El libretto, por hábil e ingenioso que sea quien lo componga, o perderá toda su gracia, o desnaturalizará la obra madre. Claro está que si, apesar de lo dicho, Vd. pone, como yo lo espero, una música excelente e inspirada al libretto de *Pepita Jiménez*, la ópera será aplaudida, pero lo será apesar mío y apesar del libretista, que sin la buena música, que nos defenderá, mereceríamos una silba.'

[14] Letter to Albéniz of 21 May 1895 from Madrid, signed 'Abraham' (Bc, 'A').

[15] 'Correspondencia', Franco (ed.), *Albéniz y su tiempo*, 86.

thrust by suggesting not only, yet again, *Lo mejor del tesoro* but also a work entitled *Asclepigenia*. This story was based on a supposedly historical episode dealing with a philosopher's daughter who befriends Proclus, regarded by Valera as 'one of the most glorious and famous Neoplatonic philosophers'.

Clearly, Albéniz the nationalist and Valera the classicist operated on different wavelengths when it came to subject matter. Albéniz wanted material dealing with Spain, material that he could adorn with his particular brand of local colour. But in the same letter of 15 March, Valera had this to say about that:

In the first place, Andalusian stories of majos, majas, bullfighters, Gypsies, etc., are already so worn out, overdone, and ubiquitous, that they lack any novelty and frequently bore the public. There are other stories that would be more entertaining and novel, and that would lend themselves to a music more beautiful and with fewer reminiscences of *jotas, fandangos*, and *boleros*, of which in Spain we are already tired.[16]

All of this is not to suggest that Valera was never reconciled to the opera of Coutts and Albéniz. In a letter of 7 August 1895, he declares: 'I note with pleasure, by your letter of the 4th, that the opera *Pepita Jiménez* will see light this coming season in no less a venue than the Royal Theatre of this city and court',[17] referring to a production that never came off. He even makes this surprising concession:

Moreover, as I am not infallible, and as the taste of the public, which I know nothing about, is at the heart of my criticism, it could well be that the public will enjoy the story and the libretto, contrary to my opinion. With respect to *Lo mejor del tesoro*, the opposite could occur.[18]

Two years later, in a letter of 27 July 1897, he exulted in the recent success of *Pepita Jiménez* in Prague: 'I recently received a telegram signed by Sr. Angelo Neumann, who gives me pleasant news of the brilliant success that *Pepita Jiménez* has had in Prague. Of that I am happy in spirit, and I give to you the most cordial congratulations.'[19] He concluded the letter with a wish for the

---

[16] 'Es la primera que los asuntos andaluces de majos, majas, toreros, gitanos, etc., están ya tan manoseados y tan traídos y llevados por todo el mundo, que carecen de novedad y son muy ocasionados a fastidiar a la gente. Otros asuntos hay, que serían más divertidos y nuevos, y que se prestarían a una música mas peregrina y con menos reminiscencias de jotas, fandangos y boleros, de que en España estamos ya ahitos.'

[17] 'Veo con gusto, por la carta de Vd. del 4, que Pepita Jiménez, ópera, está próxima a salir a luz y nada menos que en el teatro Real de esta villa y corte.'

[18] 'Además, como yo no soy infalible y como por cima de mi crítica está el gusto del público que desconozco, bien puede ser que el público guste del asunto y del libreto, contra mi opinión. Respecto a *Lo mejor del tesoro* puede ocurrir lo contrario.'

[19] 'Últimamente ha llegado a mi poder un telegrama, firmado por el Sr. Angelo Neumann, el cual me da la agradable noticia del brillante buen éxito que ha tenido en Praga la ópera Pepita Jiménez. De ello me alegro yo en el alma y doy a Vd. la más cordial enhorabuena.'

continued success of the opera, but only after having expressed once again his misgivings about its dramatic merits.

Though the correspondence between Valera and Albéniz never bore any fruit in terms of actual professional collaboration, it does establish beyond doubt two facts. One, that Valera did approve, if at times grudgingly, Albéniz's proposal to write an opera on the novel. There can be no valid legal objection to the opera on that basis, as the author's daughter Carmen later initially claimed in attempting to obstruct future performances of it.[20] Second, that Albéniz had a much freer hand in choosing librettos and librettists than one is led to believe in reading accounts of his 'slavery' to Coutts as a result of the 'pact of Faust'.

Now that Valera had removed any real obstacles from the path of Albéniz and Coutts, work proceeded rapidly. Coutts completed the libretto well before September of 1895, when the surviving manuscript of the score is dated.[21] When he began it, however, is not certain. A letter from Coutts to Albéniz dated 3 December 1894 makes reference to a libretto apparently in the works:

I will send you the libretto, *if you like*, as soon as it comes from the typewriters. *But* I should have much preferred to read it to you *first*. Because the first impression is important, and you might not understand from reading it yourself, how I meant it to go. Besides, there are many things I have left for discussion with you, which it would take too long to write, but which we could speak of, as I went along, if I read it to you. Again, why do you want the book *in English*? I want you to study it in *Spanish*. Leave the English to me! but tell me all about the Spanish.

This is clearly a reference to their new opera. Albéniz and Coutts had been hatching this idea several months before they finally notified Valera of their intentions, thus presenting him with a *fait accompli*. This accounts for Coutts's tone of alarm in his letter to Albéniz of 26 June 1895, for if Valera disallowed their use of his novel, all of Coutts's work would have been in vain.[22]

Whenever the libretto was written, Coutts's transformation of the novel confirmed many of Valera's fears. He jettisoned all of Don Luis's high-flown

---

[20] See Ch. 8 for more on this.

[21] Albéniz signed and dated the autograph of the orchestral score of *Pepita Jiménez* 'Paris Setiembre de 1895' (Bc, M981). It bears the designation 'Comedia Lírica en un acto y dos Cuadros'. An undated holograph of the 'Intermezzo' was given by Rosina to Manuel de Falla and is now in the Archivo Manuel de Falla in Granada.

[22] Bevan, 'Albéniz,' 66, observes that 'Spanish laws protecting intellectual property date from 1834, and in 1879 translation was assimilated into author's rights. The United Kingdom made a bilateral copyright agreement with Spain in 1857.' With his background, Coutts undoubtedly understood the potential legal ramifications of what they had done.

mystical soliloquizing, and not a trace of Valera's language or subtle social and spiritual commentary remains. Instead, Coutts begins the story *in medias res*, just before the climactic encounter between Don Luis and Pepita, by which point in the novel Don Luis's correspondence has ceased and the Dean is relating the conclusion of the tale. He clearly produced a text leaving much to be desired in dramatic action and psychological interest. As in *Henry Clifford* and *Merlin*, there is a sense of dramatic and musical continuity in the beginning followed by a series of numbers that retards the action and conduces to anticlimax. But before we blame Coutts exclusively for this, we must remember that the writing of the libretto, as with *Henry Clifford*, was a collaborative process. If Albéniz had felt that the book was seriously flawed, before it premiered or at any time during its career, he could easily have initiated changes. But this he did not do. Though he began an extensive reorchestration of the opera in 1899,[23] the structure of the work was left untouched, despite the fact that he recognized its lack of dramatic interest. In a letter to Rosina after the successful production in Prague, he shared these insights into the libretto:

Pepita will undoubtedly have a long, but precarious, career; the text does not excite interest except in the final scene, and one has to know the novel to understand what happens in the first act; therefore, I believe that it is essentially a work for Spain and Latin America. Thanks to the originality and beauty of the music, it will be given in German theatres, but without gaining popularity.[24]

Coutts made the perhaps unavoidable decision to telescope and condense what action there was in the novel into the space of a few hours rather than the many weeks that elapsed in the original. His structuring of the libretto thus reflects an interest in preserving the three unities of time, place, and action. The setting for the climax is the Festival of the Cross, which takes place in the novel on 3 May (as the Day of the Cross) and is referred to by Don Luis in his letter to the Dean dated the following day.[25]

---

[23] The autograph of the revision is bound in two volumes (one act per volume). The first is signed and dated 'Nice Octobre 1903', and the second, 'Nice 15 Janvier 1904' (Bc, M982). It was published in Leipzig: Breitkopf und Härtel, 1904. The firm of Max Eschig in Paris retains a copy of the printed 1904 orchestral score with corrections in Albéniz's own hand, signed by the composer and dated 'Westende Bains (Belgique) 23 Aout 1904'.

[24] 27 June 1897 (Mm, 10.374). 'Pepita tendra indudablemente larga, pero precaria carrera; el libro no logra interesar mas que en la ultima escena, y hay que conocer la Novela para entender lo que en el primer acto sucede; por esto, creo, que es obra esencialmente para España y América Española, y gracias a la originalidad y belleza de la musica se daran en los teatros Alemanes, pero sin lograr popularidad.'

[25] This represents a departure from the original, however, in that Valera centred the climax of the story around the Feast of St John, on 24 June. The activities on 3 May were of minor importance, and it is not clear why Coutts chose to make this change, unless he deemed it more suitable or appealing theatrically.

The lack of action in the story is not the only liability in the libretto. Coutts's poetry, though containing some fine passages, is often stilted and contrived. Couplets such as 'To me he seemed so ample | An apostolic sample' seemed to Ernest Newman to 'read like a bad translation from some foreign tongue'.[26] It is perhaps fortunate that the work was never done in English[27] but in Italian, German, and French only. There were two Italian translations, one by Angelo Bignotti for the premiere,[28] and one by Carlo M. A. Galateri for the two-act revision executed in 1896 and published in 1897 (Leipzig: Breitkopf und Härtel). Both of these are free translations of Coutts's text with no changes in its content or structure. The same can be said of the German translation by Oskar Berggruen. The French translation by Maurice Kufferath, used for the Brussels production and published separately in 1905 (Leipzig: Breitkopf und Härtel), makes a useful change, one that ties up an otherwise conspicuously loose thread. In Act II he replaces a short and unimportant passage of dialogue between Antoñona (Pepita's maidservant) and Pepita with text informing Pepita that Don Luis has wounded the wicked Count in a duel. He also renames the Festival of the Cross the Festival of the Infants, and at the end of the opera Don Pedro (Don Luis's father) appears with Antoñona to share in her exultation. None of these changes appears in any of the other translations, however.

Joseph de Marliave, a friend of Albéniz, made a new French translation for the 1923 edition of the piano–vocal score (Paris: Max Eschig). He also made several changes in the text, which he claimed were sanctioned by the composer himself. These alterations, however, were relatively slight. In Act I, Don Luis is accused by the Count of being Pepita's lover. In Act II, the scheming Antoñona alludes to the duel fought between the Count and Don Luis without actually telling Pepita. Finally, in the last scene Pepita intends to commit suicide by drinking the contents of a vial, but Don Luis prevents this and thus saves her. This may have provided the unfortunate inspiration for Pablo Sorozábal's drastic reworking of the libretto for the 1964 Madrid production (discussed in Chapter 8), in which Pepita commits suicide by actually drinking the poison, thus converting the work from a comedy to a tragedy.

One question remains, however, and that concerns the historical period during which the action is supposedly taking place. The novel itself leads one

[26] 'Albéniz and his "Merlin"', *New Witness* (London, 20 Sept. 1917), 495–6. Cited in Bevan, 'Albéniz', 99.

[27] A recent recording of selections from the opera featuring Josep Pons conducting the chamber orchestra of the Teatre Lliure (Harmonia Mundi CD HMC 901537, 1995, liner notes by Jacinto Torres), however, does preserve the English.

[28] Libretto published separately in Barcelona by Juan Bta. Pujol, 1896.

to assume that the events narrated in the papers 'found' by the author took place during the nineteenth century, though it is never stated explicitly. The version by Bignotti, published separately for the premiere, indicates that the 'época' is the early nineteenth century. The 1923 piano–vocal score published by Eschig, however, places the action in the eighteenth century (as did the Paris production of that year). None of the versions published in Leipzig specifies a time period. Because nothing in the libretto of *Pepita Jiménez* refers to events in the world beyond the village, the resulting sense of timelessness may have rendered unimportant, in the opinion of Breitkopf und Härtel, the issue of exact historical context.

The outstanding musical characteristic of the opera *Pepita Jiménez* is the tightly knit organization of the thematic material. Specifically, Albéniz adapted the technique of leitmotif to his own purposes, creating something that falls in between Wagnerian and Italian practice. That is to say that, although Albéniz readily assigns musical ideas to persons, locales, and emotional states, these ideas are most often in the form not of motives but rather of themes. Albéniz achieves a remarkable balance between unity and variety through the repetition and variation of themes, by the generation of new themes from previously stated material, and by the motivic interrelationship among themes. But he does not weave them into a complex matrix of motivic ideas such as one finds, for instance, in *Die Götterdämmerung*, an opera Albéniz admired. Yet their recurrence is far more frequent—and in some cases seemingly more arbitrary—than one would find in any opera by Puccini, much less by Verdi.

The vocal style is often declamatory, and the recitative resembles that of Massenet in its use of repeated notes.[29] Arias and other separable vocal numbers predominate only in the second act, whereas the first places a premium on continuity and the sections flow into one another without pause. Thus, as in Wagner, the musical interest usually resides in the orchestra, not the voices. But the instrumental forces are not unusually large in the 1896 version of the orchestration, which calls for piccolo, two flutes, two oboes, cor anglais, two B♭ clarinets, bass clarinet, two bassoons, contrabassoon, two F horns, two E♭ horns, two trumpets, three trombones, tuba, timpani, bass drum, cymbals, harp, and strings. All of this further forbids too ready a comparison between *Pepita Jiménez* and *Cavalleria rusticana*, which was a reaction against Wagnerism and aimed at sustained emotional intensity

---

[29] Especially that composer's verismo-style opera *La Navarraise* (1894), a copy of which Albéniz had in his own library (now in the Bc, M994) and in which the composer wrote a dedication to Albéniz. Other points of comparison with Massenet's operas include the use of an epistolary novel (*Werther*) as well as an interest in female characters and the conflict between sacred and profane love (*Manon*).

in long lyrical passages rather than textual clarity through the renunciation of fioritura and subordination of the voice to the orchestra. What follows is a summary of the action in the two-act revision of the opera, executed by the authors in 1896 after its Barcelona premiere as an opera in one act.

Act I takes place in Pepita's garden, where a series of conversations gives the audience some background on a story that, outside Spain, would probably have been unfamiliar. In the manner of Puccini in *La Bohème*, Albéniz provides no prelude or overture, save a few measures in which a theme is briefly presented, one that will not reappear until the Prelude to Act II.[30] This theme possesses a pastoral character, the result of colourful added-note sonorities and an open-fifth 'drone' in the bass, on the dominant. Its association with the garden is thus appropriate (Ex. 21).

Ex. 21. *Pepita Jiménez*, Act I: 'Garden' theme, bars 4–7

Don Pedro and Antoñona enter the garden. The elderly Don Pedro seeks the hand of Pepita in marriage and does not yet realize that Pepita has fallen in love with his son Don Luis, who secretly loves her in return. Accompanying their conversation is a running arpeggiation, pianistic in character, that of itself possesses little interest but which serves as an excellent 'backdrop' for their dialogue. Its neutral quality has the added advantage of not competing for attention with the more prepossessing themes with which it alternates. Albéniz uses it as a kind of refrain, and it recurs throughout Act I, providing not only contrast but unity.

When Antoñona reveals to Don Pedro that Pepita loves his son, Don Luis's theme first appears. Its upward thrust in halting dotted rhythms suggests the tentativeness of his religious aspirations. The subsequent earthward flow of the melodic contour portends the eventual attenuation of struggle between sacred and profane. In purely musical terms, it is the logical

---

[30] In fact, Albéniz did begin a prelude to the opera but never finished it. The MS is in the Mm, Lligall 6.

Ex. 22. *Pepita Jiménez*, Act I: Don Luis's theme, bars 65–9

direction of resolution in the Phrygian mode. Rhythmically as well as mod-
ally this theme has its roots in Andalusian folk music with what amounts to a
hemiola metre of alternating 3/4 and 6/8 (accomplished through ties over
the bar) in the right hand with a consistent 6/8 metre in the left. The general
type is *malagueña* (Ex. 22).

After a brief return of the 'Conversation' theme, Antoñona declares
Don Luis's spiritual pretensions mere 'humbug' and berates his plan to
run away from his feelings and return immediately to the seminary. She
goes on, then, to explain how the two fell in love, during an excursion in
the countryside. The music associated with Antoñona here endows her with
a cleverness central to the novel but unapparent in the libretto. Albéniz
assigns to this conniving busybody the busiest of all musical textures, a
four-voice fugato, complete with countersubject, tonal answers, and a
lengthy episode. The comic seriousness of her scheming is conveyed in the
key of C♯ minor, while the theme itself evokes the *malagueña* in its rhythm,
arabesque contour, and downward skipping thirds. The employment of a
folk-dance melody in the context of a learned fugue establishes her character
as a clever peasant. Albéniz's fascination with counterpoint is no mystery,
considering his studies in this subject with d'Indy at the Schola Cantorum
(Ex. 23).

When Don Pedro explains to Antoñona his instruction of Don Luis in the
gentlemanly arts of riding and fencing, Albéniz employs a theme that in its
rhythm and contour strongly suggests the graceful, prancing movements of a
horse. The patina of elegance is further enhanced by a trill on the third beat.
This material signifies not so much Don Pedro himself as the worldliness
he represents and can be labelled the 'Caballero' theme (Ex. 24). This
'Caballero' theme leads to the conclusion of the duet and Don Pedro's
gracious acceptance of Pepita's preference for Don Luis. He is quickly
reconciled to their relationship and will seek Pepita now as a 'daughter'
and not a wife. Antoñona extracts his promise to assist in her stratagem to
bring the two together, then leaves just as Don Luis arrives to inform Don

Ex. 23. *Pepita Jiménez*, Act I: Antoñona's theme, bars 163–73

Pedro of his intention to return to the seminary. The musical setting is chordal, with fleeting allusions to the 'Caballero' theme, as Don Pedro intimates what *he* would do if he were in Don Luis's position. But their conversation is cut short by the appearance of Pepita in the company of the Vicar and the disreputable Count Genazahar.

   Perhaps the most beautiful theme of the opera accompanies the entrance of Pepita, who chats briefly with Don Luis. The graceful, curvilinear contour, elegant length, even rhythms, and major key of her theme evoke the serene feminine charm of the young widow who has captured Don Luis's heart (Ex. 25). The Count, however, is jealous of Don Luis and ridicules him. The music associated with the Count is essentially monorhythmic,

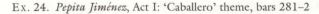

Ex. 24. *Pepita Jiménez*, Act I: 'Caballero' theme, bars 281–2

lending his character a two-dimensional quality. In addition, Albéniz employs an open-fifth drone in the bass, making the theme not only rhythmically but harmonically static, thus portraying the Count as an annoying bore. The Count's theme dominates the encounter between him and the Vicar.

A restatement of Don Luis's passionate theme precedes a lengthy duet between Pepita and the Vicar. Pepita is distraught at her condition of seemingly unrequited and hopeless love and expresses her emotion to the Vicar in a memorable passage whose chromatic inflections give it an Andalusian flavour (Ex. 26). But the Vicar merely enjoins her to calm down, and the following eleven bars of B♭ pedal convey a sense of stability as a counterpoise to her emotional tumult. He then proceeds to assuage her grief with sage spiritual counsel. The long note values and upward leap of a sixth in bar two of his theme establish a character of high-minded assurance.

Pepita submits to the Vicar's exhortation to forsake Don Luis, and their duet comes to a close as Antoñona enters, to her own theme, still berating Don Luis to herself. When Pepita informs her of the Vicar's counsel, she expresses astonishment to music that is rhythmically busy and insistent. Don Luis now enters to take his leave of Pepita. The rhythms and phrasing of this 'Farewell' section are even and symmetrical, suggesting a veneer of calm and order over the underlying distress. A crucial juncture is reached as Pepita surrenders to the situation and exits sadly, leaving Don Luis to wallow in shame. This represents the nadir of the lovers' fortunes and is expressed musically by a theme that makes its most significant appearance at the end of the second act, at the point of their being brought together through Antoñona's intervention. The entry of this 'Union' theme is unusual for the

Ex. 25. *Pepita Jiménez*, Act I: Pepita's theme, bars 346–61

(Enter Pepita from garden R.C. with roses, Vicar and Count)

opera—and therefore significant—in that it appears first in the voice (Pepita) and is then taken up by the orchestra ten bars later (Ex. 27).

Antoñona, ever the schemer, returns to upbraid the young man for the pain he is causing Pepita. She persuades him to visit the ailing Pepita that evening, in order to give her a private farewell. She then tells Don Luis that the Count is attempting to extort marriage from Pepita, by promising to forgive a debt she owes him only if she will be his wife. This, of course, arouses the seminarian's jealous rage, though he has not yet confessed his love for Pepita to anyone, including himself. The Count now enters with two officers, and his mocking of Pepita is accompanied by staccato semiquavers, which peck away in derision. Don Luis overhears this slander and comes to

Ex. 26. *Pepita Jiménez*, Act I: 'Pepita's Lament', bars 537–40

Pepita's defence, relating her history as the widow of Gumersindo, a wealthy but elderly gentleman who died after only three years of marriage. The act concludes with a recapitulation of the themes associated with Don Luis and Pepita as the Count and Don Luis stride off to fight a duel, which the audience never sees.

Unlike the first act, the second commences with a Prelude, which consists of two sections. The first section is a recapitulation of the 'Garden' theme, followed by a beautiful melody (which one reviewer found reminiscent of Puccini), high in the violins, accompanied by the 'Conversation' theme. The second section of the Prelude is in a faster, dance-like tempo and contains six distinct thematic ideas or segments. Two of these segments will appear later in the act as independent motives with their own dramatic associations.

The setting of Act II, scene i, is still Pepita's garden, as the villagers prepare to celebrate the Festival of the Cross. Antoñona is the first character to appear, and she holds the stage alone, deploring the general situation, until Pepita makes her entrance. What follows is one of the most celebrated numbers of the entire opera, Pepita's famous 'Romance', which is suggestive of *cante jondo* in its modal and rhythmic properties and especially in her initial vocalization on 'Heigh-ho', which mimics the 'ay' of the opening

Ex. 27. *Pepita Jiménez*, Act I: 'Union' theme, bars 982–9

salida in many *jondo* genres (e.g. *soleares* and *siguiriyas*).[31] The instrumental introduction evokes the chordal textures and *falsetas* characteristic of the guitar. We should know that Pepita is not a Gypsy or a *flamenquista*. The references to *cante jondo* are used simply as a vehicle for creating atmosphere and expressing profound emotion (Ex. 28).

The ensuing section presents the chorus, which sings of Pepita's virtues then prepares for the entrance of the children who are about to sing a song in praise of the infant Jesus. This villancico, the 'Children's Hymn to the Infant

---

[31] 'Yo canto por soleares' from Act II of Manuel de Falla's opera *La vida breve* provides another example of this vocalization on 'ay'.

Ex. 28. *Pepita Jiménez*, Act II, scene i: Pepita's 'Romance', bars 264–72

Jesus', counts among the most charming of Albéniz's compositions by virtue of its fetching tune, simple homophonic texture, a cappella setting (the orchestra merely provides interjections between verses), and use of bocca chiusa (hummed) passages (Ex. 29). The festival continues with a ballet danced by the children. This dance is clearly derived from the Prelude and is suggestive once again of the *malagueña* in its quick triple metre, hemiola, syncopations, and use of the augmented-second interval (Ex. 30). Towards the end of the dance Pepita faints, accompanied by a delirious succession of

Ex. 29. *Pepita Jiménez*, Act II, scene i: 'Children's Hymn to the Infant Jesus', bars 471–8

Ex. 30. *Pepita Jiménez*, Act II, scene i: Children's Ballet, bars 567–74

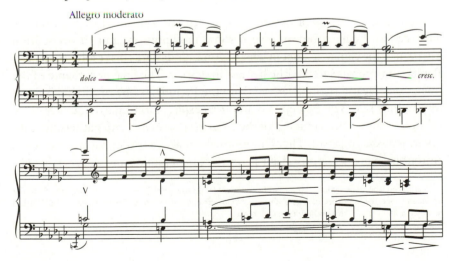

Ex. 31. *Pepita Jiménez*, Act II: Intermezzo, bars 791–4

triplets; she finally regains her composure at the close of scene i. The only number from this opera ever to be performed separately was the Inter-mezzo,[32] which occurs between scenes i and ii. Its triple metre and use of the descending minor tetrachord again evoke the *malagueña*. It is especially notable for its structure, i.e. a theme with four variations in which the accompaniment rather than the melody is subjected to change. This is reminiscent of the 'changing-background technique' of Glinka and Rimsky-Korsakov.[33] Whether Albéniz borrowed the idea from the Russians or developed it independently is unknown (Ex. 31).

Scene ii takes place in Pepita's room, which is decorated with devotional objects and paintings of saints. Don Luis enters and sings his sole aria. It begins with an instrumental introduction, which separates it from the Inter-mezzo. The text of the aria is divided into four strophes, each of which receives a different setting. The first strophe reiterates the 'Union' theme, while the remaining three strophes express Don Luis's spiritual disquiet in their rhythmic agitation. Don Luis's aria closes with a return of the Inter-mezzo theme, which serves as a bridge into Pepita's aria.

Pepita's aria consists of two themes, which are connected by a transition. The second theme is repeated with some modification, and this repetition introduces the climactic duet in which Don Luis declares his resolve to depart. Pepita now prepares to breathe her last in despair. The final new theme of the opera, the 'Death' theme, derived from the Prelude, is one of Albéniz's finest inspirations (Ex. 32). As Pepita is about to expire, Don Luis declares his love for her, to the accompaniment of the Intermezzo theme, and gathers her into his arms as she collapses. The 'Union' theme makes a triumphal appearance as Antoñona expresses approval at the result of her cunning and the curtain falls.

---

[32] It has no label in the score. Enrique Arbós conducted it during a 1917 concert of the Orquesta Sinfónica in Madrid. See the appendix in Víctor Espinós, *El maestro Arbós* (Madrid: Espasa-Calpe, 1942). Arbós recorded a 78 of it with this orchestra for Columbia.

[33] Specifically, Glinka's Second Spanish Overture (originally entitled *Recuerdos de Castilla* and composed in Warsaw in 1848, after his lengthy sojourn in Spain), and Rimsky-Korsakov's *Capriccio espagnol*, Op. 34 (1887).

Ex. 32. *Pepita Jiménez*, Act II, scene ii: 'Death' theme, bars 1273–9

The original version of *Pepita Jiménez*, the one that corresponds to the MS of 1895, the Barcelona premiere of 1896, and the libretto in Italian translation by Bignotti, is quite a bit different from all subsequent versions. Why Albéniz and Coutts revised both the music and libretto is not certain, but it was probably in response to the Barcelona production. Perhaps they wanted to make the opera seem more substantial by dividing it into two acts. Very likely they thought the changes made good dramatic sense. Unfortunately, no correspondence from this crucial revision year of 1896 survives giving us any insight into the reasons for or process of the changes made. It is possible that they worked on the revision together, perhaps in London, and had no need to write letters. This would explain why none have come down to us. All we know is that Albéniz was in Leipzig in October of 1896 arranging with Breitkopf und Härtel for publication of the new two-act version.[34]

---

[34] According to documents in the Ls, including a business card of Albéniz's dated 22 Oct. 1896, which was conveyed by hand, along with the score, to the firm. Another business card of five days later expresses displeasure with the cover design for the publication.

The original opera was in one act and two scenes. Where the dramatic statement of Don Luis's theme separates Acts I and II in the revision, the music simply dies down and leads unobtrusively into a repetition of the 'Garden' theme, followed by a portion of the Prelude. During this interval the principal characters (except the Count and Don Luis, who are understood to be fighting a duel) assemble in Pepita's garden to listen to the children sing their villancico. After this comes more of the Prelude, which serves as an intermezzo between scenes. There was neither Ballet nor Intermezzo (two of the most characteristic and famous numbers of the revision), and no ensemble number.

Scene ii consisted, as it later did, of the duet between Don Luis and Pepita, commencing with an aria sung by Don Luis. But here we see the full extent of the revision made by Coutts and Albéniz. The text is substantially different, and in the absence of the Intermezzo, which was the principal organizing feature of scene ii in the revision, we have a continued use of the 'Conversation' theme. Other important themes, jettisoned in the revision, recur here as well (e.g. Antoñona's theme and Pepita's theme). In addition, there is a lot of musical material in this duet that Albéniz did not keep in his revision, making this part of the opera all the more noteworthy. The critical juncture in the drama is reached when Antoñona appears, in the company of the Vicar and Don Pedro, to inform Pepita that Don Luis has fought a duel with the Count for her sake. This opens wide the sluice gates of their love, and all the assembled characters sing together, 'Oh, happy day!' The opera concludes with a rousing restatement of Don Luis's theme (this same closing was moved to the end of Act I in the revision, and a new one was composed).

The closing key is E major, rather than F major, which leads us to suspect that Albéniz's final choice of key relationships was the product of some deliberation. In the revision, the first act opens in the key of Db, and this tonality returns at prominent points throughout the act. The act closes on a statement of Don Luis's theme in Bb Phrygian. Act II commences in Eb major, which, along with its parallel minor, enjoys pride of place until the end of scene ii, when it is displaced by F major. The overall movement, then, is upward by step, from Db to Eb to F, i.e. from five flats to three to one. The symmetry and logic of this are too conspicuous not to have been intended by Albéniz, although precisely what significance the progression had for him is not so obvious. The Bb tonality at the end of Act I forms the dominant of the ensuing key of Eb. In like fashion, the C major key signature of the opening points toward a dominant relationship to the final key area of the opera, embracing the entire work in a gesture of V–I.[35] (The key of E major survives in the revision as the transitional key area between E♭ and F in Act II.)

Was the revision an improvement? It certainly was a trade-off. Albéniz composed some of his finest music the second time around, but the original version had a continuity and unity of conception that suffered in revision. The use of the principal themes throughout the opera was the chief unifying device in the 1895 score and was appropriate to a work of that size. Although the second act of the 1896 revision presents us with more musical variety, it also neglects some themes that were central to the musical fabric of the first act. Hence, the work's structure exhibits a kind of 'split personality'.

Another appealing, and more traditional, feature of the original is the appearance of all the main characters, except Count Genazahar, on stage at the conclusion of the opera, when they all sing together. This arrangement possesses a theatrical logic that, in the opinion of this author, the revision lacks. As will be illustrated in the ensuing reception history, however, drama was never the strong point of the opera, in any of its versions. The work stands or falls on the basis of the music and the atmosphere it creates. Therefore, the incorporation of greater musical variety in the second act, even at the expense of unity and dramatic logic, was probably a wise decision, and it may well be that these changes extended the opera's career beyond the Pyrenees.

The premiere took place in Barcelona on Sunday, 5 January 1896, at the Gran Teatre del Liceu. The work was performed in Italian, the custom at the Liceu, just as *Henry Clifford* had been. What we know of the performers comes from the published libretto, which listed the names of the singers (Table 8).

TABLE 8. *Cast of Pepita Jiménez, premiere, Barcelona, Gran Teatre del Liceu, 5 January 1896*

Pepita	Emma Zilli (or Zilly)
Don Luis	Oreste Gennari (or Genaro)
Antoñona	Carlotta Calvi-Calvi
Don Pedro	Marco Barba
Vicar	Oreste Luppi
Count Genazahar	Achille Tisseyre
Officer 1	Antonio Oliver
Officer 2	Alfredo Serazzi
Conductor	Vittorio Vanzo

[35] It should be pointed out, however, that the orchestral scores, both in MS and printed versions, do not use key signatures, though the individual parts have been transposed. This is a curious omission that may stem from a weariness on the composer's part at having to write in so many key signatures with every new page. In this context, then, the issue of the key signature of C major forming the dominant of the final key area of the opera would be meaningless, as the actual tonality of C major appears only in the Caballero theme.

The opera received two performances on the 5th, one on the 6th, two on the 8th, and one each on 11, 12, and 19 January, on which day it closed. The dances from *Henry Clifford* were presented with *Pepita Jiménez* on the 11th, 12th, and 19th, proving once again their popularity with the public in Barcelona.[36] The 11th was announced in the press as the last day, but it was held over to the 12th and repeated on the 19th.[37] The run was a good one, and the premiere could be deemed a success on the basis of that fact alone.

One of the most flattering appraisals of the work came from Amadeu Vives (*La vanguardia*, 6 January 1896, 5), a leading zarzuela composer of the time:[38] 'In truth and justice we can proclaim that our art is coming to life and that already blood is flowing in its veins, blood regenerated and vivified, whose power and force all feel and experience.'[39] Regarding the use of leitmotif, he declares it was 'applied in a magisterial fashion'.[40] This was especially true for Antoñona, who was 'painted by a master hand': 'Her meddlesome, brusque, vehement, and light character is perfectly expressed in her halting, lively phrases and in the contrapuntal rhythms in the orchestra.'[41] The story itself did not, in his view, possess much 'theatrical relief', but it could best be described as an 'idyll', a word that appears in many characterizations of the work. The best scenes were the dialogue between Pepita and the Vicar, and between Don Luis and Pepita. For these Vives says Albéniz wrote his finest music, the latter dialogue having been 'enthusiastically applauded' by the public. He concludes by praising the work as one of the foremost of Spanish operas and superior to many celebrated foreign works (unnamed).

An anonymous reviewer in *El correo catalán* (8 January 1896, 5–6) confirms that the public reserved its greatest applause for the duet between Pepita and Don Luis, which had to be repeated at the audience's insistence. Albéniz was subsequently called to the stage to receive the accolades of the public, something that occurred after other 'fragments' of the work, as well as at its conclusion. He praises the orchestration as possessing 'originality and great richness', though this may, he speculates, have worked against the voices in the soprano–tenor duet, causing them to appear 'languid and

---

[36] An undated clipping in the Mm, Prov. M-987b1, indicates that the dances were performed again at a benefit at the Teatre Líric for the families of reservists in the nearby town of Gracia.

[37] Announcing the imminent end of an opera's run might have been a ploy to increase attendance.

[38] Vives (1871–1932) is best known for his zarzuelas *Los bohemios* (1904) and *Doña Francisquita* (1923).

[39] 'Con verdad y con justicia podemos proclamar, que nuestro arte comienza á vivir y que ya corre sangre por sus venas, sangre regeneradora y vivificante, cuyo poder y fuerza sentimos y experimentamos todos'.

[40] 'La teoría del "leit motiv" está aplicada a ella de un modo magistral.'

[41] 'Su carácter entrometido, brusco, vehemente y ligero, está perfectamente expresado en sus frases entrecortadas, movidas, y en los ritmos contrapuntísticos de la orquesta.'

much less expressive'. The libretto itself made little more than a 'general allusion' to Valera's work, but it did possess the virtue of not presenting any scene or expression that was 'objectionable from a moral point of view'.[42] In other words, Coutts had refrained from extracting anything sensational or salacious from the story that would have offended the public's sense of propriety or misrepresented Valera's intentions.[43] But F. Suárez Bravo (*Diario de Barcelona*, 7 January 1896, 247–8) elaborates on this by observing that

> Audiences like ours are in the worst position to appreciate works of this kind, because it deals with a drama in which there is no development of important events and external movement is practically nonexistent; therefore, everything depends on that which is said...the beauties [of the music] can be grasped only after two or three hearings.[44]

Suárez Bravo concedes that, because the novel itself deals primarily with Don Luis's thoughts and feelings, which develop over a period of several weeks, the time frame must be telescoped for the theatre. He observes that Coutts had to pull out what action there was in order to 'weave the fabric of the libretto', and concludes that 'the drama, such as has remained, is sufficiently complete'.[45] As for the music:

> It is not appropriate to examine music minutely when dealing with a work so unified, executed in a single impulse, without vacillation or mistakes.... All of it is expressed in a very personal musical language, like everything of Albéniz, personal in melody, harmony, and orchestration. It possesses a colour that recalls the second act of 'Clifford', but here...it appears more spontaneous, more effortless in production, because here he is in his element, bringing to life Spanish characters, seduced by the atmosphere of the Andalusian countryside, where the action presumably transpires.[46]

Suárez Bravo praised the performance but felt that it required 'a few more days of study and rehearsals'.

---

[42] '[V]ituperable bajo el punto de vista moral.'

[43] It will be remembered that Valera had expressed precisely this concern, i.e. that an opera based on his novel would descend to vulgarity.

[44] 'Para apreciar obras de esta índole públicos como el nuestro, están en las peores condiciones, porque como se trata de un cuadro escénico en el que no se desarrollan grandes sucesos y el movimiento esterior es casi nulo, todo estriba, por lo tanto, en lo que allí se dice y de esto apenas si nos enteramos...de sus bellezas, solo después de dos ó tres audiciones nos hacemos cargo.'

[45] 'Tal como ha quedado, el cuadro resulta bastante completo.'

[46] 'No es cosa de desmenuzar la música tratándose de una obrita tan una, tan hecha de un solo impulso, sin vacilaciones, ni tropiezos.... Todo ello está espresado en un lenguaje musical, tan personal como todo lo de Albéniz, personal en la melodía, en la armonía y en la orquestación; tiene un color que recuerda el acto segundo del "Clifford", pero aquí... se le ve más espontáneo, más fácil en la producción, porque aquí se halla en su centro, haciendo hablar á tipos españoles, seducido por el ambiente del campo de Andalucía donde se supone que la acción pasó.'

Because of Albéniz's long-standing connection with London, the opera was reviewed in the *Sunday Times* by Herman Klein (5 January 1896, 6), a music critic and friend of Albéniz and Coutts who had travelled to Barcelona for the premiere. Klein places Albéniz in the same rank as Grieg, Dvořák, Smetana, Glinka, and Tchaikovsky as a nationalist composer of international stature. He praises Albéniz's handling of thematic material and his treatment of the voices, saying he writes with great 'consideration and melodic freedom'. Klein also has kind words for 'Mountjoy', citing what he perceived to be

the infinite tact and skill with which he has evolved from [the novel] a lyric comedy full of deep human interest, and combining pathos and passion with abundant contrast in the shape of characteristic humour and strong local colour. The personages are deftly drawn and true to the originals, while the plot, though much condensed, retains in a notable degree the subtle essence and delicate aroma of Valera's story. The lyrics, too, are admirable.

Many years later he published another, more extensive article on the opera (*Musical Times*, 1 March 1918, 116–17) in which he had high praise for several aspects of the work. Regarding the libretto, the most controversial aspect, he states that 'an undercurrent of deep passion compensates for lack of dramatic climax . . . its rare poetic feeling and truth to life, made it exactly *en rapport* with the temperament and imaginative qualities of the musician'. The victory of love over 'ambition and imagined duty, furnishes a story quite sufficiently charged with dramatic interest for a short two-Act opera'. With regard to the music, he draws a comparison with the work of Albéniz's compatriot and friend Tomás Bretón:

Unlike his contemporary, Bretón, whose opera 'La Dolores' I also heard during my stay at Barcelona, he disdained the crude employment of national Spanish melodies. . . . Albéniz contented himself with suggesting the idea or the rhythm of the national tune, without pushing the thing itself into the foreground; above all, he never brought it into play, either as motive or accompaniment, unless absolutely appropriate.

He deems Albéniz to have been as 'up-to-date' as Verdi in *Falstaff*, and his use of leading motives 'more ingenious, more skilful than the rather obvious method affected by Puccini, and consequently more interesting'. As for the musical dialogue, it 'flows serenely, easily, pointedly', aided by the fact that 'there are no set solos, no choral interruption—no chorus at all, indeed, except one sung in the second Act'.

We learn from Klein that the opera was to have premiered around Christmas of the previous year, but was delayed 'a fortnight' due to an 'eleventh-hour' change in the cast. He further informs us that neither the Grand Opera Syndicate nor the Carl Rosa Company in London was interested in producing the opera but reports on its favorable reception in 'the land of Dvořák and the Czechs'. There our discussion next takes us.

In spring of the following year, 1897, Albéniz travelled to the German-speaking world to promote *Pepita Jiménez*. Having studied and concertized in Germany, Albéniz had established useful connections over the years with important people there, including the editors at Breitkopf und Härtel in Leipzig. According to a journal Albéniz kept of his travels to Prague that year,[47] he arrived in Karlsruhe from Paris on 22 March and found lodging at the Hotel Germania. His friend David Popper was passing through the city and met him there. The following day Albéniz conferred with Felix Mottl,[48] director of the local opera theatre, with whom he was already acquainted. Both Popper and Mottl were favourably impressed with *Pepita Jiménez*, and the prospects for a performance there seemed bright, though not yet definite. Mottl arranged another meeting with Albéniz for 2 April, by which time he promised to have a final decision. Popper accompanied Albéniz on the final leg of his journey to Prague (Popper's home town), and they arrived on the 25th via the Oriental Express. Here Popper introduced him to Franz Schalk,[49] the conductor of the Neues Deutsches Theater. Popper was confident he could secure a production not only in Prague but also in Budapest—in Hungarian![50] By 30 March, the director of the theatre, Angelo Neumann, informed Albéniz that *Pepita Jiménez* was accepted for performance at Prague. But the timing of the production was in question. Though Neumann leaned towards an October premiere, Albéniz preferred getting on with it now, feeling that if it succeeded in Prague it would go along on its own, and if it did not it could rest in peace. In either event, he would be free of his 'obsession' with the work.[51] (He seems not to have calculated that it might gain only a partial success in Prague and thus continue to require aggressive promotion throughout its career. He might have done better to wait for a slot other than at the end of the season and when there would be more time to rehearse.) The only danger was that if it were to precede a production in Karlsruhe, Mottl might lose interest in the work. But he was

---

[47] *Impresiones*, ed. Franco, 37–58.

[48] Mottl (1856–1911) was a student of Bruckner and had assisted Hans Richter in the production of the *Ring* at Bayreuth in 1876, where he remained director until 1885.

[49] Schalk (1863–1931) was a promoter of the symphonies of Bruckner, of which he made controversial revisions. Neither did Albéniz's opera escape his editorial scalpel.

[50] According to a letter Albéniz wrote to Rosina dated 24 Mar. 1897 (Mm, 10.330). Popper was on the faculty of the music academy in Budapest.

[51] Letter to Rosina, 28 Mar. 1897 (Mm, 10.337).

willing to run that risk; perhaps Mottl would be interested in his next opera ('la otra que venga').[52] Before returning to Karlsruhe, however, Albéniz visited Leipzig in order to make the necessary contractual arrangements with Breitkopf und Härtel. His generosity ever to the fore, he also attempted to persuade them to publish Chausson's *Poème* for violin and orchestra. But they found the work 'bizarre', and he could only overcome their reluctance to publish it by agreeing to cover the costs himself. He insisted on paying a royalty of 300 marks, which was twice what Chausson had requested. The only condition was that these arrangements remain confidential. Chausson was overjoyed at this turn of events and exclaimed, 'But it is a fortune!' ('Mais c'est la fortune!')[53] However, he never learned its source. For his part, Albéniz declared in the letter, 'I am altogether a man of some importance!' ('!Soy [*sic*] todo un señor de cierta importancia!')

Albéniz now returned to Karlsruhe, where Mottl declared his intention to stage the opera. Although Albéniz was clearly delighted at this prospect, in a letter to Rosina he expressed some misgivings about Mottl and his reliability: 'there is no doubt that he will stage the work, but—when!'[54] In fact, Albéniz's worst suspicions were later confirmed, in spite of the fact that Mottl had evidently promised to send him a contract in May and to produce it the following season.[55] None the less, he crowed in his diary that 'the approbation of a man of Mottl's artistic stature fills me with satisfaction and encourages me to work hard'.[56] But our man of some importance had additional reasons to feel important. In the letter of 9 April he informed Rosina that the celebrated conductor Arthur Nikisch[57] had requested his programming advice for an upcoming series of five concerts of the Berlin Philharmonic in France. Albéniz urged him, in the interests of diplomacy, to include works of young French composers in these concerts, instead of the all-German programme Nikisch had been planning for his all-German orchestra. Nikisch responded enthusiastically to this proposal and asked that Chausson send him a half-dozen of the best works of the young French

[52] Letter to Rosina, 30 Mar. 1897 (Mm, 10.339).

[53] In a letter from Chausson to Albéniz dated simply 'lundi' and written on Société Nationale de Musique letterhead (Bc, 'C'). Of course, the money itself meant little to the independently wealthy Chausson, but it increased his self-assurance. The firm explained its reluctance to publish the work in a letter to Albéniz of 27 Apr. 1897 (Mm, car. 2, in a folder containing letters from Breitkopf und Härtel). They believed he was an 'audacious innovator' whose work was 'vague and bizarre' in form, of 'extraordinary difficulty', and thus had 'few adherents'. The next letter to Albéniz, dated 6 May, graciously accepts his offer to pay the costs himself.

[54] Dated 9 Apr. 1897 (Mm, 10.334): 'que pondrá la obra, es indudable, pero—cuando!'

[55] From a diary entry of 6 Apr. 1897, in *Impresiones*, ed. Franco, 44.

[56] Ibid. 44: 'la aprobación de un hombre del valor artístico de Mottl me llena de satisfacción y me infunde ánimos para trabajar de firme.'

[57] Nikisch (1855–1922) had been the conductor of the Berlin Philharmonic since 1885.

school. As a result, Nikisch conducted Chausson's Symphony in B flat at the Paris concert of 13 May 1897, which became a turning point in Chausson's career and gave his confidence a needed boost. Albéniz's confidence also received a boost, and he proudly reported to Rosina, 'Nikisch and his wife were delighted with my good advice.' He himself was elated that Nikisch had 'received me as an esteemed colleague'.[58]

Albéniz's German gambit seemed to have paid off handsomely, and he travelled to Frankfurt (as Neumann instructed) to await word from Prague about rehearsals. Then he returned to Paris. But what one strongly senses in the above passages is a gnawing insecurity within Albéniz, that despite his many successes he had not attained the recognition he needed. His reports of hobnobbing with the high-and-mighty likes of Nikisch, Mottl, and Schalk reflect an exalted view of German music and musicians, something already evident when he was 16 and on his way to Leipzig—and demonstrated by his repeated prevarications about having remained there for nine, eighteen, or even thirty-six months, instead of the few weeks he actually spent at the conservatory. From Prague he wrote home that the children were definitely to learn German as well as English.[59] He took pride in the fact that Schalk 'deals with me in a fraternal manner'.[60] Though he had lent his French friends, especially Chausson, invaluable assistance during the trip, his own loyalties appear to have remained on the east bank of the Rhine: 'Here in Germany my spirit has found complete fulfilment, and I hold the firm conviction that I must be appreciated by this healthy and sincere public! What horror those French aristocrats cause me . . . with so little real and positive genius!'[61]

Here we perceive another, though related, aspect of this complex man's personality, and that is a certain bitterness and resentment towards his French associates that seems inconsistent with his repeated protestations of friendship with them. Who were the aristocrats to whom he was referring? Dukas, d'Indy, and Chausson were all men of independent means, and d'Indy even had aristocratic ancestry. It seems that his insecurities extended to his station in society, insecurities perhaps exacerbated by the fact that his social standing was higher than it would otherwise have been without the

---

[58] From the letter of 9 Apr. 1897. 'Nikisch y su mujer estaban encantados de mi buen consejo.' The second quote comes from a letter written to her five days earlier (Mm, 10.364).

[59] Letter to Rosina of 26 May 1897 (Mm, 10.365).

[60] Letter to Rosina of 10 June 1897 (Mm, 10.351). '[Schalk] se está portando conmigo de una manera fraternal.'

[61] 28 Mar. 1897, from Prague to Rosina (Mm, 10.338). 'Desde que estoy en Alemania, mi espiritu se ha realizado completamente, y tengo la firme conviccion que he de ser apreciado por este publico sano y sincero! que horror me causan todos esos aristarcas [sic] Franceses con . . . tan poco real y positivo genio!'

assistance of another one of his 'betters'—Coutts. A notable example of this is found in his journal entry for 2 April describing his meeting with Nikisch and intercession on behalf of French composers like Chausson and d'Indy. He concludes this entry with the following rueful observation: 'That's one more favour they owe me, a fact that will not prevent them from thinking it well deserved and continuing to view me as [some kind of] strange beast.'[62] Paul Gilson threw interesting light on his relationship to this group that clarifies Albéniz's feelings of not quite belonging to the 'club':

Albéniz was, among them, a bit like an adopted son; friendly and smiling, his extravagance and wandering aesthetic were pardoned. He was loved because he apologized in a friendly way—and with humility!—for his intrusion in their cenacle, with whose gravity his capricious personality would seemingly have been incompatible.[63]

Albéniz's antagonistic relationship to French modernism cropped up during his first stay in Karlsruhe, when he played through his score for Popper. The following excerpt from his correpondence sheds further light on his ambivalence towards his situation in Paris:

dear Popper was a great help to me; we were up until midnight last night playing my music, and for me it was a gratifying moment when, after finishing the opera, he kissed me with tears in his eyes, saying there were few *healthy* musicians in our day who were capable of writing such a score. The truth is, that inspired and convinced me of the *urgent necessity of leaving Paris and its infected artistic atmosphere* [emphasis added]. But is not Brussels starting to be contaminated by identical miasmas?[64]

A letter from Bretón (in Paris at the time) to Albéniz of 23 August 1895 echoed this same sentiment: 'watch out for those French modernists—they are crazy.'[65] In the event, however, Coutts knew of Albéniz's desire to leave Paris but expressed a preference for his staying put, which he did.[66]

Clearly, the Prague experience was causing him a crisis of self-confidence. 'I am an animal who definitely possesses very little faith in himself', he wrote.

---

[62] *Impresiones*, ed. Franco, 42. '[Eso es] un favor más que esos señores me deben, lo cual no impedirá que se lo crean muy merecido, y sigan mirándome como una bestia rara.'

[63] 'Bruxelles', Franco (ed.), *Albéniz y su tiempo*, 30. 'Albéniz era, entre ellos, un poco como su hijo adoptivo; amable y sonriente, se le perdonaban sus extravagancias y su estética errabunda. Se le quería porque se disculpaba amablemente—-¡y con humildad!—por su intrusión en este cenáculo, con cuya gravedad su caprichosa personalidad habría tenido, en apariencia, que acomodarse bastante mal.'

[64] In a letter to Rosina, 24 Mar. 1897 (Mm, 10.330): 'el querido Popper me habra ayudado en gran manera; hasta las 12 estuvimos anoche tocando mis solfas, y cree que fue para mi un grato momento cuando al acabar la opera, y con lagrimas en los ojos el hombre me besó, diciendo que habian pocos músicos *sanos* en el dia, que fueran capaces de escribir tal partitura: la verdad es, que esto anima y me convence de la imprescindible necesidad de abandonar Paris y su infecta atmosfera artistica; ¿pero no empieza tambien Bruselas a estar contaminada por identicas miasmas?'

[65] Bc, 'B': 'guárdate de los modernistas franceses, están locos.'

[66] Letter to Rosina, 9 June 1897 (Mm, 10.366).

'The opera is beautiful, but many times I fear not being able to top it.'[67] His insecurity as a composer is also apparent in the caustic remarks he makes about contemporary operas he hears in Prague and Karlsruhe, recapitulating criticisms that had been levelled at his own stage works (especially *The Magic Opal*). For instance, he ridiculed the eclecticism and lack of originality of the Frankfurt composer Anton Unspruch (1850–1934), whose opera *Das Unmöglichste von Allem* (based on a play by Lope de Vega) premiered in Karlsruhe while Albéniz was there:

I have never in my life heard such a salad!... said little work, lengthy as a day of smelly constipation, is a review of all such music written today... we salute Mozart and Wagner, stumble into Beethoven, and fall in the arms of Offenbach, with a perception of the eclectic which, if it were accompanied by personal originality, would constitute a lovely work.[68]

Perhaps his view of Unspruch's work was affected by the fact that it was actually being produced while Albéniz's remained in limbo. Albéniz did not spare more celebrated figures his critical shafts. Comments in his journal on 3 June regarding a performance of Mascagni's *Cavalleria rusticana* reveal mixed feelings:

denying qualities to Mascagni would be absurd, but the work results in such a poverty of realization that it pains one to hear it. In all of it one sees nothing more than an excellent nature, but one that study has not developed. It would be futile work to search through the entire score for any didactic detail of interest: in a word, the workmanship is as minimal as can be.[69]

Albéniz's attitude here is rather ironic because he could well have been describing many of his own works up to that time. Of course, this is precisely the point. Under the influence of his Parisian friends and the Schola Cantorum, he was now attempting to develop a more intellectual approach to composition, and deriving some satisfaction from being able to look down his nose at composers who were not doing likewise (though they were vastly more successful than he in the opera business).

[67] Ibid. 'Soy un animal decididamente en tener tan poca fe en mi mismo, la obrita es una verdadera filigrana, y muchas veces temo no poder volver á hacer nada mejor....'

[68] Letter to Rosina, 5 Apr. 1897 (Mm, 10.335). '[N]o he oido en mi vida, ensalada semejante!... la dicha obrita, larga como un día de constipado naricero, es una revista... de toda cuanta música hoy escrita... saludamos a Mozart como a Wagner, tropiezas en Beethoven, y caes en los... brazos de Ofenbach, con una percepción de lo ecléctico, que si fuera acompañada de personal originalidad, constituiría una bonita obra.'

[69] *Impresiones*, ed. Franco, 50: 'el negar condiciones a Mascagni fuera absurdo, pero la obra resulta de una pobreza de realización tal, que da pena oírla; en toda ella no se ve más que una naturaleza excelente, pero que el estudio no ha desarrollado; no se trata de buscar en toda la partitura un detalle didáctico que interese, fuera trabajo inútil, en una palabra, la mano de obra es lo más mínimo que darse pueda.'

In mid-May he returned to Prague to attend rehearsals of his opera. He was dismayed to discover that, though the lead singers were making admirable progress, the chorus, orchestra, and dancers still left much to be desired. Even more distressing to him was the fact that Schalk and Neumann had made many cuts (with scissors already sharpened on the Bruckner symphonies), reducing the work to its original stature as a one-act opera. To be sure, a printed bill advertising the repertoire of the Königliches Deutsches Landestheater Neues Deutsches Theater for 13 to 21 June 1897 describes *Pepita Jiménez* as an 'Oper in 2 Acten und 3 Bildern', to be premiered on Saturday, 19 June, at 7.30 p.m.[70] But the opera's premiere was delayed and did not take place until the 22nd. It was announced and critiqued in the local papers as an opera in one act and two scenes. Thus, the work's format was being revised perilously close to the time of the first performance, and events were not under Albéniz's control. In a letter to his wife, dated 18 June 1897, Albéniz observed that

in effect, the alterations that have been made in the book have obliged me to write a lot of music; the opera has no more than one act!! and jumps from the duel to Pepita's Romance. Evidently the work will succeed without two acts, above all in a country like this, where they do not know Valera's novel, but you can already imagine my grief at seeing that disruption! Everything has its compensation in the end, and this arrangement, owing to the exclusive taste of Neumann, assures a long life to 'Pepita' at this theatre.[71]

Albéniz's misgivings were also mitigated by the faith he had in Schalk, which he had expressed in an earlier letter to Rosina of 6 June: 'I have the good fortune to have fallen into the hands of Schalk, who is a true artist and who has worked with absolute sincerity, appreciating the work certainly more than it merits.'[72] On 10 June, Albéniz related Schalk's feelings about *Pepita Jiménez*: 'The conductor Schalk just told me that the more he knows the work the more he finds it original, extraordinary, and full of noble aspiration.'[73]

---

[70] A copy of this bill was at the Ah when the author examined it. The family has since turned over all remaining papers and manuscripts to the Mm.

[71] Mm, 10.369: 'en efecto, las alteraciones que se han hecho en el libro me han obligado á escribir, pas mal de musique, la opera no tiene ya mas que un acto!!, y se salta desde el duelo, á la romanza de Pepita: evidentemente la obra gana con no tener dos actos, sobre todo en un pais como este, en donde no conocen la novela de Valera, pero ya puedes pensar si ha sido pesadumbre la mia, al ver ese desquiciamiento! en fin todo tiene su compensacion, y este arreglo debido al esclusivo gusto de Neumann, asegura en este teatro larga vida á Pepita.'

[72] Mm, 10.349: 'tengo la suerte a haber caído en manos de Schalk, que es un verdadero artista, y que ha trabajado con una sinceridad absoluta, apreciando la obra seguramente en mas de lo que vale.'

[73] Mm, 10.351. 'El Kapellmeister Schalk acaba de decirme, que cuanto mas conoce la obra, mas la encuentra original, fuera de lo comun, y llena de noble aspiración.'

Chausson, certainly one of Albéniz's closest friends, was in Prague to attend the rehearsals and performance of *Pepita Jiménez* and seeking to negotiate a production of his own opera *Le Roi Arthus*. He provided much encouragement to Albéniz at this crucial juncture, which Albéniz related to Rosina thus:

it is extraordinary the interest that Chausson takes in the work, and how much he likes it. I think that I have won him over a thousand percent. While talking yesterday after eating he told me again that I should not concern myself with all those composers of the so-called modern school, because not one of them is capable of writing a work of the originality of 'Pepita'.[74]

Albéniz's need to 'win over' Chausson and his evident preoccupation with the 'modern school' revisit themes treated above. In spite of his liberalism, there was a conservative, cautious element in Albéniz's creative temperament—something conspicuously lacking in his idol Wagner. This helps us to understand better his close association with the Franck circle and the Schola Cantorum in Paris, though he was not altogether comfortable with them either. Albéniz was prone to adopting ideas only after they had gained widespread approval. What he sought was acceptance and remuneration, not to play the role of martyr. Thus, *The Magic Opal* was a concatenation of numbers here in the style of Gilbert and Sullivan, there in the style of Lecocq and Offenbach (though the operetta is suffused with a Spanish flavour all his own, thus avoiding the error of composers like Unspruch). *Pepita Jiménez* owed a great deal to contemporary Italian opera—Puccini and Mascagni—despite Albéniz's private denunciations of Italian singers and opera in general (discussed further in the next chapter). *Iberia*, too, would reveal influence from precisely the modernist composers, especially Debussy, whose style he was apparently at pains to avoid, though the above passage shows he felt intimidated by them. In fact, he was already being pulled in their direction (see the discussion of 'La vega' in Chapter 6).

Our composer was clearly in an agitated state of mind as the premiere approached. He wrote to Rosina of the 'enormous pain' he would suffer if she were not present at this 'most important step in my artistic career'.[75] He had tried to arrange for her to join him in Prague and later to take a vacation together. But it proved impossible. On 6 June he complained that the absence of recent correspondence from her had increased his

[74] 15 June 1897 (Mm, 10.352): 'es extraordinario el interes que Chausson toma en la obra, y lo mucho que le gusta: creo que he ganado en su espiritu el mil por ciento, y ayer hablando despues de comer volvio á decirme, que no debia hacer caso de todos ellos pues ninguno de los compositores de la llamada escuela moderna, era capaz de escribir una obra de la originalidad de Pepita.'

[75] Letter of 31 May 1897 (Mm, 10.347): 'paso mas importante de mi vida artistica.'

'habitual melancholy'. (Given the heartache, tragedy, and physical suffering he experienced throughout his life, such 'melancholy' is not surprising.) The day before, he wrote to her that the fact she would not be at the premiere caused him 'profound sadness', 'without being able to give you upon returning home one of those long, loving kisses that make me so happy'.[76] So, he now faced this ordeal on his own. Not even Coutts could make the trip, for he was busy in London trying to arrange a production of *Pepita Jiménez* at Covent Garden.[77] At least Chausson was there, and Albéniz appreciated his support: 'He is decidedly a charming boy!'[78] Indeed, Chausson said the work possessed musical and dramatic qualities he had not suspected in Albéniz.[79] And the Frenchman was providing physical as well as moral support. For to make matters worse, Albéniz had been very ill, and Chausson was nursing him back to health. He was 'suffering the pains of purgatory', and his stomach would not let him 'live in peace'.[80] At one point he even changed hotels because the food was upsetting his stomach. Albéniz expressed to Rosina the desire to recuperate at a spa somewhere in northern Spain during the summer. Interestingly, the notion of taking the waters at his birthplace, Camprodon, did not appeal to him because it was 'too rustic'.[81]

But worst of all were the rehearsals. He wrote in his journal that the dress rehearsal on the 21st was a 'true disaster' and lamented the orchestra's 'absolute incomprehension of the work'.[82] A letter to Rosina described it simply as 'fatal'.[83] All this notwithstanding, the premiere took place the following day (cast in Table 9). Since the opera lasted only an hour and a half, it was followed by a 'Ballet–Divertissement'. No miraculous transformation had taken place, and in Albéniz's own mind the performance was less than satisfactory. None the less, he was exultant over the reception of his opera and wrote immediately to Rosina:

It is midnight and I am alone in my room, the window open, and with a sweet melancholy that invades my spirit at the thought of you. That may be very lyrical, but it is very true, and I feel an irrepressible need to communicate with you. Of all that comes to memory, the triumph in Prague is the greatest satisfaction I have had in my

---

[76] '[S]in poder darte al volver á casa uno de esos largos y cariñosos petones que tan feliz me hacen.' The letters of 5 and 6 June are in the Mm but their numbering is inverted (10.350 and 10.349 respectively).

[77] Letter to Rosina, 4 Apr. 1897 (Mm, 10.364).

[78] Letter to Rosina of 5 June 1897 (Mm, 10.350). '¡Decididamente es un charmant garçon!'

[79] Letter to Rosina of 15 June 1897 (Mm, 10.353).

[80] Letter to Rosina of 16 June 1897 (Mm, 10.368).

[81] Letter to Rosina of 15 June 1897 (Mm, 10.353).

[82] *Impresiones*, ed. Franco, 54.

[83] 22 June 1897 (Mm, 10.370).

TABLE 9. *Cast of* Pepita Jiménez, *Prague, Neues Deutsches Landestheater, 22 May 1897*

Pepita	Frl. Wiet
Don Luis	Herr Elsner
Antoñona	Frl. Kaminski
Don Pedro	Herr Dawison
Vicar	Herr Sieglitz
Count Genazahar	Herr Hunold
Conductor	Franz Schalk
Stage direction	Herr Ehrl

entire artistic life. The profound respect that my work has been able to inspire was one of the results that until now I had tried in vain to obtain, and here I have acquired it fully. The enclosed newspaper is the most hostile to the theatre management, and we had discounted its review from the start, in the certainty that in any event it would be bad. It is palpable evidence of what I am telling you. Having made a detailed study of the work and criticizing gently its faults, he proclaims that it is the work of a complete musician, a connoisseur of the most recondite secrets of his art and, what is more, of an originality obsolete in our time.[84]

An anonymous critic writing for the *Deutsches Abendblatt* (23 June 1897, 2) praised Albéniz's training and ability. He especially appreciated his handling of the orchestra, though he conceded that it often overwhelmed the singers. He also commented on the predominance of triple metre, citing the exact number of measures in duple out of the whole (277). He further revealed a knowledge of the score by complaining about Albéniz's predilection for double accidentals and the difficulties they posed to reading. But he concluded by declaring that 'through its rich polyphony and wealth of ideas it will arouse the interest of the musician, though it may otherwise be caviar for the public'.[85]

---

[84] 23 June 1897 (Mm, 10.371). The present author has not yet encountered a review that conforms precisely to the description offered by Albéniz. 'Son las 12 de la noche, estoy solo en mi cuarto, la ventana abierta, y con una dulce melancolía que a tu recuerdo invade toda mi alma; todo esto será muy lírico, pero es muy verdad, y siento una invencible necesidad de comunicar[me] contigo. De todo lo que a mi memoria acude, el triunfo de Praga, es la satisfacción más viva que en mi vida artística he tenido; el profundo respeto que mi obra ha sabido inspirar, era uno de los resultados que hasta la presente, en vano había tratado de conquistar, y que aquí de lleno he conseguido: el Diario adjunto, el más hostil a la dirección del Teatro, y cuya crítica de antemano habíamos descontado, por tener la seguridad de que de todas maneras había de ser mala, es una prueba palpable de lo que te digo; todo y haciendo un minucioso estudio de la obra, y criticándola dulcemente en sus debilidades, proclama que es la obra de un músico de cuerpo entero, conocedor de los mas recónditos secretos de su arte, y a más, de una originalidad desusada en nuestros tiempos.'

[85] '[W]elche durch ihre überreichte Polyphonie und Gedankenfülle sehr hohes Interesse der Musiker erregen darf, wenn sie auch im übrigen Caviar fürs Volk sein mag.'

It is well that Albéniz received the accolades of the public and certain segments of the press. Not all the critics were as kind, though some tempered their reservations with thoughtful objectivity. Writing in the *Beilage zu Bohemia* (24 June 1897, 3), the reviewer 'K' expresses the opinion that the outcome of Don Luis's 'spiritual struggle' was too much delayed in the opera as opposed to the novel. He continues: 'The libretto does not contain any exciting event and exercises no arousing effect, while the religious scruples of the devoutly Catholic lovers are not able to elicit any profound interest in the context of present-day spiritual trends.'[86] As for the music itself:

The composer has labelled his work a 'lyric opera', by which apparently is meant that a simple character of feeling prevails and the poetic sensitivity of the external world is directed inward, whereas one normally would be entitled to assume that, with a lyric presentation, human passion would overflow restraint in the fullness of emotion. Albéniz, however, does not give the singers any absolute melodies, but rather cultivates exclusively the declamatory singing style, in which the sensually pleasant is subordinated to the characteristic. A deliberate and thought-out method of composition prevails in the work, so that not infrequently profundity has as a consequence heaviness and lack of melodic grace in the voice.... Even the experienced music listener is often compelled to direct his keen attention only to the orchestra and to ignore the phrases of the voices.[87]

Two reviews appeared in the 24 June edition of the *Prager Zeitung*, the first one on page 2 by an anonymous critic. His criticism of the libretto echoes that of 'K': 'The plot offers no event with which the music can direct itself toward external effect. The musical figures can only reflect what feelings the souls of the two lovers exhibit.'[88] The other review, written by Julius Steinberg, appears on the following page of the newspaper and could hardly have made Albéniz feel any better about what he read on page 2: 'The composer demands of his public that they follow him through labyr-

---

[86] 'Das Textbuch enthält mithin kein spannendes Ereigniß und übt keine zündende Wirkung, während die religiösen Bedenken des strengkatholischen Liebespaares bei der gegenwärtigen geistigen Strömung ein tieferes Interesse zu erregen nicht im Stande sind.'

[87] 'Der Componist hat sein Werk als "lyrische Oper" bezeichnet, womit wohl angedeutet werden soll, daß in derselben ein einfacher Gefühlscharakter vorwaltet und die poetische Empfindung von der Außenwelt sich nach dem Innern wendet, wobei man übrigens zu der Annahme berechtigt sein könnte, daß bei einer lyrischen Darstellung in der Fülle des Gefühls das menschliche Gemüth in Gefang überströmt. Albéniz jedoch gibt den Singenden keine absoluten Melodien, sondern cultivirt [*sic*] ausschließlich den deklamatorischen Gesangstil, bei welchem das sinnlich Wohlgefällige dem Charakteristischen hintangesetzt wird. In dem Werke herrscht zumeist eine in sich gekehrte, beschauliche Compositionsweise, bei welcher das Vertiefen nicht selten eine Schwerfälligkeit und einen Mangel an melodischer Grazie der Singstimme zur verhängnißvollen Folge hat.... Selbst der geübte Musikhörer wird oft genötigt, seine gespannte Aufmerksamkeit nur dem Orchester zuzuwenden und die Phrasen der Singstimmen unbeachtet zu lassen.'

[88] 'Kein Ereigniß bietet die Handlung, mit welchem die Musik auf den äußerlichen Effekt abzielen könnte, ihre Tonfiguren haben nur wiederzuspiegeln, was an Empfindungsgehalt die Seelen zweier Liebenden aufweisen.'

inthine ways of musical speculation, and listen more with reason than with the ear.'[89]

Appearing as it did at the end of the regular season, *Pepita Jiménez* ran only two nights; it was performed once more on the ensuing Friday, 25 June. The negative reception the opera received in some quarters does not seem to have played a role in its short run, and it was well received by the public. The critic writing for the *Deutsches Abendblatt* (cited above) claimed that the premiere was not sufficiently advertised by the management, implying that the attendance was not what it should have been. But according to another reviewer, *Pepita Jiménez* 'engaged the lively interest of the audience. The premiere of the interesting work was a success. The composer was repeatedly called [to the stage] and received more laurels.'[90] The critic for *Beilage zu Bohemia* stated unequivocally that 'with the premiere of the new work both the public and the composer himself could be completely satisfied'.[91] None the less, it did not find the permanent place in the theatre's repertoire Albéniz had hoped for and was never produced there again. He seems, however, to have been resigned to this. Reference has already been made to his letter of 27 June to Rosina in which he predicted a 'precarious' career for his opera outside Spain and Latin America because of its lack of dramatic action and the unfamiliarity of foreign audiences with the novel. And he believed that *Henry Clifford* would be done in Prague the following winter.[92] As recently as 6 June he had written to Rosina that *Mar y cel* would be 'the result of the boost I am receiving in Prague'.[93] And he had his sights set on new possibilities.

In the letter of 23 June cited above, Albéniz tells Rosina about a contract he has signed for the composition of a stage work which, he claims, was originally intended for Mascagni but which Neumann gave instead to him in light of his achievement with *Pepita Jiménez*. He provides no more details of the project except to say that the libretto is to be assigned to the author [José] Echegaray. Four days later another letter informs her that the opera is to be based on a libretto entitled *La voglia*, which he enthusiastically

[89] 'Der Tondichter stellt an sein Publikum die Aufforderung, ihm durch labyrinthische Gänge musikalischer Spekulazion zu folgen und mehr mit der Vernunft als mit dem Ohr zu hören.'

[90] 'Dr. A. G.', *Prager Tageblatt* (23 June 1997), 10: 'begegnete der lebhaften Theilnahme des Publicums. Die Aufführung des interessanten Werkes . . . war eine vortreffliche. Der Componist wurde wiederholt gerufen und erhielt mehre Kränze.'

[91] 'Mit der Aufführung der Novität konnte das Publicum und selbst der anwesende Componist vollkommen zufrieden sein.'

[92] Letter to Rosina, 4 Apr. 1897 (Mm, 10.364). At this time he expressed 'the complete assurance that I am a musician for these people, and if not now, in time' ('tengo la completa seguridad de que yo soy un musico para esta gente, y si no, al tiempo').

[93] 'Mar y Cel sera el resultado de este empuje que recibo en Praga' (Mm, 10.349).

describes as 'simply colossal', with a plot of the 'most dramatic' kind.[94] With this he firmly believed he had finally found a libretto that 'must bring me name and fortune'.[95] He had also signed another contract to write a ballet on the novel *Aphrodite* of Pierre Louÿs (1870–1925).[96] His thoughts then turned toward the 'pact': 'Of course, the question of poor, dear Coutts must be resolved, but he is so fond of me and is so sensible that I don't believe he will put the least difficulty in the way of realizing these projects.'[97]

Albéniz had good reason to believe that Coutts would not place any obstacles in his path. In a letter from Coutts dated 5 February 1897 (Bc, 'C'), the Englishman had thrown interesting light on his view of their professional relationship:

But, my dear fellow, you don't quite understand me about the librettos. . . . there is (in England, anyhow) absolutely no *career* for a librettist. That is to say, that I must write things that a bookseller will publish. The composer has his career, yes! But the librettist, no! . . . my career must be, finally, in *literature*. If I can have the pleasure & privilege of starting you on your great career, with really well written librettos, *all right*! But I cannot go on writing librettos all my life! I assume there are plenty of people capable of good ones, besides me—.

This not only addresses the very informal character of their partnership but also demonstrates beyond question that Coutts saw himself first and foremost as an author, not a banker whose 'weakness' was 'writing dramatic verse in his leisure hours'. And the sword of professional 'infidelity' cut both ways. Several years later, on 15 February 1905 (Bc, 'C'), Coutts apprised Albéniz of the following: 'I have finished my libretto for Pitt and read it to him (The Winter's Tale). He likes it, though I wrote it in one fortnight! You are not to be jealous! It will be a most excellent thing for you & me, if I can get a footing in Covent Garden.'[98]

[94] Although this letter (Mm, 10.374) does not clarify to which of the Echegaray brothers (José or Miguel) he is referring, a letter from Neumann to Albéniz makes it clear that José (1832–1916) was the one (Bc, 'N'). The dramas of José Echegaray enjoyed great popularity in Prague. *La voglia* ('The wish') was an idea for a libretto Neumann had, and he hoped Echegaray would consent to write it.

[95] '[H]a de darme el nombre y la fortuna.' This little quote speaks volumes about his motivation for writing for the stage. The adulation and remuneration he sought were simply not to be found either in piano performance or composition. In Spain and elsewhere in Europe, particularly Italy, the path to fame and fortune lay through the theatre.

[96] This popular novel (pub. 1896) depicts courtesan life in ancient Alexandria. According to Deledicque, *Albéniz*, 405, some years later a publisher in Milan offered Albéniz the opportunity to set a libretto based on Louÿs's 1898 novel *La Femme et le pantin* ('Woman and puppet'), set in Spain. By then, however, Albéniz was too ill to accept the invitation.

[97] 'Naturalmente, habrá que sortear la cuestion del pobre querido Coutts, pero, me quiere tanto, y es tan sensato, que no creo ponga en la realizacion de estos projectos la mas minima dificultad.'

[98] Percy Pitt (1869–1932) was the conductor and musical adviser at Covent Garden. In a letter to Albéniz of 14 Jan. 1905 (Bc, 'C'), Coutts states that he declined an invitation from Pitt to write a libretto for the Ricordi prize. Evidently Albéniz was not the only composer who esteemed Coutts's literary abilities.

However, Albéniz's enthusiasm in this hour of triumph proved unprophetic. *Pepita Jiménez* would continue to receive its warmest reception outside Spain and the Spanish-speaking world (indeed, it has never been produced anywhere in the Americas), while *La voglia* would remain naught but a pipedream. *Aphrodite* died on the vine as well. There are two postcards and two letters extant from Louÿs to Albéniz (Bc, 'L'). The first is dated 9 June 1897 and accepts Neumann's proposal, with one exception: the ballet must not be done in France. He promised to send Albéniz the scenario by 30 September. The next three missives attempt to set up appointments to meet, but finally Louÿs's illness interfered, and there was no more correspondence.

Albéniz continued to importune Coutts for texts on Spanish subjects even after the completion of *Pepita Jiménez* and at the same time he was entertaining ideas of adapting other works of Valera for the stage. In a letter of 28 December 1896 (Bc, 'C'), Coutts states, with a perceptible tone of exasperation, 'I have ordered a vol.... containing Tom Moore's "Lalla Rookh"—a Moorish poem, about Mokhama—It may be that you will like *that* subject.' Though Albéniz did nothing with it, during this period of intense involvement with the theatre he also took increasing interest in music for solo voice. While in London he had composed 'Il en est de l'amour' to a text by M. Costa de Beauregard (Paris: T. Cée, 1892). This was followed three years later by the *Deux Morceaux de prose de Pierre Loti*, 'Crépuscule' and 'Tristesse' (San Sebastián: A. Díaz, 1897). In the Loti songs especially we perceive the essential elements of Albéniz's mature style: syllabic declamation, in the manner of the French *mélodie*, and the absence of a memorable melody in the voice; a preference for flat keys (typical of all his music) with abundant chromaticism (especially double flats) and frequent modulations; and difficult piano accompaniments. In 1896 Albéniz began collaborating with Coutts on songs as well as operas. Among these are *To Nellie: Six Songs* (Paris: Au Ménestrel-Heugel, 1896?) set to texts of Coutts.[99] The individual numbers are entitled: 'Home', 'Counsel', 'May-Day Song', 'To Nellie', 'A Song of Consolation', and 'A Song'. Coutts's song texts resemble his opera librettos in their somewhat stilted and archaic style, though there are some appealing images and phrases. But as Bevan points out, what Coutts has manufactured for Albéniz are 'skilfully-written lyrics in the style of the Victorian ballad, or parlour song'.[100] This may have been unconscious

---

[99] See Falces, *Pacto de Fausto*, for an excellent study of all the Coutts songs, especially from a textual point of view.

[100] For a brief but insightful treatment of these songs, see Bevan, 'Albéniz', 210–21. This quote is on page 215, as is the stanza from 'The Rosary'. Both Falces and Bevan have built on the foundation of José María Llorens Cisteró's article 'El "Lied" en la obra musical de Isaac Albéniz', *Anuario musical*, 15 (1960), 123–40.

imitation, but a simple comparison proves the point. The following is the first stanza of Rogers and Nevin's 'The Rosary' (1898):

> The hours I spent with thee, dear heart,
>   Are as a string of pearls to me;
> I count them over ev'ry one apart,
>   My rosary, my rosary!

This bears an unmistakable resemblance to the first stanza of Coutts's 'A Song of Consolation':

> Again, dear heart, we snatch an hour
>   From Time, who grudges bliss:
> Thy lips unfold, like morning flower
>   To pout the promised kiss!

Albéniz had no more idea than Coutts what kind of verse this was; both probably thought it was high art. As a result, his setting of the text is virtuosic and contrived, out of step with the simple, homespun sentiments Coutts expresses. As usual, Albéniz invests most of the musical interest in the accompaniment, while the voice declaims in a syllabic fashion that is at once tricky to sing and melodically forgettable (false relations further exacerbate the conflict between voice and piano). This collision of styles renders the songs somewhat less than convincing, though a happy exception to this is 'To Nellie'. For once Albéniz relegates the piano to a supportive role, and the voice has a lovely melody to sing in B Aeolian (Ex. 33).

Other Coutts songs from 1896 include 'Will you be mine?' and 'Separated' (the only extant numbers from a collection of six songs), completed in Brighton on 29 November and 4 December, respectively.[101] As their titles suggest, they are in the same vein of Victorian sentiment as the *Six Songs*. 'The Gifts of the Gods' (Brussels: Dogilbert, 1897) later appeared with 'The Caterpillar' as a set of two songs.[102] The latter song is charming and makes effective use of the Dorian mode. Like 'To Nellie', it succeeds by giving preference to the voice over the piano. One other song, composed in 1906 but never published during his lifetime, is 'Art thou gone for ever, Elaine?'.[103]

---

[101] MS in the Oc (pub. Madrid: Instituto de Bibliografía Musical, 1997).

[102] Though most catalogues list these as a group of two songs, based on the Édition Mutuelle publication of 1913, Falces, *Pacto de Fausto*, 157–8, argues against considering them a pair. 'The Caterpillar' was composed at least six years later than 'The Gifts of the Gods', in 1903. Moreover, Albéniz always took his poems for groups of songs from the same collection. 'The Gifts of the Gods' comes from Coutts's *Poems* (1896), whereas 'The Caterpillar' appeared in *Musa Verticordia* (1895). Both songs were translated into French by Henry Varley for the 1913 edition (entitled 'Les Dons des dieux' and 'La Chenille').

[103] Discussed in Llorens Cisteró, 'Lied', 15. The MS is dated Paris, Apr. 1906. He examined it at the Ah, but it may now be at the Mm.

Ex. 33. *To Nellie: Six Songs*: 'To Nellie', bars 1–8

Albéniz was not confined to Coutts's poetry, and around this same time he composed the lovely 'Chanson de Barberine' to a text by Alfred de Musset (Madrid: Unión Musical Española, 1972). But, in fact, his future was more than ever bound up with that of his benefactor, and the following four years would absorb him in a project beyond the dimensions of anything he had previously attempted. It would ultimately prove beyond his abilities as well— and irrelevant to his importance in the history of music.

6

The Imperfect Wagnerite
(1898–1904)

———

THE next product of Albéniz's professional association with Coutts was an operatic project on a truly grand scale, one that held tremendous importance for Coutts, if not as much for Albéniz. This was a trilogy of operas based on the Arthurian romance *Le Morte d'Arthur* by the fifteenth-century English author Sir Thomas Malory. The constituent parts of the *King Arthur* trilogy were to be *Merlin*, *Launcelot*, and *Guenevere*. The urgency Coutts felt about this project is already apparent in a letter of 4 January 1895 (previously quoted in connection with his quest for a suitable title for *Henry Clifford*), in which he relates the following:

I am feeling very much upset by the coming production of a drama at the Lyceum taken from the King Arthur legend. 10 years ago I projected writing 3 operas on that theme, and have amassed a large quantity of material. I could finish all 3 in a year, whenever opportunity offered. But now this wretch, this author, has got my precise idea! Instead of using Tennyson, he has gone back to the original legend as told in the book called 'Morte d'Arthur'. He has taken Morgan Le Fay as one of the principal characters (which Tennyson never did) and in fact, seems to me to have sucked my brains, probably through the perfidy of some kind friend to whom I may have talked of the scheme! I have always done myself an infinity of harm by speaking of my projects to others. I get carried away by my subject & forget that theatrical authors, critics, & managers are thieves and vagabonds! But it is very hard and makes me feel very depressed.

His devotion to *King Arthur* did not wane with the passage of time. On 23 May 1903,[1] Coutts wrote to Rosina in response to her concerns about the financial arrangements between him and her husband. She felt that Albéniz was not producing a quantity of music commensurate with the generous stipend he was affording them. To this he responded:

[1] Letter in the Mm, car. 2.

The process, in the case of music, is of course slow; but it has been no slower than I anticipated, & when it is finished, my dear Madame, remember this: whatever 'The Public' may think of our operas, we shall have done, to the utmost of our ability, a work that in England can never be disregarded; we shall have written *The National Trilogy.*

Of course, no country would be complete without a National Trilogy, and it would indeed have been difficult for the redoubtable duo of Albéniz and Coutts to set their sights much higher than this. We begin to appreciate the fact that Albéniz was not only involved in the creation of Spanish national opera, but English as well. However, this could raise the question as to what national opera really is, when it consists of a Wagnerian opera composed by a Spaniard on an English libretto. But Coutts's vision was neither prophetic nor was it shared by Albéniz himself. In fact, if one reads between the lines in the letter, it becomes clear that other, more personal dynamics were coming into play. Rosina was probably using the composer's snail pace as an expedient for getting him out of a project she felt weighed too greatly upon him. Be that as it may, Albéniz's wonted facility of composition did, in fact, fail him as he waded into a musical bog from which he had increasing difficulty extricating himself. It took him several years to finish the first opera,[2] and the trilogy as a whole remained incomplete at his death.

Rosina was not the only one who harboured doubts about the merits of the project. In a letter to Albéniz dated 15 April 1897, Count Morphy offered these reflections on the trilogy: 'Let us suppose the work is finished. What will be its result? In the first place, it will have to endure the attacks of fanatical Wagnerites who presume it to be imitating or competing with the famous Trilogy.'[3] Morphy does not suggest that Albéniz go back on his word and withdraw, but he questions whether the result will be worth sacrificing his health and efforts, which could be more profitably directed elsewhere. After all, Wagner had enormous resources at his command. Where, Morphy asks, is Albéniz's Bavarian King Ludwig, his Liszt? At all events, he urges him to end his self-imposed exile and return to Barcelona or Madrid to finish the work.

This Arthurian episode is treated in the secondary literature as an incredible aberration in Albéniz's career, a totally misguided effort that was foisted

---

[2] To be sure, Albéniz, nearly completed *Merlin* in 1898, but he then got mired down in numerous and extensive revisions. In fact, he never finished the orchestration of Act I. After Albéniz died Coutts sent it to León Jehin, director of the Monte Carlo orchestra, for completion. There was a possibility of a production there in 1920–1, but it never took place. This information is from Coutt's letters to Rosina in the Mm (car. 2).

[3] Bc, 'M'. 'Supongamos la obra concluida. ¿Cual va á ser su resultado? En primer lugar ha de sufrir los ataques de los fanáticos Wagnerianos por suponer que imita o quiere competir con la famosa Trilogía.' Although Wagner's *Ring* is usually referred to as a tetralogy, in fact the composer himself described it as a trilogy with a 'Prelude-evening' (*Vorabend*), and this is undoubtedly what Morphy had in mind in this excerpt.

on him by the eccentric Maecenas in whose hands he had unwisely placed his
financial well-being. Edgar Istel was particularly harsh in his assessment of
this episode in Albéniz's career:

So, the poor Spaniard was forced to torment himself writing in Wagner's manner and
to compose a 'Merlin'... textually as well as musically nothing but an uninspired
Wagner imitation; in vain poor Albéniz tried to find a way out of the labyrinth of his
leading motives, which he handled 'improvisationally'. How entirely disoriented, with
what an absolute misconception of his own most personal gifts, Albéniz was at that
time, may be deduced from the fact that he, the charming improvisor of the pianistic
miniature, when he composed 'Merlin', made a special trip to Munich, in order to
hear 'Die Götterdämmerung', and upon his return confided to a friend, amid sobs,
that he felt he must confess an evil thought he had entertained—he had envied
Wagner.[4]

The notion that he would regard envy of Wagner as an evil thought and
sob about it seems a fatuous exaggeration. In a journal entry of 20 May 1897
he reports hearing a barrel organ ('organillo') playing the 'religious march'
from Act II of *Lohengrin* in waltz time outside his room at the Hotel Saxe in
Prague. '¡Oh la popularidad!' he exclaims, with a discernible trace of envy.[5]
But Albéniz was a confirmed Wagnerite, if an imperfect one, and envy of the
Master was not evil but inevitable.

Indeed, one could see the project as consistent with Albéniz's ever-waxing
devotion to Wagnerism, a love affair that went back perhaps as far as his days
as a student of Louis Brassin in Brussels. We have noted that during his
London years he made a deep impression on Bernard Shaw with his performance of Brassin's transcriptions of selections from *Das Rheingold* and *Die
Walküre*. Albéniz attended performances of Wagner's operas whenever possible. During his stay in Karlsruhe in 1897 he stated in a diary entry of 3 April
that he had spent the entire day studying the score of *Tristan und Isolde*
before attending a performance of it in the evening, conducted by Felix
Mottl. 'Wagner has written nothing better', was his estimation of the work.[6]
While in Prague for the rehearsals of his own opera, Albéniz attended
productions of *Das Rheingold*, *Die Walküre*, *Siegfried*, and *Die Götterdämmerung*. His diary contains enthusiastic commentary regarding the whole
cycle, and he praised the performance of *Siegfried* in this way: 'Never have I

---

   [4] 'Isaac Albéniz', 136–7.
   [5] *Impresiones*, ed. Franco, 46. Albéniz achieved a similar popularity many decades after his death, when the
rock group The Doors used excerpts from 'Asturias (Leyenda)' in their 1968 recording 'Spanish Caravan'. In
the early 1990s a television commercial featured the guitarist Manuel Barrueco in the back seat of a particular
make of car playing 'Asturias (Leyenda)', to demonstrate the quietness of the ride. Unlike Wagner, however,
the name of Albéniz remains unknown to the majority of those who recognize his music.
   [6] *Impresiones*, ed. Franco, 42. 'Wagner no ha escrito nada mejor.'

felt such intense pleasure with the works of Wagner as that provided by the one yesterday.' 'Say what they will, that man has been a colossus.'[7] Detailed annotations made by Albéniz in his personal copies of the full scores to the *Ring* cycle reveal a profound knowledge of the music.[8]

The fact that Albéniz would compose an opera upon this subject should not strike us as so strange, considering the fascination with things Arthurian that gripped *fin-de-siècle* artists and musicians. The most conspicuous operatic example of this phenomenon would be *Le Roi Arthus* (premiered 1903) by Albéniz's close friend Ernest Chausson, though the Catalan composer Amadeu Vives also wrote an Arthurian opera, entitled *Artus* (1895). Other cases could be cited, however: Hubert Parry's *Guenever* (1886), Carl Goldmark's *Merlin* (1886), Theodor Hentschl's *Launcelot* (1898), Herman Bemberg's *Elaine* (1892), Max Vogrich's *König Arthur* (1893), and Adolf von Doss's *Percifal* (1883). And, of course, there was the influence on him of Felip Pedrell, who had composed his Wagnerian trilogy *Els Pirineus* only a few years earlier, in 1891.

But the unfortunate result of his Wagner worship was that he compared himself very unfavourably to his idol. On 30 May 1897 his appraisal of his own work relative to *Die Götterdämmerung* descended to the scatological: 'music must be classified in two categories: that which is a work of the spirit and that which is fecal; in effect, there is an infinity of composers—among which, alas!, I include myself—who write music the way they digest [food], yes, and the result is . . . that.'[9] His long-standing friendships with Count Morphy and Tomás Bretón were strained by their unbelief. Bretón wrote him a letter on 26 March 1897 (Bc, 'B') disparaging Wagner, and Albéniz responded contemptuously to Rosina that the letter was 'inconceivable' in its 'presumption and ignorance'.[10] One wonders if the fact that the next letter from Bretón in the archive dates from three years later indicates a rift between them as a result of this clash. Morphy kept up a steady drumbeat of opposition to Wagner and to one of the Master's chief apostles in Spain, the composer Enric Morera. Already in 1895 he had accused Albéniz of 'falling into the the pit of Morera, [where] the Wagnerian dragon is opening his jaws'. The Spanish love of song and indifference to purely orchestral

[7] Ibid. 48. 'Nunca he sentido con las obras de Wagner el intenso placer que proporcionó la de ayer.' 'Vamos, digan lo que quieran, ese hombre ha sido un coloso.'

[8] Published Mainz: Schott, n.d. These have surfaced in the library of La Escuela Superior de Canto in Madrid. They bear Albéniz's stamp, dated 16 Apr. 1896. The scores were eventually bequeathed to Enrique Arbós, who then gave them to the school. I thank Prof. Jacinto Torres for bringing them to my attention.

[9] *Impresiones*, ed. Franco, 49: 'hay que clasificar la música en dos clases: la que es obra del espíritu y la fecal; en efecto, hay un sinfín de autores, entre los cuales, ¡ay!, me incluyo, que hacen música, como hacen la digestion, si, y el resultado es . . . ese.'

[10] 30 Mar. 1897 (Mm, 10.339).

music resonates in his disdain for Wagner, 'who with such facility expresses everything with the orchestra and not with words'.[11] Albéniz evidently replied that Morphy was an enemy of progress and failed to see the importance of Wagner's reforms. To this Morphy responded that Wagner was fine for Germany but not for Spain. He regretted seeing someone like Albéniz, endowed by God with 'genius, light, and beauty', converted into a disciple of Morera.[12]

Albéniz's commitment to Wagnerian principles in the trilogy is apparent in his use of leading motives and their presentation and development almost exclusively in the orchestra. It is also apparent in his avoidance of simultaneous singing and his treatment of the voices, i.e. in the emphasis on clarity of declamation and renunciation of fioritura. Indeed, during his stay in Prague he wrote to his wife that the Italian tenor Tamagno was residing in his hotel, and this fact brought forth from him a denunciation of 'the most stupid liberties of the most stupid Italian school'.[13] A few years later, while in Milan looking for a publisher for *Merlin*, Albéniz declared in another letter to her that the Ricordi firm represented 'all the horror of the Italian school'.[14] Since Ricordi was Puccini's publisher, it is possible that this was an expression of his feelings about that composer's works. What Albéniz apparently objected to in contemporary Italian opera, then, was what he perceived to be a lack of academic rigour (in the case of Mascagni) and its penchant for 'horrifying' story lines (not to mention the liberties taken by Italian singers). This is not to say, however, that there is no trace of Italian influence in his own operas. *Henry Clifford* owes a great debt to Verdi, while much of the flowing lyricism in *Pepita Jiménez* is reminiscent of Puccini; we have already commented on that plot's similarity to *Cavalleria rusticana*. Albéniz's derogation of things Italian (we recall his critique of Mascagni) had a cultural basis and reflected resentment of the surpassing influence of Italian music and musicians in Spain during the eighteenth and nineteenth centuries. On a personal level, his snobbery undoubtedly masked envy of the success of composers like

---

[11] Letter of 23 Dec. 1895, signed 'Tu padre Abraham' (Bc, 'A'): 'que solo con la orquesta y sin palabras con tal facilidad todo lo expresa.'

[12] Letter of 15 Mar. 1896, signed 'Papa Abraham' (Bc, 'A').

[13] Dated 19 May 1897 (Mm, 10.343): 'las mas estupidas libertades de la mas estupida escuela Italiana.' Francesco Tamagno (1850–1905) was an international musical celebrity. According to Enrique Franco, *Impresiones*, 69 n., Tamagno was especially popular at the Teatro Real in Madrid. Albéniz made his remarks about Tamagno in regard to his appearance in Meyerbeer's *Le Prophète* in Prague at that time. In this same letter he states he has made the acquaintance of Tamagno, 'which is to say I have met the ideal of an ass' ('que es lo mismo que haber conocido el ideal del Burro').

[14] Dated 17 Nov. 1902 (Mm, 10.280): 'todo el horror de la escuela italiana.' In his 5 Jan. 1896 review of the Barcelona production of *Pepita Jiménez*, Herman Klein, friend of Albéniz and Coutts, stated: 'An opera with a happy ending is as great a rarity nowadays as one that does not deal with the lowest passions and the most sordid motives.'

Mascagni and Puccini, success that he himself craved but never came close to achieving in the theatre.

Albéniz's opinion of the 'Italian school' was in sympathy with Coutts's. In his dedication to Albéniz in the *King Arthur* librettos (1897), 'Mountjoy' took the Italians to task in this way:

The experience thus gained has revealed many things to us, and among them the strange and unjustifiable separation that has taken place between literature and music...the fault [for this] lies chiefly at the door of the composers themselves, especially those of the Italian school; who have asked for words as a decorator asks for nails, in order to hang upon them ready-made gew-gaws.

Coutts went on to praise Albéniz by invoking Wagner:

But such has never been your demand.... On the contrary, you clearly recognize how 'twin-born' are the 'harmonious sisters', music and poetry; truly appreciating that portion of Wagner's teaching which would carry us back to the wisdom of the Elizabethan composers.

So now they would show the Italians how opera was properly to be done. When precisely the Arthurian project commenced is not known. Coutts wrote to Albéniz on 15 January 1897 (Bc, 'C'), stating that the libretto for *Launcelot* was finished. All three librettos were published that same year, in a limited edition of 200 copies, by the publisher John Lane in London. The manuscript for the Prelude to Act I of *Merlin* is dated Paris, October 1898.[15] Albéniz's copy of the trilogy libretto bears the date 20 January 1901 at the end of *Merlin*. He autographed the full score 'Barcelona 25 de Abril de 1902'. A piano–vocal arrangement was published in 1906 by Édition Mutuelle in Paris.[16] Unfortunately, Albéniz completed only the piano–vocal score of the first of *Launcelot*'s three acts.[17] Marginalia in the libretto represent his furthest progress with the four acts of *Guenevere*.

Even a casual glance at the Prelude to Act I reveals that Albéniz had taken an impressive leap to a new level of composition. It is scored for piccolo, three flutes, two oboes, cor anglais, three Bb clarinets, bass clarinet, three bassoons, contrabassoon, four F horns, four trumpets, three trombones, bass

---

[15] In the Mm, Lligall 7, with parts and score in Catalan and English. This was probably used for the 1950 production. There are, in fact, two MS orchestral scores of the Prelude, one consisting of only 30 bars, and the other, cited above, containing 105. Torres, 'La producción escénica', 192, points out that both share the same 30 bars of music, and that the extra material in the latter case seems simply to consititute elaboration. Which was composed first is unknown, but the longer version may well have been intended for concert use.

[16] In both English and French, translated by Maurice Kufferath. The libretto was at the Ah when the author examined it. It is now at the Mm. The MS full score is in the Bc, M977.

[17] The MS is in the Bc, sig. M983, and is dated Sept. 1902. Albéniz had begun work on the full score of Act II, working from the piano part written directly below the orchestral parts. But he only completed thirty-one pages. This MS is in the Mm, Lligall 6, and is dated Cannes, 17 Jan. 1903.

trombone, tuba, timpani, tam-tam, snare drum, two harps, and strings. The orchestration is not only rich but highly imaginative. It opens with a timpani roll juxtaposed against sustained notes in the string basses, horns, and contrabassoon, with the gradual addition of bassoon, bass clarinet, clarinet, and cello. Later on, he pits tremolandi strings against a melody in the low woodwinds (cor anglais, clarinet, and oboe). In addition, he employs divisi strings to fill out the texture called for by the rich harmonies. His mixing of colours is also remarkable, if one reflects on the scoring of *The Magic Opal* of only a few years earlier. At one point in the Prelude, a trombone choir plays triple pianissimo against a melody in the string basses. This is followed by a haunting theme in the cor anglais. Such mixtures of strings and brass are frequent throughout the score and reveal a new-found confidence in orchestration, the product not only of his experience in the theatre but also of the assistance he received from Paul Dukas. Federico Sopeña's derogation of Albéniz's skill as an orchestrator, citing his 'perplexity before orchestral work', is simply unsupportable here.[18]

The orchestral score reveals a rhythmic verve and variety not found in the piano–vocal version.[19] The subtle dynamic contrasts are also noteworthy, while the chromatic harmony, avoidance of separable numbers, Arthurian subject matter, and overall conception of an operatic polyptych clearly derive from Wagner. Moreover, Bevan has identified four significant leading motives in *Merlin*, and these in turn were apparently inspired by or taken directly from the *Ring*. One is associated with Arthur's destiny and appears first in the Prelude to Act I. It is identical to the 'Friedensmelodie' from Act III of *Siegfried*. The motives appear singly and in combination, and they migrate to the only completed act of the second opera, *Launcelot*.[20] This opera also presents new motives, similarly derived from the *Ring*. But, as in *The Magic Opal* and *Henry Clifford*, Albéniz finds a way to sneak out from behind the façade of the work to reveal his true identity as a Spaniard, and in the middle of Act III occur two enchanting Spanish-style dances.

The opera is in three acts. Act I takes place outside St Paul's church, in London, where the famous sword Excalibur is embedded in a marble block. Inside the church, monks are chanting; it is Christmas Day. Coutts states in the libretto that he has employed two hymn texts attributed to St Ambrose (340–97 CE), but Albéniz himself composed the melodies for the a cappella 'chant' sections in Act I. He has carefully contrived to simulate the metric

---

[18] *Historia de la música*, 2nd edn. (Madrid: EPESA, 1970), 124: 'perplejidad ante el trabajo orquestal.'
[19] The first two acts were arranged for piano by Albéniz, the third act by Mr J. M. d'Orellana.
[20] See Bevan, 'Albéniz', 191–9, for a discussion of Albéniz's Wagner borrowings.

Ex. 34. *Merlin*, Act I: 'Veni redemptor gentium', bars 1–6

freedom of Gregorian chant by eschewing a time signature (Ex. 34). Merlin appears and is soon confronted by Nivian, a Saracen dancing girl, who demands that she and her sisters be released from a spell Merlin has cast upon them. Merlin, however, will not yet accede to her demand. Various nobles now enter in preparation for choosing a king, to be determined by drawing the sword from the stone. Morgan Le Fay, queen of the land of Gore and an enchantress, steps forward to protest that the proceedings are nothing but Merlin's magic, claiming that her son Mordred is the rightful heir to the throne. Undeterred, the Archbishop of Canterbury permits Gawain, son of King Lot, to attempt to withdraw the sword from the stone. He is unsuccessful, as is Mordred who follows him. The assembly then quits the scene to attend a tournament, and guards are placed by the stone. Arthur now appears, in the company of Kay, son of Sir Ector. Arthur is making haste to the tournament but has forgotten his sword. He sees Excalibur and advances to seize it. Though warned away by the guards, he persists and succeeds in wresting the sword from its marmoreal sheath. Word quickly spreads, as Arthur reflects apprehensively on the fate now befalling him. The monks reappear, more chanting takes place, and the knights who were guarding the stone bear solemn witness to what they saw. Merlin reveals Arthur's royal lineage to an otherwise incredulous multitude, and the Archbishop triumphantly proclaims Arthur king, while Morgan and Mordred seethe with contempt. The act ends with an ensemble passage (six soloists, chorus, and orchestra) whose grandeur is without precedent in any of Albéniz's earlier stage works.

Act II transpires in a hall in Tintagil [*sic*] castle. Merlin conveys to Arthur the glad tidings that the rebellion of Morgan and Mordred has been put down and that they have been taken captive. Merlin is aware, however, that Arthur is in love with Guenevere and advises him against giving in to his passion, which advice Arthur sternly rejects. Sir Ector, Kay, and Gawain now enter in the company of nobles and knights. Their joint victory over Morgan and Mordred is celebrated, and the captives, along with the captain of their forces, Sir Pellinore, are brought forth for royal judgment and sentencing. Morgan feigns repentance for her sedition and pleads for mercy. The assembly's call for their execution notwithstanding, Arthur magnanimously pardons them, after which he knights Gawain. Morgan and Mordred are more determined than ever to overthrow Arthur, and Morgan intimates that his union with Guenevere will be the agency of his downfall. None the less, as long as Merlin remains puissant, Arthur is safe; therefore, Morgan casts about for a way to incapacitate Merlin. At this juncture, Nivian enters and explains the nature of the spell Merlin has cast upon her and her dancing sisters. It seems they are compelled by his magic to dance for the Gnomes, who, thus enticed, leave their grotto unguarded so that Merlin is able to steal their gold.[21] Nivian implores Morgan to break this spell, whereupon she enters into a scheme of Morgan's devising. This involves robbing Merlin of his staff so that he will be powerless to escape from the grotto, once a giant rock near its entrance rolls into place behind him. Nivian is advised that she must rely on her feminine wiles to secure the staff from Merlin, as no spell exists that can otherwise prevail over his powers. At this point Nivian leaves to answer a summons by Merlin, and the curtain descends with Morgan's wishing her 'good speed'.

An enchanting prelude is heard at the beginning of Act III, while the curtain is still down (Ex. 35). The curtain's ascent reveals a sylvan scene in the month of May. There is a cavern on one side and a lake in the distance, while Arthur lies resting at the foot of a beech tree. A chorus extols the joys of spring, and Arthur sings of his love for Guenevere. Merlin enters and warns Arthur yet again about the perils of his attraction to Guenevere. For his pains, however, Merlin is merely dispatched to ask Guenevere's hand in marriage on Arthur's behalf. Before setting out, Merlin decides to raid the Gnomes' store of gold. Nivian now appears with her troupe of dancers, captivating Merlin and the Gnomes with their undulations. They perform in time to Spanish-style music that has reminded most commentators of the

---

[21] The original tale by Malory was devoid of any such gold lust or exchange of wealth. Clearly, the banker in Coutts could not leave this unaltered. Of course, the model for this trilogy, Wagner's *Ring*, was based precisely on the theft and recovery of gold. See Bevan, 'Albéniz', 115, 120, for a discussion of this issue.

Ex. 35. *Merlin*, Act III: Prelude, bars 5–12

Ex. 36. *Merlin*, Act III: Dance of Nivian and the Saracens, bars 493–7

polo on which the entr'acte before Act IV of *Carmen* is based (Ex. 36).[22] The Gnomes are seduced out of their cavern and disappear in pursuit of the Saracens, leaving Nivian and Merlin alone. Night descends, and a choral number is accompanied by a bewitching play of lights across the stage. Nivian now dances alone for Merlin, so enchanting him that he agrees to her request to hold his staff. This dance is also very stylized but seems most akin to the *malagueña* (Ex. 37).[23]

All the while, Morgan is observing these developments in secret. Soon Merlin descends into the cave to plunder the gold, whereupon Nivian strikes a nearby boulder with the staff, causing it to roll over and seal the cave. Nivian rejoices in her new-won freedom and determines to return to her homeland. Morgan exults in her victory, and the curtain descends. The story

[22] See Ch. 7 for a further discussion of the *polo* in *Iberia*, 'El polo'.
[23] Bevan, 'Albéniz', 80, states that this dance was performed by the New Queen's Hall Orchestra in London on 12 Sept. 1917, Sir Henry Wood conducting. The dance numbers compensate for a lack of dramatic action in Act III, a solution Albéniz resorted to in *Pepita Jiménez*. This produces an effect that, while entertaining, retards the momentum towards the conclusion and is anticlimactic.

Ex. 37. *Merlin*, Act III: Nivian's Dance, bars 937–40

continues in the next two operas. In *Launcelot*, Guenevere, now the queen, is falsely accused of poisoning one of Arthur's knights, and Launcelot steps forward to be her champion. This development is accompanied by their mutual romantic attraction. In *Guenevere*, Launcelot is caught with the queen in her chamber (where he has been lured by a forged letter), and Arthur declares war on him. Arthur soon realizes, however, that Mordred is his real enemy, and they slay one another in mortal combat. Guenevere retires to a convent, and Launcelot is left alone to reflect ruefully on the demise of chivalry.

One of the chief problems any composer would have working with this libretto is Coutts's penchant for archaisms and stilted poetry. Even Coutts himself acknowledged as much in a letter to Albéniz of 26 June 1905 (Bc, 'C'), saying that he was 'anxious to eliminate ancient & obsolete words'. This was fortunate, for some of the expressions he uses definitely impede comprehension (though Coutts thoughtfully included a glossary in the published libretto): 'Not yet! More treasure I need | Foolish one, hark what I rede' (*Merlin*, Act I, 4); 'O fate uncouth! | O ban and bale' (*Merlin*, Act I, 13); 'Sore disworship shall be your guerdon, | Ruth and ruin to home and State!' (*Merlin*, Act II, 19). What agonies must the composer of 'Córdoba' have endured when he attempted to wrap his music around the following:

> Citadel isle of the wardering waters!
> Moated tower of the marching main!
> England! mother of sons and daughters
> Ruled to be monarchs, governed to reign! (*Merlin*, Act I, 16)

Or this:

> When flowerets of the marigold and daisy are enfolden,
> And wingless glow-moth stars of love englimmer all the glades,
> The paynim fairies footing forth in every forest olden
> Dance hand in hand the saraband with fair enchanted maids! (*Merlin*, Act III, 30)

Still, one must give Albéniz credit. He always managed to set Coutts's poetry with a sure sense of the accents of the language, no matter how contrived it was. But it is also easy to see why Albéniz resorted to a recitative style of vocal writing. Making any sort of lyric material out of this poetry would have stymied him completely.

Above and beyond his penchant for stilted and archaic language, Coutts's prudishness comes to the fore in the following instructions to Albéniz:

It is very important to maintain the strict idea of the Opera that Nivian wins the rod from Merlin without any *sexual* cajoleries at all. Such a disagreeable episode, however inevitably suspected by the *French* mind, would go far to ruin the Opera in England, besides being contrary to the *plot* of the Opera, which is that Nivian merely acts under Morgan's directions, in order to gain her liberty, and that Merlin regards her as *a child*, and for that very reason is quite off his guard.[24]

Coutts was evidently not very familiar with Freud or he would have seen that, even without 'sexual cajoleries', Nivian's 'winning the rod' was already heavily freighted with erotic innuendo. Interestingly, we once again encounter the 'woman-as-child' motif that runs like a thread through their correspondence. And, again, such a woman-child has yet the ability to rob a man, even a mighty sorcerer, of his powers and imprison him.

Merlin was never produced during Albéniz's lifetime (see Chapter 8 for a discussion of the 1950 premiere). The Prelude to Act I, however, was well received at its premiere in Barcelona on 14 November 1898, during the third in a series of four concerts Vincent d'Indy conducted with the Asociació Filarmònica, normally under the direction of Mathieu Crickboom.[25]

The process of composition and working at close quarters with Coutts took a toll on Albéniz. In March of 1898 he and Coutts were holed up in the Hotel Excelsior Regina Cimiez in Nice working on *King Arthur*. Albéniz wrote to Rosina that they had finished studying the libretto and that he himself had wanted to begin composing when Coutts suddenly declared that, in order to preserve Albéniz's health, they should wait to continue until after they returned from an excursion to Florence. This upset Albéniz, who was prepared to make the 'new sacrifice' of getting on with the job. Although he appreciated Coutts's friendly concern for his health, he then had to spend two 'interminable' hours with him and Nellie at dinner 'tête á

[24] From an undated list of corrections (Mm, 10.295).
[25] See *Diario de Barcelona*, 19 Nov. 1898, 12566–8, by F. Suárez Bravo. Bravo refers to his friend Albéniz as the 'untiring Catalan artist, never satisfied with what he has done and always fatigued by greater aspirations' ('incansable artísta catalán, nunca satisfecho con lo que ha hecho y fatigado siempre por aspiraciones mayores'). According to Bevan, 'Albéniz', 80, Crickboom himself conducted this Prelude at a concert of the Filarmònica at the Teatre Líric in Barcleona, possibly in 1908.

tête (triste á triste debiera decir [I should say])'. When he tried to extricate himself due to an upset stomach, Nellie accused him of inventing an excuse to leave. 'They hold me in their grasp like limpets', he complained.[26] He was understandably anxious to return home.

In the event, the family Coutts departed for Florence without Albéniz, who remained behind due to a cold and a bout of constipation. However, he was soon well enough to venture south to join them. A letter from Genoa indicates that his love of travel had not dimmed with the passage of time, and he promised Rosina that one day they would make this same Italian excursion together.[27] After Rome and Florence, he returned to Paris and his family.

We are indeed fortunate to have Albéniz's diary entries from this period to give us a glimpse of the inner man. However, he did not imagine his journal would remain private; he was clearly writing for an audience. He labels this portion of his diary 'Thoughts, Aphorisms, Paradoxes, and other Trifles, with Autobiographical Points and Elaborations, Nice, 1898'.[28] He began these entries at the Hotel Excelsior Regina Cimiez in Nice on 1 April 1898, expressing his long-standing desire 'to leave to posterity a permanent record of my important passage on this enchanting planet', a desire he claimed to have had since the age of 10. He tells us that his poor command of grammar and orthographics is due to 'the simple and lamentable reason of never having been in any school, much less in a lecture hall'.[29] He is on his way to Rome to join Coutts, and once there marvels at the beauty of the place, though he feels it a form of 'infidelity' to be doing so without his 'dona Perpetua' Rosina at his side. For this reason he will separate from Coutts and return to Paris in the hope of making the journey another time with her. By 10 April he is once again in Paris, and Spain's conflict with the United States over Cuba and the state of musical culture in his homeland weigh on his mind in an entry of ten days later. His reflections contain more than a bit of sarcasm:

My poor country will never change; to read the Madrid and Barcelona papers amidst the cruel circumstances through which it is passing, is truly dispiriting. . . . I read that the Orchestra, the Orchestra of Arévalo! has agreed to contribute to the national

---

[26] Letter of 29 Mar. 1898 (Mm, 10.346): 'como lapas me tienen agarrado.'

[27] Letter to Rosina of 4 Apr. 1898 (Mm, 10.357).

[28] 'Pensamientos, Aforismos, Paradojas y Otras Zarandajas, con sus puntos y Ribetes de Autobiografia, Niza, 1898.'

[29] '[D]ejar á la posteridad un imperecedero recuerdo de mi importante paso por este encantador planeta'; 'la sencillísima y lamentable razon de que no habiendo estado jamás en escuela alguna de primeras letras, y menos pisado un aula.' The original of this journal is in the Mm, car. 4. It is reproduced in *Impresiones*, ed. Franco, 59–67, though Franco did not consult the original MS and his edition contains omissions and errors. The excerpts that follow are based on the original manuscript.

subscription by organizing—what?—a concert?—no, sir—a bullfight with young bulls!!! And ... I read with satisfaction and pride that Spanish music has a new composer. The young Señor Grasses!!! What work has said señor produced? is it some kind of quartet? a symphony? a lyric work that gives off brilliant flashes of genius? perhaps a well thought-out and well-written sonata? ... no, sir, Señor Grasses has limited himself at the early age of twenty years to writing a set of waltzes ... and that is all.

Nothing ... there we are all heart, that is agreed ..., but an encephalitic mass ..., for what?[30]

What we find lacking here is any indignation over the actions of the United States. Count Morphy was at the centre of this crisis as the royal secretary and had written to him at this time complaining of 'Yankee treachery'.[31] But Albéniz's venom is reserved for his own country. No doubt the celebration of Grasses's modest attainments aroused memories of his own mistreatment at the hands of the critics in Madrid when he tried to do something beyond the ordinary. Of course, what had Albéniz written by the time *he* was 20? Nothing more than a 'military march' for piano. But his bitterness was intense and perhaps caused him to be a bit unfair. Around this time he wrote to Clementina and expressed himself on the subject of Spain with great candour:

I do not have to tell you the state of nervousness in which I find myself because of the numerous calamities that are befalling our unfortunate country. What remedy does it have? We have not corrected ourselves, nor will we ever. Ill-intentioned chauvinism blinds us in such a way that our faults appear to us virtues and our crass ignorance, inspired science. Send me your news, but do not tell me one word about anything else going on there, as I have decided to ignore what is happening and what will happen in Spain.[32]

---

[30] *Impresiones*, ed. Franco, 63. In the following original, the passages in brackets were omitted by Franco in his edition. Albéniz began interrogative sentences with a question mark placed not upside down but turned backwards (they are rendered here in normal position). He did not place his exclamation points upside down at the beginning of an emphatic statement. Albéniz was fond of using ellipses, and these are indicated by three points together followed by a space. Normal ellipses indicate editorial deletions. Albéniz was generally careless in his use of accents and punctuation. 'Mi pobre tierra no cambiará; el leer la prensa de Madrid y Barcelona, en medio de las crueles circunstancias porque atraviesa, es realmente desconsolador.... leo que la Orquesta, !la Orquesta de Arévalo ha acordado contribuir a la suscripcion nacional [organizado—que?—un concierto?—no senor—una novillada!!!] Y ... leo con satisfacción y orgullo que la España Musical cuenta con nada menos que con un nuevo compositor. El joven señor Grasses!!! ?que obra ha producido dicho senor? ?es algun cuarteto?, ?una sinfonia?, ?una obra lirica que despide brillantes destellos de genio? ?quiza una bien pensada y bien escrita sonata? ... no señor, el señor Grasses se ha limitado a la temprana edad de 20 años a escribir una tanda de valses ... et voila tout. Nada ... alli somos todo corazon, esto esta convenido ..., pero masa encefálica ... para qué?

[31] 15 Apr. 1898 (Bc, 'M').

[32] Letter to Clementina, cited in Sopeña, 'Gracia y drama', 129. 'Excuso decirte el estado de nerviosidad en que me hallo con motivo de las cuantiosas desdichas que sobre nuestro malaventurado país están cayendo. ¡Qué remedio tiene! ¡No hemos corregido, ni nos corregiremos jamás! El chauvinismo mal entendido nos

The year 1898 was one of severe health problems for Albéniz, which were even reported in the Barcelona press.[33] He devoted that summer to seeking relief at a health spa in Plombières. His intestines had always been a source of discomfort, and his penchant for overeating only made matters worse. A number of sources comment on Albéniz's large appetite and manner of eating. When dining out, he was wont to order all the dishes at once and then to stir them together into a mishmash, which he devoured rapidly and with great relish.[34] He also had a love of cognac in addition to his habitual 'puro' cigars, of which he was a genuine connoisseur. Arbós reported that Albéniz enjoyed strong foods, especially Catalan sausage. He liked nothing more than to curl up with a big salami and wash down the slices with generous swigs from a flask of gin. But these habits did not agree with his stomach and sometimes caused him to lose its contents. Undaunted after such episodes, he would return to his chair and continue eating.[35] Count Morphy upbraided him sharply for his abuse of food, drink, and tobacco. He accused him of being an 'obese musician' and deplored the 'terrible force' his 'gastronomic instinct' held over him. But he blended his chastisements with some home remedies like drinking lots of milk in small quantities and not taking fluids during meals, advice Albéniz probably disregarded.[36]

By the end of August Albéniz was ready to return home. He was still suffering some abdominal distress and feeling a bit weak, but at least the diarrhoea had stopped. However, old habits died hard. On 27 August 1898 he wrote to Rosina to have a box of Upman cigars (cost: 22 francs) in the house upon his return. He also wanted warm milk, which was all he was taking.[37] Clearly, with his new milk-and-cigars diet, Albéniz was trying to serve two masters at once. At least he never denied his gluttony and concomitant corpulence, as we have noted that he often signed his letters 'Saco' ('Sack'), 'El Gordo' ('The Fat One'), or 'Saco gordo' ('Fat Sack').

In his diary on 2 February 1899, he reported having completed the orchestration of the first half of Act I of *Merlin*, in spite of his poor state of health. 'The intimate satisfaction that completing one's *duty* provides is a lenitive for all moral and physical pain,' he wrote.[38] Albéniz's stoic attitude is

ciega de tal modo que nuestras faltas nos parecen virtudes y nuestra crasa ignorancia ciencia infusa. Dame noticias vuestras, pero no me hables una palabra de la cosa pública, pues he decidido ignorar lo que pase y lo que pasará en España.'

[33] Untitled clippings from 1898 in the Mm, Prov. M-987c.

[34] According to Joan Llongueres, 'Cómo conocí a Isaac Albéniz', in *Evocaciones y recuerdos* (Barcelona: Dalmau, 1944), excerpted in Franco (ed.), *Albéniz y su tiempo*, 111–13.

[35] From Arbós's autobiography, excerpted in 'Santander 1883', Franco (ed.), *Albéniz y su tiempo*, 118–19.

[36] Letters of 19 Oct. 1897, 23 Dec. 1895, and 27 Apr. 1898 (Bc, 'A' and 'M').

[37] Mm, 10.363.

[38] 'La íntima satisfacción que produce el cumplimiento del *deber*, es un lenitivo a todo dolor moral y físico.'

reflected in a letter from Coutts several years later in which the Englishman says, 'I can agree with all your ideas concerning the chastening and pacifying effects of suffering.'[39] But the state of his homeland as well as his health was still weighing on his mind. Five days after the previous entry, Albéniz wrote the following: 'One of the things that most saddens me when I reflect on the character that predominates in Spain is the petulant ignorance in which we live.'[40] It is worth noting that literacy rates in Spain around 1900 were remarkably low, and less than half the population could read and write.[41] None the less, there was in Spain at this time a renaissance in letters, music, and art, and Albéniz was one of its chief representatives. Ironically, it was precisely at this moment that the nation reached the nadir of its imperial fortunes and seemed in a state of irreversible decline.

The death of the Spanish empire in the conflict with the United States paralleled personal losses in Albéniz's life that proved far more painful. On 10 June 1899 Ernest Chausson died in a freak bicycling accident that shocked and saddened his friends and admirers, who rightly felt that he was just beginning a distinguished career as a composer (he was only 44 years old). Albéniz participated in the funeral ceremonies, and from Paris he wrote a moving tribute to his late friend that appeared in the Spanish press on 5 July 1899.[42] In it he reminded his readers that although Chausson had been

immensely rich, he never employed his wealth in vain ostentation, nor tried to use it to gain easily a position that he did not deserve solely on the basis of his intrinsic artistic merit. . . . his left hand never knew the benefits that his right hand was lavishly dispensing. His death has been a widespread sorrow and the emptiness that it leaves among his friends is impossible to fill!!

That Albéniz was upset about this loss is apparent from a letter of 17 June 1899 (Bc, 'C') that Coutts wrote to console him, a letter that reveals some of Albéniz's own thoughts on his friend's untimely demise:

[39] Letter of 6 Apr. 1905 (Mm, 10.341).
[40] *Impresiones*, ed. Franco, 64. 'Una de las cosas que más me contristan cuando reflexiono sobre el carácter que en España predomina, es la petulante ignorancia en que vivimos.'
[41] But the 19th cent. had witnessed great improvement. Jacinto Torres, *Las publicaciones periódicas musicales en España (1812–1990)* (Madrid: Instituto de Bibliografía Musical, 1991), 15, cites a study by Sánchez Agesta, *Historia del constitucionalismo español* (Madrid: IEP, 1974), 507, stating that in 1803 only 5.96% of the Spanish population was literate. By the end of the century, this figure had increased to 33.45%. It now stands at above 95%.
[42] This clipping, without the newspaper's name, is in the Mm, Prov. M-987c: 'inmensamente rico, nunca empleó sus riquezas en vana ostentación, ni procuró, gracias á ellas, escalar facilmente un puesto que tan solo quería deber á su intrínseco mérito artístico. . . . no sabiendo nunca su mano izquierda los beneficios que prodigamente dispensaba la derecha. Su muerte ha sido un duelo general y el vacio que deja entre sus amigos, imposible de llenar!!'

Is it not certain, rather, that however altruistic we may become, through subsequent 'planes' of being, we can never lose our ego, unless at the cost of annihilation? The children [of Chausson],—yes, it is wonderful to remark their insusceptibility; but who would rob them of it? The contrary instinct will develop. Life will teach it them; and which is greater,—their egoism, in not realizing their father's death, or his egoism, if he wished them to realize it? Dear friend,—be still the poetical philosopher; do not let your philosophy fossilize into a religion. You will find nothing in philosophy half so full of wisdom as that complexity of nature which causes us so many pangs of thought.

The 'complexities of nature' continued unabated into August, when Albéniz's patron and friend Count Morphy passed away on the 28th of that month. The following year brought Albéniz further 'pangs of thought' with the death of his mother in April. This loss provoked the following reflections from him:

for myself it appears to me that I have lost an integral part of my being. . . . death is the most regular and necessary thing and . . . to die at a certain age . . . is not only regular and necessary, but rather a supreme relief and a supreme pleasure, especially when during life, whether because of character or minimal intellectual development or because of circumstances surrounding the individual, one lived in eternal torment. Our poor mother has been a good example of that![43]

Albéniz had been conveying money to his father through Clementina for at least ten years. In 1892 his parents had attempted a reconciliation of sorts. By living with Dolores, Ángel hoped to benefit from her part of his pension. But he insisted on bringing his mistress and children with him, and Dolores understandably chose to move back in with her daughter in Madrid; Ángel returned to Barcelona. Thus, Ángel's death in March of 1903 occasioned a different response from his son. Albéniz wrote to Clementina that there was 'no reason for hypocritical lamentations' concerning the death, and his bitterness (which Clementina felt even more intensely) was a lasting monument to their complex and trying relationship.[44]

Charles Bordes had appointed Albéniz to teach piano at the Schola Cantorum in 1897; on account of his intense involvement with composition, however, Albéniz was now less interested in teaching that he had been before. He took a more casual approach, and a couple of episodes from

[43] Letter to Clementina, cited in Sopeña, 'Gracia y drama', 131: 'a mi mismo me parece que me falta una parte integral de mi ser. . . . el morir es la cosa más regular y necesaria y . . . morir a cierta edad . . . no tan sólo es regular y necesario, sino un supremo alivio y un supremo goce, máxime cuando durante la vida, ya sea por el carácter, ya por el escaso desarrollo intelectual o por las circunstancias que rodearon al indivíduo, éste vivió en un eterno tormento. ¡Nuestra pobre madre ha sido de ello un buen ejemplo!'

[44] Letter from Château Saint-Laurent in Nice dated 19 Mar. 1903. Cited in Ruiz Albéniz, *Albéniz*, 103.

his tenure there illustrate the point.[45] On one occasion, Albéniz was so engrossed in his creative endeavours that he neglected his teaching at the Schola Cantorum for several days. The director sent someone to his house to check up on him, and when the door opened, a plump, bearded visage delivered this news: 'I am not the Albéniz you are looking for. I am his twin brother. The maestro died last week.' When the envoy returned to the Schola Cantorum with this distressing report, Bordes, d'Indy, and Alexandre Guilmant, the organ teacher, went to see for themselves. Of course, the joke was on them, and Albéniz got a good laugh out of it. On another occasion, one of Albéniz's piano students at the Schola Cantorum was rather timid in his performance of the 'Appassionata' Sonata of Beethoven, and Albéniz interrogated him about his love life. When the young man answered that he had no girlfriend and had never had relations with the opposite sex, Albéniz replied that he should leave off making music, as certain works could not be played with 'blood of tiger-nut milk'.[46] The boy's father was not happy with this sage counsel, however, and protested to the administration. But the affair was forgotten. In fact, what the father hoped to accomplish, Albéniz's ill health succeeded in doing by forcing him to give up the position in 1900. D'Indy wrote to Albéniz in this year expressing regret that his Spanish friend would not be able to continue on as an instructor.[47] None the less, Albéniz did have two students who went on to distinguish themselves: René de Castéra and Déodat de Séverac. Castéra (1873–1955) composed a wide variety of pieces, including *Jour de fête au Pays Basque* for orchestra. In 1902 he founded Édition Mutuelle, which published many of the works of Schola Cantorum students, as well as Albéniz's *Iberia*. Séverac (1872–1921) actually had Aragonese ancestry and was a student of d'Indy at the Schola Cantorum. He was a prolific composer of songs who also completed Albéniz's *Navarra*.

Albéniz's association with the Schola Cantorum inspired his most charming work for piano, *Yvonne en visite!*, whose two movements bear the titles 'La Révérence' ('The curtsy') and 'Joyeuse Rencontre, et quelques pénibles événements!!' ('Joyous encounter, and some painful events!!'). It appeared

[45] From a typewritten document by the Catalan violinist Marià Perelló (b. 1886) entitled 'Apuntes para una biografía de Isaac Albéniz: recuerdos personales' (Mm, car. 1), 7–8. See also Collet, *Albéniz*, 60–4. We do not know if this was Perelló's source for the stories.

[46] Collet relates a similar story in which Albéniz chided a student for his coldness and ascribed it to a lack of amorous experience—the student happened, however, to be a priest! Whether this was on another occasion or simply a variant of the above tale is impossible to say.

[47] Many of the records of the Schola Cantorum from this period have evidently not survived, and the exact years of Albéniz's work there are difficult to document. Kalfa, 'Albéniz à Paris', 33, gives the period of his instruction as 1897–1901. But the letter from d'Indy (Bc, 'I'), dated 7 Oct. 1900, refers to his having left his position there due to sickness. This is cited in Llorens Cisteró, 'Inéditas', 96.

in a collection of pieces for children 'small and large' by musicians at the Schola Cantorum.[48] This delightfully humorous work contains Albéniz's annotations (in the manner of Erik Satie) describing a visit of the young pianist Yvonne Guidé,[49] who is forced to perform by her mother. Yvonne gets a bad case of nerves and stumbles through her repertoire, while her increasingly unhappy mother threatens her with ten days of Hanon exercises!

Albéniz was also involved with another important musical institution in Paris at this time, the Société Nationale de Musique (founded 1871). Letters from Chausson reveal that Albéniz's services as a performer and composer were in demand at Société Nationale de Musique concerts, and that his music, including *Rapsodia española*, was also featured on several programmes.[50] Albéniz's single most important work for orchestra, *Catalonia*, premiered at a concert of the Société Nationale de Musique on 28 May 1899 in the Nouveau-Théâtre.[51] The critic Lomagne declared it 'the most brilliant Spanish fantasy' since Chabrier's *España*.[52] *Catalonia* (Paris: Durand, 1899), dedicated to the Catalan artist Ramón Casas (1866–1932), was conceived as a 'Suite populaire' of compositions inspired by his homeland. But Albéniz abandoned work on the other pieces and contented himself with the first number.[53] The work is scored for a large ensemble consisting of piccolo, two flutes, two oboes, cor anglais, two clarinets, bass clarinet, two bassoons, contrabassoon, four horns, two trumpets, three trombones, tuba, timpani, cymbals, harp, and strings. It was supposedly inspired by a trip to a small village in the Catalan countryside where a festival with music and dance was taking place. It is one of the few works in which he quotes pre-existing

---

[48] *Album pour enfants petits et grands. Recueil de pièces de piano, à deux et quatre mains, composées par un groupe de musiciens de la Schola Cantorum* (Paris: Édition Mutuelle, n.d.). *Yvonne en visite!* was later published separately in 1909 by Rouart, Lerolle et Cie. and by Édition Mutuelle.

[49] His 'dear little friend' to whom the work is dedicated; she may have been the daughter of G. Guidé, co-director of the Théâtre Royal de la Monnaie in Brussels.

[50] There are eighteen letters from Chausson in the Bc, and sixteen of them pertain to Société concerts. Letters 10 and 14 (both undated) request his services as pianist in a Duparc transcription for two pianos of a Franck chorale, and the Fourth Trio of Lalo, respectively. No. 17 has already been cited in regard to the publication of Chausson's *Poème*.

[51] Most sources give 27 May as the date, but it was announced in *Écho de Paris* on the 28th, as the 'Suite Espagnole'. It received a brief but favourable appraisal of its 'tumultuous Catalan joy' in that paper following day (clipping in the Mm, Prov. M-987e).

[52] According to Collet, *Albéniz*, 69.

[53] The MSS for *Catalonia* are in the Bc, M984. The work was begun in Jan. 1899 in Paris. Albéniz's shaky orthography is in evidence, as he reverses the orientation of the exclamation points, *!Catalonia¡*. Although this was apparently to be the first piece in the suite, he began work on another piece, the MS of which is labelled 'Primer Fragmento del No. 1 (Comacho)' and dated 20 Apr. 1899. This second piece bears a dedication to the Catalan artist Josep-Marià Sert (1874–1945). It remained incomplete. Interestingly, another MS in M984 is *Rapsodie Almogávar*, also begun in Jan. 1899. Although it is only a single page, it is identical to the opening of *Catalonia*. Almogávars were Catalan soldiers of the Middle Ages. This raises a question as to Albéniz's initial programmatic conception of the work.

melodies, in this case the Catalan folk songs 'El pobre terrisaire' and 'La Filadora', which form the thematic material of the piece. The woodwinds evoke the *flabiol*, a fipple flute used in the *coblas* (groups of strolling musicians) of the *sardana*, the famous Catalan circle dance.[54] The work is in free sonata form, and the exposition moves from tonic to dominant in E♭ major; the development evolves seamlessly out of the secondary area. The retransition is dominated by augmented chords and whole-tone scales (a device he would later employ in *Iberia*), but a shock awaits purists with the arrival of the 'recapitulation' at rehearsal 47 in E major rather than E♭. The score calls for the entrance of a group of 'strolling musicians' (*musiciens ambulants*), and the wayward tonality of their rendition of the principal theme lends a humorously out-of-tune character to it. But the theme soon settles into a dominant preparation for the correct key (E♭), in which the secondary theme returns in a new rhythmic guise (2/4) in the concluding presto section.

Dukas was tutoring Albéniz in orchestration during this time and assisted him in the instrumentation of both *Catalonia* and the Prelude to Act I of *Merlin*.[55] But the musical debt Albéniz owed Dukas extended beyond that. The principal theme of *Catalonia* bears a marked resemblance to that of Dukas's *L'Apprenti sorcier* (1897) in its grouping of three measures of 3/8 into a seeming 9/8 phrase. The rhythm is also similar, as the comparison between fragments of the two themes in Example 38 makes clear. The whole-tone scales and augmented chords Albéniz employs also suggest the assimilation of a French harmonic idiom alien to his earlier compositions, and further reinforce the impression that Dukas's famous tone poem served as a model for *Catalonia*. Despite this, the work possesses great originality and may well be the finest nineteenth-century orchestral work

Ex. 38. (*a*) *L'Apprenti sorcier*, principal theme, bars 3–5,
(*b*) *Catalonia*, variant of principal theme, bars 10–12 (cello)

---

[54] According to José Luis García del Busto, trans. Michael Fink, liner notes for *España* (Philips CD 432 826-2, 1992). The work's programme and the titles of the folk melodies appear in a set of programme notes now in the Mm, car. 3.

[55] A letter from Dukas of 17 Mar. 1902 (Bc, 'D') enquires about Albéniz's handling of trumpets, trombones, and harps in the Prelude to Act I of *Merlin*. Paul Gilson was also giving him advice, as evidenced by a letter without date (Bc, 'G') that concludes with a brief lesson in orchestration advising him not to put clarinet and oboe on the middle notes of a chord.

by a Spanish composer; it is certainly the only one to remain in the standard repertoire.

Though Albéniz was unsuccessful in getting *Merlin* produced, the Prelude to Act I of the opera enjoyed some popularity during his day. After the premiere in Barcelona under d'Indy in 1898, it was performed at the Conservatoire de Nancy on 22 January 1899. During this concert Albéniz also executed the solo keyboard part in Bach's 'Brandenburg' Concerto No. 5. In the words of the conservatory's director, Joseph Guy-Marie Ropartz (1864–1955), his was an 'incomparable interpretation'.[56]

We should not be surprised that Albéniz's involvement in Parisian life extended beyond music. He was an ardent Dreyfusard and supported the Jewish officer in the French army wrongly accused of espionage. There is a letter in the archive in Albéniz's hand defending Dreyfus, though we do not know to whom it was addressed.[57] In it Albéniz insists that

the Dreyfus affair was a question of humanity... we came to speak in passing, and I do not see why I should hide my opinions about the French who do not think as I do when my way of thinking greatly pleases many others.... Long live France, because that is to cry Long Live the Universe, France is its honor and its glory. (trans. Kathleen Comfort)

Albéniz also refers in this letter to the invasion of Spain in 1823 by a large French army (an invasion his maternal grandfather resisted). He had every right to express an opinion about these matters as long as the French felt they had every right to interfere in the affairs of his country! Coutts shared his indignation over the scandalous proceedings and published a poem entitled 'To Liberty' in his *Musa Verticordia,* decrying the injustice to Dreyfus.

Albéniz occupied three different residences during his Paris years. The first was at 49 rue d'Erlanger (building no longer standing) until about 1905, when he moved for a short time to 21 rue de Franklin. The years 1906–9 were spent at 55 rue de Boulainvilliers in a fashionable, upmarket district. The building, completed in 1905, was virtually brand new in the year Albéniz moved there and still stands today. Thus, though he also had addresses elsewhere in France and Spain, Paris was his 'home base', and he became a fixture in the French capital's cultural life. Though he had reservations about French modernism, Albéniz held Debussy in high regard, despite

---

[56] There are sixteen letters from Ropartz to Albéniz (Bc, 'R') concerning the arrangements for this concert and requesting Albéniz's help getting Novello to publish his music. Albéniz interceded, but without success.

[57] Dated 9 June 1899 (Mm, 10.299). This quote is from Kalfa, 'Albéniz à Paris', 35, who owns a copy of this letter: 'l'affaire Dreyfus est une question d'humanité...., nous sommes venus à parler incidemment, et je ne vois pas la raison pour laquelle je devrais cacher mes opinions envers des Francais qui ne pensent pas comme moi, quand il y en a d'aussi bons auxquels ma façon de penser fait le plus grand plaisir.... Vive la France, car c'est crier Vive l'Univers, elle en est l'honneur et la gloire!!'

Collet's erroneous statement to the contrary.[58] In a letter to Adolfo Salazar, Rosina faulted that famous musicologist for repeating in an article Collet's falsehood that Albéniz detested Debussy, insisting that they were 'united by a cordial friendship and a mutual and sincere admiration'.[59] Further evidence of this is at hand in a 1902 letter from Coutts thanking Albéniz for sending him the score of *Pelléas et Mélisande*, a gift that provoked this enthusiastic response: 'Thanks for Pelleas et M[elisande]. I did not hear it in London. Nellie did, & liked it greatly.'[60] Deledicque, who became acquainted with Manuel de Falla during Falla's exile in Argentina, wrote to the family on 2 August 1946 telling them of Falla's insistence that Albéniz felt a great admiration for Debussy and his music.[61] But we know from a letter by Laura that though Albéniz admired Debussy and was a friend, he found it 'repugnant' when Debussy left his wife (who then attempted suicide) to live with Emma Bardac in the autumn of 1904. Like d'Indy and Dukas, he withdrew his friendship for some time after that tragedy. She goes on to say that Albéniz was very close to Séverac, Dukas, and especially Fauré. Dukas and Albéniz 'loved one another like brothers', while Fauré confided in him 'his most intimate secrets', more than in his own family.[62] Marguerite Long reports that Albéniz 'worshipped' Fauré, and that one of his last requests before he died was to hear her perform Fauré's Second Valse-caprice, which he thought 'divine'.[63] Fauré's letters to Albéniz include poems he wrote to his friend, and these reveal as nothing else could the depth of feeling between the men.[64] They appear below for the first time in translation.[65] Though at first glance they suggest a homosexual relationship, there is no other evidence to support such a conclusion; they were clearly

[58] Collet corresponded with Albéniz's widow and daughter but did not show them his manuscript prior to publication. Thus, one reads in Collet, *Albéniz*, 59, about Albéniz's supposed dislike of Debussy ('Et il n'aima jamais Debussy').

[59] Mm, car. 2. The letter was written on 10 Dec. 1931 from Barcelona to Madrid: 'les unió una cordial amistad, y una mutua y sincera admiración.'

[60] Mm, 10.334, dated 19 Dec.

[61] Mm, car. 2, Deledicque correspondence. 'Albéniz sentía una gran admiración por [Debussy], circun-scrita a su obra musical.'

[62] Mm, car. 2. The letter is dated '1/3/35' but there is no indication to whom it was written. Perhaps it was merely intended for posterity. From her father's close relationship with Fauré, Laura learned that the Frenchman led a double life. He did not get along with his wife or children (though better with the latter than the former), and he carried on an affair with Marguerite Hasselmans (the daughter of the orchestra conductor Luis Hasselmans). When they were together in public, they gave the impression of father and daughter, and they were so discreet that it appeared nothing more than an excellent friendship.

[63] *Gabriel Fauré*, 56.

[64] There are twenty-seven items (letters, cards, poems) from Fauré to Albéniz in the archive (Bc, 'F'). These three poems are undated.

[65] They appear, with the rest of Fauré's correspondence to Albéniz, in Jean-Michel Nectoux, 'Albéniz et Fauré: Correspondance inédite', *Tilas* (Travaux de l'Institut d'Études Ibériques et Latino-américaines) (1977), 173–4.

meant in jest. At all events, they speak to the uncommonly profound affection that Fauré felt for his Spanish friend.

O very handsome, very dear Albéniz, receive the greetings
from a heart that beats and suffers, alas, far from your eyes!
Have you kept the smell of my ebony hair?
Have you kept the sound of my Siren's voice?
Have you kept the honey of my fiery lips?
Do you sometimes feel my breath in your hair?
And my fingers in your beard, and my foot on your corns,
pressure which made you cry: more, more!!
Do you remember everything? . . . Oh, do not answer: 'shut up!'
Because making you drunk with love is my only goal![66]

Take care of your little wandering stomach
Ignore the bad dishes, stuff yourself with the good ones;
Always wash them down with good champagne
and then, take a walk in the green countryside.
Spurn alcohol: little kirsch, no rum,
as the Schola Cantorum prescribed!
Do not work too much, that gives you a headache,
and anyway, it is useless: people are so stupid![67]

I want to give you a thousand and three kisses
longer than the recitation of the Trojan War![68]

(translations by Kathleen Comfort)

Despite his illness, in 1899 Albéniz began an extensive reorchestration of *Pepita Jiménez*, no doubt inspired by the lessons he had learned from the other orchestral works of this period.[69] In the absence of vocal polyphony, Albéniz sought to imbue the orchestra with contrapuntal variety. His concern for this was so great that he insisted in a letter to his publisher of 11 April 1904 (Ls) that the lack of polyphonic interest in the earlier score had

---

[66] 'O Albéniz très beau, très cher, reçois les vœux | d'un cœur qui bat et souffre, hélas, loin de tes yeux! | As-tu gardé l'odeur de mes cheveuz d'ébène? | As-tu gardé le son de ma voix de sirène? | As-tu gardé le miel de mes lèvres de feu? | Sens-tu pas quelques fois mon souffle en tes cheveux? | Et mes doigts dans ta barbe, et mon pied sur tes cors, | pression qui te faisait crier: encor, encor!!! | Te souviens-tu de tout? . . . Ah, ne réponds pas: "zut!" | Car t'enivrer d'amour est mon unique but!' Jackie Pritchard, OUP copy-editor for this book, had the following insight regarding these poems: '[They are an] over-the-top parody of something like Baudelaire, full of the right clichés.'

[67] 'Soigne ton petit ventre aux instincts vagabons. | Laisse les mauvais plats, empiffre-toi les bons; | arrose-les toujours de bon vin de champagne | et puis, promène-toi dans la verte campagne. | Méprise l'alcool: peu de kirsh, pas de rhum, | ainsi que le prescrit la Schola Cantorum! | Ne travaille pas trop, ça fait mal à la tête, | et puis, ça sert à rien: les gens ils sont si bêtes!'

[68] 'Je voudrais te donner des baisers mille et trois, | plus longs que le récit de la guerre de Troie!'

[69] In Rafael Moragas, 'Epistolario inédito', 43, Albéniz states in a letter of June 1899 that he is reorchestrating *Pepita Jiménez*.

necessitated a revision to make it more 'modern'. In characteristically French fashion, his conception of polyphony had more to do with sonority and colour than with lines. Indeed, he never made any alteration of the piano–vocal score. To begin with, Albéniz changed the instrumentation. He sought to lighten the texture by eliminating some of the bass instruments, such as the tuba, contrabassoon, and bass drum. He dispensed with the cymbals as well. He also homogenized the horn section by jettisoning the two E♭ horns in favour of four in F. He did, however, add another harp, perhaps to reinforce the plucked-string sonority associated with the guitar. But he made his biggest strides as an orchestrator in his handling of the strings. The revision presents a much greater exploitation of the resources of the string section (e.g. through the employment of harmonics, muting, divisi, and rapidly alternating arco and pizzicato). The writing for the woodwinds is also more idiomatic, and Albéniz invests greater rhythmic vitality in these parts in order to animate the texture. Only the treatment of the brass remains relatively unchanged, and they continue to provide mostly chordal textures accompanying the other sections. Little melodic use is made of the trumpets, trombones, or even horns.

The net effect of this, of course, is to enhance the prominence of the orchestra at the expense of the voices, exacerbating the imbalance that several critics had found disturbing. But at least by this time Albéniz had liberated his instrumentation from his pianism and was conscious of the orchestra as an entity unto itself, rather than a mere projection of the keyboard. In 1904 Breitkopf und Härtel published the revision in German–English, French–English, and German–Italian versions, in addition to a piano–vocal score (unchanged) solely in French (Kufferath translation). In 1905 it issued the libretto in French to coincide with the Brussels production in January of that year.

The extant correspondence between Albéniz and Breitkopf und Härtel gives us some interesting insights into his relations with that firm.[70] The most important thing we learn from it is that Albéniz had to assume most of the actual cost of translation and printing. For instance, on 16 November 1896, he sent a payment of 590 francs to them, in part to pay Oskar Berggruen for his translation of the libretto into German. On 22 November 1897, he sent 2,000 francs to cover the Italian and French

[70] This is now located in the Ls under Signatur 3226. There are fifty-one items in all from Albéniz, including business cards, letters, and telegrams. In addition, copies of all the firm's letters to Albéniz have been preserved (eight of the originals of these letters are located in the Mm, car. 2). All the items from Albéniz are in French. The exact date of Albéniz's initial contract with Breitkopf und Härtel is not yet known. The earliest piece of correspondence is a business card of Albéniz's, dated 22 Oct. 1896, which simply accompanied corrected proofs of the score.

translations. When Albéniz finished the orchestration of his opera, he had to pay 900 francs for publication of the new version. Since he was hard-pressed to pay this sum all at once, the firm agreed to accept trimestral payments of 300 francs.

But Albéniz's relations with Breitkopf und Härtel were not altogether rosy. Some of his complaints were minor, for instance, about their occasionally writing to him in German, which he could not read reliably, rather than French or English, as he had requested. A letter of 4 October 1904, however, expresses extreme irritation with mistakes that had persisted in the newly printed version, in spite of the corrections he had conveyed to them in the proofs. Though absolving the firm itself of 'ill will', he accuses their editorial personnel of carelessness. A letter dated 21 April of the following year makes the more serious accusation that the firm has not displayed sufficient interest in his work and has not accorded him due respect. The last letter from Albéniz is dated 31 October 1906, from Barcelona, and concerns the liquidation of their contract.

Albéniz's interest in orchestral writing around 1900 received further impetus from another collaboration with Coutts. The Englishman wrote several letters[71] to Albéniz about a series of poems entitled *The Alhambra* that the composer had evidently requested for setting to music and which were based on the composer's suggestions ('I have only versified your ideas!' Coutts states in the final letter[72]). Albéniz decided not to use these poems for songs but rather commenced a suite of pieces for orchestra inspired by them.[73] At some point Albéniz again changed his mind and chose to write the suite for piano rather than orchestra, but he completed only the first number, 'La vega' (composed 1897 but not published until 1908, by A. Diaz in San Sebastián). Coutts published his poems separately in 1898.[74] José Vianna da Motta, the work's dedicatee, premiered it at a Société Nationale de Musique concert on 21 January 1899. 'La vega' is a clear sign that Albéniz had entered a new phase in piano composition. Its nearly fourteen-minute length is unprecedented in his nationalist piano pieces, and

[71] Dated 15, 16, and 26 Jan. 1897 (Bc, 'C').

[72] On 16 Jan. 1897 (Bc, 'C'), Coutts had written to Albéniz: 'I suppose the sonnets (as you call them) need not be in strict sonnet form? All you want is short verses—3 or 4—forming a little poem? Is that so?' This sheds more light on their collaboration, as it is clear Albéniz valued Coutts's poetic services and was no mere slave of the Englishman.

[73] '!La Alhambra¡ [sic] Poème Symphonique de F. B. Money-Coutts. Musique de Isaac Albeniz.' The suite was to consist of six pieces, but only Nos. 1 and 3 ('La vega' and 'Generalife') were begun (in 1896 and 1897, respectively). The MS is now in the Bc, M984.

[74] London: John Lane. The MS of 'La vega' is in the Bc, M980, and is dated Paris, 14 Feb. 1897. There is a piece in the Mm, Lligall 12, that bears the title *Fantaisie espagnole pour le piano*, dated 'Auteuil-Paris 22 Mai 1898'. This work is identical to 'La vega', but why Albéniz changed the title is unknown.

Ex. 39. 'La vega', principal theme, bars 9–17

its layout conveys something of the majesty of Franck's variations.[75] But, in fact, it is structured in clear-cut sonata form. The haunting principal theme in Ab minor resembles a *petenera*[76] and is obsessive in its melancholy. The Ab pedal persists for the first thirty-six bars, and the ostinato pattern clearly suggests the repetitive accompaniment of the guitar. The entrance of the 'voice' at bar 9 on a sustained note evokes the introductory *salida* (vocalization on 'ay') of a flamenco singer (Ex. 39).

The extensive transition to the secondary theme includes some of his most virtuosic writing to date. The Gb major secondary area commencing at bar 137 (which begins with a four-bar introduction to the actual theme) contains added-note sonorities that were not previously characteristic of his style and that strongly suggest the influence of Debussy. Still, though one may be reminded here of *Images*, it is well to remember that the first set of those pieces did not appear until 1905 (an earlier set of *Images*, composed in 1894, was not published until 1978). At the very least, Albéniz was no mere imitator. The secondary theme at bar 141 is very symmetrically built of antecedent and consequent four-bar phrases.

---

[75] Gauthier, *Albéniz*, 93. *L'Automne (Valse)*, composed in 1890, is almost thirteen minutes long, while the first movement of Sonata No. 5 lasts over eleven minutes, but they are not 'Spanish'.

[76] In the opinion of Iglesias, *Albéniz*, ii. 401. It is so stylized, however, that the interpretation is loose at best. According to Pohren, *Flamenco*, 132, the lyrics of the *peteneras* deal with a beautiful prostitute, Petenera, who is killed by a jealous lover.

Ex. 40. 'La vega', secondary theme (with introduction), bars 137–48

This is a free evocation of a *jota copla*, particularly in the consequent phrase at bar 145, whose rhythm clearly reflects the octosyllabic lines of that verse style (Ex. 40). There is no clear demarcation between exposition and development, and the one merges seamlessly into the other around bar 190. Augmented sonorities starting at bar 306 exude a faint fragrance of impressionism. The recapitulation commences at bar 348, with the secondary theme appearing first in E♭ at bar 484 as a dominant preparation for its arrival in the new home key of A♭ major at bar 500. The principal theme itself modulates to the parallel major in the coda at bar 524, and the piece ends in the tonality of A♭ major, a rare instance of 'progressive' tonality in his work.

The pianist José Tragó said of 'La vega': 'One sometimes hears distant sounds produced by Arab instruments; there is something of . . . the nostalgia and the flavour of our precious Andalusian songs.'[77] The abundant added-

---

[77] In a letter to Albéniz of 10 Dec. 1899 (Bc, 'T'). 'Se oyen de vez en cuando ruídos lejanos producidos por instrumentos árabes; hay algo de . . . la nostalgia y el déjo de nuestras hermosas canciones andaluzas.'

note sonorities and fuller texture of this music as well as the application of sonata form to his folkloric style are a clear premonition of *Iberia*, and without doubt 'La vega' was the product of Albéniz's years in Paris and his efforts at writing large-scale stage works. If he had persisted in writing zarzuelas—nothing more than a series of short, charming numbers—he would not have come to this pass. We have observed his steadily increasing interest in thematic and tonal organization, in formal unity over large spaces of his musical canvas. This certainly reflects the influence of the Franck circle in Paris, who in turn shared his reverence for Wagner. In a letter to his friend Enrique Moragas, Albéniz enthused about his latest piano work: 'What I have composed is the entire plain of Granada, contemplated from the Alhambra.' He claimed that Debussy had already heard it and wanted to go to Granada himself. He had also played it for his painter-friend Ignacio Zuloaga, who praised its colour. Albéniz elaborated on this, saying, 'I understand his enthusiasm for colour. I, you see, am no painter, and yet I paint—but my brushes are the keys.'[78]

But Albéniz was by no means ready to give up on opera yet. He was convinced of the merit of his efforts in that arena, including *Merlin*, a production of which he did everything in his power to secure. Indeed, in his diary on 11 March 1901 he wrote, 'My misfortune is great; I am foolish with aspirations!!!'[79] These aspirations began to take material form in June 1901 when Albéniz, Morera, and Granados entered into an agreement to establish a Teatre Líric Català in Barcelona.[80] The plan was to produce a series of twelve presentations of their works the following spring at the Teatre de Novetats, including *Merlin* as well as Morera's *Emporium* and Granados's *Follet*. A meeting on 2 July explored the possibility of constructing a new theatre (apparently Albéniz's brainchild; he was in a building mood that year) whose repertoire would consist of 'classical works' and some new ones. Morera, however, soon betrayed the confidence of his friends and applied to Ruperto Chapí in Madrid to have his opera produced at the Teatro

---

[78] Cited in Llorens Cisteró, 'Inéditas', 100. 'Comprendo su entusiasmo por el color. Yo, ya lo ve usted, no soy pintor y pinto, pero mis pinceles son las teclas.'

[79] Mm. car. 4. 'Gran desgracia es la mia; ser tonto con aspiraciones!!!'

[80] The actual contract is located in the Mm, car. 4, and is dated 18 June 1901. It is also signed by Miquel Utrillo (secretary) and Antoni Niubó. They evidently had made an arrangement with the El Dorado theatre for performances in Aug. and Sept. and placed a guarantee on the contract. But they lacked enough time to prepare and lost their 1,500 pesetas (letter of Juan Molas y Casas dated Barcelona, 8 July 1901 (Bc, 'M')). A notice of the new season appeared in *Veu de Catalunya*, 9 Aug. 1901. According to Roger Aliér, 'Musical Life in Barcelona 1888–1936', in *Homage to Barcelona: The City and its Art 1888–1936* (London: The Arts Council of Great Britain, 1985), 279, Morera and other composers had already started a season of Catalan lyric theatre at the Tívoli in Feb. 1901, but it did not arouse public interest (still drawn to zarzuela and Italian opera) and lost money.

Lírico in that city.[81] Albéniz wrote to Chapí on 9 November 1901[82] to give
him the details of Morera's betrayal and deceit, stating that a contract had
already been signed with the Teatre de Novetats for producing the operas.
At some point Albéniz approached the Liceu about producing *Merlin*. But
he merely encountered the suspicion and hostility of the theatre's management, which insisted on his submitting the score to a panel of 'experts' for
evaluation. This was an unconscionable affront to an artist of Albéniz's
stature, and his wife and friends objected strenuously to any capitulation
on his part.

Albéniz and Granados gave up in disgust, and the entire Catalan lyric
theatre project came to naught. Years later, Granados was apparently referring to this episode when he wrote in a letter to Albéniz, dated 26 May 1907
(Bc, 'G'): 'you worked hard on Morera's behalf...he repaid you with
ingratitude.'[83] Albéniz expressed his new attitude toward Morera in a letter
to Pedrell of 23 November 1901, warning him that the 'so-called maestro
Morera has invaded that capital!!'[84] The whole episode merely reinforced
Albéniz's hostility towards Spain, and his diary contains a bitter entry for 3
April 1902: 'The Spanish people sing a lot but think little.'[85]

Albéniz's interest in Catalan lyric theatre and his association with Morera,
viewed so negatively by Count Morphy, stimulates reflection about his
relationship with Catalan nationalism and the modernist movement in Barcelona, of which Morera was a leader. The late nineteenth century in Barcelona was a period of cultural florescence. First the *Renaixensa* (a revival of
Catalan culture, especially language and literature) then *modernisme* transformed the city into one of Europe's most vibrant centres. Music and
musicology flourished during this period, initially under the inspiration of
Pedrell (who wrote Catalan zarzuelas), then with Morera (a Pedrell pupil),
Vives, and Lluís Millet (1867–1941). The journal *Revista musical catalana*
(1904–36) was an important manifestation of this renaissance, as were *La*

[81] In the Albéniz archive there is a letter from Chapí to Morera dated 25 Oct. 1901 (Bc, 'C') accepting
Emporium for the Teatro Lírico.

[82] This letter, written from Barcelona, was at the Ah when the author examined it. It has since been given to
the Mm. Though not in Albéniz's own hand, it is written in the first person and thus must have been dictated
by him. Albéniz states that he had removed to Barcelona in May 1901 on the advice of his doctors, who
prescribed a more healthful climate for him. He had entered into the agreement with Morera to assist his
faltering Catalan lyric theatre project.

[83] 'Tu hicistes fuerte a Morera...el, te pagó con desagradecimiento.' An example of Albéniz's generosity
was his warm review, dated 26 April 1895, of Morera's *Las monjas de Sant Hyman* at the Teatre de Novetats
(written in Catalan, periodical unknown, clipping Mm, Prov. M-987b1). Morera returned the favour by
warmly reviewing *Henry Clifford* the following month (*La Renaixensa—Diari de Catalunya*, 16 May 1895,
2763–5). Morera was the dedicatee of Albéniz's 'Córdoba'.

[84] Bc, 'Epistolario de Felipe Pedrell', M964: ' "soit disant" [*sic*] maestro Morera, ha invadido esa capital!!'

[85] This is found only the original, not in *Impresiones*, ed. Franco. 'El pueblo Español, canta tanto, como
piensa poco!!!'

ilustración musical española y americana (1888–96) and *La música religiosa en España* (1896–9), both edited by Pedrell (who also contributed numerous articles to *RMC*).[86] Albéniz's pan-Hispanic nationalism was indebted to the more conservative *Renaixensa* philosophy as articulated by Pedrell. Catalan nationalism, *per se*, seems to have held little appeal for him. Albéniz did, of course, write several pieces named after or inspired by Catalonia: the zarzuela *Catalanes de gracia*; 'Capricho catalan', from *España: Six Feuilles d'album*; the orchestral suite *Catalonia*; 'Cataluña (Curranda)', from the *Suite española* No. 1; and the *Escenas sinfónicas catalanas*. And contrary to what Istel claimed, Albéniz was fluent in Catalan.[87] The family often spoke it at home,[88] and he received numerous letters in Catalan. He also sprinkled his prose with Catalan expressions, though he customarily expressed himself in Spanish or French. To be sure, Catalan pieces are no more numerous in his output than those dedicated to a single Andalusian city, Granada. Interestingly, he completed only one vocal work with a Catalan text, i.e. the *Tres romanzas catalanas* (*c*.1886, now lost). He did make it through eleven bars of a choral-symphonic poem entitled *Lo Llacsó* to a text by the Catalan artist and author Apel.les Mestres (b. 1854), but for whatever reason he soon lost interest.[89]

Yet, Albéniz was well connected with all the *modernistes*, not only those in music but also the artist Casas (dedicatee of *Catalonia*) and the playwright and painter Santiago Rusiñol (1861–1931), and many of his own inclinations were in harmony with theirs. For instance, the *modernistes* idolized Wagner just as he did. In 1901 an Associació Wagneriana was founded at the famous Els Quatre Gats[90] tavern by Catalan Wagnerites, including Granados and Albéniz.[91] The proscenium of the fabulous Palau de la Música Catalana in Barcelona (completed 1908) displays a high relief depicting the 'Ride of

---

[86] See Torres, *Las publicaciones*, 476–7 and 704–5, for a detailed history of these journals.

[87] 'Isaac Albéniz', 118, wrote that Albéniz 'did not consider himself a Catalan and never spoke the language'. This is a demonstrable untruth. Llongueres, in 'Cómo conocí', Franco (ed.), *Albéniz y su tiempo*, 113, records a brief conversation with Albéniz in Catalan. Ruiz Albéniz, *Albéniz*, 33, affirms that Albéniz enjoyed speaking Catalan with family and friends, mixed with Spanish, French, and English, which prompted one acquaintance to refer to his home as the 'Tower of Babel'!

[88] Louis Bonafoux interviewed Laura Albéniz for a Mar. 1909 article in *Heraldo de Madrid* as Albéniz lay dying in Paris. She declared that they spoke fluent Catalan at home. Clipping in the Mm, Prov. M-987c.

[89] MS of three pages only, in the Bc, M984, dated Paris, 1 Apr. 1896. It is labelled 'Poema Sinfónico en un Prologo y tres actos' and is scored for orchestra, chorus, soprano, mezzo-soprano, tenor, and baritone.

[90] From 1897 to 1903, Els Quatre Gats ('The Four Cats', Catalan slang for 'just a few people') was the principal hangout for Barcelona's bohemians. It was established by the painters Rusiñol and Casas, who along with the folklorist Miquel Utrillo and the café's manager Pere Romeu constituted the feline foursome. Picasso's first public exhibition took place there in 1900, and both Albéniz and Granados gave recitals there. For an excellent introduction to this subject, see Vincent and Stradling, *Cultural Atlas of Spain and Portugal*, 142–5.

[91] *La vanguardia*, 6 June 1909, 3, reported that he was one of the founding members of the Wagner Association.

the Valkyries'.[92] Many choral societies sprang up during this time, devoted not only to performance but to music education. Foremost among them was the Orfeó Català, founded by Vives and Millet in 1891 and a direct offshoot of the Schola Cantorum in Paris. Morera in turn established the Societat Coral Catalunya Nova in 1896. In fact, there was a close association between the Catalan modernist group and the Franck circle in Paris.[93] This helps us to understand better the significance of d'Indy's conducting stints in Barcelona in 1895 and 1898, which Albéniz helped arrange, and Albéniz's attraction to the Franck circle while living in Paris. It also places in sharper relief Albéniz's Wagnerism, which was logical and natural in the context of Catalonian culture during that period. Composing *Merlin* may have been a burden for Albéniz, but he clearly saw the potential for achieving a success in Barcelona with the composition of a Wagnerian opera. Indeed, his writing an Arthurian trilogy does not seem strange at all when compared to the prospect of a collaboration with the Belgian symbolist Maurice Maeterlinck, whose *Pelléas et Mélisande* inspired Fauré, Debussy, and Schoenberg. In fact Maeterlinck *was* interested in working with Albéniz on a project, but nothing ever came of it.[94]

Albéniz's renewed interest in establishing himself in Barcelona had inspired him to look for a building site for a new home there. A flurry of letters[95] went back and forth between Rosina in Paris and Albéniz in Barcelona during June of 1901, at the same time as Albéniz was laying plans for the Catalan lyric theatre project. The home was to be located at the intersection of Funicular and Bonanova. The reason for choosing this site was that his doctor had recommended he reside at a higher elevation, and this hilly western district of Barcelona seemed ideal to Albéniz. He described the house as a 'torre' ('tower'), which would get him as high off the ground as possible. In the meantime he rented a 'piso' ('floor') in Barcelona at 110 passeig de Gràcia, at the intersection with Diagonal, where they could live

---

[92] The structure was built by the celebrated Catalan architect Lluís Domènech i Montaner (1850–1923), who also designed the stage.

[93] Items in the archive reinforce the importance of his Catalan connections. A letter in Catalan from J. Cabot (dated Barcelona, 9 Dec. 1908 (Bc, 'C')) seeks his help in arranging a concert of the Orfeó Català in Paris. Albéniz in turn appealed to the Spanish embassy in Paris, but a letter from F. de Leon y Castillo (31 Dec. 1908 (Bc, 'L')) makes it clear they did not have the money. Another letter, from Joaquim Casas-Corbó (dated Barcelona, 23 Apr. 1897 (Bc, 'C')), asks him to use his London connections to locate a person in connection with L'Avenç, the modernist publishing concern in Barcelona. It is also signed by Josep-Marià Sert, Ramon Font, Ignasi Iglesias, Morera, and Alejandro Cortada. Albéniz received an undated 'get well' card signed by Rusiñol, Utrillo, and others from Sitges (Bc, 'R').

[94] Three undated letters from Georgette Leblance concerning such a collaboration with Maeterlinck survive in the Bc ('L'). Maeterlinck proposed a lyric opera on *Alladine et Palomides*, but Albéniz demurred. He likewise parried Maeterlinck's suggestion of an opera entitled *Beatrice*.

[95] Mm, 10.375–90.

until the house was built. This was also well above ground. Purchasing the land and drawing up plans absorbed much of his time and energy, but he made sure to study Wagner and asked Rosina to send him the *Ring* scores (except *Das Rheingold*, which was his least favourite) and *Tristan und Isolde*. He also requested other books and scores (Pergolesi and Lully), which she should bring with her when she moved to Barcelona, as well as furniture. He was especially interested in her buying a standing electric fan and electric cigarette lighter, as they cost too much in Barcelona. Although he expressed concern about money and was attempting to economize, he could not restrain his appetite for luxury (an impulse already apparent during his trip to Budapest). It is clear that his income from Coutts permitted him to live as lavishly as he did, with apartments in different cities, buying property on which to build a home, and purchasing the latest conveniences. It is hard to imagine where else such large sums of money could have come from, as he was no longer concertizing.

His impatience to be reunited with Rosina is a constant thread running throughout this correspondence. By 4 July 1901 everything was in readiness and nothing was left except for her to arrive 'subito y allegro con brio'. Three days later he is growing very impatient for her arrival and complains that 'the days turn into centuries for me... I cannot take it anymore, I cannot take it anymore, I cannot take it anymore'.[96] This last phrase becomes a refrain throughout the letter and even in the next one of the following day. His use of repetition and exclamation reminds one of his penchant for exaggerated dynamic markings in his works of this period and in *Iberia*, where quintuple fortissimo and pianissimo are not uncommon.

In addition to this heartache, his bowels were in their usual state of rebellion, and a 'frightful diarrhoea!!!!!!!' was causing him great pain. He was consulting with a Dr Sojo, who diagnosed his condition as colitis with symptoms of dysentery ('entero-colitis membranosa con manifestaciones disentéricas'). Taking waters was again the principal treatment, and Albéniz advised Rosina, also in poor health, to do the same. Albéniz thought they could take the waters at Caldetas and finish up at Sobrón, which Sojo had recommended as stronger and more effective than most. But Albéniz soon decided against Sobrón for reasons of economy.

These physical ailments could not keep Albéniz from embarking on a brief career as a critic during this period in Barcelona. He wrote reviews for *Las noticias* under the pseudonym Cándido, and as the name suggests, he could be just that—even acerbically and sarcastically so. In reference to a

---

[96] 'Los dias se me converten en siglos... no puedo mas, no puedo mas, no puedo mas!!!!!'

production of *Die Götterdämmerung* at the Liceu, Albéniz excoriated the German conductor (a 'señor Fischer') by asking, 'Does not said señor believe that with a gram more of enthusiasm on his part the relative monotony of the orchestral execution yesterday evening would have disappeared?'[97] On other occasions, however, his praise was unstinting, as in the case of Pedrell's *Els Pirineus* already mentioned.

But, as was his wont, Albéniz did not remain long in one place. In the spring of 1902 he followed Morera to Madrid in hopes of gaining an audience for *Merlin* or *Pepita Jiménez*.[98] Before leaving Barcelona, however, a dinner was given in his honour at the Hotel Sant Jordi de Vallvidrera, and many friends and luminaries were in attendance, including the conductor Crickboom and the critic Suárez Bravo.[99] In spite of the festive mood, Albéniz expressed with some bitterness his reasons for moving to Madrid. He found in Barcelona an environment hostile not only to him but to artists like Pedrell, Vives, and Morera, all of whom had likewise emigrated to the capital city. The final straw, however, was the Liceu's reaction to his *Merlin*. This, perhaps more than any other single reason, impelled him to abandon Barcelona.

So, now he would return to a city that, in fact, had not been altogether kind to him either. On 18 May 1902[100] Albéniz reported enthusiastically to Rosina from Madrid that he had met with Chapí and that *Merlin* would be produced in that city between October and December. His desire now was to move to Madrid, not only for the sake of the *Merlin* premiere but because he was determined finally to make his mark as a *zarzuelero*. In 1902 he committed to writing a zarzuela entitled *La real hembra* ('The royal woman') on a libretto by Cristóbal de Castro, a journalist in Madrid. Castro had signed a contract with the Circo de Parish to write the libretto for a zarzuela grande in three acts and in verse.[101] In this same letter, Albéniz told Rosina of his plans to spend the summer near Santander to make the translation of *Merlin*, with the help of Eusebio Sierra, as well as to work on *Launcelot* and a new operatic project, *Rinconete y Cortadillo*, based on an episode from *Don Quijote* (libretto by Henri Cain).

---

[97] Clipping without date (other than year), Mm, Prov. M-987c. '¿No cree dicho señor, que con un gramo más de entusiasmo de su parte, la relativa monotonía de la ejecución orquestal de anoche, hubiera desaparecido?'

[98] Chapí, however, had already made it clear to Albéniz in a letter of 22 Mar. 1901 (Bc, 'C') that he only wanted to produce new, unpublished works, which would have eliminated *Pepita Jiménez* from consideration.

[99] The exact date of this event is not yet known. It is reported in clippings in the Mm, Prov. M-987c, especially Joaquim Pena, 'Musichs que fugen', *Joventut*, 3 (1902), 383–5.

[100] Mm, 10.391.

[101] Notice of this was printed in *La época*, 5 Aug. 1902, 3.

In the summer of 1902, Madrid appeared to be Albéniz's oyster. In addition to the prospect of *Merlin* in the autumn and the new zarzuela, he was attempting to bring *Pepita Jiménez* to the capital city. It was certainly not his first attempt to do so. In his letter of 23 August 1895 (already cited), Bretón wrote that he had read that *Pepita Jiménez* might be produced at the Teatro Real that year. This production, as we know, never got off the ground. Undaunted, Albéniz wrote to his publisher on 22 September 1897 (Ls), saying that he was going to use his influence with the Queen to get a staging at the Teatro Real, and that he was also angling for a reappearance at the Liceu. Neither of these prospects bore fruit.[102] Now, in 1902, Albéniz determined to try a new tack. In early August, a hearing of *Pepita Jiménez* was arranged by one Sr. Romeo at the offices of the newspaper *El evangelio*. The event was attended by critics, writers, and music *aficionados*, as well as by Albéniz's friends, including Coutts. Contemporary press accounts relate that Albéniz played through the score at the piano, at times singing the parts, giving the assemblage at least some idea of the music. Sr. López Muguiro wrote a flattering account of the session: 'When we heard the presentation of *Pepita Jiménez* we felt pleasure and pain, pride and discouragement. We knew that here was a purely Spanish opera, replete with beautiful ideas, fresh, inspired, with an irreproachable form.'[103] He went on to lament its obscurity in Madrid, in spite of its successes elsewhere in Europe: 'Our brilliant musical culture!...We do not deserve more than what we have: up above—the style of Echegaray—'la Circe'...down below... 'the tango of the saucepans.'[104] He refrained from any further commentary on the opera, preferring to wait 'for a more opportune occasion, which will not be long in presenting itself, with the premiere that some music theatre will offer us'.[105]

The event was reported in other newspapers as well. *La época* (6 August 1902, 3) stated that Albéniz was the 'object of sincere and enthusiastic congratulations on the part of those who were fortunate to hear the music of *Pepita Jiménez*'.[106] In addition, a telegram was sent to Juan Valera, 'giving

---

[102] From Bretón's letter to Albéniz of 5 Mar. 1901 (Bc, 'B'), it is clear that they hoped to get *Pepita Jiménez* on Chapí's festival in the autumn, along with *Merlin*, and in a Spanish translation.

[103] In *El evangelio*, 2/118 (7 Aug. 1902), 2. 'Cuando escuchamos la lectura de *Pepita Jiménez* sentimos placer y pena, vanidad y desconsuelo. He aquí—nos decíamos—una ópera castizamente española, repleta de ideas hermosas, fresca, inspirada, con una forma irreprochable.'

[104] '¡Brillante cultura musical la nuestra!...No nos merecemos más de lo que tenemos: allá arriba—estilo Echegaray—"la Circe"...allá abajo..."el tango de las cacerolas".' Though the second reference is somewhat obscure, the first one, to *Circe*, is to Chapí's opera of that title (prem. 1902).

[105] '[P]ara ocasión más oportuna, que no tardará en presentarse, con el estreno que nos ofrecerá cualquier teatro lírico.'

[106] 6 Aug. 1902, 3: 'objeto de sinceras y entusiastas plácemes por parte de cuantos tuvieron la fortuna de oír la música de "Pepita Jiménez".'

him notice of the brilliance of the occasion just celebrated'.[107] No trace of this telegram has come to light, and neither has any reply from Valera been found. In spite of the encomiums of those who heard Albéniz's rendition of the piano score (which, by one account, was too difficult even for its author), the work failed to fulfil López Muguiro's hopes and received not a single offer from any of the local theatres.

Albéniz did come close, however. He wrote to his publishers from Madrid on 24 July 1902 (Ls), urgently requesting that they send off the score and parts of the French–Italian version to a Sr. Marabini, director of the Teatro del Retiro, where the opera was to be auditioned on 15 August. A letter of 22 August of that year from Albéniz to Leipzig informed them, however, that the deal fell through when it became clear that Marabini wanted to be provided with the music free of charge, a suggestion Albéniz characterized as 'the height of impudence'. At this same time, Coutts was trying unsuccessfully to secure a performance in London, especially at Covent Garden. Albéniz gave up on Madrid and retreated once again to the north, his well-laid plans having come to naught. *Rinconete y Cortadillo* never made the journey from mind to manuscript, and Castro finished only the first act of the libretto for *La real hembra* before leaving town and losing interest in the project. Albéniz got no further than the Prelude and first two scenes.[108] Finally, Chapí did not live up to whatever assurances he had given Albéniz, and *Merlin* was never produced in Madrid.

Albéniz persisted in his efforts to secure performances of *Pepita Jiménez*. There was a definite possibility of its production in Leipzig, and Karlsruhe continued to be a prospect for some time. Indeed, several commentators believed it was performed in those cities. Herman Klein, in the 1918 *Times* article already cited, stated that the opera was done in Karlsruhe and Leipzig the same year as the Prague premiere. López Muguiro wrote in his *El evangelio* review that it had already been presented in Leipzig, Munich, and Prague. Georges Jean-Aubry[109] claimed that *Pepita Jiménez* was performed in Karlsruhe in 1905. Jean-Michel Nectoux[110] chides Albéniz's biographers for overlooking the Leipzig performance—for which he fails, however, to provide a date—citing a letter from Fauré referring to performances in

---

[107] '[D]ándole cuenta de la brillantez del acto que acababa de celebrarse.'

[108] The MS is in the Bc, M984. The first number is dated 7 Sept. 1902, and the final additions were made twenty-two days later. The work is heavily orchestrated, while the vocal lines seem incidental to the music (in fact, pitches are not indicated, only rhythms).

[109] See his *Notices sur quelques compositeurs contemporains* (no publisher or date given, though it bears a 1910 dedication to Albéniz); also stated in his article 'Albéniz', *Les Musiciens célèbres*, ed. Jean Lacroix (Geneva: Éditions Contemporaines, 1946), 218–20.

[110] 'Correspondance inédite', 167.

Brussels and Leipzig. Other examples could be noted, but these suffice to illustrate the confusion that surrounds the exact course of the opera's career. Available records in Leipzig and Karlsruhe reveal no such performances, and the *Deutscher Bühnen-Spielplan* (Leipzig: Breitkopf und Härtel) for the years 1896–1905 mentions nothing except the Prague performances. Moreover, not a shred of memorabilia in the archive recalls stagings in any of the German cities mentioned above. Neither does anything in the extant correspondence mention actual productions, only prospects for production. It is reasonable to assume that references to such performances appeared in the press (and later in articles and books based on these accounts) for the purpose of enhancing the opera's reputation, as a promotional gesture. Three years elapsed between Albéniz's Madrid gambit at *El evangelio* and the next production, in 1905 in Brussels. This was the last, and without doubt the most successful, to take place during his lifetime.

The autumn of 1902 was spent recuperating from his habitual malaise, this time in the beauty of the Swiss Alps. In the company of Frank and Nellie, Albéniz stayed at the Grand Hotel in Territet. 'God Almighty!! how insipid is the life of a rich man!!!!', he exclaimed facetiously in a letter to Rosina.[111] Coutts hoped to rent a chalet where he and Albéniz could finish the trilogy, and though Albéniz liked the idea of working amidst the natural beauty of the place, there were forest murmurs of discontent:

The situation, lovable young woman, is complicated; these nice people believe in God and adore us; I see neither means nor manner of detaching ourselves from them, and as recently as yesterday afternoon, they told me again and again that their affairs are in a prosperous state and they intend to persist in this theatrical madness, setting the trilogy until it is finished!!! . . . but I do not know, I do not know, how I will get out of the commitment I made to Real Hembra, and this pains me in the extreme, to mislead a man [Castro] who is less deserving of deception than any I can imagine!![112]

In addition to this, Albéniz was evidently homesick, and a planned trip to Florence would retard his return to Paris.

One has to ask at some point if there was not a slightly disingenuous quality to Albéniz's carping about Frank and Nellie. Albéniz seems to have spent a very great deal of time away from home, and it is not too hard to imagine that home life appealed to him less than his repeated assertions of

---

[111] 19 Oct. 1902 (Mm, 10.392). 'Dios de Dios!! que soseria la vida del rico!!!!'

[112] La situación, joven amable, se complice; esta buena gente, en Dios creé, y en nosotros adora; no veo medio ni manera de desasirnos de ellos, y no mas tarde que ayer tarde, me dijo y me repitio, que hallandose sus asuntos en muy prospero estado, entendia hacer la ultima locura teatral poniendo en escena la trilogia en cuando esta se halle terminada!!! . . . pero no se, no se, como voy á salir del compromiso de la Real Hembra, pues me duele en estremo, engañar al hombre menos merecedor de engañas que pueda imaginarse!!'

longing for the family suggest. Coutts once made reference to all of Albéniz's terrible domestic difficulties,[113] and allusions to Rosina's nervousness appear in their correspondence. Chausson wrote to his wife Jeanne from Prague about a conversation with Albéniz and Schalk in which Albéniz was seeking 'to prove to Schalk that there is not a single married man who does not have a few brief adventures which entail no consequences and which would not affect marital fidelity in any way'.[114] This does not prove Albéniz had extramarital affairs, but it indicates a rather liberal attitude towards marriage and suggests that Albéniz prized a certain amount of freedom and independence. Thus, it may have seemed expedient to blame his absences on Coutts, posing in his letters as a helpless prisoner of the Englishman's every whim who, but for the necessity of finishing the trilogy, would be at home with his family. Since Rosina was most likely the source of the anti-Coutts campaign waged by all biographers, one could surmise that Albéniz succeeded in convincing her that duty alone and not desire caused him to spend time in the company of Coutts pursuing Arthurian glory. Still, the process of writing the trilogy was draining and did make it more difficult for him to devote time to other, perhaps more suitable, projects.

November found Albéniz and his travelling companions in Milan searching for a publisher for *Merlin*. His letters home reveal that Coutts is still urging him to delay his work for a while longer so that they can enjoy their time together and so that his health will not be too greatly taxed by the effort. This once again puts the lie to Istel's thesis that Coutts's relentless pursuit of this project drove Albéniz to an early grave! Albéniz urges his children to write to Nellie, who has been extremely kind to him, though he finds it a 'great shame that she has the head of a mosquito!!!!'[115] What prompted this outburst can be discerned in his remarks of a few days later, in which his patience with her diminutive cerebrum is wearing thin in spite of her kindness.[116] After a month together, Alpine splendour notwithstanding,

[113] In a letter dated 6 June 1906 (Mm, 10.283), Coutts exclaims: 'I can't understand how you manage to get through all your dreadful domestic troubles, keeping still the brightness of your spirit . . . you go on & on, giving up your life to those around you, and still remaining full of love & charity to them all! Ah! compared with you, I am a devil.'

[114] Letter written in June 1897. Cited in Jean-Pierre Barricelli and Leo Weinstein, *Ernest Chausson: The Composer's Life and Works* (Norman: University of Oklahoma Press, 1955), 92. Chausson refused to support Albéniz's argument.

[115] Letter of 11 Nov. 1902 (Mm, 10.396): 'que lastima tan grande de que tenga esa cabeza de mosquito.' Albéniz refers to himself in this passage as 'Puts', which was evidently the agnomen given him by his daughter Laura, to whom he sent a postcard on 15 Nov. 1902 (Mm, 10.308) signed with that name. That its Spanish pronunciation rhymes with Coutts may or may not be coincidence.

[116] Letter of 14 Nov. 1902 (Mm, 10.298). 'Un santo, si santos hubiere, no es capaz de resistir tal cumulo de nimias y estupidas frivolidades, . . . que yo habre dominado mi caracter y mis nervios . . . realmente, es la mas grande prueba de cariño y de *devouement* que puedo darle á Coutts, y á ella misma!!' It is important to note that Nellie did not reciprocate Albéniz's disdain at all. Coutts wrote to his friend on 8 Feb. 1906 (Bc, 'C')

Albéniz cannot wait to get away from her. 'A saint, if there were saints, could not bear such an accumulation of trivialities and stupid frivolities, . . . that I will have controlled my character and nerves . . . really is the greatest proof of affection and *devotion* that I can give to Coutts, and to her!!' Coutts himself had often complained of her behaviour and blamed their rocky marriage on it. In fact, his complaints grew more exasperated with the passage of time. On 9 July 1904 (Bc, 'C') he elaborated on Albéniz's women-are-children philosophy presented earlier:

You never see that it is easy enough for a man to treat a woman as an amusing baby, if he has his home, his friends, & his work. But if that amusing baby deprives him of home & friends & work, how does the philosophy work out then? It amounts to becoming the slave & nurse of that baby, at the sacrifice of all the man's higher instincts.

On another occasion he summed up the situation by declaring her a 'neurasthenic lunatic'.[117]

But he had no cause to complain of Albéniz, whose saintliness he regularly rewarded. On 23 May 1903 (Mm, car. 2), he wrote to Rosina to reassure her about their financial arrangements and to extol his composer: 'I might have given other composers £10,000 a year, without securing the services of one who would have worked in such exact harmony and exact fellow-feeling with myself.' He may not have been giving him such a sum, but the allowance was extremely generous and permitted Albéniz to establish yet another residence in 1903, at the Château Saint-Laurent in Nice (more will be said of their precise financial arrangements in the next chapter). Albéniz would now divide his remaining time on earth between Paris, Nice, and Tiana, just as his hero Liszt had done in his twilight years between Weimar, Rome, and Budapest.

Albéniz made the final entries in his diary in Tiana and Nice between August 1903 and April 1904. What one perceives in these brief inscriptions is an increasing bitterness, a frame of mind inconsistent with his normal approach to people and life but the seeds of which we have encountered throughout this story. The combination of his acute physical distress and the repeated frustrations he had experienced in the theatre, particularly in Spain, combined to accentuate this facet of his personality. For Albéniz's struggle with chronic inflammation of the kidneys, known as Bright's disease, was now in full career.[118] This ailment produces extreme discomfort, and Albéniz

declaring that 'she always speaks of you with the greatest affection'. But according to Rosina Moya Albéniz de Samsó, Rosina did not like Nellie, and neither woman was very intelligent.

[117] Letter of 17 May 1906 (Bc, 'C').

[118] This disease is named after the English physician Richard Bright (1789–1858), who undertook the first systematic study of it. The more technical term for the illness is glomerulonephritis. Albéniz claimed that he

was often in excruciating pain during the last years of his life. He needed to rely more and more on Laura as his secretary to assist him with his correspondence. When precisely he developed the condition is hard to say, though the severe bout of illness experienced in 1898 may have been its onset. In these entries, Albéniz expressed himself on a wide range of subjects—women, politics, love, philosophy, religion—but not music. His view of women as children had now degenerated into an intense misogyny, but what prompted this is hard to know. Though he excluded Rosina from the circle of his contempt for women, it is hard to imagine that his dislike of women in general was completely disconnected from his feelings about his wife in particular. Though he clearly did not want to hurt *her* feelings, he carelessly neglected to exclude his daughters from his general condemnation of the opposite sex! His proximity to death only hardened his religious scepticism. His ruminations on God as an impersonal force seem to reflect the influence of Schopenhauer and Nietzsche, though we have no evidence he read those philosophers' writings. What is most striking here is his use of the second person plural in the second, lengthy entry. To whom was he addressing these thoughts that were so important to him? His family? Posterity? He seems to be carrying on an argument that had perhaps started earlier and in which he was determined to have the last word. Whatever the case, through the excerpts below we get a window into the tortured soul of a genius driving himself towards the final and greatest achievement of his career.[119] Given the tenor of his remarks, it is no wonder that they have never appeared in any previous biography, but we must question the wisdom of concealing thoughts and feelings Albéniz clearly intended others to read. Pleasant or not, these passages reveal his state of being at a supremely difficult juncture in his career. By confronting this dimension of his interior life, we gain a greater appreciation of the irrepressible buoyancy, colour, and optimistic good spirits in *Iberia*, and a better understanding of the brooding melancholy that underlies so much of that work.

What frightens me about death is not *dying*, but rather *ceasing to comprehend*! (Nice, 27 July 1903)[120]

developed the condition after a bout of yellow fever, supposedly contracted on a tour of Latin America in his youth. According to the *American Medical Association Encyclopedia of Medicine* (New York: Random House, 1989), glomerulonephritis can indeed be caused by some common tropical diseases, like malaria, though yellow fever is not mentioned specifically as a potential cause.

[119] These excerpts appear in *Impresiones*, ed. Franco, 65–7, except for the first two, which are inexplicably absent. Moreover, consultation of the original reveals that the wrong dates and places are assigned to the entries in the printed edition. The entry for 25 Aug. in Tiana does not appear and instead that heading is given to the entry from the following day. As before, the passages appear with Albéniz's original spelling, punctuation, and orthography.

[120] 'Lo que me espanta en la muerte, no es el *morir*, sino el *cesar al comprender*!'

They say *the lofty judgements of God are inscrutable*!! Say more readily that stupidity and human vanity, within his very ignorance, are and will be eternal. Concede to me that God is the sum and compendium of the *unconscious*, and to give you pleasure, I will admit his existence. God is force, force is brutality and perfect equilibrium, but equilibrium that emanates directly and in consequence of the former, not because a divine mind has desired *consciously* that it should be thus. In short, I deny the personality of a supreme being. (Tiana de la Costa, 25 August 1903)[121]

Goodness, generosity, and intelligence form a whole; it is an error to qualify someone as good when his goodness is not accompanied by the other qualities that are related and inseparable. In most cases this merely superficial goodness conceals a passivity that is in the highest degree egotistical, joined with a cowardice and lack of sincerity that horrify. (12 September 1903)[122]

Faith is the abdication of one's intelligence; wretched is he who believes and does not create. (16 September 1903)[123]

Of all the animals in creation, only *man* consents to abdicate the dignity of his bearing; I would like to know the wisdom of a quadruped, on judging the ridiculous and offensive capers of the mentality of the human biped. (Nice, 7 February 1904. First day of Carnival)[124]

Love is a mere exacerbation of the most subtle egotistical instincts that characterize the human *being*; it engenders all evil and base passion, and the most curious aspect of this is that, with a deliciously unconscious hypocrisy, love pretends to poeticize (and the majority belive it) to the point of sanctifying his diabolical mischief!!! ... people do not want to be convinced that ultimately, for the preservation of the *race*, the lovely and potent genital passion is more than enough, without the necessity of requesting assistance from a hypocritical sentimentality that vanishes for the slightest reason, laying bare the entire sad skeleton of hatred, jealousy, possessiveness, mental disturbance, and other *lovely* little things of which it consists; *love* was never an *altruistic* passion, as *friendship* can and should be, ... [it is] one of the most voracious and stupid passions that embitter human existence!!!! (Nice, 28 February 1904)[125]

---

[121] 'Dicen; *los altos juicios de Dios*, son *inescrutables*!! decid mas pronto que la estupidez y la vanidad humana, dentro de su misma ignorancia son y seran eternas!!! Concededme que Dios es la suma y compendio de la *inconsciencia*, y por daros gusto, admitire su existencia!! Dios, es fuerza; fuerza es brutalidad y perfecto equilibrio; pero equilibrio que emana directamente, y en consecuencia de la primera, no porque un divino cerebro haya querido *conscientemente* que asi fuera; en suma, niego la *personalidad* de un ser supremo.'

[122] 'Bondad, generosidad, inteligencia, forman un todo; es un error calificar de bondadoso á una persona, cuando su bondad no va acompanada de las otras cualidades afines inseparables; las mas de las veces esta bondad meramente superficial esconde una pasividad en alto grado egotistica, unida á una cobardia y falta de sinceridad que espanta.'

[123] 'La *Fe*, la que se tiene en la creacion agena, es la abdicacion de la propia inteligencia; desgraciado aquel que cree y no crea.'

[124] 'De todos los animales de la creacion, tan solo el *hombre*, consiente en abdicar la dignidad de su *porte*; me gustaria conocer el juicio de un cuadrupedo, al juzgar por sus ridiculas y antiesteticas cabriolas de la mentalidad del humano bipedo.'

[125] 'El *amor*, es una mera exacerbación de los mas sutiles instintos egoistas que caracterizan al *ser* humano; toda mala y baja pasion, es por él engendrada, y lo mas curioso del caso, es que con una hipocresia

A woman is deceitful *per se*, and from the time she leaves the womb; unfortunate is the man who runs up against one who pretends to be *sincere*!!! Her sincerity will always be the most splendid specimen of *gross cruelty*, and the most incontrovertible proof that every woman is a *solitary entity*, full of unconscious hatred for everything around her and absolutely convinced of her omnipotent superiority!!! Are there exceptions? Naturally... my wife. (Nice, 28 February 1904)[126]

The idea of *Fatherland* can be considered an excusable egoistic sentiment, but never a *virtue*. (Nice, 20 April 1904)[127]

Albéniz liked to discuss philosophical issues, and a letter from the noted author Louis Bertrand (dated simply Nice, 25 November (Bc, 'B')) expresses his regret that work on a novel will prevent him from continuing their discussions on aesthetics and metaphysics. His correspondence with Coutts also reveals a lively dialogue on politics and religion. Albéniz, in spite of his lack of formal education, was fluent in Spanish, French, English, Italian, and Catalan, knew some German, and was well read. His library included novels of Daudet and Flaubert, the writings of Berlioz, plus the works of Voltaire, Byron, Hugo, Racine, Corneille, de Musset, Molière, Balzac, Plato, Louÿs, Maeterlinck, France, Plutarch, Shakespeare, Goethe, and Schiller (these last two in French translation). He also read works of his compatriots, some of them collaborators, who wrote inscriptions in the volumes. Rusiñol, Feliu i Codina, Guimerà, and Serrano are all represented. Of course, there are several volumes of Coutts's works. His music library, consisting of much sheet music and several books on music, was also large. Of special interest are Eslava's *Escuela de composición: Del contrapunto y fuga*, 2nd edn. (Madrid, 1864) and *Les Mélodies grégoriennes* (Tournai, 1881). Significantly, there are only two books dealing with folk music: *Cantos y bailes de Valencia* by José Hurtado (n.p., n.d.) and *Old English Popular Music* (London: Macmillan, 1893). Unfortunately, none of these contains any marginalia.[128] He loved to

deliciosamente inconsciente, pretende poetizar (y la mayoria opina como el) y hasta santificar sus diabólicas fredaines!!! ...la gente no quiere convencerse de que en suma, y para la salvaguardia de la *raza*, con la hermosa y potente pasion genital, basta y sobra, sin necesidad de pedir ausilio a un hipocrita sentimentalismo, que se desvanece al menor motivo, dejando al desnudo toda la triste armazon de odios, celos, posesion exclusiva, obcecacion, y demas *hermosas*¡! zarandajas de que se compone; nunca fue el *amor*, una pasion *altruista*, como puede y debe serlo la *amistad* ... [es] una de las mas voraces y estupidas pasiones que amargan la existencia humana!!!!'

[126] 'La mujer es embustera *per se*, y desde que deja el materno claustro; desgraciado el hombre, que topa con una que pretenda ejercer de *sincera*!!! su sinceridad sera siempre el más espléndido especimen de *grosera crueldad*, y la mas incontrovertible prueba de que cada mujer, es un *ente solitario*, lleno de inconsciente odio por cuanto la rodea, y absolutamente convencido de su omnipotente superioridad!!! ?que hay excepciones? Naturalmente... mi mujer.'

[127] 'La idea de *Patria*, puede considerarse como un excusable egotistico sentimiento, pero jamas como una *virtud*.'

[128] Albéniz's library is kept at the Ah. His sheet music and books on music are at the Mm. Many manuscript and published scores by other composers are in the Bc.

collect books, and the generous income from Coutts facilitated his buying. In addition, he collected fans and paintings. Though he could have built a valuable collection of impressionist paintings, he preferred to patronize Spanish artists such as Joaquín Sorolla (1868–1923), Rusiñol, Zuloaga, and Casas. His daughter Laura become a noted artist in her own right, and her drawings adorned the first edition of *Iberia*.

With his interest in literature, Albéniz was not oblivious to the fact that his talents would be better devoted to librettos more consonant with his love of Spain, or at least outside the realm of the medieval English lore that so fascinated Coutts. This was the whole *raison d'être* for *Pepita Jiménez*. In 1899 he began composing a one-act lyric drama entitled *La Sérénade* (author unknown), but he soon abandoned the project.[129] In 1905 he commenced work on another lyric drama, *La morena* ('The dark woman'), on a text by Alfred Mortier. This, too, was left incomplete.[130]

A reversal in Albéniz's operatic fortunes was on the way, but once again it would take place outside Spain. Ironically, it would prove the beautiful sunset and not the glimmering sunrise of his theatrical ambitions. Albéniz, dispirited by his inability to succeed as an opera composer, would thereafter pour his declining energies into writing once again for the piano, a decision greatly supported by friends and family alike. The result of this was, of course, his immortal masterpiece *Iberia*.

---

[129] Bc, M984. Seventeen pages, dated Paris 20 June 1899. There is also an MS in the Mm, Lligall 6, consisting of only twenty-two bars in six pages. It is dated Paris, 20 June 1899. It seems that Albéniz often waded into composition in a burst of enthusiasm without having thought the work through. As soon as his improvisatory muse tired, he had little in the way of structure to sustain his effort. This is especially true of sets of pieces such as *The Alhambra* and *Catalonia: Suite Populaire*, which yielded only a single complete number each.

[130] *La morena* was to be a four-act lyric drama, but Albéniz composed only three pages. The MS is dated Nice, 21 Apr. 1905 and is now in the Bc, M984.

7

Iberia
(1905–1909)

ALBÉNIZ and Brussels went back a long way, and he retained many friends and professional connections there. In 1905 he finally succeeded in securing a production of *Pepita Jiménez* and his zarzuela *San Antonio de la Florida*[1] at the Théâtre Royal de la Monnaie,[2] with which he had kept up a long correspondence on this very matter.[3] The opera and the zarzuela premiered together on 3 January, 1905, with additional performances on 6, 10, 13 January, and 1 February. Maurice Kufferath translated the opera libretto into French[4] and the work appeared as a *comédie lyrique* in two acts and three scenes (cast in Table 10). The production was apparently a huge success, though its total of five performances might not suggest this.

Albéniz's friend Octave Maus (*Le Courrier musical*, 8/3 (1 February 1905), 76–8) found that 'in the place of banal and artificial exoticism, conventional picturesqueness, he has substituted a colour more discreet but more truthful, which marvellously evokes the places, customs, and distinctive characters of Spain.'[5] He praised in particular the character of Antoñona, the duet of the Vicar and Pepita, the dances and children's chorus, and the Prelude to Act II, as well as the love duet between Pepita and Don Luis. These are precisely the features earlier reviewers found so endearing.

---

[1] Now entitled *L'Ermitage fleuri*, in a French translation by Lucien Solvay and Robert Sand. The libretto was published Brussels: T. Lombaerts, 1904. In marked contrast to the reception accorded it in Spain, the Brussels critics had nothing but praise for the zarzuela's elegance, humour, and popular melody. It ran with *Pepita Jiménez* on 6, 10, and 13 Jan., and 1 Feb. It was presented alone on 16 and 29 Jan.

[2] See Jules Salès, *Théâtre Royal de la Monnaie 1856–1970* (Nivelles: Éditions Havaux, 1971), 140.

[3] According to Deledicque, *Albéniz*, 330.

[4] Kufferath (1852–1919) was music director at the Monnaie and a friend of Albéniz. (His father, Hubert Ferdinand Kufferath, had taught counterpoint at the Conservatoire Royal when Albéniz was a student there.) According to the composer, in a letter to Breitkopf und Härtel of 28 May 1901 (Ls), Kufferath had previously promised to try to secure a performance of the opera at the Monnaie.

[5] 'A l'exotisme banal et artificiel, au pittoresque de convention il a substitué un coloris plus discret mais plus véridique, qui évoque à miracle les sites, les coutumes, les caractères distinctifs de l'Espagne.'

TABLE 10. *Cast of* Pepita Jiménez, *Brussels, Théâtre Royal de la Monnaie, 3 January 1905*

Pepita	Mme Baux
Don Luis	M. David
Antoñona	Jeanne Maubourg
Don Pedro	Pierre d'Assy
Vicar	M. Belhomme
Count Genazahar	Alexis Boyer
Officer 1	Armand Crabbé
Officer 2	M. Lubet
Conductor	Sylvain Dupuis

Other critics, however, had some reservations. A reviewer named Labarbe, from the local *Le Peuple* (5 January 1905, 2), complained of the fact that

Two roles dominate the entire work, that of Pepita and that of Don Luis, and the rest remain in the shade. Fatally, the situations are repeated without providing much variety. This fault is common in all works inspired by short stories or novels, and very exceptional are those that conserve in their adaptation to the stage all their interest and that which creates their charm.[6]

He singled out the orchestration, however, as 'lively, varied, and rich' and, from the point of view of the music alone, he judged *Pepita Jiménez* 'a very expressive, coherent work, of an absolute sincerity and beautiful lyric flight, which is worthy of gaining and retaining attention'.[7]

Le Patriote (4 January 1905) placed Albéniz 'among the colourists, possessing innate melody and musical thought'.[8] It drew the inevitable comparison with *Manon* in terms of the characters and theme of the opera, and the closing duet between Don Luis and Pepita, which smacked of the one between Manon and Des Grieux at Saint-Sulpice. But Albéniz's approach to the number was different from Massenet's and provided a solution to the problem of presenting the drama's climax at the very end of the opera:

He has made this scene a symphony rather than a duet: with successive exposition, simultaneous development, transformation in the course of the struggle, and the final triumph of one of the themes. All of this is academic work. But this work is a

---

[6] 'Deux rôles dominent toute l'œuvre, celui de Pepita et celui de Don Luis, les autres restent dans l'ombre, et fatalement les situations se répètent sans apporter beaucoup de variété. Ce défaut est commun à toutes les œuvres inspirées de nouvelles ou de romans, et très exceptionnelles sont celles qui conservent dans leur adaptation à la scène tout leur intérêt et ce qui fait leur charme.'

[7] '[U]ne œuvre très expressive, très suivie, d'une sincérité absolue, d'une belle envolée lyrique et qui est digne d'attirer et de retenir l'attention.'

[8] '[P]armi les coloristes, ayant la mélodie innée, la pensée musicale.'

revelation. And, as elsewhere, there reigns from one end to the other a discreet emotion and an inimitable something called sincerity; this act is delicious to listen to.[9]

Interestingly, though he found Albéniz's opera more 'moral' than *Manon*, he did not approve of the work's 'vague scorn for religious matters, an atmosphere of Voltaire-style libertinism'.[10]

Pepita Jiménez attracted a great deal of attention in other cities in Belgium (e.g. Bruges and Liège), and abroad as well (Leipzig, London, Barcelona, and Madrid).[11] Pierre Lalo, writing in the Parisian *Le Temps* (11 April 1905), viewed the libretto as the major weakness of the work but attributed 'charming qualities' to the music, praising its handling of leitmotif, transformation of themes, and symphonic development. None the less, he regarded the work as redolent not of Bayreuth but of Spain and its fragrance, flavour, and colour, enthusing that Albéniz was 'one of the greatest inventors of rhythms in the entire universe'.[12] And he lauded his handling of the orchestra: 'And to add to his subtle eloquence, M. Albéniz has the most lively, the most supple, the most brilliant orchestra, an orchestra in ceaseless movement, changing, glistening, an orchestra that flows . . . like a stream.'[13]

Pierre Lalo's enthusiasm for the opera certainly indicated a potential market for *Pepita Jiménez* in Paris, and this thought was not lost on either Albéniz or Coutts. But that would not take place during Albéniz's lifetime, which in four years would run its course. The movement towards a Paris performance seems to have begun a few months after the Brussels triumph. A letter from Fauré to Albert Carré, director of the Opéra-Comique, written in August or September of 1905, makes a good case for an audition of the opera: 'But the music of *Pepita Jiménez* is better than very interesting. What is more, it reflects the atmosphere of his homeland in the most intense fashion.'[14] In a letter to Albéniz dated 23 September 1905, Fauré refers to Carré's acceptance of an audition.[15] Fauré also suggested to his friend André

---

[9] 'Il fera de ce tableau une symphonie plutôt qu'un duo. L'exposé successif, le développement simultané, la transformation au cours de la lutte, le triomphe final de l'un des thèmes, tout cela c'est du travail d'école. Mais ce travail est une trouvaille. Et comme d'ailleurs il règne de l'un à l'autre bout une émotion discrète, et ce quelque chose d'inimitable, la sincérité, cet acte est délicieux à écouter.'

[10] [U]n vague mépris des choses religieuses, une atmosphère de libertinage voltairien.'

[11] Clippings from newspapers in these cities are to be found in the Mm, car. 3. In most cases they lack the name and date of the newspaper.

[12] '[U]n de plus grands inventeurs de rythmes de l'univers entier.'

[13] 'Et pour ajouter à leur subtile éloquence, M. Albéniz a l'orchestre le plus vif, le plus souple, le plus brillant, un orchestre sans cesse mouvant, changeant, chatoyant, un orchestre qui coule . . . comme un ruisseau.'

[14] Nectoux, 'Correspondance inédite', 167. 'Or la musique de Pepita Jiménez est mieux que très intéressante. De plus elle reflète l'atmosphère de son pays d'origine de la façon la plus intense.'

[15] Ibid. 168.

Messager, artistic director at Covent Garden, that he mount the opera.[16] Nothing came of either of these efforts.

Neither was Albéniz successful in getting *Merlin* produced there, though serious consideration was given to staging it at the Théâtre Royal de la Monnaie the following season. However, the lovely Prelude to Act I was performed in Brussels in 1905 for a festival of orchestral music (organized by Henri Merck) at the concert hall Grande Harmonie. In addition, a M. and Mme Tassel sponsored a private audition of the opera at their mansion in Brussels, with Albéniz accompanying the singers at the piano.[17] Though *Merlin* would remain unfamiliar to the Belgian public, the possiblity of a new stage work materialized as a result of the Brussels success. Ramon Cattier was a journalist with *La Gazette* in the Belgian capital, and he and Albéniz now laid enthusiastic plans for an opera entitled *La loba* ('The she-wolf'). There are three letters in the archive (Bc, 'C') from Cattier to Albéniz, and the final one, dated 4 October 1905,[18] accompanied an outline of the drama, which he was still revising. But the project never advanced beyond that point.

This episode in Belgium marked both the high point and the end of Albéniz's musico-theatrical career. A combination of discouragement with the continued lack of interest in Spain in his operas, and inability to get a production of *Merlin* anywhere, persuaded him that his waning strength should be focused on what he did best, writing for the piano. However, his theatrical ventures had not by any means been a waste of time and effort. First, they had brought forth from his pen some of his finest numbers, especially in *Pepita Jiménez*. Second, they had given him the best composition lessons he could have received, and he was now far beyond where he had been fifteen years earlier in terms of his handling of texture, sonority, and large-scale form.

So, Albéniz now set about composing a monumental set of works for the piano entitled *Iberia*, whose creation would occupy him during the years 1905–8. It belonged to what the composer referred to as his 'second manner',[19] of which 'La vega' was a clear harbinger. But whether *Iberia* should actually be called a 'suite' is open to question. Albéniz's title simply refers to it as twelve *nouvelles impressions* ('new impressions') for piano. Performers usually programme at most a few of them on a concert; all

[16] Ibid. 170.

[17] See Deledicque, *Albéniz*, 336. The concert took place on 13 Feb. 1905.

[18] The others are dated 4 Mar. and 1 Oct.

[19] Letter to Joaquim Malats from Paris dated 2 Oct. 1907. This correspondence was first published in Joan Salvat, 'Epistolari dels nostres músics: Isaac Albéniz a Joaquim Malats', *Revista musical catalana*, 30/357 (Sept. 1933), 364–72; repr. in Franco (ed.), *Albéniz y su tiempo*, 129–36. The originals are in the Mm. It is worth noting that many of them are in Laura's hand, as she was serving as his secretary.

together they make for a long evening (total playing time is about eighty-five minutes). It could more justifiably be called a collection, as the pieces are quite distinct and are not laid out in a sequence of any significance. That is, the pieces could be rearranged in any order without upsetting the collection at all (in fact, Albéniz's original ordering of them in the manuscript was changed in the printed editions). This is certainly untrue of a suite in the traditional sense of the term. The harmonic and rhythmic richness and complexity of these pieces are quite extraordinary, especially in comparison to his piano pieces of the 1880s and 1890s. They abound in counter-rhythms, interweaving of the fingers, hand crossings, difficult jumps, and nearly impossible chords, while the innumerable double accidentals make them difficult to read. As a result, *Iberia* requires almost superhuman tech-nique, and Albéniz himself was hardly capable of playing it. Manuel de Falla and Ricart Viñes encountered Albéniz on the rue d'Erlanger one day during the period he was composing *Iberia* and found the master in a state of extreme discouragement. He confided to them that the previous evening he had come close to destroying the manuscripts of the new work because he deemed them unplayable. Artur Rubinstein threw some intriguing light on the subject of Albéniz's own execution of *Iberia*. The Polish pianist described a visit to Albéniz's widow and daughter during which they requested he play selections from *Iberia*. At first Rubinstein demurred, stating, 'It might shock you to hear me leave out many notes in order to project the essence of the music.' But they insisted. When he finished 'Triana', the composer's widow turned to Laura and expressed her amazement that Rubinstein played it 'exactly as your father used to play it'. Laura concurred, approving of his omission of the 'nonessential accompaniment'.[20] Of course, when Albéniz played this music he had one foot in the grave and was only a shadow of his former pianistic self. Blanche Selva, who premiered the entire collection, did not leave out any 'nonessential accompaniment', and neither would Albéniz have forgiven her for doing so (though most pianists find they have to make some slight changes in the music to be able to play it).

The twelve pieces of *Iberia* are arranged into four books of three pieces each. Each number evokes a peninsular locale, city, festival, or song and dance, largely concentrating on the south of Spain. But it is important to understand that the density of folkloric references is unprecedented in his output, and though a piece may bear the title of a particular song or dance, Albéniz feels no constraint to confine himself to that genre. It is good to remember that, when one refers to this or that theme as a *zapateado* or

[20] *My Young Years*, 480–1. Albéniz's encounter with Falla and Viñes appears in Collet, *Albéniz*, 158.

bulerías, one means that it is a freely composed melody utilizing the essential rhythmic and melodic components of that genre. However, these references are often so stylized that it is difficult to ascribe them to any specific category of song and dance. Despite the profusion of ideas, there is a clearly defined structure underlying them. The year before beginning work on *Iberia,* Albéniz had written in his diary on 20 April 1904 that 'The ideal formula in art ought to be "variety within logic".'[21] *Iberia* is a musical expression of this aphorism, in so far as its abundant musical variety is for the most part contained within the 'logic' of sonata forms and generally symmetrical phrasing.

The first book, consisting of 'Evocación', 'El puerto', and 'Fête-Dieu à Séville' (the original title, but usually referred to as 'El Corpus en Sevilla'), bears a dedication to Madame Jeanne Chausson and was composed during the month of December in 1905.[22] 'Evocación' is one of the most hauntingly reflective pieces Albéniz ever composed.[23] There is a strong fragrance of wistful nostalgia, and we feel that we have immediately penetrated to some inner core of being, not only of the culture but of the man himself. The movement is laid out in modified sonata form. The opening theme is sometimes described as a *fandanguillo* (see the International edition), but, as is usual with Albéniz, such pat labellings are misleading. Certain elements do suggest a member of the *fandango-malagueña* family, e.g. the triple metre combined with minor key (in A♭), descending minor tetrachord (in the bass in bars 13–19), use of the augmented second (in the middle line, bars 3–4), and certain arabesque turns of musical phrase (bars 11–18). But it is not a *fandanguillo per se,* especially in its slow tempo. It could also be seen as a *jota copla* in Andalusian disguise. This ambiguity of type is fitting, given its introductory position in the collection. Albéniz utilizes a syncopated ostinato figure in the bass, his favourite device for animating a texture. The tonic pedal for the first twelve bars provides an element of stability while the harmony is similarly 'animated' by increasing chromaticism in the melody and the middle line. The theme itself possesses a curiously offbeat quality, as there is an agogic accent on beat two. The shape of the line and the ties and phrase markings reinforce this emphasis. Thus, the effect of

---

[21] Mm, car. 4. 'La formula ideal en Arte, debiera ser, "variedad dentro de la logica".' The composer made this entry while in Nice.

[22] The three numbers of Book 1 were completed in Paris on 9, 15, and 30 Dec., respectively. The autograph for 'Evocación' is located in the Bc, M980. 'Evocación' actually bears the title 'Prélude' on the manuscript. This title would be more suggestive of a suite. It remains a mystery how the printed version acquired its present title. The manuscripts for 'El puerto' and 'Fête-Dieu à Séville' are located in the Lc and Oc, respectively.

[23] The author acknowledges the debt the following analysis of *Iberia* owes to Mast, 'Iberia'.

Ex. 41. *Iberia*, 'Evocación', principal theme, bars 1–4

the syncopation in the left hand is intensified by the metric ambiguity in the right (Ex. 41).[24]

The melody itself retains a folk-like character in the way it circles first E♭ (bars 1–6) then A♭ (bars 11–17) within the narrow compass of an octave. In contrast to the tenuous connection of the principal theme to the *fandanguillo*, what emerges in the second theme at bar 55 is a clear reference to a *copla* of the *jota navarra*, stated in the relative-major key of C♭ over a dominant pedal on G♭. This theme is remarkably similar in rhythm to the opening melody and obviously grows out of it,[25] but the ascending melodic contour and major key clearly establish the appearance of something new (Ex. 42). Starkie[26] has suggested that this combination of a southern principal theme with a northern secondary theme constitutes a sweeping musical gesture embracing the whole of Albéniz's peninsular subject. In any event, the development that follows is brief, about twenty bars long, and the retransition is dominated by the distinctly French sounds of the whole-tone scale. The use of this scale and the concomitant French augmented-

Ex. 42. *Iberia*, 'Evocación', secondary theme, bars 55–8

---

[24] This may be why Alicia de Larrocha (London CD 417887-2) lengthens this first note, in order to emphasize its place on beat one.

[25] Iglesias, *Albéniz*, i. 226, considers this movement actually to be monothematic, with the B theme a variation of the opening melody.

[26] Walter Starkie, *Spain: A Musician's Journey through Time and Space*, ii (Geneva: Edisli—At Editions Rene Kister, 1958), 122.

Ex. 43. *Iberia*, 'Evocación', Iberian-sixth chord, bar 102

sixth chord in *Iberia* may seem at first hearing to be a merely colouristic feature, but in fact it serves a structural function in several movements. Mast has identified a curious kind of augmented-sixth chord at bar 102 that will recur throughout the collection. It is a combination of German and French, with a clashing semitone in the middle. He has dubbed it the 'Iberian-sixth chord' (Ex. 43).[27] The restatement of the opening theme at bar 103 takes place over a dominant pedal, so that the ensuing twelve bars serve as a lengthy preparation for the return of the *jota copla* in the tonic major, over a tonic pedal. This emphasis on the dominant in the restatement is characteristic of Albéniz's treatment of sonata form throughout *Iberia*. The surprising harmonic twists in the coda, such as the Ab with a major seventh suddenly shifting to Cb minor (bars 134–5), and the penultimate chord of G major lurching to Ab major with an added sixth, serve notice that Albéniz has updated his Spanish style and is now thoroughly *au courant*.

In addition to *Iberia*'s bold harmonies and chordal planing, the abundant indications in both French and Italian regarding nuances of tempo, dynamics, and sonority (*très souple, très lointain, absolument atténué*, quintuple pianissimo) point to French impressionism as the inspiration for this renovation. Albéniz himself strenuously rejected the notion, but he did not help his case by referring to the collection as 'impressions'. Joaquín Turina relates an incident that further confirms Albéniz's awareness and assimilation of contemporary trends. In 1907 Turina attended a concert of the Parent String Quartet at the Salle Aeolian in Paris. The ensemble presented a modern composition, and Turina overheard a spirited conversation nearby regarding its merits. One person objected to its highly dissonant harmony, but the other responded in defence of the new work: 'What do you want? These things are in fashion now, and I myself am writing a series of pieces in which I employ the same procedures.'[28] That person was Albéniz talking

---

[27] See Mast, 'Iberia', 228.

[28] 'Encuentro en París', in Franco (ed.), *Albéniz y su tiempo*, 115–16 (originally appeared in *Arriba*, 14, Jan., 1949). '¿Y que quiere usted? Estas cosas están de moda ahora y yo mismo estoy escribiendo una serie de piezas en las que empleo los mismos procedimientos.' Debussy's first book of three *Images* (1905) may have provided the inspiration for Albéniz's first book of three 'impressions'. Debussy also composed an *Iberia* (for orchestra, however) during the period 1905–8, but we cannot prove this was anything more than coincidence.

about his *Iberia*. He was simply doing what he had always done, wading into
the waters of innovation after it was safe to do so.

'El puerto' exudes a completely contrasting atmosphere of noisy good
spirits, the hustle and bustle of a sea port. In fact, this was inspired by the
fishing-port town of El Puerto de Santa María near Cádiz on the Guadalete
River, a region Albéniz knew very well. This is clearly in the style of the
zapateado, a lively genre that is danced but not sung. It is in 6/8 metre with a
frequent but not regular use of hemiola.[29] After an accompanimental introduction, the incisive principal theme enters just before bar 12, its accented,
staccato line contrasting with the legato arpeggios of the left hand (Ex. 44).

Ex. 44. *Iberia*, 'El puerto', principal theme, bars 11–17

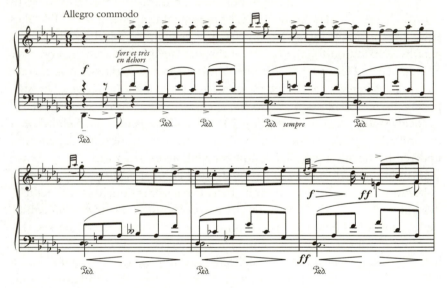

The overall form of the piece resembles that of 'Evocación', except that
there is no contrasting secondary theme in another key but rather a development section. Thus, its form is simply A–development–A′ with an introduction and coda. In spite of the increasing modal inflections, taking us from
major to Mixolydian to Phrygian, the entire A section is united by a D♭ tonic
pedal. This provides a stabilizing element within an otherwise exuberantly
riotous clash of syncopations and chromatic alterations. One particularly
arresting bit of colour is the suggestion of *rasgueado* in the flourish in bars

---

[29] The author's interpretation of this melody is supported by Cecilio de Roda, 'La "Suite" Iberia',
Programas de conciertos, Sociedad Madrileña (1911–13); repr. in Franco (ed.), *Albéniz y su tiempo*, 73–5.
Iglesias, *Albéniz*, i. 232, also concurs in this assessment.

Ex. 45. *Iberia*, 'El puerto', 'rasgueado' flourishes, bars 45–7

45–7 (Ex. 45). The development section at bar 83 tosses around the principal thematic material in transpositions of the Phrygian mode before another whole-tone retransition leads to the return of the home key at bar 123. In spite of the extroverted character of this music, the piece concludes in a subdued way, triple pianissimo, just like the other two numbers in this first book. In fact, six of the twelve pieces of *Iberia* end softly, as if the introspective mood of 'Evocación' were casting a long shadow over the whole work.

'Fête-Dieu à Séville' is one of the most frequently performed numbers from the collection, and one of the most difficult. Unlike most of the selections in *Iberia*, it is programmatic in nature and describes the Corpus Christi Day procession in the city of Seville, during which the statue of the Virgin is carried through the streets accompanied by marching bands, singers, and penitential flagellants. The opening 'rataplan' conveys the sound of the drum rolls as the procession nears. For dramatic effect, Albéniz would rest his hands on his ample abdomen during the rests in between these strokes.[30] The march-like theme that dominates the A section of this work exhibits very symmetrical phrasing, spiced up with some rather jarring dissonances that suggest the less-than-perfect intonation and execution of a band on parade in the streets of Seville (Ex. 46). It is inspired by the *estribillo* of the popular Castilian song 'La Tarara'. The *saeta* (literally 'arrow') is 'a piercing cry of religious ecstasy'[31] sung in free rhythm during the procession. Although it will dominate the B section, it makes its appearance at bar 83 underneath the march theme, now played quadruple fortissimo in semiquavers alternating between right and left hands. Albéniz resorts to a musical canvas of three staves here to contain his panorama (Ex. 47). The march theme passes from the scene, but the vivacious accompaniment continues in contrast to the freely expressive rhythms of the *saeta*, which are heightened by the placement of fermatas every two bars and the 'molto rubato' tempo marking. All of this suggests movement through space and time. A pensive,

[30] Collet, *Albéniz*, 160.
[31] Mast, 'Iberia', 245.

Ex. 46. *Iberia*, 'Fête-Dieu à Séville', 'rataplan' and march theme, bars 4–14

Ex. 47. *Iberia*, 'Fête-Dieu à Séville', march and *saeta* themes, bars 83–8

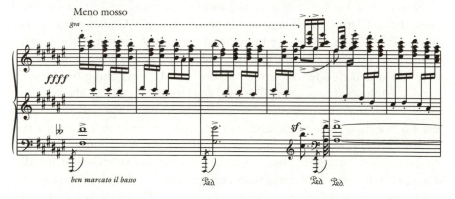

mystic air settles over the scene with the advent of greater harmonic instability and hushed dynamics (quadruple pianissimo). It was, of course, standard
procedure in Albéniz's earlier ABA forms to provide such a contrasting
mood in either section. But we see here how deftly he now merges the
sections, by overlapping themes and by providing a continuous accompanimental pattern. The seams are much less obvious than in his earlier style, and
this serves to convey the continuously unfolding sequence of events during
the celebration. Another departure from earlier practice is the avoidance of
exact repetition in the return of the A section, at bar 255. The march theme
appears in a greatly elaborated fashion, again very noisily, and concludes with
a spirited transformation in 3/8. The coda creates a captivating mood. The
distant strains of a lugubrious *copla* float over chords that remind the listener

of Debussy's *La Cathédrale engloutie* (composed in 1910 after Albéniz's death). Then Albéniz blends in the sound of church bells, *très lointain* ('very distant'), while an F♯ pedal exudes the tranquillity of an Andalusian night, with its black star-studded sky and palm fronds gently fluttering in the cool evening breeze.

In the autograph score, 'Triana', which he composed less than a month after the first book was complete, appears as the first selection in Book 2 (dedicated to Blanche Selva), followed by 'Almería' and 'Rondeña', which were composed later that year. This chronological order was reversed in the first published edition, however, so that 'Rondeña' leads off Book 2 followed by 'Almería' and 'Triana'.[32]

The title 'Rondeña' poses a problem, for there is little about this piece to remind one of a true *rondeña*, or even *rondeñas*. This flamenco genre is named after the city of Ronda in the south-west part of Spain. The *rondeña* (singular) is a rather oriental-sounding guitar solo, nowadays done scordatura and filled with melisma-like *ligados* (slurred runs) in free rhythm. It is true, however, that before the guitarist Ramón Montoya (*c.*1880–1949) developed the *rondeña* into its present form, it was somewhat synonymous with *malagueña*,[33] and that was probably what Albéniz had in mind. It would have been what is now called *rondeñas* (plural), which *is* a triple-metre song related to the *malagueña*, but it does not employ a regular hemiola and does not resemble what Albéniz has written here. Perhaps the title is simply a free evocation of that region, using the adjectival form of the city's name. The strict alternation of 6/8 and 3/4 that begins 'Rondeña' reminds Iglesias of the Cuban *guajiras*, as it does this author. But the *guajiras compús* begins on the dominant not the tonic, and it is not as fast as this number. In fact, its metre and tempo might remind us of the *bulerías*. But the metric alternation begins to go astray, and often four bars of 6/8 ensue before a return of 3/4. This must be viewed as a hybrid from Albéniz's fertile imagination. The first seventeen bars of 'Rondeña' constitute a simple instrumental introduction, but this accompaniment becomes more melodic at bar 17 and provides intimations of the principal theme, which appears definitely at bar 41 (Ex. 48). The principal theme group moves through the subdominant, G major, to arrive at a contrasting area in the dominant at bar 93, marked 'poco meno mosso'. After ten bars of introduction, a comparatively languid *copla* emerges. Though it exhibits the rhythm of an

---

[32] The autograph for 'Triana' is in the Oc and is dated Paris, 23 Jan. 1906. The MSS for 'Almería' and 'Rondeña' are in the same library and are dated Paris, 27 June 1906, and Nice, 17 Oct. 1906, respectively.

[33] In Redford, 'Iberia', 42, there is a reproduction of a piece labelled 'Malagueña o Rondeña (Rasgueada)' from Eduardo Ocón (ed.), *Cantos españoles: Colección de aires nacionales y populares* (Málaga: Cuarta, 1906). See Pohren, *Flamenco*, 136–7, for further discussion of this genre.

Ex. 48. *Iberia*, 'Rondeña', principal theme, bars 41–4

Ex. 49. *Iberia*, 'Rondeña', secondary theme, bars 103–6

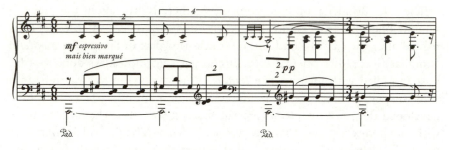

octosyllabic *jota* verse, it relies on the technique of 'iterance' (repetition of a note) common to Spanish *jondo* singing. It thus makes for an interesting blend of styles (Ex. 49).

The entire four-bar phrase is repeated several times at different pitch levels, enhanced by Phrygian colouring, to intensify its effect. When the original introductory theme returns in D♭ major at bar 149 and leads to modulatory exploration of the other themes, it creates the impression of a development section. But if we have so far established the essential elements of sonata form, including a retransition (bars 189–200, all in 6/8) employing the whole-tone scale, the juxtaposition of the principal and secondary themes at bar 201 presents us with a most unusual recapitulation (over a dominant pedal, as Albéniz so often does at this juncture). The recapitulation, if it be such, progresses through some daring modulations, even bringing back the D♭ major passage of the development. The coda at bar 233 recalls the dreamy quality of the B section, which prevails nearly to the end of the movement, only to give way to a very animated variation of the principal theme in the final nine bars. The form of 'Rondeña', then, is closer to sonata than anything else (Iglesias sees it simply as ABAB'A'Bcoda), but, however one chooses to analyse it, Mast's judgement holds: 'the parameter of metric alternation, the gradual formation of the whole-tone scale, and the various contrapuntal thematic combinations are handled with the touch of a master.'[34]

'Almería' presents no such problem in formal analysis, as it is clearly in sonata form. What is evidently elusive, however, is the rhythmic category. Unlike 'Rondeña', Almería is a place (a seaport in south-eastern Spain where Albéniz's father worked for a time in the 1860s), not a kind of music. At first glance, however, there is a striking resemblance between the two pieces in the steady alternation of 6/8 and 3/4. Even the downward motivic thrust in the right hand against the rising, widely spaced arpeggio in the left is familiar. But evidence of Albéniz's genius lies in the fact that appearances are deceptive. For a closer examination reveals that now strict metric alternation is indicated in the left hand only while the right alternates more freely, though it remains mostly in 6/8. But the real significance here is not so much in the metre but in the accents, which are conspicuously placed over the second and third beats in the 3/4 bars preceding 6/8 time in the hemiola pattern. This *compás* of two beats of duple, two beats of triple, followed by one beat of duple (unaccented, though it is on the downbeat), is strongly suggestive of the *siguiriyas*, i.e. *8* 9 *10* 11 *12* 1 2 3 4 5 6 7.[35] This genre, whose name is a Gypsy corruption of *seguidillas*, is the most *jondo* of all flamenco rhythms. One can easily imagine its persistent undulations in this opening (Ex. 50).

Ex. 50. *Iberia*, 'Almería', principal theme, bars 3–7

Siguiriyas is in the Phrygian mode, which, though 'Almería' starts out in major, is not long in appearing (bar 7). After ten bars of introduction, another member of the principal theme group pours forth in the upper register. As he has done several times now, Albéniz resorts to a sustained G pedal to provide a foundation for the increasing modality and chromatic inflection. This pedal does not relent until bar 54, where it is supplanted by a

---

[34] 'Iberia', 264. Iglesias's analysis is in *Albéniz*, i. 256.

[35] This is one way to count it, though not the normal way. Pohren, *Flamenco*, 143, makes the excellent point that the *compás* of siguiriyas is idential to that of *soleares*, except that it starts on 8 and not 1.

brief melody in the bass. A transition commences at bar 68 that will take us
to a new theme group, in the subdominant. Twelve bars of chords alternating Mixolydian-wise between C major and B♭ major over a C pedal serve as a
frame to prepare for the secondary theme, a *copla*, at bar 101 in the bass. As
in 'Rondeña', this theme combines the iterance of *cante jondo* with an
octosyllabic rhythm vaguely reminiscent of a *jota copla*. The melody is in
4/4 on a third staff, while the lower two staves continue the pedal and a
gently rocking accompaniment in 6/8 (articulated 3/4). This passage is one
of Albéniz's most extraordinary conceptions (Ex. 51). The C pedal persists
through to the commencement of the development at bar 154, initially in F
Phrygian. Again, a whole-tone scale and French augmented-sixth chord
dominate the retransition to G major and a restatement of the main themes
of the piece, followed by a coda at bar 246 over a G pedal. 'Almería' is thus
typical of Albéniz's handling of sonata form, with a couple of modifications,
especially in the subdominant secondary theme group.

Ex. 51. *Iberia*, 'Almería', secondary theme, bars 101–4

'Triana' is named after the famous Gypsy quarter in Seville, considered one
of the cradles of flamenco. This number resounds with all the clamour of a
juerga, the strumming of guitars, clacking of castanets, and percussive *taconeo*. Oddly, though it is marked throughout in 3/4 metre, it begins with a
descending rhythmic motive, outlining a tetrachord from F♯ to C♯ in the
melody, whose accents and syncopations create the sensation of duple metre.
This has reminded most commentators, including Mast and Iglesias, of the
pasodoble (two-step) or a march of some kind. As usual, a tonic pedal, here on
F♯, anchors this passage (Ex. 52). This rhythmic motive (short–short–long)
informs and generates the thematic material of the entire piece, especially at
bar 9 where a second principal theme in the style of the *sevillanas* emerges in
unambiguous triple metre (the syncopation continues over a pedal in the left

Ex. 52. *Iberia*, 'Triana', first principal theme, bars 1–2

Ex. 53. *Iberia*, 'Triana', second principal theme, bars 9–11

hand, however) (Ex. 53). The percussive interjections suggesting heelwork and castanets add brilliant local colour to Albéniz's musical canvas in the transition to the secondary theme in the relative major at bar 50, which presents a *copla* of effervescent gaiety (Ex. 54). The development section starting at bar 66 imposes terrific technical demands on the performer. The retransition for once is not grounded in the whole-tone scale, but it is suffused with triplet arpeggiations that recall patterns idiomatic to the guitar. A restatement of themes in the tonic minor and major begins at bar 102, leading to a coda that diminishes in intensity until the final, strident statement of the second principal theme.

Albéniz wasted little time in commencing work on Book 3 (dedicated to Marguerite Hasselmans), completing the three numbers 'El Albaicín', 'El polo', and 'Lavapiés' during November and December of 1906 while spending the winter in the temperate climate of Nice.[36]

---

[36] 'El Albaicín' was completed in Nice on 4 Nov. 1906 and bears a dedication (dated Nice, 15 Feb. 1907) 'To the artist whom I admire most; to the friend whom I love most' ('Al artista á quien mas admiro, Al amigo á quien mas quiero'). This refers to the pianist Joaquim Malats, whose interpretations gave the composer complete satisfaction. 'El polo' was finished in Nice on 16 Dec. 1906, while the third number in the book, 'Lavapiés', was actually finished a few weeks earlier, on 24 Nov. 1906. It bears a dedication 'To Malats the charmer !!! His adorer, despite being married to another !!!! Albéniz' ('A Malats l'encisador !!! su adorador, apesar de estar casado con otra !!!! Albeniz'). The autographs for these numbers are located in the Bc (M980), Oc, and Mm, respectively.

Ex. 54. *Iberia*, 'Triana', secondary theme, bars 50–3

El Albaicín is the fabled Gypsy quarter in Granada, a city of which Albéniz was intensely fond and from which he repeatedly drew inspiration in his music. This number is structured as a series of three alternations between a dance-like principal theme, highly motivic and rhythmic in character, and the freer, *copla*-style secondary theme. The unmistakable reference in the opening gambit is to the *bulerías*, with its twelve-beat *compás* (Ex. 55). The texture here simulates a guitar technique in which the thumb of the right hand

Ex. 55. *Iberia*, 'El Albaicín', principal theme, bars 1–9

alternates with the fingers in plucking the strings. The similarity between this number and his earlier 'Prélude' from *Chants d'Espagne* is conspicuous. We might once again imagine that the rhythm of the guitarist's *falseta* is shadowing the disciplined *taconeo* of the dancer. The triple-pianissimo dynamic marking gives this opening an air of both mystery and intensity, of controlled energy that must at some point blaze forth. Albéniz's abundant directions to the performer shed further light on the atmosphere he is creating. The opening is marked 'Allegro assai, ma melancolico' ('spirited allegro, but melancholy'), while the pianist is to use the una corda pedal and to play 'très estompé' ('very blurred'). The 'toujours nonchalant' ('always nonchalant') is revealing, in so far as it is typical of a flamenco number to start out in a quasi-improvisatory way, and then to build in strength, intensity, and confidence as the *duende* (lit. 'magic', the equivalent of 'soul' in the blues) deepens. That is, of course, precisely what will happen here. Interesting, too, is how tightly coiled is the melodic contour of the first five bars, packed into a tetrachord from the tonic B♭ to E♭, while the supertonic C is iterated incessantly in the upper voice as a pedal, like an open string on the guitar.

What most intrigues about this forty-eight-bar introduction is the rhythm. The hemiola pattern of the *bulerías* (or its more stately relation the *soleá por bulerías*) begins on beat twelve of the *compás*, and Albéniz displaces this strong beat to beat two in his 3/8 bar through an agogic accent. (This reminds us of 'Evocación', where he accented in similar fashion the second beat of the bar in the opening theme.) The *compás* repeats on the second beat of bar 9. The first beat of bar 1 is clearly perceived as an anacrusis to a downbeat, the twelfth count in the *compás*. This persists until bar 49 at which point the dynamic level rises to triple fortissimo and something extraordinary yet subtle occurs in the rhythm—the downbeat shifts to beat one, made abundantly clear by the accents placed there. Although Mast regards this as the arrival of real *bulerías* after some preludial improvising on the 'guitar', in fact we say goodbye to *bulerías*, and the rhythm of the first forty-eight bars never reappears. The regular triple metre to which the rhythm now conforms has nothing at all to do with *bulerías*, as the hemiola vanishes altogether. What this is, really, is hard to pin down, but what Albéniz considered it to be is obvious—a *malagueña*. If we look at either 'Rumores de la caleta (Malagueña)' from *Recuerdos de viaje* or his 'Malagueña' from *España: Six Feuilles d'album*, we see precisely this species of downbeat-oriented triple-metre rhythm animated by frequent triplet *falsetas*. This change is so smoothly executed, however, that one scarcely notices it. The persistence of the rhythmic motive of four semiquavers followed by a quaver on beat three, prominent before and after bar 49, aids the transition. The B section at bar 69

Ex. 56. *Iberia*, 'El Albaicín', secondary theme, bars 69–74

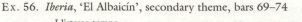

avec la petite pédale, et bien uniforme de sonorité,
en cherchant celle des instruments à anche

presents an evocation of *cante jondo* and is marked 'L'istesso tempo sempre'
('always the same tempo'), in order to avoid any loss of momentum. Its
manifold contrasts stimulate much reflection (Ex. 56). The clearest difference here is that though there is no reduction in tempo or loss of beat sense,
the downbeat is obscured by the fact that the melody begins on the anacrusis
of beat one and the downbeats of the second and fourth measures are
weakened by a tie. One can easily imagine this melody as a melisma vocalized
on 'ay'. The contour of the line is especially noteworthy in its similarity to
medieval liturgical chant. It ascends rapidly to a 'reciting tone', which it
embellishes with upper and lower neighbours before descending back to the
'final' in F Phrygian. Of course, one of the origins of *cante jondo* is in
liturgical singing. Though the tempo is strict, there is none the less a sense
of chant-like rhythmic freedom in this line. Even more arresting is its
monophonic texture in which the theme is doubled at the fifteenth. This is
one of Albéniz's favourite devices for delivering such a melody and is reminiscent of the lovely B section of the 'Prélude' from *Chants d'Espagne* cited
above. Albéniz's instruction to the performer at this point may give us
insight into what this signifies to him. He calls for a uniformity of sonority
in the manner of reed instruments ('instruments à anche'). Mast offers the
following interpretation of this:

Even though the style of this melody is that of cante jondo, Albéniz seems to be
emphasizing the Moorish aspect of the Albaicín in Granada in this work. Malm states,

'The standard Western imitations of Near Eastern music are inspired by its nasal, outdoor sound'. He then describes a double clarinet common in pan-Islamic music, stating, 'One may play parallel melodies on the two pipes or use one as a drone'.[37]

There are regular interruptions of the *copla* every four bars, signifying the interjection of the guitarist. After the second such interjection the *copla* is extended two bars by a 'melisma' skipping downwards by thirds. The interjections become more insistent in their frequency and lead to a return of the dance music. Both A and B sections continue to alternate, a pattern typical of flamenco performance, becoming ever more elaborate and extensive in texture and range. The piece concludes with downward thrusting exclamations of the 'interjection' motive and the tonic chord on B♭ with a raised third.

'El polo (Chanson et danse andalouses)' is named after one of the oldest and most serious of *cantes*. In fact, there are two kinds of *polo*. The first is a composed sort of art music of the early nineteenth century, the most famous examples being those by Manuel García (1775–1832), especially the one entitled *El criado fingido* that Bizet borrowed for the entr'acte before Act IV of *Carmen*.[38] The other, unrelated kind of *polo*, is the actual flamenco *polo*. The last of the *Siete canciones populares españolas* of Falla is a *polo* inspired by this type, which exhibits the *compás* of the *soleares* family of rhythms.[39] Though Albéniz's thematic material bears little resemblance to this and is more akin to García's style, it possesses the inconsolably melancholy quality of the flamenco *polo*. What the composer has captured here is not so much the substance of this *cante* as its spirit. (None the less, Albéniz still had his keen sense of humour, and he inscribed on the manuscript that the *polo* 'should not be confused with the sport of the same name'.)

The obsessive character of this melancholy mood is expressed in the basic rhythmic pattern, which is incessant from the first beat to the last and appears straightaway in the now customary 'instrumental' introduction. This metric pattern is quite distinctive and does not fit into any flamenco category this author is familiar with. Mast views it as a kind of hemiola in which two bars of 3/8 become one bar of 3/4. But the accents fall on one and three of such a

---

[37] Mast, 'Albéniz', 214. The quotation is taken from William P. Malm, *Music Cultures of the Pacific, the Near East, and Asia* (Englewood Cliffs, NJ: Prentice Hall, 1967), 42–3. Another possible reference is to sections of monophonic group singing in flamenco, during which the men and women sing an octave apart.

[38] The melody itself, however, apparently derived from a folk source and was not a thoroughly original composition by García. See Theodore S. Beardsley, 'The Spanish Musical Sources of Bizet's *Carmen*', *Inter-American Music Review*, 10/2 (Spring–Summer 1989), 143–6. Enrique Franco, 'La Suite Iberia di Isaac Albéniz', *Nuova rivista musicale italiana*, 7 (1973), 68, finds the 'rhythmic formula' of Albéniz's *polo* identical to García's *El criado fingido*.

[39] This family includes the *caña*, which is very similar to the *polo*. A typical *polo* verse is as follows: 'Everyone asks God | for health and freedom, | I ask for death | and he will not grant it.' Cited in Pohren, *Flamenco*, 113. The *polo* often employs long melismas on 'ay', a practice derived from religious sources.

Ex. 57. *Iberia*, 'El polo', principal theme, bars 17–23

larger unit and are not necessarily perceived in that way, especially when the principal theme arrives at bar 17 (Ex. 57). However we choose to view the rhythm, the predictable symmetry of the phrasing and the natural-minor scale on F over a persistent tonic pedal in the left hand heighten its almost fatalistic affect. Another aspect of the rhythm that contributes to the forlorn quality of the music is the little sigh-like rest that occurs on the downbeat of the even-numbered measures. This dovetails with Albéniz's instructions at bar 17 to play 'dolce en sanglotant' ('sweetly sobbing') and again at bar 49 to play 'toujours dans l'esprit du sanglot' ('always in the spirit of a sob'). The obsessive quality continues into the secondary theme at bar 111, which is closely related to the principal theme rhythmically but is in the relative-major key (Ex. 58). The abundant added-note sonorities in 'El polo' further contribute to its emotional intensity. The form of the piece is once again sonata, with the usual French-augmented-sixth-based retransition and dom-

Ex. 58. *Iberia*, 'El polo', secondary theme, bars 111–14

inant return. In spite of the depressive character of the music, the movement ends with a bang (in the form of a virtuosic flourish of rapid triplets) and not the whimper we might have expected.

Lavapiés is a district in Madrid named for the local church where a foot-washing ritual was performed on Holy Thursday.[40] This locale was known in Albéniz's time for its low-class denizens called *chulos*. There was a great deal of noisy street life, and its accidental sounds are represented by the abundant surface dissonance in this piece. Thus, Albéniz indicates that the music is to be rendered 'joyfully and with freedom'. As Mast points out: 'The "wrong-note" technique in Lavapiés injects humor—a portrayal of the constantly misfiring valves of a Madrid street-musician's hand-organ...[but] the underlying harmonic functions are quite simple.' The principal thematic material is based on the *habanera*, which became all the rage in Madrid in the late nineteenth century in response to the turmoil in and eventual loss of Cuba (Ex. 59).[41] The density of the score (employing three staves at times), the sheer profusion of notes in a riot of dissonance, makes 'Lavapiés' almost unplayable, and it was this work that nearly drove Albéniz to destroy his manuscripts.[42] It would be hard to improve on Mast's description of this music, which exhibits 'elements of melodic disorder, brought about through a complex technique of sporadic imitation, changes of register, cross-relations, and cross-rhythms'.[43] Such 'unpredictability' must somehow be counterbalanced by stabilizing elements in the music to prevent chaos, and this is where Mast finds 'Lavapiés' a disappointment. For the sonata-allegro

Ex. 59. *Iberia*, 'Lavapiés', principal theme, bars 2–5

[40] Linton E. Powell, *A History of Spanish Piano Music* (Bloomington: Indiana University Press, 1980), 80.

[41] Franco, 'Iberia', 69, finds that this theme is derived from a popular Andalusian villancico, 'Campanas sobre campanas'.

[42] Mast, 'Albéniz', 40, states that when Selva heard of his intention to destroy *Iberia*, 'she asked to see [Lavapiés] first, and returning within a day or two, she played the piece from memory'. Selva herself had earlier said that *Iberia* was unplayable, but Albéniz insisted, 'You will play it!' (Collet, *Albéniz*, 160).

[43] Mast, 'Albéniz', 310.

Ex. 60. (*a*) *Iberia*, 'Lavapiés', secondary theme, bars 78–81

(*b*) *España: Six Feuilles d'album*, 'Tango', bars 3–6

format is clear-cut and close to the surface. The opening tonal area is D♭ major, which leads through a complex transition to the secondary theme in the dominant, A♭ major. As Albéniz so often does, the actual theme at bar 78 is prepared by several bars of introductory rhythm. This secondary theme possesses a more reposeful character than the first, but it is still of the *habanera* type. Despite his new style, the similarity of this melody to his earlier 'Tango' from *España: Six Feuilles d'album* is conspicuous (Ex. 60*a*, *b*).

The development section lasts some forty-three bars before a retransition commences, employing the Iberian-sixth chord. A restatement of themes in the tonic is followed by a coda in which the secondary theme is dressed up in whole-tone garb as the melodic line descends in register and dynamic level through a series of sequences before the sudden triple-fortissimo authentic cadence at the end. Mast finds in 'Lavapiés' 'a disappointingly high degree of predictability at the large-scale formal' level, as if the thematic materials had been poured into a 'sonata-derived "mold"'.[44] Iglesias, however, views this movement as a mere ABA with coda, which is an understandable perception. Albéniz does not repeat his expositions, and there is no definite seam between the exposition and development sections. But this is a bit too simple, for it does not take into account the clear use of transition material to modulate from principal to secondary key areas. It also ignores the fact

---

[44] Mast, 'Albéniz', 311. Iglesias's analysis is in *Albéniz*, i. 314–19.

that much of the 'B' section is developmental in nature, employing both principal and secondary themes. The restatement of themes includes both A and B, something a regular da capo structure would not do, and the placement of these ideas under the same tonal 'roof', so to speak, is one of the hallmarks of a sonata recapitulation. For these reasons, we cannot view the form of this and other sonata movements in *Iberia* as mere ABA structures. In the 1880s Albéniz *had* observed a clear distinction between his sonatas on the one hand and his Spanish-style character pieces (usually in da capo form) on the other. In maturity, however, he combined the two styles under the influence of the Parisian circles in which he routinely moved. Edgar Istel is certainly correct in asserting that had Albéniz remained in Spain and not settled in Paris he would never have written anything like this music.[45]

The final book (dedicated to Madame Pierre Lalo) took longer to finish. 'Málaga' and 'Eritaña' were composed in the summer of 1907 in Paris, but the final number, 'Jerez', which occupies the middle position in the book, was not completed until January 1908.[46] The explanation for this is quite simple. Albéniz had originally planned to conclude the collection with *Navarra*, a work he left incomplete at his death (the last section was finished by Déodat de Séverac). He felt the style of *Navarra* was, after all, 'shamelessly cheap' ('descaradamente populachero')[47] and that it did not fit in with the other numbers. So, he composed 'Jerez' as a substitute.

'Málaga' is another example of Albéniz's application of sonata form. This is one of the shortest pieces in the collection, lasting around five minutes. Here again the opening is supported by a pedal, this time the final of F Phrygian, though the overall key is B♭ minor. The abundant syncopations in the melody above are counterbalanced by the regularity of the phrasing in four-bar units. The rhythmic freedom, triple metre, and modality evoke the *malagueña* (Ex. 61). The second principal theme grows out of this at bar 17 and exhibits a hemiola pattern in which two bars of 3/4 sound like three bars of 2/4, all against a very even accompaniment. The secondary theme in D♭ major at bar 58 evokes the *jota malagueña* in its octosyllabic rhythm and cadential flourish

---

[45] 'Isaac Albéniz', 143.

[46] The autograph of 'Málaga' is dated Paris, July 1907; of 'Eritaña', Paris, Aug. 1907; and of 'Jerez', Nice, Jan. 1908. They are all located in the Bc, M980. Mast, 'Iberia', 1, raises the question as to the exact completion date of 'Jerez', pointing out that a letter from Albéniz to Malats dated 30 Nov. 1907 (citing from Llorens Cisteró, 'Inéditas', 99) indicates that the work was already completed. The state of the manuscript itself, however, may give us a clue, as it contains numerous corrections. Bits of manuscript paper were pasted over passages to be altered and the new material written on them. The work was probably done by Nov., but revisions were not finished until Jan. of the following year, when Albéniz felt satisfied enough to date it.

[47] Letter from Albéniz to Malats dated Nice, 30 Nov. 1907, in Salvat, 'Epistolari', Franco (ed.), *Albéniz y su tiempo*, 135–6. Albéniz may have regarded *Navarra* as insufficiently sophisticated for inclusion in *Iberia*, but it exhibits the modified sonata form typical of that collection.

Ex. 61. *Iberia*, 'Málaga', first principal theme, bars 1–4

Ex. 62. *Iberia*, 'Málaga', secondary theme, bars 58–61

(Ex. 62). Its consequent phrase in bars 62–4 is closely related to the second principal theme. In the context of the entire collection, the *jota* theme takes on the character of a leitmotif, unifying the various numbers through its recurrence. This is a procedure we have already noted in his *Escenas sinfónicas catalanas* of 1889 and which reflects a well-established interest on his part in formal unity. As usual, Albéniz simply modulates his way out of the secondary theme group into the development without a perceptible seam. The retransition is based on the French augmented-sixth chord before a dominant-oriented restatement of the principal theme group and the establishment of B♭ major in the secondary theme, in which tonality the work concludes.

'Jerez',[48] as we know, substituted for *Navarra* and presumably exhibits a level of complexity and sophistication more in keeping with the character of *Iberia*. For the first and last time, we get a key signature of no flats or sharps, and the first sixteen bars are utterly diatonic and contain not a single accidental. This is unusual in Albéniz's music, as the composer exhibited a marked predilection for flat keys and abundant accidentals. The E pedal that persists through these measures gives an unusual case of pure Phrygian, before G♯ creeps in at bar 17. Because we are unaccustomed to hearing

---

[48] The English corruption of the word Jerez (through the Portuguese for Jerez, 'Xerez', where the X is pronounced 'sh') has provided the name for a famous liquor made there—sherry.

Ex. 63. *Iberia*, 'Jerez', first principal theme, bars 1–3

this in Albéniz's music, however, the lingering impression is of Aeolian with a lot of emphasis on the dominant. This duality between E and A as tonics will characterize the tonal relationships until the end of the piece. (As we have earlier observed, the G♯ does not necessarily function as the leading tone in A minor and does not clear up the matter of tonality, because it is characteristic of Spanish modality to harmonize the final of a Phrygian mode as a major chord, in this case E major.) Although the metre is 3/4, we tend to hear the quaver as the unit of pulse, as the tempo is a leisurely andantino with the crotchet at seventy-six per minute. The *falseta*-style skipping in thirds in the right hand, outlining a descending minor tetrachord, constitutes a phrase of twelve quaver 'beats' evenly divided over the barline, six before and six after. The seeming presence of an underlying twelve-beat *compás* has perhaps led most commentators to agree with Collet that this is a kind of *soleares* (a Gypsy corruption of *soledades*, or 'loneliness'). Though the accents do not fall in the right places, the desolate mood of that *cante* prevails here (Ex. 63). A second principal theme and lengthy transition lead to the secondary theme, over a C pedal, at bar 67. Though this *copla* possesses a freely lyric quality (marked 'rubato'), the 'guitar' interjections are twice as long as the phrases they separate and are clearly based on the rhythmic motive from the end of the first principal theme (Mast refers to this motive as a 'reverbera-tion') (Ex. 64). Albéniz's metrical shifts in 'Jerez' are the most complex in the collection, as he now moves from 3/4 to 3/8, then to alternating bars of 1/4 and 2/4. It is not readily apparent what musical purpose these serve, as they have nothing to do with hemiola. One suspects they may be intended more for the eye than the ear. Planing is used throughout the development and into the coda, and gives the harmony a Debussian quality. The custom-ary dominant pedal during the restatement of themes at bar 155 creates greater confusion here than before because it can be viewed as either the

Ex. 64. *Iberia*, 'Jerez', secondary theme, bars 67–72

dominant of A minor or the final of E Phrygian. An Iberian-sixth chord (spelled Gb–Bb–C–Db–E) precedes the coda, in which the conflict between A and E as tonal centres is finally resolved in favour of the latter.

'Eritaña' was not originally to have concluded the collection. Albéniz stated in a letter that he had originally intended 'Eritaña' to be second, while another work, entitled 'L'Albuféra' (based on a 'jota valenciana'; L'Albuféra is a seaside area near Valencia), was to have completed the book.[49] But this work never saw the light of day, and 'Eritaña' took its place. The name came

[49] Albéniz explains this in a letter to Malats dated Paris, 22 Aug. 1907. See Salvat, 'Epistolari', Franco (ed.), *Albéniz y su tiempo*, 134. This portion is also reproduced in Iglesias, *Albéniz*, i. 346. The original is in Laura's hand, not Albéniz's.

Ex. 65. *Iberia*, 'Eritaña', first principal theme, bars 1–4

from a popular inn on the outskirts of Seville, called the Venta Eritaña, where flamenco was performed. Artur Rubinstein described a visit there, 'where the flamencos sang and danced. I watched them with delight, sipping *Jerez* (sherry) and devouring *jamón crudo*, that delicious smoked ham.'[50] Thus, the collection concludes with the light-hearted strains of the *sevillanas*, identified as such by Albéniz himself in the letter cited above. Of all the works in *Iberia*, this one received the highest praise from Debussy. The rhythms of the *sevillanas* permeate the piece from the very beginning (Ex. 65), and there is no strongly contrasting *copla* section. Sonata form is apparent, but the themes are so interrelated through rhythm that only the contrasting key areas decide the issue. The profusion of added-note harmonies and accidentals in 'Eritaña' gives the impression of tone clusters. But it is all surface colour, and the tonal relationships are normal. The principal theme group is in E♭ major, while the secondary theme at bar 47 is in the traditional area of B♭. A curious feature of the metre, one not encountered in the collection before, is the use of a dotted line to divide almost randomly interspersed measures of 4/4 into one beat followed by three, though Albéniz does not indicate a metre change. In rhythmic terms, this is analogous to the 'wrong notes' and tone clusters in its quirky, offbeat effect. These elements certainly help suggest the *jaleo* of a festive *juerga* in which there is a virtual cataract of sound made by stomping, clapping, finger-snapping,

[50] *My Young Years*, 465.

shouting, singing, and guitar playing. Interestingly, what has been missing since 'Lavapiés' is the whole-tone scale. Perhaps out of sensitivity to the suggestion that he was influenced by Debussy, Albéniz abandoned it in the final book, as if he had bidden 'good riddance' to it at the end of 'Lavapiés'.[51]

The works were first published in Paris by Édition Mutuelle of the Schola Cantorum (1906–8), and this edition was reprinted in Madrid by Unión Musical Española (1906–9).[52] As already mentioned, the four books of *Iberia* were premiered at various locales in France by the French pianist Blanche Selva,[53] dedicatee of the second book. Working from the manuscripts, she presented them as indicated in Table 11.

TABLE 11. *Premieres of* Iberia *performed by Blanche Selva*

Book no.	Date	Venue
One	9 May 1906	Salle Pleyel, Paris
Two	11 September 1907	Saint-Jean-de-Luz, France
Three	2 January 1908	Salon of Mme Armand de Polignac, Paris
Four	9 February 1909	Salon d'Automne, Paris

But in fact the Catalan pianist Joaquim Malats (1872–1912) was Albéniz's favourite interpreter of these pieces, and they were composed for him. Though Selva was the first to present entire books in concert, Malats premiered many of the individual numbers in concerts in Spain. For example, he performed 'Triana' in Barcelona on 5 November 1906 at the Teatre Principal and five weeks later in Madrid on 14 December at the Teatro de la Comedia. This was fully ten months before Selva's performance of that piece. He performed both 'Triana' and 'El puerto' in Barcelona the following year at the Teatre Principal on 23 March 1907. Albéniz and his family were in attendance, and the event was a huge success. Thus, Rubinstein's assertion that it was his 'privilege to introduce . . . *Iberia* . . . to [Albéniz's] own country and the rest of the world' was entirely untrue.[54] Malats had done it a decade

---

[51] Mast, 'Albéniz', 368.

[52] See Baytelman, 'Albéniz', 86, for a complete list of publishers. Baytelman notes a discrepancy between the publication date of 'Jerez' in 1908 and what she reads as the year 1909 on the autograph. This author's examination of the autograph yielded the year 1908, but in the process of binding the page was cut off at the bottom, and the date is hard to read. Iglesias, *Albéniz*, i. 335, however, confirms the autograph year of 1908.

[53] Selva (1884–1942) later became director of a music academy in Barcelona.

[54] *My Young Years*, 140. Rubinstein performed *Iberia* in Madrid and Barcelona during the 1916–17 concert season, according to a newspaper clipping in the Mm, Prov. M-987g. His recollection on p. 481 of his memoirs that no one had played them in Madrid before and that they were a 'complete revelation' to the public there does even less credit to Malats, whom Rubinstein evidently regretted never having heard play. Malats had performed them again in Madrid at the Teatro de la Comedia on 10 Dec. 1909.

earlier, and no doubt more capably. Albéniz laid great plans for a tour that would take Malats and *Iberia* throughout Europe and win plaudits for himself. Albéniz was especially keen to have a Spaniard introduce the works.[55] But Malats fell ill and could not realize these plans. Albéniz's letters to Malats certainly reveal the composer's uncommonly great admiration and affection for his countryman and merit some discussion.

Albéniz addressed him as 'Querido Quinito' ('Dear Quinito'), a diminutive construction of the final syllable of his given name (Joaquín in Spanish). In a letter from Nice of 9 November 1906, Albéniz lavished the following praise on his friend:

You are not unaware of the high artistic esteem in which I hold you; for many years you know that I have predicted you would reach the pre-eminent position you have attained; in my opinion you belong in the small number of pianists worthy of that name in the musical world, having in your favour that special idiosyncrasy your race bestows and which enhances with special brilliance everything you interpret.

Now with respect to my *Triana*, you know the profound emotion that I felt when I heard you play it at your house. I owe you the greatest satisfaction that I have experienced in my already long career as a composer; your magnificent interpretation has succeeded in convincing me that not in vain have I scribbled on so much paper during my life, and though I had achieved nothing more than that an artist of your calibre took an interest in my work, I should consider it a worthy prize for me and sufficient reward for my labours.

A million thanks to you, my dear Quinito; continue along your glorious road; you already know you can count on the unconditional and powerful love of your fraternal friend.[56]

That Albéniz had Malats and not Selva in mind when composing *Iberia* is clear from a letter dated Paris, 22 August 1907, in which he declared, 'this work, this *Iberia* of my sins, I write essentially through you and for you'.[57]

---

[55] Perelló, 'Apuntes', 16. Another one of Malats's admirers was Fauré, who offered him a professorship in piano at the Paris Conservatoire. Malats turned the offer down because it required his adoption of French nationality.

[56] Salvat, 'Epistolari', repr. in Franco (ed.), *Albéniz y su tiempo*, 130. 'No ignoras el alto concepto artístico en que te tengo; desde hace muchos años sabes que te tengo predicho alcanzarías el preeminente puesto a que has llegado; en mi concepto formas en el corto número de pianistas dignos de tal nombre en el mundo musical, teniendo en tu abono esa especial idiosincrasia que da la raza y que avalora con especial brillantez todo cuanto interpretas.

Ahora bien con respecto a mi *Triana* y sabes la profunda emoción que resentí cuando te la oí en tu casa; le debo la más grande satisfacción que he experimentado en mi ya larga carrera de compositor; tu soberbia interpretación ha logrado convencerme de que no en vano he emborronado tanto papel durante mi vida, y aun cuando no fuera más que el haber alcanzado el que un artísta de tu calibre se interesara a mi obra lo consideraría digno galardón para mí y suficiente premio a mis trabajos.

Un millón de gracias, mi querido Quinito; prosigue en tu glorioso camino y ya sabes que cuentas con el incondicional y fuerte cariño de tu fraternal amigo.'

[57] Ibid. 134. '[E]sta obra, esta *Iberia* de mis pecados, la escribo esencialmente por ti y para ti.'

Nine months earlier (Nice, 27 December 1906) Albéniz informed Malats that
he had just finished composing, 'under the direct influence of your marvellous interpretation, the third book of *Iberia*. . . . I believe that in these numbers I have taken "españolismo" and technical difficulty to the ultimate
extreme, and I feel compelled to confirm that you are at fault for it.'[58] In
spite of the joy he derived from Malats's exquisite interpretations of *Iberia*, his
old bitterness towards Spain lingered like a foul odour during an otherwise
savoury meal: 'you already know that Madrid is the region of perpetual
insipidness, of concealed envy, and . . . I believe that the more modest part I
personally appear to take, the more success your effort will have.'[59]

Of course, pianists other than Selva and Malats performed *Iberia* during
Albéniz's lifetime. Albéniz himself evidently performed 'Almería' and 'Triana' at a concert of the Libre-Esthétique in Brussels in 1908.[60] This was his
last public appearance. The composer's friend and former student José Tragó
performed some numbers from the collection in Madrid in April of that same
year.[61] Albéniz's student Clara Sansoni gave perhaps the first Italian performances of *Iberia* in 1909.[62] Alfred Cortot was fond of these pieces and after
receiving a copy of *Iberia* directly from Albéniz responded that it was 'truly
of the first order'.[63] The Portuguese virtuoso José Vianna da Motta performed 'Triana' and 'Almería' on 14 January 1908 in the Beethoven-Saal in
Berlin. Unfortunately, in a letter to Albéniz of 29 May 1906 he suggested
that *Iberia* revealed French influence, especially of Debussy. This incurred
the composer's wrath, and Vianna da Motta recanted in early 1908, apol-
ogizing for the unintentional insult.[64] Albéniz's preference for direct and
immediate effect is, in fact, quite dissimilar to Debussy's symbolist perchant
for allusion and implicit statement.

The papers in France took scant notice of Selva's *Iberia* premieres. In
Spain, however, a Malats concert was always worthy of mention in the
press, and the critics gave unqualified praise to the works. Malats's Barcelona
performances were hailed by *La vanguardia* as compensation for the

[58] Salvat, 'Epistolari', repr. in Franco (ed.), *Albéniz y su tiempo*, 131. '[B]ajo tu directa influencia de
intérprete maravilloso el tercer cuaderno de *Iberia* . . . creo que en estos números he llevado el españolismo
y la dificultad técnica al último extremo y me apresuro a confirmar que tú tienes la culpa de ello.'

[59] Ibid. 134. Letter from Paris of 2 July 1907. '[Y]a sabes tú que Madrid es la región de la guasa perpetua,
de la encubierta envidia y . . . yo creo que cuanto más modesta sea la parte que personalmente me toca
representar, más éxito tendrá tu tentativa.'

[60] Collet, *Albéniz*, 75.

[61] Letter from Tragó to Albéniz, dated 2 Aug. 1908 (Bc, 'T'). He acknowledges receipt of the third and
fourth books.

[62] According to a newspaper clipping without date or title in the Mm, Prov. M-987c.

[63] Undated letter in French (Bc, 'C'), 'Vraiment de tout premier ordre'.

[64] There are eight letters from Vianna da Motta (1868–1948) to Albéniz in the Bc ('M'). This one is dated
16 Feb. 1908. This and the letter of 29 May 1906 are reproduced in Llorens Cisteró, 'Inéditas', 19–20.

'collective ingratitude' shown to the composer. 'El puerto' was a 'poem of admirable naturalness and freshness' with a 'classically Spanish ambience'. *El noticiero* concurred that it contained a 'popular flavour that is very Spanish'.[65] In Madrid, Malats had to repeat 'Triana' at his December 1906 concert, just as he had had to do in Barcelona. *La época* declared its novelty 'enchanting' and noted a 'great distance' between it and his earlier works such as 'Sevilla' and 'Granada':

The Spanish ambience has lost nothing in freshness or character, and despite that, the harmonic ambiguities, the novel rhythms, the form of the work, the pianistic technique have been so improved and enhanced that it could well be cited as a little piece worthy as a model to be imitated, as an example of an orientation that many ought to follow.[66]

All this surprises, given the previous hostility of the Spanish press towards Albéniz's 'foreignized' music and anything 'Frenchified'. In truth, the work's sympathetic reception in Spain was probably aided by the composer's ill health and premature death. Then again, purely instrumental music did not raise the critics' hackles the way stage works did, especially when it was played by an artist of Malats's stature. In the case of musical theatre, Albéniz was running up against a long tradition and a deeply entrenched establishment. But in the sphere of piano music, he himself had defined the tradition and could do as he pleased. After hearing 'Triana', Bretón wrote approvingly to Albéniz, 'That is your great road.'[67]

Olivier Messiaen was also a great admirer of Albéniz's *Iberia* and placed it in the highest category of works for the piano.[68] Pierre Boulez is of the opinion that it is 'the wonder of the piano, the masterpiece of Spanish music which takes its place—and perhaps the highest—among the stars of first magnitude of the king of instruments'.[69] Though Debussy thought Albéniz's penchant for exaggeration and superabundance was tantamount to 'throwing music out the window', he had warm praise for the work:

[65] *La vanguardia* reviewed the two concerts of Malats on 6 Nov. 1906 (by 'M. J. B.'), 9; and 24 Mar. 1907, 8–9. *El noticiero* also reviewed both concerts, on 6 Nov. 1906 and 25 Mar. 1907.

[66] 17 Dec. 1906, 3, by Cecilio de Roda. 'El ambiente español no ha perdido nada ni en frescura ni en carácter, y a pesar de ello, las vaguedades harmónicas, las novedades rítmicas, la disposición de la obra, la técnica pianística se han mejorado y avalorado tanto, que bien puede señalarse esa piecita como modelo digno de imitarse, como ejemplar de una orientación que muchos deberían seguir.'

[67] Letter of 15 June 1907 (Bc, 'B'). 'Ese es tu gran camino.'

[68] Notes for a recording of *Iberia* by Yvonne Loriod (Ducretet-Thomson 8557/8). Cited in Kalfa, 'Albéniz à Paris', 36. See also Gauthier, *Albéniz*, 99, 111, for more Messiaen quotes concerning *Iberia*. Regrettably, he does not indicate his source for these. The above recording does not appear in his discography. According to Gauthier, Messiaen considered 'El polo' to be Albéniz's masterpiece.

[69] Cited by Gonzalo Badenes, trans. Angela Buxton, in liner notes for a recording of the *Concierto fantástico* and Arbós's transcriptions of *Iberia* (Auvidis Valois V4661, 1992).

Isaac Albéniz...acquired a marvellous knowledge of the craft of composition....
There are few works in music to compare with *El Albaicín*....Although...the
popular themes are not exactly reproduced, it is the work of one who has absorbed
them, listening until they have passed into his music, leaving no trace of a boundary
line....Never has music attained to such diverse, such colorful impressions [as in
Eritaña]. One's eyes close, dazzled by such wealth of imagery. There are many other
things in this *Iberia* collection, wherein Albéniz has put what is best in him.[70]

Several orchestrations of *Iberia* have been made over the years. Albéniz
made his own of 'El puerto' but was evidently not happy with it.[71] The ones
most commonly played are by Arbós, the violinist and conductor.[72] Others
have since been rendered by Carlos Surinach (complementing Arbós's) and
Leopold Stokowski ('Fête-Dieu à Séville'). It is regrettable that Ravel did not
orchestrate one of the numbers from *Iberia*. The dancer Ida Rubinstein had
requested a ballet score from him, and he immediately thought of arranging
something from *Iberia*. But he gave up the idea when he learned that Arbós
had the rights to the work.[73]

During Albéniz's lifetime other arrangements were made of these pieces.
The complexity of the music forbids a transcription for solo guitar, but there
was a Trio Iberia from Granada consisting of bandurria (Sr. Devalque), lute
(Sr. Artea), and guitar (Sr. Barrios) that performed the collection widely and
whose arrangements Albéniz hugely enjoyed. A copy of one of their programmes[74] reveals that their repertoire included not only *Iberia* but transcriptions of others of Albéniz's works as well as Spanish-style compositions
by Bretón and Arbós. The works were further popularized during the 1920s
and 1930s by the Gypsy dancer 'La Argentina' (whose real name was Antonia
Mercé) and her Ballets Espagnols, who danced to Arbós's transcriptions of
'Triana', 'El Albaicín', and 'Fête-Dieu à Séville'.

In addition to giving Spanish performers national music of the highest
order to present to the public, Albéniz was always keen to help compatriot

[70] Leon Vallas, *The Theories of Claude Debussy*, trans. Maire O'Brien (New York: Dover Publications,
1967), 162–3. The original appeared in the *Bulletin français de la Société Internationale de Musique*, 9/12
(Dec. 1913), 42–4. Debussy was reviewing a concert of the 'Concerts Colonne—Société des Nouveaux
Concerts' given on 29 Oct. that featured Spanish musicians performing Spanish works.

[71] The MS is in the Bc, M980, dated Nice, Jan. 1907, on the first page and Nice, Feb. 1907, on the last.
According to Baytelman, 'Albéniz', 87, 'It was to be included in a multi-movement work called *1re. Suite
d'orchestre*.' But that suite remained unfinished. Istel, 'Isaac Albéniz', 142, wrote that Arbós told him of a
private audition of Albéniz's arrangement by the orchestra of León Jehin, in Nice. It was not to anyone's
liking, and he left it to Arbós to do.

[72] According to Arturo Reverter, 'Albéniz–Arbós: Amistad, relación musical, escenarios', *Notas de música*
(Boletín de la Fundación Isaac Albéniz), 2–3 (Apr.–June 1989), 25, Arbós completed orchestration of
'Evocación' in 1910, 'Triana' in 1917, 'El Albaicín' in 1924, 'Fête-Dieu à Séville' in 1925. He also orche-
strated *Navarra*, in 1927.

[73] Kalfa, 'Albéniz à Paris', 31–2.

[74] Located in the Mm, car. 3.

composers in any way he could. The two extant letters in the archive from Manuel de Falla (1876–1946) to Albéniz make it clear that Falla held Albéniz in affectionately high esteem and had come to Paris hoping to study with him and Dukas.[75] In early January 1908 Falla was residing in Paris and wrote to Albéniz explaining his difficulties securing a production of his opera *La vida breve* (1905) in Madrid and complaining of his inability to focus on composition because of all the lessons he needed to give just to survive. The second letter, written several days later, expressed his great gratitude to Albéniz for working behind the scenes to secure Falla a stipend of 1,000 francs from the Spanish King through the Marqués de Borja.[76] Now he could compose in relative tranquillity. This no doubt prompted him later to write that Albéniz 'was an example of loyal and disinterested comradeship to all of us who are working towards the creation of a new Spanish art'.[77]

Around this time Albéniz came to the assistance of another of his countrymen, Joaquín Turina (1882–1949). Only a month before he assisted Falla, Albéniz heard from Turina, also in Paris, that René de Castéra at Édition Mutuelle would not cover more than half the cost of publishing his Quintette because it was too long. Albéniz was a close friend of the publisher of his own *Iberia*, and he instructed Turina not to talk to Castéra until he, Albéniz, had a chance to clear things up. In the event, Albéniz agreed to cover all necessary costs beyond Turina's means to pay.[78] It is worth noting that both Falla and Turina performed selections from *Iberia*. Turina wrote a letter sometime after this incident, telling Albéniz he planned to play some of *Iberia* in Seville that April.[79] Falla wrote to Albéniz's daughter Laura from Madrid on 15 June 1915 informing her that he had played 'Evocación'— 'which every time seems to me more admirable'—during a conference he had organized on new music at the Ateneo.[80] Several years earlier, in 1891, Albéniz had gone to hear a young Pau Casals perform at a restaurant in Barcelona and gave the young man a letter of introduction to take to Count Morphy in Madrid for assistance. Three years later, the young cellist used this letter to gain the support of the Queen Regent, María

[75] The two letters are dated 11 and 17 Jan. 1908 and are located in the Bc ('F').

[76] Another letter in the Bc ('N'), from Marquesa Vda. de Nájera in Madrid, dated 28 Dec. 1908, assures Albéniz that the King will assist Falla. Evidently Albéniz continued to seek help for him after the 1,000 frances ran out.

[77] Manuel de Falla, *On Music and Musicians*, trans. David Urman and J. M. Thomson (London: Marion Boyars, 1979), 32 (original appeared in *Música*, 2 June 1917).

[78] The correspondence (see n. 79) makes it clear, however, that Albéniz would receive the rights to the work.

[79] There are four extant letters from Turina to Albéniz in the Bc ('T'), dated 8, 12, and 20 Dec. 1907. The final, undated letter (which mentions *Iberia*) must have been written after this time because Turina states he has not talked to René de Castéra for a while since their disagreement over publication of his Quintette.

[80] This and one other letter (dated 31 Oct. 1923) to Laura are located in the Bc ('F') with the two mentioned above: 'que cada vez me parece mas admirable.'

Cristina.[81] Granados, too, benefited from Albéniz's intercession with a publisher, and wrote to him that 'you know how to be, as you always were,
generous with your friends'. Josep Plá tells a touching story of Albéniz's
generous financial assistance to the Spanish sculptor Manolo Hugué in 1905
and how Albéniz's home (then on the rue Franklin) was a harbour of warmth
and hospitality for struggling young artists from Spain.[82]

Albéniz rendered assistance in ways other than merely financial. We recall
that he helped organize d'Indy's concerts in Barcelona in 1895 and 1898. He
also secured for Fauré the title of Knight Commander of the Royal Order of
Isabel the Catholic, and helped arrange a festival of Fauré's music that took
place in Barcelona in March 1909.[83] Albéniz's correspondence indicates that
other composers wrote to him for musical counsel. Eugène d'Albert wrote on
4 August 1902 for advice about a *seguidilla* that he planned to use in the
intermezzo of an opera he was composing.[84] The author Henri Cain (one of
the librettists of Massenet's *La Navarraise*) wrote to him seeking suggestions
about staging, set designs, and music for Beaumarchais and Mozart.[85]

To be sure, Albéniz's generosity also extended to less celebrated people. In
the autumn of 1906 (Perelló says it took place in the Sala Giralt on 14
September) he organized a concert in Tiana to benefit the poor of that
community and invited Malats to join him on stage to perform some two-
piano music of Saint-Saëns and his own *Rapsodia española*. This was but one
of many benefit concerts he gave throughout his career. The illustrious
guitarist Miguel Llobet (1878–1938), a close friend of his, also appeared
on this programme playing Albéniz's 'Granada' and other transcriptions.
Finally, Perelló recalled another instance of Albéniz's kind-heartedness.
After Albéniz facilitated his becoming a student of Mathieu Crickboom, he
undertook to give the aspiring violinist a lesson in life. One day as they were
walking down a street in Barcelona, a pale and wizened old woman
approached them seeking alms. Albéniz gave her five pesetas and then
admonished the young man to 'learn to be generous'.[86]

---

[81] Corredor, *Conversations with Casals*, 28. H. L. Kirk, *Pablo Casals* (New York: Holt, Rinehart &
Winston, 1974), 63, elaborates on this by stating that Albéniz encouraged Casals to flee the 'provincialism
of Catalonia and . . . the cultural shortcomings of Barcelona'.

[82] Barcelona, 25 May 1907 (Bc, 'G'). Granados does not specify which publisher other than that it was a
Parisian firm: 'sabes ser, como siempre fuistes, generoso con tus amigos.' Plá's account is in 'La generosidad',
Franco (ed.), *Imágenes de Isaac Albéniz*, 17–19 (excerpt from 'El poeta Moréas y Albéniz', *Vida de Manolo
contada por él mismo*, Barcelona: Ediciones Destino, 1947).

[83] Fauré informed Albéniz of the award and thanked him for his assistance in a letter of 21 Dec. 1908
(Collection Fauré—Fremiet). Cited in Kalfa, 'Albéniz à Paris', 23, and Nectoux, 'Correspondance inédite',
161 (actual letter on 168).

[84] Letter in Italian, from Lago Maggiore (Bc, 'A').

[85] Albéniz wrote the date 29 Dec. 1906 on this letter (Bc, 'C').

[86] Arturo Llopis, 'En el centenario de Isaac Albéniz', *Destino* (13 Feb. 1960), 14 (clipping in the Mm,
car. 4). Llopis interviewed Perelló for this piece.

Albéniz continued to teach piano as well as philosophy, but he never established a school of pianism as Granados did. He seems to have remained indifferent to pedagogy, though he did produce an outstanding student during this period, Clara Sansoni. At Fauré's invitation, he also served on the jury at the Conservatoire in 1905 and 1907. His assessments of auditioning hopefuls survive from the trials of 1907 and indicate that he was generally charitable in this arena as well, at least to the women. But on 17 October a Mr Aube's piano playing failed to please: 'Oh non non non non.' Mr Bousquet merited a '*Non; helas!*', while Mr de Fleurian a '*Non decidement*'. Mr Coutine was a '*petit co-co-co-chon*' ('little pig'). Albéniz expressed to Malats his view that it was criminal to encourage artistic aspirations that had no hope of realization, and he considered even himself guilty of it.[87]

But Albéniz was not only on the dispensing end of charity, and in fact we cannot understand the evolution of *Iberia* without acknowledging and probing further into the continuing importance of his remunerative relationship with Coutts. Albéniz's granddaughter Rosina Moya Albéniz de Samsó has stated that Coutts's ongoing patronage permitted Albéniz to compose in peace without having to work or worry about finances. Without such help, he would not have been able to bring forth *Iberia*. Those who claim that Albéniz was merely Coutts's slave and that their collaboration was a marriage of Spanish poverty and English vanity need to explain why Coutts continued to support his composer after Albéniz ceased all work on the trilogy and devoted his time almost exclusively to piano music. They also do not have the luxury of ignoring, as all biographers have done, Coutts's letters to Albéniz and what they reveal about their relationship. For we understand clearly from the correspondence that these erstwhile business associates had become the most intimate of friends. Coutts never once in the letters expresses the slightest impatience with the pace of composition or makes any demands on Albéniz at all. Coutts's patronage was now divorced from any mercenary considerations and was based solely on his fraternal love for Albéniz.

To begin, how much financial assistance did Albéniz receive from Coutts? As of 1893, the amount stated in L1453 was £800 a year, in addition to three-eighths of all his earnings. This was a substantial sum of money at that time. And it seems to have increased, thanks to the largess of Coutts. We can now clarify the issue of remuneration because records of Coutts's payments to Albéniz and members of his family have come to light in the Latymer Archive at Coutts & Co. The records do not indicate whether the money was purely an allowance or included earnings from concerts, productions, and

---

[87] Letter of 2 July 1907, in Salvat, 'Epistolari', Franco (ed.), *Albéniz y su tiempo*, 133.

TABLE 12. *Amounts paid by Coutts to Albéniz, 1894–1908*

Year	Total payments (£)
1894	670.00
1895	2,156.67
1896	1,578.68
1897	2,000.00
1898	1,370.00
1899	1,650.00
1900	1,400.00
1901	1,575.00
1902	1,375.00
1903	1,036.00
1904	800.00
1905	1,600.00
1906	2,225.00
1907	954.70
1908	1,957.00
Total	22,348.05

publications. We still do not know to what extent, if at all, Coutts was handling Albéniz's finances. Albéniz's correspondence with his publishers in Leipzig indicates, however, that he was paid directly by them. Thus, we can safely assume that he had income apart from the amounts in Table 12, which cover the period 1894 to 1908. In the year of his death, Albéniz received a final payment of £260 on 2 January. In October of that year, Rosina began receiving a sum of £100 monthly.

The very large sums in the years 1895–7 and 1905–6 might well reflect income from performances of their operas, but in other cases these figures demonstrate that Coutts's generosity was great, and did in fact increase over the course of time. Indeed, in *Chances and Changes* (99), Coutts's son states that upon his own marriage in 1900, Coutts gave him and his wife a yearly allowance of £1,000. Along with his annual salary of £500, he declares, '£1500 a year was a very good income to get married on, in the year 1900, and went as far as a nominally very much larger income nowadays [early 1930s]'. Coutts gave Albéniz an allowance equal to or greater than that which he was giving his own son. Combined with the money Albéniz made from other sources, this income was more than sufficient to meet his needs, and these were many.

In addition to Albéniz's own health problems, his wife and children (especially Alfonso and Enriqueta) also required medical treatment for various ailments, and he had to provide for his parents during their final years.

We also know, from letters written by him to the firm of Breitkopf und Härtel, that he had to pay substantial amounts for the publication of his opera *Pepita Jiménez*. Moreover, his inveterate generosity was a drain on the treasury. We recall that he paid for the publication of Chausson's famous *Poème*, which the firm had declined otherwise to publish because of its modernity, and assisted Turina in publishing his work.[88] He also incurred expenses travelling widely and frequently to promote his own music, while maintaining residences in several cities. Finally, Albéniz had a prodigal temperament and did not always manage his money wisely. In a letter to Rosina of 23 May 1903 (Mm, car. 2), Coutts addresses her concerns about the disparity between Albéniz's small operatic output and the large income they were receiving from him. Coutts reflects on Albéniz's handling of money in the following way:

Sometimes, it's true, Albéniz & I quarrel concerning his expenditure; & I am still inclined to think that his methods of house management might be amended & brought more into accord with English habits. He can never persuade me that taking about furniture from place to place is less expensive than having furnished apartments; nor that to send out to shops for articles as they happen to be wanted is less expensive than keeping a store in the house & giving it out, as required! But these matters are, after all, detail, & the chief difficulty he has had to contend with has been his health: I trust this is now better established; though he will always, I fear, have to keep a curb on the appetite, which unfortunately he once indulged too largely! If he can do this, all will go well, *and without any further enlargement of his income.* (Emphasis added.)

It is obvious that without the patronage of Coutts, Albéniz would have had to navigate some very narrow financial straits. He made money from his publications, including *Pepita Jiménez*, the performances of which also produced income. But this would hardly have been enough to support his lifestyle. He had taught piano for a time at the Schola Cantorum in Paris, but he was forced to give this up in 1900 due to his poor health. As his physical condition deteriorated so did his fabled virtuosity, and resuming his peripatetic existence as a touring concert artist was out of the question. The frequent need for rest and recuperation occasioned by his malady made holding any kind of regular job impossible.

Thus, far from precipitating his 'untimely end', as Istel asserted, Coutts kept Albéniz afloat not only economically but physically, and in so doing played the traditional role of a patron. The Englishman himself understood

---

[88] It should be pointed out, however, that Albéniz does seem to have profited from the *Poème*, as Breitkopf und Härtel conveyed the royalties to him after the death of Chausson in 1899.

this perfectly well and made a striking reference to it in the letter to Rosina cited above:

Suppose I went tomorrow to the Uffizzi [*sic*] gallery at Florence and suppose they were asses enough to sell me the Botticelli 'Holy Family' for £100,000; would you not say that I had obtained value for my money? But what is the difference, if instead of honouring a dead artist by purchasing his work, I give a living artist the opportunity to produce his work? I hope I have made my meaning clear and that if it is at all true that financial relations between Albéniz & me have been a source of worry to you, you will henceforth put them out of your mind; because indeed, though in modern days this is rarely done, it is no more than what was constantly done in times when art and trade were not confused in men's minds as now they are.

The final question that arises, however, is this: if Albéniz was making so little progress towards completing his commission, i.e. *King Arthur*, and indeed virtually abandoned the work during the period he composed *Iberia*, why did Coutts persist in supporting him? The answer is at once simple and complex: Albéniz was the best friend he had.

    For his commitment to writing, Coutts seems to have paid a heavy emotional price. His letters to Albéniz are often very personal in nature and reflect the turmoil of his private life, occasioned in part by his decision to break with family tradition and expectations. According to the current Lord Latymer,[89] the great-grandson of Coutts, the family, even Coutts's own son, greatly disapproved of his having left his wife for poetry and music (he and Nellie separated at least once). This, he continues, may account for the 'absence of any other documents in the family' pertaining to their activities. This is indeed an unfortunate loss, for Albéniz's letters to Coutts would have provided many valuable insights. However, the letters Coutts wrote to Albéniz suggest that he left his wife not for poetry and music but because of extreme differences in personality. He complained bitterly of her indifference to his career as a writer. At other times he accused her of 'dementia' and 'lascivious mania'. In the same letter in which he made these charges,[90] he declared that 'her condition would break down far stronger men than I am. ... I often wonder what J.C. would have done, if he had lived with a woman, not like Mary, who was content to sit at his feet, but with one who *sat on his head*.' Finally, in a letter of 3 February 1901,[91] he clarified the issue: '*But*—inasmuch as I had left home, society, career, & children, because I will not & cannot live with a woman *who does not love me*,—so, I should most assuredly do the same again, *however much I might love the woman*.'

---

[89] In a letter addressed to this author of 21 July 1990.   [90] Dated 24 Aug. 1904 (Mm, 10.276).
[91] Mm, 10.274.

In short, Coutts was not a happy man. Among his most plaintive outpourings is this lament from a letter of 6 March 1905 (Mm, 10.279):

My dearest friend: Don't be anxious about me. It is true that I suffer a great deal. . . .
First there is the *physical* suffering of constant, wearying interruption & the terrible
struggle to do my work, in spite of such annoyance. I cannot get physical quiet,
except when I am away from Nellie. Secondly, there is the mental suffering of the
most violent detestation & contempt of myself, & the constant effort to crush down
my egotism. . . . Lastly, I suffer, because Nellie's fearful hysteria communicates itself to
me, & I have to act the part of trained nurse.

Thus, in all fairness to Coutts, we should realize that there were two sides,
at least, to the story. According to his son, when Coutts's mother died in
1899, he 'lost the one being in the world, perhaps, who had an entirely
disinterested love for him'.[92] This could be construed to imply that Albéniz's
love for Coutts, unlike his mother's, was not 'entirely disinterested'. Coutts
himself, however, placed Albéniz on the same pedestal occupied by his
mother. We find evidence of this in the final stanza of his poem 'In Memory
of I. Albéniz', from *Egypt and Other Poems* (published in 1912):

> Farewell, and farewell; and when I too can burst
> From this chrysalis world to another less curs'd,
> May you, as of old, with my coming elate
> By the side of my mother my footsteps await.

Coutts touched on the subject of emotional support in a letter to Albéniz
dated 27 August 1906 (Bc, 'C'), responding to encouragement offered by
his Spanish friend: 'Dear boy! It is good to have *someone* in the world who
admires one a little! I don't want flattery; but a small amount of admiration is
perhaps necessary to one's work.'[93]

Coutts's troubled marriage and estrangement from his family increased his
sense of alienation. As a result, he found in Albéniz—the sympathetic,
generous, and jovial Spaniard—a friend in whom he could confide his
troubles, a fellow artist whose struggles, though of a different kind, were
no less severe than his own. This relationship, as much as any other consideration, inspired him to assist Albéniz financially. Indeed, what emerges
most strongly from their correspondence is a deep and abiding affection.
Nothing could more effectively refute the thesis that their co-operation was
based solely on money, that Albéniz had 'prostituted' his art, than the

---

[92] Latymer, *Chances*, 98. That Coutts's son disapproved of his father's artistic associations is suggested by
the lack of any mention whatsoever of Albéniz in the book.

[93] Encouragement flowed both ways. On 13 Jan. 1908 (Bc, 'C') Coutts wrote to Albéniz: 'all that you have
done is noble, high, full of the best kind of beauty.'

expressions of endearment to be found with almost embarrassing frequency in the letters. A sampling of these is appropriate here to lay once and for all to rest the vicious and inaccurate assertions of writers like Istel.

Most charming and generous of men! I can only hope to be worthy of such a friendship as yours, and so strong & noble an affection. (4 February 1897, Mm, 10.271)

Your deep affection for me, dear boy, is a great comfort to me, and your letters are often a great consolation. My curse in life really is that *I feel everything too much*. (15 August 1900, Mm, 10.273)

Life tries me sorely; but you are my best help. (15 February 1905, Bc, 'C')

Your bad account of your health troubles me much. If only you & I could have lived a calm philosophic & artistic life together! (6 April 1905, Bc, 'C')

Your letter is full of *rubbish*, dear boy. So long as you *love* me, I want no more. To *admire me* is absurd. (20 July 1905, Mm, 10.285)

You are, with me, (because you love me so well) like a woman—you read 'between the lines' in my letters! (8 February 1906, Bc, 'C')

Dearest friend, indeed I do love you, & if it were not for the feeling that no matter what I say or do, you would love me still, I don't think I could support the dreadful eternal worry of my existence. (17 May 1906, Bc, 'C')

Dearest friend: Indeed you must not praise me in that extravagant way. I am quite unworthy of it; and my chief goodness consists in loving you. (6 June 1906, Mm, 10.283)

Would to God we were neither of us wedded! (11 October 1907, Bc, 'C')

My dearest, dearest friend, do try not to be an ASS!! I love you better than I love even Nellie. . . . If it were not for your affection, what on earth would become of me? (29 October 1907, Mm, 10.289)

Yes, we are twin-souls—But, we are also unfortunately also twin-bodies *now*. (14 May 1908, Mm, 10.290)

As with the poems of Fauré, we confront once again the question of sexual orientation. It is worth repeating that there is no evidence that Albéniz was either homosexual or bisexual. According to Barbara Peters, head of the Latymer Archive, however, Coutts possessed 'wide-ranging tastes'. Documents in the archive indicate payments to a mistress, and perhaps to a male companion. We will never know. What is certain is that, by his own admission, he possessed an extremely sensitive, poetic temperament. This probably accounts for the feelings he had for Albéniz and the intimate way he expressed them. Certainly his declarations of love were platonic in character.

What were Albéniz's feelings? These we must infer from his correspond-ence with his wife, because his letters to Coutts have evidently not survived.[94] It would be too cynical to assume that his apparent expressions of endear-ment to Coutts were a mere ploy to maintain his patronage. Albéniz's letters to Rosina indicate that he truly liked Coutts, but Albéniz obviously played somewhat the role of psychotherapist in their relationship. His own tempera-ment, though prone to melancholy, was too sunny and optimistic to need as much support. And his marriage was, if not ideal, definitely more stable.

By the period of *Iberia*, then, Albéniz's association with Coutts had ripened into a deep friendship, and Coutts's letters to his Spanish friend shed light on very intimate aspects of their lives. Coutts's neurosis did not dim with the passage of time, and his marriage continued to be a source of frustration. He understood Albéniz's physical plight and own domestic troubles, and he was now giving Albéniz an extraordinary amount of money for producing virtually nothing at all in the way of the trilogy. But his understanding of Albéniz's plight was filtered through his own essentially solipsistic view of the universe. He did not fully comprehend just how much Albéniz was suffering; otherwise, he could not have written as he did on 20 February 1905 (Bc, 'C'): 'But oh! dear friend, I think I would gladly take half your sickness to have the peace and leisure that you have. Life is one long eternal WORRY!' Neither would he have dispensed such tripe as the following of 24 October 1908 (Bc, 'C'): 'all is well, if you will only think it so.' Only a week later he promised to send Albéniz 'the book of the Christian Scientists' because of its 'power over some minds to translate them into a spiritual plane of thought'.

Despite all this, their collaboration did produce one more work, the *Quatre Mélodies* for solo voice and piano of 1908, dedicated to Gabriel Fauré. They appeared in a bilingual edition in 1909 (Paris: Rouart, Lerolle; French trans. by M. D. Calvocoressi) with the titles 'In Sickness and Health' ('Quand je te vois souffrir'); 'Paradise Regained' ('Le Paradis retrouvé'); 'The Retreat' ('Le Refuge'); and 'Amor summa injuria'. These very expressive songs are ex-amples of Albéniz's late style and resemble *Iberia* in the technical demands they place on the pianist and in their chromatic harmony and abundant modulations. They also exhibit a very sophisticated formal design, avoiding repetition and following the dictates of the text in a through-composed manner. Typically, all are in flat keys (with abundant double flats) and all

[94] According to the current Lord Latymer, Coutts's son probably burned Albéniz's letters. This conflicts with a letter Coutts's son wrote to Rosina, dated 1 Aug. 1923 (Mm, car. 2), in which he promised to send her the composer's letters *if he found them*. Perhaps he never did. It is also possible that the family, remembering the Oscar Wilde affair, sought to destroy any documents that were suggestive of scandal.

Ex. 66. *Quatre Mélodies*, 'Amor summa injuria', bars 9–13

exhibit a syllabic setting of the text that cedes musical interest to the accompaniment. A good example of this comes from 'Amor summa injuria' (Ex. 66). This is not to say that the voice has an easy time of it, as the declamatory line, full of accidentals and awkward skips, provides the singer with ample challenges. The combination of virtuosic piano writing with an unmemorable vocal line typifies his song style. Whether the results merit the effort expended to learn them is debatable, but the infrequent appearance of

these songs on recital programmes (there are no recordings) is not merely a
matter of oversight.

With the completion of *Iberia* and *Quatre Mélodies*, Albéniz began a
precipitous decline into terminal illness. He spent the summer of 1908 in
Bagnoles de l'Orne taking the waters and relaxing with his friend Carlos
Salzedo (1885–1961), the famous harpist. It was during this time that he
also met a future biographer, Deledicque, who found it hard to believe that
Albéniz was actually ill, he was 'so happy, so animated'.[95] The following
account of Albéniz's final weeks on earth is indebted to his nephew Víctor
Ruiz Albéniz, a doctor who aided the composer during that most difficult
period.[96] Albéniz and his family spent a trying winter on the Riviera, where
they had gone in the futile hope that its mild climate would stimulate a
recovery. A brief return to Paris in the spring and the ministrations of various
specialists there did little to retard the deterioration of his health. A regular
stream of visitors came by, and Dukas appeared religiously every day. Albéniz's heart was sorely taxed by excessive urea in his blood, due to the
inefficiency of his kidneys. He was even forced to give up his beloved cigars,
his 'smoky inspiration' as he called them, which he gave away to his friends
and students. Now the family retreated once again to the south, this time to
the French Basque country on the Atlantic side of the Pyrenees, in the small
resort town of Cambo-les-Bains. Here he and his wife and daughters settled
into a suite in the Château Saint-Martin, complete with a garden in an
adjacent patio (the spring was late in arriving, and the rose bushes were not
yet in bloom). Uremia plagued Albéniz, now confined to his bed, and
necessitated daily visits from a doctor in nearby Bayonne. Víctor was summoned from Madrid to assist in Albéniz's care, and the arrival of his beloved
nephew lifted the composer's spirits. Víctor instituted a new regimen of
treatment that included saying nothing to upset Albéniz, especially about
his prodigal son Alfonso, and satisfying his every desire, as long as it did not
conflict with the doctor's instructions. These injunctions in tandem with
Víctor's efforts to detoxify Albéniz's system began to bear fruit, and the
composer declared, 'I again have the desire to live.'

Albéniz was eager to know about the current music scene in the Spanish
capital, especially the reception of his *Iberia*, and Víctor assured him it had
won over the public. According to Víctor, Albéniz reflected philosophically
on his earlier piano works in the following way:

There are among them a few things that are not completely worthless. The music is
a bit infantile, plain, spirited; but, in the end, the people, our Spanish people, are

---

[95] Letter to Vicente Moya, 14 Oct. 1944 (Mm, car. 2).   [96] Ruiz Albéniz, *Albéniz*, 115–42.

something of all that. I believe that the people are right when they continue to be moved by *Córdoba, Mallorca*, by the *copla* of the *Sevillanas*, by the *Serenata*, and *Granada*. In all of them I now note that there is less musical science, less of the grand idea, but more colour, sunlight, flavour of olives. That music of youth, with its little sins and absurdities that almost point out the sentimental affectation . . . appears to me like the carvings in the Alhambra, those peculiar arabesques that say nothing with their turns and shapes, but which are like the air, like the sun, like the blackbirds or like the nightingales of its gardens. They are more valuable than all else of Moorish Spain, which, though we may not like it, is the true Spain![97]

Víctor undertook musical as well as medical duties and amused his uncle by playing on the violin excerpts from Wagner, especially the *Siegfried Idyll*. Albéniz plied his nephew with many questions about the current fare in the theatres and about the latest musical fashions in Madrid. He became so excited about a *garrotín* that Víctor sang for him that he got up from his bed and toddled to a nearby piano to improvise on the tune, already hoping to use it in a new book of *Iberia* pieces. But the fabled fingers of old were no longer up to the task. The few pathetic sounds he produced were the last his hands would ever elicit from the instrument of which he had once been a past master.

Coutts was in Paris during this time, but he wrote from the Ritz on 25 April 1909 (Bc, 'C') that he and Nellie could not accept Laura's invitation to Cambo because Nellie had business in London and he had to accompany her. He either could not or would not comprehend the gravity of the situation, something he and his wife would later regret. But there were several other visitors during this final struggle. Casals visited him, in the company of Cortot and the violinist Jacques Thibaud. So did René de Castéra, who related an incident concerning the invalid's continuing lack of religion. On one occasion they walked together to a nearby church, where Albéniz remarked that though he visited that church every day, he still had no faith.[98] There would indeed be no deathbed conversion for Isaac Albéniz.

[97] Immediately after this lengthy quotation, on pages 123–4, Ruiz Albéniz vouches for its accuracy, claiming the composer's words made a deep impression on him and the others present. 'Hay entre ellas algunas cosas no despreciables del todo. Es música un poco infantil, llana, caliente; pero, al fin, el pueblo, nuestro pueblo español, es también algo de todo eso. . . . Yo creo que la gente tiene razón cuando aun sigue emocionándose con *Córdoba*, con *Mallorca*, con la copla de *Sevillanas*, con la *Serenata*, con *Granada*. En todas ellas ahora noto yo que hay menos ciencia musical, menos idea-grande, pero hay más calor, luz de sol, sabor de aceitunas. Esa música de juventud, con sus pecadillos y ridiculeces que casi apuntan la afectación sensiblera . . . a mí me parece que son como los alicatados de la Alhambra, aquellos arabescos, raros, que no quieren decir nada con sus giros y formas, pero que son como el aire, como el sol, como los mirlos o como los ruiseñores de sus jardines, lo que más vale de toda la España mora, que es, aunque no lo queramos, ¡la verdadera España!'

[98] Collet, *Albéniz*, 62.

The most heartening development was a surprise visit by Albéniz's dear friend Enric Granados. Víctor described their relationship as one of son to father, on Granados's part, and of older to younger brother on Albéniz's. We have a letter from Granados to Albéniz that encapsulates his father-figure view of the elder composer: 'I see your protection as a sign of virility. You are strong, and as the possessor of a great force, you do not conceive evil toward anyone.'[99] Granados now entertained his dying friend with renditions of his own compositions, including 'La maja y el ruiseñor' and the lovely 'Intermedio' from *Goyescas*.[100] He then launched into a performance of the master's own *Mallorca*, which reduced all those present to tears. Granados subsequently read a letter from Debussy informing Albéniz that, upon the recommendation of himself, Fauré, Dukas, and d'Indy, the French government had awarded him the Croix de la Légion d'Honneur. Later, in private, Granados broke down weeping when he learned from Víctor that Albéniz was on his deathbed. 'His work has hardly begun! It is now, with *Iberia*, that Isaac has come into his own!', he lamented.[101] Some months later, Rosina conveyed to Granados the manuscript of Albéniz's newest but incomplete set of piano pieces, *Azulejos*, with the request that he complete them as soon as possible. This he faithfully and skilfully did, describing Albéniz's 'delicious' creations as something he guarded 'like gold in a cloth'.[102] Granados sent a telegram to the Barcelona press dated Bayonne, 9 May 1909, in which he reported the sentiments of Fauré and the Conservatoire: 'He told me that here we all adore Albéniz; we consider him a very great artist and man; we hope with all our heart for his speedy recovery.' Granados himself extolled the music of Albéniz as 'graceful; it is of a very nervous tranquillity; it is of an elegance that smiles with sadness and progresses by degrees until it achieves a mastery both commanding and serene, like Goya's *Maja*. *Iberia* evokes memories of our "golden century".'[103]

[99] 26 May 1907 (Bc, 'G'). 'Yo veo tu protección como un signo de virilidad. Eres fuerte, y como poseedor de una fuerza grande, no conocibes el mal para nadie.'

[100] According to Carol Hess, *Enrique Granados: A Bio-bibliography* (New York: Greenwood Press, 1991), 25–6, in 1909 Granados began reworking earlier sketches to create *Goyescas*, but the process of revision continued into the following year. Even if Víctor's memory serves him well here, it seems unlikely that the versions Granados played for Albéniz were precisely the ones with which we are familiar.

[101] '¡Su obra está apenas iniciada! Es ahora, con las *Iberias*, cuando Isaac se ha encontrado a si mismo'.

[102] '[C]omo oro en paño' (the idiom does not translate well). From a letter to Joaquim Malats dated 11 Dec. 1910 (Mm, 10.034). *Azulejos* are porcelain tiles, which the pieces are meant to suggest. Granados finished the first number, 'Preludio', on 25 May 1910, and it was published by Édition Mutuelle in 1911. It is not clear, however, how much of the published work is by Granados, as the MS is lost.

[103] This clipping is in the Mm, Prov. M-987c. 'Aquí todos adoramos a Albéniz me dijo; le consideramos muy grande como artista y como hombre; deseamos de todo corazón su pronto restablecimiento.... concienzuda, graciosa, esbelta; es de un nerviosismo tranquilo; es de una elegancia que sonríe con tristeza y va por gradaciones hasta llegar al imperio dominante y sereno de la maja de Goya. Iberia evoca los recuerdos de nuestro siglo de oro.'

The intense emotion of Granados's visit may have caused Albéniz's condition to worsen, and death moved much closer to his doorstep. The morphine he was receiving lessened his pain, but it also weakened his heart—and he was developing an addiction to it. At one point he lashed out at his nephew for denying him a shot, in his delirium accusing Víctor of being an 'assassin' who enjoyed watching him suffer. On this occasion he was given a placebo with mere water in the syringe, but on 18 May he was given an actual injection of morphine, which caused arrhythmia and initiated the end. Víctor sent a telegram to Alfonso in London to come immediately to Cambo. When Albéniz heard of this, he was anxious to see his son one last time, to achieve some reconciliation in what had been a trying relationship. But that was not to be. Albéniz had lapsed into unconsciousness during the morning, but in the afternoon around three he opened his eyes and requested that Rosina massage his hands, as she had often done during their life together. Later that evening Laura presented him with a red rose from the bushes that just that day had begun to bloom in the garden. Albéniz admired it feebly before closing his eyes forever at exactly eight o'clock on the evening of 18 May 1909. In eleven more days he would have reached his forty-ninth birthday.

Albéniz's body was embalmed and interred temporarily in Cambo before being sent by train to Barcelona, where elaborate funeral preparations had been made by Granados and others. Malats declined Granados's invitation to serve as president of the commission in charge of organizing these ceremonies,[104] but he continued to champion *Iberia* in Madrid and Barcelona. Unfortunately, the sands of his own life were running out, and he died three years later. Letters of condolence poured in from such notables as Albert Roussel, Jeanne Chausson, Octave Maus, and Charles Bordes.[105] Both Frank and Nellie Coutts, of course, were devastated by their friend's passing. Perhaps the finest, most sincere tribute Albéniz received was written by Nellie (Helen) to the children:

My Darling Ones: I cannot say to you all I would I cannot! I am broken hearted. I have been with you all the sad days and even night I need not tell you all your Darling Father was to me. he was so *Noble Good*! a kind word for everyone! I never met a Nature like his. how I shall miss him he was the one bright spot in my life. I dare not ask you about your Poor Mother. Poor soul, and you two Poor darlings! try and comfort Mother. I do so regret we were not with you at the end. I thought the poor

---

[104] Letter from Granados to Malats of 21 May 1909 (Mm, 10.030).
[105] These four letters are in the Mm, car. 2.

darling would fight the battle but it was too much for him. . . . I love you always. Your Helen Coutts.[106]

Coutts himself continued to support the family for many years, writing to Rosina to 'rely upon me to do all that can be done . . . to alleviate this dreadful blow of fate'.[107] In one letter to Laura he insisted, '*I must trust to you* (and I say this very seriously) to let me know if your mother finds her present allowance from me insufficient'.[108] In addition, he placed the legal services of his own solicitor (a certain Mr Maugham, probably the father of Somerset) at her disposal without charge and without any obligation for her to take advice given by either himself or Maugham.[109] In 1915 Coutts was obliged to reduce Rosina's annual allowance to £200, explaining that 'in this dreadful time of war, I am compelled to scrape together all the money I can, as the taxation is so terrific'.[110] With reluctance, he finally suspended payments and legal support in 1918, explaining that 'the war has made me quite a poor man'.[111] Coutts died in 1923, leaving to Rosina the rights to the texts he wrote for Albéniz, and a cash sum of 500 francs. Rosina lived to see not only her husband but all her children pass away, before her own death in December of 1945.

[106] This letter appears here unedited. It is dated simply London, Monday (Mm, 10.297). The poor style gives us insight into her apparent inability to appreciate Coutts's literary bent.

[107] Letter dated London, 19 May 1909, from Coutts to Rosina (Mm, car. 2).

[108] Dated 28 Nov. 1909 (Mm, car. 2).

[109] It seems that Alfonso was not co-operating in Coutts's attempts to turn over to Rosina the rights to Albéniz's compositions and wanted to retain some of the rights for himself. The rights were eventually transferred to Alfonso's mother in their entirety. By 5 Feb. 1918, Coutts had had his fill of Albéniz's troublesome son and wrote to Rosina that 'I never want to have anything to do with him, and moreover I do not trust what he says' (Mm., car. 2).

[110] Letter of 30 June 1915 (Mm, car. 2). He also justifies his action by pointing out that the children were grown and no longer dependent on her.

[111] Letter of 5 Feb. 1918 (Mm, car. 2). This may have been true in a relative sense, but archival records (L1406, an inventory of his assets) indicate that at his death Coutts still possessed considerable wealth.

8

The Legacy of Albéniz

THE impact of Albéniz's life and work obviously did not end with his funeral.
The fact that a major publisher has contracted this book strongly suggests
that Albéniz continues to be a vital presence in the canon of western music.
Thousands of recordings of his music have been made, and no less than forty
publishing houses have printed his works.[1] And Albéniz exerted a discernible
influence on succeeding composers. Yet, his output was undeniably uneven
in quality, and the only part of it to hold a place in the repertoire is a portion
of the piano music. The rest of the piano pieces, stage works, and songs have
slid into obscurity. Despite the enormous creative energy he poured into his
operas in particular, his reputation has reaped relatively little benefit from
them. Why? We might begin to answer this question by briefly tracing the
fate of his operas to the present day.

All of Albéniz's extant completed stage works except *Henry Clifford* and
The Magic Opal were produced after his death. *San Antonio de la Florida* was
revived on 18 November 1954 at the Teatro Fuencarral in Madrid, in a
revised version by the composer Pablo Sorozábal (1897–1988).[2] It played
again on 19, 20, 22, 23, and 24 November. The critics were only slightly
kinder on this occasion than their grandfathers had been in 1894. Even
though the music was praised for its freshness and verve, the libretto was
still condemned on account of its 'lack of interest'. The work has remained
absent from the stage ever since.

Merlin finally premiered on 18 December 1950 at the Tívoli in Barcelona,
performed by the Club de Fútbol Junior, whose annual custom it was to

---

[1] See Baytelman, 'Albéniz', 33, for a list of publishers. Appendix E of her book, 107–14, is a discography of
piano works alone. See Clark, *Guide to Research*, 139–219, for a complete discography.

[2] Few details of this revival are available. It was, by his own admission, unsuccessful. See Pablo Sorozábal,
Mi vida y mi obra (Madrid: Fundación Banco Exterior, 1986), 281. The orchestral score of the work was
evidently lost during the Spanish Civil War (1936–9), and Sorozábal had to orchestrate it anew. Whatever
other changes he made are unclear. Score and parts of his revision are in the Se. His correspondence with
Vicente Moya (Mm, car. 2) indicates that he had approached the dancer Antonio with the idea of staging the
zarzuela as a ballet. This deal seems to have fallen through, however, as did his attempts to get Hispavox to
record it.

TABLE 13. *Cast of* Merlin, *premiere, Barcelona, Tívoli, 1950*

Morgan Le Fay	Teresa Fius
Nivian	Concepción Alsina
Merlin	Teodoro Torné
Arthur	Esteban Recasens
Sir Ector	Antonio Cantín
Kay	Manuel Conde
King Lot	Jose María Nogueras
Gawain	Jaime Carbonell
Mordred	Manuel Lobo
Sir Pellinore	José María Carbonell
Archbishop of Canterbury	Santiago Such

produce an opera. The text was translated into Spanish by Manuel Conde, and José Sabater conducted the Orquesta Clásica de Barcelona (cast in Table 13). The opera received many encomiums. U. F. Zanni, writing in *La vanguardia española* (20 December 1950, 14), found the opera 'very worthy' and that 'the writing is noble, frank, and intelligently adapted to the inspiring themes. The orchestration reveals a firm and skilled hand in the conception of instrumental combinations.'[3] Alfredo Romea, critic for *El noticiero universal* (19 December 1950, 8), noted the Wagnerian influence (as did Zanni), particularly in 'the robustness with which the orchestral commentary is handled'.[4] However, though the first and third acts offered 'much that was spectacular', the second was 'frankly boring'.[5]

These reviews echoed earlier appraisals during Albéniz's lifetime, for example by Rafael Mitjana in *Revista musical de Bilbao* (October 1902), who praised the score's 'technical solidity, knowledgeable organization of the structure, stylistic elegance, intimate co-penetration of the text with the music'.[6] Mitjana also pointed to the connection between the Arthurian legend and the 'epic of the Holy Grail', and thus to Spain (not to mention Wagner and *Parsifal*). The opera found another advocate in Ernest Newman, who extolled the 'magical beauty' of the music. He recommended the score 'to anyone who is on the look-out for something at once original, strong and

[3] '[L]a escritura es noble, franca e inteligentemente adaptada a los temas inspiradores. La orquestación revela una mano firme y hábil en la concepción de combinaciones instrumentales...es una ópera dignísima.'
[4] '[L]a robustez con que está tratado el comentario orquestal.'
[5] The performance was also favourably reviewed by M. Casamada in *La Vie musicale* (2 Dec. 1951–Jan. 1952), 8–10. The article presents a useful summary of the action both musical and dramatic, along with examples of the various leading motives.
[6] Reproduced in *¡Para música vamos!* (Valencia: Casa Editorial F. Sempere, 1909), 206: '[S]olidez de la técnica, la sabia ordenación de la estructura, la elegancia del estilo, la íntima compenetración del texto con la música.' Collet, *Albéniz*, 128, discounts the value of Mitjana's views because he was a '*musicographe*' and 'not at all' a musician. In fact, Mitjana *was* a skilled musician.

beautiful', and who could appreciate with him the fact that 'the best opera on our sacrosanct British legend has been written by a Spaniard'.[7] Like *Henry Clifford*, however, the opera sank into oblivion after this one brief incarnation and never inspired another company to mount it.

After many years of behind-the-scenes manœuvring by Max Eschig, the Albéniz family, Fauré, Dukas, and others, *Pepita Jiménez* finally appeared at the Opéra-Comique in Paris on 18 June 1923.[8] Joseph de Marliave rendered a new French translation, which appeared in the piano–vocal score published by Max Eschig that year.[9] It was performed in conjunction with the two-act opera *Nausicaa*, composed by Reynaldo Hahn on a poem by René Fauchois. It appeared again on 19, 21, and 23 June, for a total of four performances.[10]

Henry Malherbe (*Le Temps*, 20 June 1923, 3) did not care for the libretto but rhapsodized about the music as

vital and of an agile animalism, hardy and inflamed. It shudders like a beast of prey, it shimmers like a fleece. Languid and ardent, chaste and passionate, it blends mysticism and voluptuousness, the sacred scents of incense and candles with the odours of wet and whirling dancers. The rhythmic frenzy of the composer suffices to our pleasure.[11]

'Le Capitaine Fracasse' (*L'Écho de Paris*, 18 June 1923, 5) found Albéniz's ideas 'gushing, spontaneous, fresh, abundant, lyrical…unified, vivified, transfigured, by an interior happiness, a joy in inventing melodies'.[12] Dukas, who played a central role in arranging the production, wrote a review in *Le Quotidien* (5 July 1923, 6) in which he had high praise for the work:

but the music, here, is animated by all the life lacking in the play. It breaks the bonds of the little story and sings by itself the most evocative song of Spain, the most sparkling [song] of popular verve, or the most poetical languor of delicate melancholy one can hear. Without pause, without any trifle entering to break its flight, it is

---

[7] 'Albéniz and his "Merlin"', 495–6.

[8] For more on Dukas's role in the revival, see M. T. Preckler (ed.), *Cartas de Paul Dukas a Laura Albéniz* (Bellaterra: Universidad Autónoma de Barcelona, 1983).

[9] In 1923 Eschig also published two 'fantasies' or arrangements of selections from the opera for piano trio (with bass ad lib.) by Pierre Letorey.

[10] The role of Pepita was realized by Marguerite Carré. Max Bussy played Don Luis, and Lucienne Estève Antoñona, while M. Azéma played Don Pedro and Pierre Dupré the Vicar. M. Bourdin appeared as the Count, and MM. Pujol and Goavec played the officers. The ballet was choreographed by Mme Chasles. The production was directed by Albert Wolff.

[11] '[E]st vivante et d'une animalité agile, hardie, enflammée. Elle a des frissons de bête de sang, le luisant d'une toison. Alanguie et brûlante, chaste et passionnée, elle mêle le mysticisme à la volupté, les senteurs sacrées des encens et des cierges aux odeurs de danseuses moites et déhanchés. La frénésie rythmique du compositeur suffit à notre plaisir.'

[12] '[J]aillissent, spontanées, fraîches, abondantes, chantantes…unifiés, vivifiés, transfigurés, par une allégresse intérieure, une joie d'inventer des chants.'

elevated in the orchestra, quivering on wings of rhythm, and spreads in charming caprices across each scene . . . so alive, so spontaneous, so delicious.[13]

The inevitable accusation of verismo cropped up in a review by Raymond Charpentier in *Comœdia* (18 June 1923, 1–2), who found a 'regrettable' influence of 'Italianism' in *Pepita Jiménez* and dismissed it as a kind of 'Cavalleria Iberica'. In the context of post-First World War neoclassicism, Albéniz was probably bound to run afoul of those who regarded his unrepentant nationalism and melodious sentimentality as *passé*, but the objections of this critic seem to us now singularly myopic. At all events, the work did not remain in the repertoire of the Opéra-Comique.

Family and friends made more attempts to extend the opera's life. These efforts were impeded for some time by Carmen Valera, daughter of the novelist and executrix of his estate. She wrote to Laura Albéniz on 2 September 1923 expressing her indignation that any credit should go to Coutts as 'author' and declaring herself sole proprietor of rights to her father's works. But Max Eschig, who now had the rights to the opera, found a way out of the difficulty by proposing to Carmen Valera the addition of the subtitle 'Tiré d'une nouvelle de Juan Valera'. That did the trick, and the way was cleared for a revival in Barcelona.

Pepita Jiménez opened at the Liceu on 14 January 1926, in honour of Albéniz and the thirtieth anniversary of the opera's premiere in that very place. It was also a benefit concert for the Junta de Protección a la Infancia. It was repeated on the 20th and closed on the 26th. It was done in Italian translation, but this time using the version by Carlo Galateri rather than the original by Angelo Bignotti.[14] After the opera, the Banda Municipal performed arrangements of excerpts from *Iberia*.

Perhaps because of the nature of the production, as a memorial to Albéniz and a benefit for children, the press had nothing but praise for the opera. An anonymous review in *La noche* (15 January 1926, 1) is typical of the reception, declaring that it was a 'triumphal evening for the name of Albéniz', and that the audience listened to the opera 'full of devotion'. Such a reception

---

[13] '[M]ais la musique, ici, est animée de toute la vie qui manque à la pièce. Elle s'élance d'un bond audessus de cette petite intrigue et chante pour elle-même le chant d'Espagne le plus évocateur, le plus étincelant de verve populaire ou le plus poétiquement alangui de mélancolie délicate qu'on puisse entendre. Sans arrêt, sans que rien vienne rompre son essor, elle s'élève de l'orchestre, tout frémissant de ses rhythmes ailés, et se déploie en caprices charmants à travers chaque scène . . . si vive, si spontanée, si délicieuse.'

[14] Carmen Valera had stated (15 Mar. 1924) that the Madrid music director Rivas Cherif was interested in executing a Spanish revision of the libretto. Why this suggestion was not taken up and why the work persisted in Italian remain unanswered questions. (Her correspondence was at the Ah when the author examined it.) The cast included Hina Spani, Pepita; Sra. Davydoff, Antoñona; Constantin Folco-Bottaro, Don Luis; Massin Pieralli, the Vicar; and Segura Tallien y Jordá as Don Pedro. José Sabater conducted; Sr. Castells painted the decorations; and Rafael Moragas served as scenic director.

would, of course, have been very gratifying to Albéniz and would have done much to reconcile him to his homeland. But despite this, almost four decades would pass before another production in Spain.

Pepita Jiménez finally found its way onto the stage in the Spanish capital sixty-two years after Albéniz's abortive attempt to arrange a performance there. Unfortunately, this was not the *Pepita Jiménez* Albéniz wrote, nor one that he would have embraced as his own work. Pablo Sorozábal was a prominent composer of zarzuela who, as already mentioned, revised and conducted *San Antonio de la Florida* in 1954. In the late 1950s he set out to revive *Pepita Jiménez* in time for the centenary of Albéniz's birth. Due to wrangling between the heirs, impresarios, publishers, and arrangers, it did not come to light, though, until 1964, as part of an opera festival celebrating twenty-five years of fascist rule. Sorozábal, however, deemed the work as it stood inadequate and in need of major revision, which he himself undertook. In his autobiography, Sorozábal states that he altered the declamatory style of much of the vocal writing to make it more lyrical, adapted the libretto from French to Spanish, reorchestrated large sections of the score, divided the second act into two separate acts, and transformed the drama from a comedy to a tragedy.[15] Claiming that the ending was ambiguous, he chose to have Pepita commit suicide rather than succeed in her attempt to seduce Don Luis away from his vocation.[16]

In a letter to Vicente Moya of 4 February 1958, Sorozábal reassured Albéniz's descendants concerning his motives: 'As I told you, in this matter I am guided solely by my admiration for Albéniz.'[17] Repeatedly, however, Albéniz's son-in-law asked for more than admiration. He expressly requested that Albéniz's music not be changed, particularly in regard to the orchestration, which 'should be respected without introducing any modification'.[18] These wishes were not heeded, and thus the groundwork was laid for perhaps the saddest episode in the history of *Pepita Jiménez*.

[15] Sorozábal, *Vida*, 317–18.

[16] Feminists might view this revision as the reassertion of a patriarchal paradigm requiring the demise of temptresses (e.g. Carmen) who seduce men away from military or religious duty. It is possible that the plot change was prompted by the conservative political climate during the Franco dictatorship. For instance, Federico Moreno Torroba's zarzuela *Monte Carmelo* (1939) told a similar story of a woman falling in love with a priest, and the Franco regime banned the work. However, Sorozábal, of Basque descent, was not a fascist. In all likelihood he based his choices on aesthetic rather than political grounds.

[17] Mm, car. 3. 'Como ya le dije en este asunto sólo me guía en éste mi admiración a Albéniz.'

[18] Letter dated 27 Mar. 1959: 'debe respetarse esa orquestación sin introducir modificación alguna.' This statement reflects sentiments expressed by Albéniz himself in his correspondence with Breitkopf und Härtel. In a letter of 18 Aug. 1897 (Ls), he gave the firm permission to make corrections to the 'bad' translation by Oskar Berggruen, *but not to the music*.

The three-act opera premiered on 6 June 1964 at the Teatro de la Zarzuela and was done only once more, on the 10th. Pilar Lorengar and Alfredo Kraus sang the lead roles, and María Clara Alcalá appeared as Antoñona. Sorozábal conducted the Orquesta Filarmónica. Carmen Polo de Franco, the wife of the Spanish dictator, was in the audience for the premiere. Most accounts describe the production as a success. Though the press deferred to the popular Sorozábal and received his revision politely, Federico Sopeña, writing in *ABC* (7 June 1964, 109), objected to the plot change, describing it as 'irritating' in view of the wide currency of the novel. He called for a new arrangement of the opera with a restoration of the original ending.

Sorozábal subtitled the portion of his autobiography dealing with his revision of Albéniz's opera 'Mi aportación a Pepita Jiménez'.[19] His unintentional 'contribution', however, has been to reinforce the notion that Albéniz's creation is fatally flawed and not worthy of a revival in its original form. He has offered up an alternative that is neither completely Albéniz nor Sorozábal (nor Valera nor Coutts) and is consequently unconvincing. It has not found a place in the repertoire, due primarily to the absurd changes made in the plot. Sadly, the result of his 'contribution', then, has been to bury the work deeper in ignominy than all the political machinations of all the theatres and all the intrusions of Carmen Valera were able to do. A recording of the work in its newly revised form was made in 1967 on the Columbia label (SCE 931/2), with Teresa Berganza singing the role of Pepita and Julián Molina as Don Luis. This was for many years the only recording of *Pepita Jiménez* available. A new recording has recently appeared that does a much better job of presenting Albéniz's intentions, even to the point of using the original English version.[20]

Obviously, Albéniz's operas have had a chequered career and have failed to capture the public's imagination, in Spain and elsewhere. What are the reasons for this? To begin, Henri Collet was of the opinion that Albéniz simply did not have a 'sense of theatre', and he elaborated on this idea in the following way:

Albéniz, pianist and musician, but not dramaturge, does not concern himself with [dramatic] effect and scenic operations. His orchestra delivers its overabundance, without nuances, in a pianistic conception of the work. The voice merely declaims.

---

[19] 'My Contribution to *Pepita Jiménez*.' Also to be found in an article in *Arriba*, 6 June 1964, 25; in the liner notes of the recording; and as a preface to the photostatic copy of the MS, in the Bn. Score and parts are in the Se.

[20] This recording (already mentioned in Ch. 5 n. 27) is a concert suite arranged by Josep Pons, the conductor, and features Susan Chilcott and Francesc Garrigosa in the lead roles. This author would prefer to hear the work sung in Spanish and believes that that would also have been Albéniz's preference.

All the ideas of the author are blended in an instrumental ensemble comparable to an immense piano.[21]

Collet also cited the following portion of Armando de la Florida's review of *Henry Clifford*, declaring it '*la vérité même*' ('the truth itself'): 'Enthusiast of the modern school, [Albéniz] reserves his preference for the orchestra and relegates the voices to a secondary role. . . . His characters, within the musical drama, possess complete uniformity in their manner of being, feeling, and thinking.'[22] Edgar Istel asserted unequivocally that Albéniz had 'not the faintest suspicion of dramatic composition, and forges . . . straight ahead absolutely without contrasts or strettos'.[23]

We must admit the validity of these criticisms in regard to all his operas. His sense of dramatic pacing was not well developed, as we noted in his tendency to introduce a series of numbers towards the end of the drama, retarding its momentum and conducing to anticlimax. One could argue that Albéniz never had a first-rate libretto to work with and was instead saddled by Coutts with mediocre texts against his will. But the librettos were the product of considerable collaboration, and we know that the composer was not confined to texts by Coutts. Clearly, Albéniz himself was at least partially to blame, as he could not readily distinguish a good libretto from a mediocre one, nor see what changes had to be made in a libretto to make it a better vehicle for his musical purposes.[24]

Albéniz might have been able to rise above his dramaturgical limitations if he had possessed another essential quality in an opera composer, and that is the musical instinct to express himself through the human voice. Time and again Albéniz has been criticized for his poor orchestration, but the best orchestrator in the world would not be able to make Albéniz's stage works any more compelling than they already are. Next to the issue of the libretto, what the critics harped on most was the lack of impact made by the singers. Either they were not given material that showed off their voices, or they were occluded by the thematic interest of the orchestra, or the *Sprachmelodie* that Albéniz cultivated lacked sufficient force and appeal. For instance, throughout much of *Pepita Jiménez* the voices seem almost incidental to what is

[21] *Albéniz*, 123–4, in regard to *Henry Clifford*. 'Albéniz, pianiste et musicien, mais nullement dramaturge, ne se soucie guère de l'effet et des opérations scéniques. Son orchestre, sans nuances, doit ses surcharges à la conception pianistique de l'œuvre. La voix se borne à déclamer. Toutes les intentions de l'auteur sont fondues dans l'ensemble instrumental comparable à un immense piano.'

[22] *Lo teatro català*, 6/226 (11 May 1895), 4. 'Entussiasta de l'escola moderna, tè preferencias per l'orquesta, relegant á las veus a'l desempenyo d'un paper secundari. . . . Sos personatjes, dintre 'l drama musical, tenen uniformitat completa en la manera de sèr, sentir y pensar.'

[23] 'Isaac Albéniz', 138, in reference to *Pepita Jiménez*.

[24] One recalls his attraction to Valera's *El maestro Raimundico*, which Pilar Aparicia stated contained no more dramatic interest than *Pepita Jiménez*.

happening in the 'accompaniment'. Yet, in a work of folkloric character, especially one influenced by contemporary Italian models, the absence of a memorable lyric style is a difficult liability to overcome. Albéniz's revision of the orchestration in *Pepita Jiménez* exacerbated his central handicap as an opera composer, namely, that his musical impulses took instrumental rather than vocal form, a tendency reinforced by his desire to be *au courant* and adopt Wagnerian principles of speech-melody. The very same shortcomings explain why the songs have not become popular. In most cases they could be played as piano solos without any loss of musical interest. One is, therefore, inclined to agree with Istel that Albéniz's operatic writing, as well as his songs, frequently 'has almost nothing to say, in a musical sense, that his best piano compositions do not adequately reveal'.[25]

Albéniz's desire to write for the stage possessed a significance beyond the inherent musico-dramatic quality of the works. There was a powerful movement towards national opera in nineteenth-century Spain, and *Pepita Jiménez* (as well as the nationalist operas he left incomplete) must be understood as an attempt on Albéniz's part to foster this development. Pedrell's *Els Pirineus* of 1891, Bretón's *La Dolores* of 1895, and Granados's *María del Carmen* of 1898 were also important contributions, but like Albéniz's opera, none of them captured the public imagination or held a place on the stage. The only two Spanish operas that continue to be performed with any regularity today are Granados's *Goyescas* (prem. 1916) and Falla's *La vida breve* (prem. 1913). Tellingly, both premiered outside Spain (in New York and Nice, respectively). The inability of Spanish composers to bring to life a school of Spanish opera comparable to that of France, Italy, or Germany was the result of the public's ongoing love of the zarzuela. Opera was patronized largely by the upper classes, who thought of it as primarily an Italian genre (we recall that both *Henry Clifford* and *Pepita Jiménez* premiered at the Liceu in Italian). The masses preferred the zarzuela's alternation of spoken dialogue and music to the continuous music of opera.[26]

In spite of all this, Albéniz's operas contain some of his most enchanting musical inspirations and should not be allowed to languish in their current state. There is every good reason for restoring to concert programmes the numbers from *San Antonio de la Florida*, the dances, choral, and orchestral selections from *Henry Clifford*, and the Prelude to Act I and the dances from Act III of *Merlin*. They would provide performing organizations with fresh

[25] 'Isaac Albéniz', 138.

[26] For an excellent treatment of this phenomenon, see Ramón Barce, 'La ópera y la zarzuela en el siglo XIX', in *España en la música del Occidente: Actas del Congreso Internacional celebrado en Salamanca 29 de octubre–5 de noviembre de 1985*, 2 vols. (Madrid: Instituto Nacional de las Artes Escénicas y de la Música, 1987), ii. 145–53.

repertoire by a composer who continues to prove his popularity with the concert-going public around the world in hundreds of guitar and piano recitals and recordings every year. They would also enlarge and refine our appreciation of Albéniz's stature as a composer, one who is now known almost exclusively for *Iberia* and a handful of other piano pieces. Despite the foregoing commentary, *Pepita Jiménez* deserves a revival and could hold a place on the stage if it were done well and with sensitivity to the composer's original intentions. The musical conceptions contained in that work are so consistently engaging, the local colour and atmosphere so charming, that regardless of the lack of vocal or dramatic impact, the opera could win an audience over—as it has done several times. If it were staged in conjunction with *San Antonio de la Florida*,[27] as was done in Brussels, it could make for a very satisfying evening. Better yet, however, is an idea that Max Eschig had in the 1920s, i.e. to programme it with Manuel de Falla's *La vida breve*. The two scores complement one another perfectly in style and subject matter, and their combined duration would be no longer than three hours.[28] Failing this, however, *Pepita Jiménez* still contains several numbers that can be performed separately or as a suite. For, as Istel has said, Albéniz's score 'impresses most favorably where, detached from the dramatic events, it pours itself out in lyric detail'.[29] And the opera has the added advantage of being available in both piano–vocal and orchestral printed versions (parts and score available from Max Eschig in Paris). Unfortunately, the full scores for his other stage music remain only in manuscript, sometimes with parts of the same score located in different collections in the Barcelona area. It would be a daunting, if worthwhile, task to prepare modern editions of them for the purposes of revival.

   The most important legacy of the operas lies in the role they played in Albéniz's evolution as a composer. Though Albéniz himself broke his output down into two 'manners', it makes more sense to divide it in the traditional fashion of early, middle, and late. The early works include his zarzuelas of 1881–2 (now lost), the many salon pieces of the 1880s, and the suites of Spanish pieces composed up to 1894, including such well-known collections as *Recuerdos de viaje* (1886–7) and *España: Six Feuilles d'album* (1890). The works of the middle period include all the stage works, the piano piece 'La vega' (1897), and the orchestral work *Catalonia* (1899). These last two works are clear premonitions of Albéniz's late period, represented chiefly by

---

[27] That is, if someone were first to orchestrate it, as Sorozábal did.

[28] *Pepita Jiménez* lasts approximately one hour and forty-five minutes. *La vida breve*'s two acts and four scenes last about sixty-five minutes.

[29] 'Isaac Albéniz', 138, regarding *Pepita Jiménez*.

Iberia (1905–8) for piano solo, and *Quatre Mélodies* (1908), for voice and piano, on poems by Coutts.

Albéniz's three-phase career as a composer can be seen, then, to correspond roughly to the final three decades of his life, from 1880 to 1909. Each decade brought with it a new level of development, culminating in an undisputed masterpiece, *Iberia*. The other conspicuous feature of his career is that, aside from his beginnings as a zarzuela composer, the first decade was devoted largely to the composition of works for piano, while the second decade was given over primarily to musical theatre. The final creative period presents a return to piano composition. This seeming ABA form poses, however, an important variation in the da capo. For Albéniz the composer of *Iberia* was light years beyond Albéniz the composer of *Recuerdos de viaje* in terms of musical sophistication and technical control, something he himself acknowledged. To be sure, some aspects of *Iberia* are observable in the early works, e.g. the use of Spanish dance rhythms, modality (especially the Phrygian mode), characteristic melodic and rhythmic flourishes, the descending minor tetrachord, and evocations of flamenco *cante jondo* and guitar. But many of the chief characteristics of *Iberia* are completely absent in the early period, and these are summarized below.

In terms of formal structure, the early nationalist works are nearly always in simple sectional forms, usually ABA. The typical *modus operandi* regarding thematic material is repetition, not development. Albéniz's melodies, no matter how charming, were suited to little more than transposition, a characteristic Romantic device. By contrast, eight of the twelve pieces of *Iberia* are in freely adapted sonata form. Albéniz's juxtaposition of contrasting material and development of ideas create a richness and variety unprecedented in his early piano works. This is aided in part by melodies built from motivic cells that render them more capable of development.

The early works offered harmonies that were suited to the melodic material in their charm and poignancy but rarely ventured beyond the conventional. *Iberia*, on the other hand, reveals the influence of contemporary French music in its chromaticism, use of whole-tone scales, and its myriad modes and modal mixtures.[30] Dissonance is far more prominent, and not simply as a surface feature. For example, the use of augmented-sixth sonorities for modulating to distant tonal areas is conspicuous, and we have noted Albéniz's own jarring brand of augmented-sixth chord. There is also a high concentration of added-note sonorities and the use of secundal and quartal

---

[30] This point must not be stressed too much, however. Albéniz's use of modes and modal mixtures was derived from folk music; but the musical context in which this trait appears does exhibit the influence of the Parisian circles in which he moved.

harmonies, which do not occur in the early suites. The sophistication of his harmonic language, moreover, enables Albéniz 'to sustain interest for much longer periods than in the earlier works'.[31]

Although Albéniz's style was always characterized by lively rhythms, *Iberia*'s use of superimposed metres, rapidly shifting metres, and complex patterns of accentuation represents a quantum leap over his earlier practice. The textures of *Iberia* and the early works are essentially homophonic, but those of *Iberia* are much more animated and often exhibit a contrapuntal use of countermelodies, especially during developmental sections. Finally, the virtuosic exploitation of the resources of the piano, the sheer range of timbres and effects Albéniz elicits from that instrument in *Iberia*, finds no parallel in the compositions from the early period.

To what can we attribute this dramatic evolution in Albéniz's style, then, and what role did the stage works, in particular *Pepita Jiménez*, play in that development? We recall that Albéniz wrote opera in several of the major styles of his day. He wrote English operetta in *The Magic Opal*; French and German operetta in the additional numbers for *Incognita* and *Poor Jonathan*; Spanish operetta (zarzuela) in *San Antonio de la Florida*; Italian grand opera in *Henry Clifford*; Spanish national opera in *Pepita Jiménez*; and Wagnerian opera in *Merlin*. In *The Magic Opal* and *San Antonio de la Florida* Albéniz was called upon to do no more nor less than what convention demanded, i.e. write a series of self-contained numbers that would be separated by spoken dialogue. *Henry Clifford*, too, was essentially a number opera, but with the important difference that the music was now continuous and not broken up by spoken dialogue. This meant that the various numbers had to flow into one another and that there had to be some sense of connection between them. This was a challenge he had never before faced. In *Iberia* Albéniz relied heavily on pedal point as a device for clarifying the structure of a sonata-form movement. Although we find no sonata forms in *Henry Clifford*, pedal point is frequently employed in making a transition from one number or section of a number to the next. On occasion, the apparent goal of the pedal point is supplanted by an unexpected key, usually by means of a common tone.

In *Pepita Jiménez*, Albéniz for the first time abandoned the 'number' format and strove, at least in Act I, to create a continuous flow of musical and dramatic action. Act II, scene i, conforms to his earlier model by presenting a series of pieces, but in the closing scene between Pepita and Don Luis the music and drama once more flow unimpeded toward the

---

[31] Mast, 'Iberia', 377.

climactic conclusion. Here again Albéniz employed pedal point as a structural device, even endowing it on occasion with dramatic significance. But the demands of continuity and unity required the use of recurring or 'leading' themes, which he subjected to variation and reinterpretation. Like the melodies in *Iberia*, these are built up of motivic cells that allow not only for development but for dramatic association among the various themes. The pattern of recurrence and variation of thematic material provides an alternative structure to the earlier number format and possesses its own symmetry and dramatic sense. Occasional set pieces do appear, and they are organized along traditional formal lines, e.g. AB or ABA. Even these set pieces, however, are integrated into the larger structure by their thematic or motivic connection to previously stated material. In *Merlin* we find the nearly complete dissolution of numbers and the kind of uninterrupted musical development associated with Wagner. This is aided by the use of leading motives that permit actual *Fortspinnung*. In *Merlin* Albéniz imbued entire acts with the kind of structural cohesion that had previously characterized his piano pieces of merely three or four minutes in length.

Albéniz's harmony in *The Magic Opal* was, if anything, less daring than that employed in his *Chants d'Espagne* of the same time period. The larger scale of *Henry Clifford* demanded greater harmonic variety and interest, and Albéniz responded by resorting to more frequent and bolder modulations. This process continued in *Pepita Jiménez*. But here for the first time we find evidence of long-range tonal planning, a product of Albéniz's conception of the work as a continuous and ultimately self-contained fabric of themes. The harmonic organization evident in *Pepita Jiménez* is also an attempt to counterbalance the proliferation of key areas with some underlying logic and direction. In *Merlin* Albéniz freed himself from the fetters of key signatures altogether, and wrote virtually the entire opera in a signature of no flats or sharps, which has nothing to do with the key of C major or A minor.[32] The harmony is highly chromatic and reveals a penchant for false relations and distant modulations (reminiscent of Fauré). But the most remarkable feature of *Merlin* is its rhythmic variety, the fluid alternation of metre, and the juxtaposition of duple and triple rhythms. The subtlety of the rhythm exceeds even that of *Pepita Jiménez*, not to mention the earlier works. In addition, Albéniz's use of animated homophony and even of imitative counterpoint in the operas gave him a command of handling complex textures that clearly separates his early from his late works.

---

[32] However, the numerous accidentals, especially the double sharps and flats of *Pepita Jiménez* that so bedevilled the poor critic in Prague, are still abundant here.

Albéniz gained his knowledge of orchestration mostly from his experience writing and conducting musical theatre, and what he learned from Dukas was then applied to *Merlin* and to the reorchestration of *Pepita Jiménez*. Albéniz's increased appreciation of the expressive potential of sonority found ready expression in his late piano works, and one encounters in *Iberia*, for example, the fullest possible exploitation of the timbral resources of the piano. As an orchestrator, then, Albéniz may originally have thought of the orchestra as a big piano, as Pedrell and others have asserted, but in his late works he had come 180 degrees and was thinking instead of the piano as a self-contained orchestra. It is no coincidence that *Iberia* and *Navarra* have inspired several composers and conductors to orchestrate them.

On the basis of the above summary, then, it is clear that Albéniz acquired a more sophisticated musical language and ability to organize large-scale pieces as a result of his composition of opera. The particular significance of *Pepita Jiménez* lies in the fact that it represents Albéniz's first attempt to apply all of the elements of technical control discussed above to the national idiom that was his real calling. It thus forms an important milestone on the road to *Iberia*, and this author concurs with Turina's assessment that the 'great' Albéniz, the Albéniz of *Iberia*, first stands revealed in *Pepita Jiménez*.[33]

Many have argued that, had Albéniz not been shackled to the 'pact of Faust', he might well have written a more nationalist kind of musical theatre that was both beneficial to his development as a composer *and* found a permanent place on the stage. But speculation as to what heights Albéniz would have attained as a composer of Spanish opera had he not been burdened with the trilogy is simply idle. It is obvious that the contract was not binding and that he had, in fact, the opportunity to write national opera, had he been so inclined. The extant manuscripts indicate that his efforts in this regard were desultory and incomplete. Can we assume that he would have come any closer to realizing these ambitions with the crushing financial burdens that the absence of Coutts's patronage would have imposed? Absolutely not. Laplane's description of the 'pact' as productive of naught but 'abortions' is ludicrous. In fact, the piano repertoire owes one of its crown jewels to the generosity of this obscure, misunderstood, and oft maligned Englishman and to the operatic endeavours his support sustained. Where the idea of the 'pact of Faust' came from is unclear. It may have originated with Albéniz in jest, or it may have been an invention of acquaintances who could not understand the real nature of his association with Coutts. According to

[33] Cited in Collet, *Albéniz*, 110. The statement was made in a review by Turina that appeared in the *Revista musical* (Bilbao) in Feb. 1911. Collet's translation is as follows: 'Nous savons tous que le Grand Albéniz commence avec sa *Pepita Jiménez*.'

Rosina Moya Albéniz de Samsó,[34] Albéniz's wife Rosina viewed the composer's relationship with Coutts in a negative light. It was possibly through her influence that Arbós and Istel arrived at their unflattering conclusions. Albéniz's daughter Laura, on the other hand, regarded Coutts's support of the family as benign, and rightly so. We can only speculate concerning Rosina's seeming ingratitude for the assistance her family received from Coutts. Albéniz's supposed Faustian pact is the most flagrant misconception in his entire legacy, and we ought now to consign it to the nether world, where it belongs, so that a more accurate and just assessment may take its place.

With this understanding we are in a better position to evaluate Albéniz's achievements in comparison to his contemporaries in Spain who were writing instrumental music in a similar vein. There are basically two things that differentiate Albéniz from Pablo de Sarasate, Joaquim Malats, Francisco Tárrega, Miguel Llobet, and other popular composers of Spanish music in the nineteenth and early twentieth centuries. First, though they all began their compositional careers at roughly the same level of skill, through his relentless quest to develop his talent Albéniz went far beyond the realms of salon music, in which they remained firmly entrenched. He transcended mere folklorism and forged a new style of Spanish music based on the incorporation of advanced harmony and form, to give his works more emotional weight and intellectual depth than those by the performer/composers mentioned above. What, then, differentiates his Spanish style from that of a Debussy or Ravel? His knowledge of the rhythms of Andalusian flamenco was more thorough and extensive. He placed more emphasis on the *jondo* genres than foreign composers, who had only a superficial knowledge of Spanish folk music and simply mimicked the lighter genres, especially the *jota* and *habanera*. This is also what distinguishes him from the eminent zarzuela composers of his time, such as Bretón, Vives, Chapí, and Chueca, whose stage works are animated by *zapateados*, *seguidillas*, *jotas*, *habaneras*, *boleros*, and *pasodobles* (as well as foreign dances like polkas, mazurkas, and waltzes); rarely do the Gypsy genres such as *bulerías*, *soleá*, or *siguiriyas* make an appearance in any serious way. Moreover, we must remember that, unlike Sarasate, Bretón, and even Granados, Albéniz avoided quoting folk melodies and preferred to compose his own. This is precisely what Debussy noted in 'El Albaicín', that Albéniz had not reproduced popular melodies but rather had 'absorbed them, listening until they have passed into his music, leaving no trace of a boundary line'. As Albéniz himself said, 'I never utilize the "raw material" in its crude state myself. You have only to listen to *Pepita* to

---

[34] In a letter to this author dated 21 Apr. 1992.

perceive that. What I like is to suggest our national rhythms, and infuse the spirit of our national melodies into my music.'[35]

This brings us to the second point, which is that Albéniz utilized not only the 'raw materials' but also the process of flamenco. Improvisation was central to his method of composition, and this is why his music has the freshness and spontaneity of the folk models that inspired it.[36] Many of his musical vignettes go beyond being mere 'souvenirs', for Albéniz pours much of himself into his pieces, in their effervescent gaiety and in their wistful reflection. He does not conceal himself behind a charming folkloric façade but actually reveals his inner self through it. In this sense he is more deeply romantic than a mere dispenser of exotic, escapist entertainment, for he infuses an autobiographical element into otherwise impersonal clichés. In short, much of his music possesses something approaching *duende*, the powerful emotion of *jondo* flamenco.

Though Albéniz's piano music sounds, therefore, very Spanish, when we examine it we immediately perceive that it is in fact an eclectic mixture of style elements from various sources, especially Chopin, Weber, Schumann, and, later, Debussy. But flamenco—all folk music, really—reflects an ongoing dialectic between 'high' and 'low' art, between upper and lower social classes, between foreign and native. Flamenco is a complexly syncretic blend of various traditions, Gypsy, Moorish, Jewish, native Spanish, and Latin American. And it has consistently borrowed elements from the European classical tradition both in guitar technique and harmony. It is not a static entity, frozen in time and place, but dynamic and ever-changing. So, Albéniz's eclecticism does not at all diminish the 'authentic' sound or feeling of much of his Spanish music. The music may be idealized, but it is based on essential musical and compositional ingredients that give it a certain genuineness. And it possesses the one ingredient Albéniz himself considered indispensable for the eclecticist—originality. The renowned author Miguel de Unamuno (1869–1936) could well have been writing of Albéniz when he stated that 'those whom many simple-minded folk regard as exotic spirits, anglicized, gallicized, Germanized, Norwegianized, are the ones whose roots intermingle the most closely with the roots of those who created the Spanish soul'.[37]

[35] From a letter to Herman Klein, who quoted it in his *Musicians and Mummers* (New York: Cassell, 1925), 256. Cited in Bevan, 'Albéniz', 204. Of course, on occasion he did directly quote folk songs, as in *Catalonia*, but this is merely an exception that proves the rule.

[36] Three of his improvisations survive on wax-cylinder recordings and are available on CD in *The Catalan Piano Tradition* (Vai Audio, VAIA/IPA 1001).

[37] From *Essays and Soliloquies* (New York: Knopf, 1925), cited in John Crow, *Spain: The Root and the Flower* (Berkeley and Los Angeles: University of California Press, 1985), 271.

Much is made of the fact that he was Catalan and that he necessarily wrote his flamenco-inspired music as an outsider peering through a prism of romanticism, that 'Andalusia [was] as musically strange to the Catalan Albéniz as the Hebrides to a Welshman'.[38] Again, though, this fails to take into account the fact that he spent an enormous amount of time touring in the south as a youth. It is safe to say that he knew that part of Spain as well as he knew the north. And one does not have to be from Andalusia to develop a deep understanding of its music, any more than one has to be from the Mississippi Delta region to sing the blues. Albéniz himself referred to this in a letter to Enrique Moragas[39] when he declared that

Malats, a Catalan, interprets like an Andalusian; Granados, from Lleida, becomes absorbed like no one else in the melancholy of the Andalusian fields; Miguel Llobet, the Barcelona guitarist bordering on the wondrous, surprises, not with Gypsy rhythms, but rather in the way he impresses on the strings of his guitar a stamp of elegant authenticity that is amazing.

This paradox, that through northern art music Albéniz approached so closely the spirit of southern folk music, is his most singular trait as a composer, one that only Falla possessed to as great a degree. The spontaneity, intensity, and immediacy of his work are not the hallmarks of an undeveloped talent but the true measure of his musical genius.

Albéniz is often spoken of in the same breath as Granados, and we have observed that there was a close and affectionate relationship between them. Certainly Granados's works contain the same melodic charm and rhythmic buoyancy as Albéniz's, and he was rather more successful than Albéniz on the stage.[40] But in terms of piano music, Granados never wrote anything comparable to *Iberia*, not even the wonderful *Goyescas*, which in fact reveals some influence from Albéniz's late style. In its emphasis on rhythm and sonority, *Iberia* lies at once firmly in the tradition of flamenco art and in the modern aesthetic. It occupies a singular position in the history of Spanish keyboard music. But it should not cause us to overlook his important contribution to

---

[38] J. Gibb, 'The Growth of National Schools', in D. Matthews (ed.), *Keyboard Music* (Harmondsworth, 1972), 291, cited in Bevan, 'Albéniz', 200.

[39] Cited in Llorens Cisteró, 'Inéditas', 101. 'Malats, catalán, interpreta como un andaluz; Granados, leridano, se asimila como nadie la melancolía de los campos andaluces; Miguel Llobet, que es el guitarrista barcelonés rayano con lo maravilloso, sorprende, no ya los ritmos gitanos, sino que imprime a las cuerdas de su guitarra un sello de casticidad elegante que asombra.'

[40] Granados was remarkably progressive in his approach to musical theatre, but the study of this part of his output has until recently been hampered by the loss of *María del Carmen* and what was thought to be the disappearance of the Catalan operas. The British musicologist Mark Larrad has recovered these latter works, which reveal a surprisingly advanced harmonic idiom. See that author's 'The Lyric Dramas of Enrique Granados (1867–1916)', *Revista de musicología*, 14/1–2 (1991), 149–66, and 'The Catalan Theatre Works of Enric Granados' (Ph.D. dissertation, University of Liverpool, 1991).

genres other than nationalist piano music, for Albéniz also revived the keyboard sonata in Spain and wrote the most successful Spanish orchestral music and concertos of the nineteenth century. Thus he laid the foundation for his successors who excelled in precisely these genres, especially Manuel de Falla.

If we consider Falla as the central point towards and from which we measure the progress of Spanish nationalism in music, Albéniz is Falla's most important predecessor. There is little of Granados in the music of Falla, for Granados drew his principal inspiration not from Andalusia but from Castile, Goya, and the eighteenth-century *tonadilla*. Falla owes an obvious debt to Albéniz in such masterpieces as *La vida breve* (1905), *Noches en los jardines de España* (1916), and *Fantasía bética* (1919) in their blending of southern Spanish folkore and elements of French modernism. Turina's style shift was the direct result of Albéniz's influence,[41] and in such guitar works as *Ráfaga*, *Fandanguillo*, and the Sonata reverberations of Albéniz's Franco-Hispanic style are clear. In the music of Joaquín Rodrigo (b. 1901) and Federico Moreno Torroba (1891–1982), we clearly hear the echoes of Albéniz's style. It was indeed he who defined what Spanish art music of our time should sound like. According to one of Spain's foremost pianists today, Antonio Ruíz-Pipó,

> When it is said that many composers of our century imitate his *españolismo*, that word is not understood in the true dimension of its definition. If they talk of the Spanish forms and melodies of Albéniz, it is because *he invented them and created a Hispanic idea of music* such that ... it persuades them to identify it with this country. (Emphasis added.)[42]

Turina put it more simply when he said, 'Our father Albéniz showed us the road that we had to follow.'[43]

His influence on French composers is harder to quantify. Given the deep impression he made on them, it would be surprising if a serious examination of this subject did not reveal that their debt to him was as great as his was to them. But that study has yet to be undertaken in a systematic fashion. Ricart Viñes used to play Albéniz's music for Debussy, and Jacqueline Kalfa suggests

---

[41] See 'Encuentro en Paris', Franco (ed.) *Albéniz y su tiempo*, 116. Turina states that after securing Albéniz's help with the publication of the Quintette, the master made him promise to stop writing that kind of music and to establish his art on the foundation of Spanish popular song—especially of Andalusia, as Turina was from Seville.

[42] *La voz de Galicia*, 26 Aug. 1994. 'Cuando se dice que muchos compositores de nuestro siglo imitaron su *españolismo* no se piensa en la verdadera dimensión de esa definición. Si se habla de las formas y las melodías españolas de Albéniz, es porque él las inventó y creó una idea hispánica de música puesto que ... logró que la identificasen con este país.'

[43] Cited in Antonio Fernández-Cid, 'Matices diferenciales y nexos afectivo-musicales de Enrique Granados e Isaac Albéniz', *Notas de música* (Boletín de la Fundación Isaac Albéniz), 1 (Dec. 1988), 18. 'Nuestro padre Albéniz nos mostraba el camino que habíamos de seguir.'

that 'Soirée dans Grenade' from *Estampes* (1903) might be indebted to Albéniz's influence, which she definitely perceives in Séverac's *Cerdaña* for piano (1910) and many of the works of Maurice Ohana.[44] The case of Ohana reminds us of his enormous impact on the repertoire for classical guitar. Albéniz died in the same year as Francisco Tárrega (b.1854) and just at the time when a young guitarist from Andalusia by the name of Andrés Segovia was preparing to take the music world by storm. Albéniz was a lover of the guitar and evidently played the instrument himself. Llobet was a close friend, as was his mentor Tárrega, who was coming of age as a concert artist in the 1880s along with Albéniz and who was the first to arrange his music for the guitar. Albéniz bequeathed a fortune in transcribable works to that instrument, and no guitar recital would be complete without some of his music. Guitarists have consequently returned the favour by giving his pre-*Iberia* piano works a degree of celebrity they would otherwise lack if they depended on the attentions of pianists alone. Though Albéniz wrote not a scrap of music for the guitar, his legacy is inextricably bound up with it.

Another important facet of Albéniz's legacy is his very humanity. Albéniz was a man of contradictions, of stoic self-discipline and of prodigal excess. He pinched pennies yet spent lavishly. He expended much time and energy attempting to restore his health through various therapies and diets, yet launched a relentless assault on his body through overindulgence in tobacco, alcohol, and food. Variety within logic was his motto, but variety at the expense of logic was often his way of life. Still, though he was a romantic, his atheism reflected a clear-eyed, rational approach to philosophical issues. In short, the classic and the romantic waged a constant struggle within him. *Iberia* certainly exemplifies his desire to contain the incessant flow of ideas in some rational formal context. But the resistless fecundity of his imagination often overwhelms any immediate impression of structural logic. An analogous conflict between truth and fantasy is readily apparent in his autobiographical dispensations. He was generous to a fault, but his generosity was made possible by the paternal figures on whom he depended for guidance and material support, and who perhaps filled a void left by the unhappy relationship with his own father. During his concert career, Albéniz composed pieces for his own performance that were charmingly evocative and sentimental. Yet, there was always a conservative, cautious, classicizing streak in his musical temperament. Thus, he generally avoided gratuitous displays of digital derring-do in his music, and on stage he retained a dignified reserve devoid of romantic posturing. The cerebral northerner coexisted with the

---

[44] 'Albéniz à Paris', 27–9, 33–6. Ohana (b. 1914) writes in a very avant-garde idiom, but his music is often inspired by flamenco, e.g. the *Tiento* for solo guitar (1955) and the Guitar Concerto (1958).

sentimental southerner; the fearless performer, with the self-doubting composer. In the event, this turned out to be a productive combination, as it
drove him to expand the domain of his compositional craft.

Albéniz's life, especially its fictional aspects, has become the stuff of legend,
and it is not surprising that movie makers have shown an interest in projecting
it on to the big screen. The first attempt, *Albéniz: Una vida inmortal*, was
produced by Sono Film in Argentina and premiered in 1947 in Buenos Aires.
It was directed by Luis César Amadori and starred Pedro López Lagar as the
composer and Sabina Olmos as Rosina. Michel Raux Deledicque believed
that, in spite of a few fabrications, it was well acted and produced and did credit
to the national film industry. A promotional flyer for the movie survives in the
archive and gives us some idea of its thrust. It shows a handsome and youthful-
looking Albéniz making 'bedroom eyes' at a glamorous Blanche Selva (played
by the pianist Marisa Regules) as she renders his *Iberia* at the piano.[45] As silly
as this seems, the movie was decidedly superior to the Spanish film of that same
year. *Serenata española*, directed by Juan de Orduña, took enormous liberties
with a story that was already sufficiently entertaining. Vicente Moya described
the movie as 'vulgar and crude' and said it was 'not a biography of Albéniz' but
instead pure fantasy. It showed him hanging around with an unattractive
assortment of 'drunks, Gypsies, and female dancers'.[46] In fact, both films
seem to have used Albéniz's life as a starting point for weaving an engaging
but fictional romantic tale. Hollywood almost got into the act with a film to be
based on the biography by Deledicque. The project, which never got off the
ground, was evidently the brainchild of the pianist José Iturbi.[47]

And yet, what is Albéniz's standing in Spain today? Had he been present in
spirit at his own funeral, he would have found the scene touching, and not a
little ironic. For Albéniz, one the most eloquent voices in the chorus of
Spanish national music, had had a complexly ambivalent relationship with
the public and critics in his homeland. Now that he was gone, however, all
was forgiven and forgotten. Or was it?

After Albéniz's death numerous attempts were made to establish memor-
ials in his honour and to convince the government to award him the Gran
Cruz de Alfonso XII.[48] But these efforts largely came to naught. The

[45] Mm, car. 3.
[46] Letter to Deledicque dated Barcelona, 19 Nov. 1947 (Mm, car. 2). Celin Romero, of the famous
Romero family guitar quartet, saw this movie in Spain and once asked this author if it was true Albéniz had
killed a Gypsy. The answer, of course, is no.
[47] Deledicque makes reference to this project in a letter to Moya dated 9 Oct. 1951 (Mm, car. 2). He
himself was in contact with Iturbi, but he never wrote to Moya to explain why these plans fell through.
[48] Clippings in the Mm, Arxiu premsa biogràfic 1872–1964, indicate that a commission was formed in
1923 to erect a monument to Albéniz in Madrid's Retiro park. Both Arbós and Vives were on it. In 1926 and
1931 commissions in Barcelona endeavoured to erect a monument on Montjuïc. Neither goal was apparently

centenary of Albéniz's birth in 1960 brought out the old resolutions to do him justice.[49] On 8 June a plaque was placed on his residence at 55 rue de Boulainvilliers in Paris. In July, concerts and an exposition took place in Camprodon, and the town established a small monument in his honour. Conferences and concerts were likewise held in Barcelona, and on 6 August there was a commemorative programme in Tiana. Yet, in the opinion of the Catalan musicologist Dr Montserrat Bergadà, there persists in Spain, especially in Catalonia, a decided ambivalence towards Albéniz.[50] There are few critical editions of his music, and there is no archive or museum devoted to the preservation and dissemination of his work.[51] Instead, when the family donated his archive to the city of Barcelona years ago, it was doled out in parcels to the Orfeó Català, Bibiloteca de Catalunya, and Museu de la Música. The correspondence and several scores were divided up between these archives, with their varying hours and facilities. The family hopes that eventually the collection will be reunited, but this is highly unlikely. There is a street named after him in the western end of town, but there are no streets, statues, or monuments dedicated to him in the areas tourists frequent. Indeed, visitors come and go in Barcelona without ever forming the idea that Albéniz—or, for that matter, Granados—had anything to do with the place. Where are the parks, statues, and historical plaques to remind them of the musical glory these two brought to the city? There is a Palau d'Albéniz on Montjuïc, which is a lovely structure. It was built for an exposition in 1930 and afterward fell into disuse. There were plans to convert it into a music museum, and the principal investor wanted to name it after his favourite composer, Albéniz. The plans fell through, but the name remained. Still, the palace has little to do with the most famous composer Catalonia ever produced.[52] There is a Teatro Albéniz near the Puerta del Sol in Madrid, but that likewise has little to do with him. Norway and the Czech Republic

accomplished. First mention of the Gran Cruz de Alfonso XII is made in a letter from Granados to Malats of 21 May 1909 (Mm, 10.031). *La vanguardia* (7 June 1909) confirmed that the proposal had been made to the Spanish government, but to the best of this author's knowledge, it was never awarded.

[49] Centenary memorabilia are in the Mm, car. 1.

[50] In a conversation with this author on 10 July 1995. She is the author of 'Les Pianistes catalans à Paris entre 1875 et 1925 (Contribution à l'étude des relations musicales entre la France et l'Espagne)' (thèse doctorat, Université François Rabelais, Tours, 1997).

[51] José Soler has edited a new edition of *Pepita Jiménez* (Madrid: Instituto Complutense de Ciencias Musicales, 1996), while one of *Merlin* by José María de Eusebio will soon appear (Valencia: Editorial Piles). Jacinto Torres and Guillermo González are preparing an urtext and facsimile edition of *Iberia*, soon to be published by Schott in Spain (EMEC-EDEMS). Antonio Iglesias has published a performance edition of this work (Madrid: Alpuerto, 1993). The Museu de la Música *does* have a lovely exhibit devoted to him that displays many of his personal items, including his monogrammed 1905 Rönisch piano. Albéniz was fond of Erard pianos as well.

[52] See José Tarin-Iglesias, *El Palacio de Pedralbes y el Palacete Albéniz* (Madrid: Editorial Patrimonio Nacional, 1974), 159.

have certainly done a better job of showcasing Grieg and Dvořák. Albéniz occasionally referred to Spain as 'mi morena ingrata' ('my ungrateful dark one'),[53] and in some respects this is still the case.

But after all, Albéniz chose to reside permanently outside of Spain. During the Franco dictatorship (1939–75) especially, Albéniz's love of France could not have earned him any points for loyalty. And though the most inflammatory passages in his diaries and correspondence were not published during the Franco era, his attitudes were no doubt generally known. Then, too, he was from a liberal, Masonic family of Basque and Catalan descent, and this would not have helped his case with the fascists. Yet, he cultivated *andalucismo* and was never a full-fledged exponent of Basque or Catalan musical nationalism. In a real sense, Albéniz comprised all of Spain in his ethnicity and music, but paradoxically he never found his place there. This was probably fortunate, for had he not moved to Paris, his art would never have risen to the heights it did. This is due not only to the associations he cultivated as a result, but also to the fact that public taste in Spain was oriented towards a much simpler type of music. One has to bear in mind that Spanish audiences were generally less educated and sophisticated than those in France, England, and Germany. The first performance of a Beethoven symphony did not take place in Madrid until 1866, and the public's overwhelming preference at orchestra concerts was for excerpts from Italian operas.[54] Chamber music died out under the influence of María Cristina (mother of Isabel II), who preferred salon music. This subsequently came into vogue among composers, especially at the Real Conservatorio (which she helped establish in 1830). This trend certainly made an impression on the young Albéniz, who wrote a great deal of salon music during his residence in Madrid.[55] The only other avenue open to young composers lay in the realm of zarzuela. But the zarzuela was primarily a commercial enterprise that conformed to the tastes of the public and resisted innovation, as Albéniz found out when he attempted to infuse even a few progressive features (such as recurring thematic ideas) into *San Antonio de la Florida*. We remember, for instance, that one Madrid critic accused him of being *demasiado extranjerizado*, or 'too foreignized'. The zarzuela was a bastion of *casticismo*, or 'genuine Spanishness', and tampering with it as Albéniz did was bound to elicit a negative response from the Madrid press. (Keep in mind, however, that the 'genuineness' of zarzuela was an illusion, as its music

---

[53] Laplane, *Albéniz*, 56.
[54] Lionel Salter, 'Spain: A Nation in Turbulence', in Jim Samson (ed.), *The Late Romantic Era*, Music and Society (Englewood Cliffs, NJ: Prentice Hall, 1991), 156.
[55] See Salazar, *La música contemporánea en España*, 117–53.

bore a strong imprint of Italian opera.) Had Albéniz remained in Spain, this was the public he would have had to placate, and his style would never have advanced beyond his first 'manner' (lovely though those pieces are). Yet by leaving, he incurred the resentment of those who felt that only composers who remained in the country should receive the public's support.

But regardless of his expatriate status, Albéniz occupies an important position in the cultural history of his homeland. There were essentially two philosophical camps in Spain around 1900. One wanted to insulate itself from the rest of Europe and preserve what it thought to be distinctly and uniquely Spanish in culture. This group frowned upon foreign influence as a kind of betrayal of national identity, of national pride. The other group sought to open Spanish culture up to the rest of Europe, just as it advocated a progressive political and economic agenda for a country in which there was a profound reverence for tradition and the old order.[56] Conservatives extolled Spain's imperial past and exaggerated her influence in the world. The government practised censorship and dismissed openly liberal professors from their university posts. It is easier in this context to understand Albéniz's derogation of patriotism as an 'egotistical sentiment' and not a 'virtue'. The folly of going to war with the United States simply to preserve Spanish 'honour' (out of a very real fear that backing down would incite a revolution) was a product of this mentality, which Albéniz condemned in his diary.[57] The political and cultural circumstances that gave rise to this disastrous conflict provoked a period of soul-searching, expressed by a group of authors known as the 'Generation of '98' (named after the year in which the war took place). Among them were some of the most famous men of Spanish letters, including Unamuno. As Falla scholar Carol Hess points out, these writers all

wrestled with the question of Spanish identity [and] all thought 'the problem of Spain' psychological in origin, rather than economic or political. For the Generation of '98 it was not only governmental ineptitude and religious fanaticism that had created moral stagnancy, but also the repeated denial of what it meant to be Spanish in the modern age.[58]

This certainly resonates strongly with Albéniz's diary entries on the subject of his homeland, and like him most of these thinkers advocated looking

---

[56] For a brilliant synthesis of this history, see Carol Hess, 'Manuel de Falla's *The Three-Cornered Hat* and the Advent of Modernism in Spain' (Ph.D. dissertation, University of California, Davis, 1994), 1–28.

[57] See George O'Toole, *The Spanish War* (New York: Norton, 1984). The Spanish policy of rounding up and confining peasants in Cuba to deny the revolutionaries support and supply was at least as provocative to US public opinion and business interests as the sinking of the *Maine*. The subsequent Spanish war effort was so inept that it would have been comical, were it not for the blood and treasure it wasted.

[58] Hess, 'Falla', 4.

outward towards the rest of Europe for guidance, particularly France. This cosmopolitan outlook was *modernismo*, which became the counterpoise to an inherently xenophobic *españolismo*. As Albéniz spent more time outside Spain and consequently came under the influence of Wagner and French music, he developed an increasing affinity with the modernists, especially in Barcelona.[59] Thus, Albéniz aligned himself with the forward-looking internationalists who sought a closer incorporation of Spain into European culture. Albéniz was not a kindred spirit of the Russophiles who disdained 'foreign entanglements', but rather of composers like Tchaikovsky, 'who wanted to join the outside world'.[60] Rodrigo (who studied with Dukas at the Schola Cantorum) has said of Albéniz that what he represents is 'the incorporation of Spain, or better said, the reincorporation of Spain into the European musical world'.[61] This was best summed up by Albéniz himself when he declared that Spanish composers ought 'to make Spanish music with a universal accent'.[62]

Iberia, then, exhibits a political and philosophical dimension we might otherwise overlook. It is more than beautiful music; in its novelty and scope it is a summing up of Albéniz's view of Spanish culture and its proper place in European civilization. But if we are to understand fully the appeal of Albéniz's Spanish pieces, especially *Iberia*, we must place them in the more personal context of his romantic nostalgia for a Spain that no longer exists, or never really existed at all. For his nostalgia is also ours, and this, more than the sum of its various parts, explains the enduring attraction of his music. In the words of Julián Gallego:

'El puerto' did not have that fresh happiness [and] 'Almería' never emitted so limpid a *copla*. . . . The dazzling 'Triana' on the piano is nothing like the New York suburb that we see today. Among cars and motorcycles, 'El Albaicín' has lost the profound charm of its silence. . . . 'Málaga' has been the victim of tourism and does not possess the simple musical grandeur it did when it was the provincial capital.[63]

[59] In the realm of painting, Darío de Regoyos y Valdés (1857–1913) pursued a course parallel to Albéniz's by residing in Paris and adopting elements of French impressionism in his depictions of Spanish subjects and scenes. There are six letters from Regoyos to Albéniz in the Bc ('R').

[60] Paraphrase of Paul Henry Lang (ed.), *The Symphony 1800–1900* (New York: Norton, 1969), pp. xxxiii–xxxiv.

[61] From the programme notes of a concert at the Liceu commemorating the centenary (Barcelona: Juan A. Pamias, 1960) (Mm, car. 1).

[62] See Ruiz Albéniz, *Albéniz*, 102, 'hacer música española con acento universal'.

[63] 'Albéniz: La España que (acaso) fue', *Notas de música* (Boletín de la Fundación Isaac Albéniz), 1 (Dec. 1988), 28. ' "El Puerto" no tuvo esa fresca alegría . . . "Almería" jamás lanzó esa copla tan límpida. . . . La rutilante "Triana" pianística poco tiene que ver con el suburbio neoyorkino que vemos hoy. Entre automóviles y motocicletas, "El Albaicín" ha perdido el hondo encanto de su silencio . . . "Málaga" ha sido víctima del turismo y no tiene aquella sencilla grandeza musical de cuando era capital de Provincia.'

So, in both Albéniz's life and his music we perceive a genuine dichotomy between fact and fiction, between the real and the imaginary—and between the old and the new. For the most enduring aspect of his legacy is that Albéniz participated in a movement of the Spanish spirit towards openness and progress and away from isolation and inertia. Albéniz was in the vanguard of those who helped Spain cross over from the past and embrace the future without losing a sense of its mythic identity, which is no less potent for residing in the imagination.

On 14 December 1935, less than a year before the ancient struggle between old and new in Spain would again turn ruinously violent, a group of Albéniz's admirers gathered at his tomb to dedicate a sculpture by Florencio Cuarían. Frank Marshall was in attendance along with other notables such as Rafael Moragas and Jaime Pahissa. But the most luminous votary present was the poet and playwright Federico García Lorca (1898–1936), whose extraordinary life was soon to be brutally sacrificed on the altar of civil war. Lorca wrote for the occasion a touching epitaph for Albéniz, the last two stanzas of which complete our portrait of this great man.

> Oh sweet death of a little hand!
> Oh music and goodness intertwined!
> Oh eye of the goshawk, pure of heart!
> Sleep in forgetfulness of your old life!
>
> Sleep sky without end, shy snow.
> Dream winter of fire, grey summer.
> Sleep in forgetfulness of your old life![64]

[64] Cuarían's sculpture is no longer at the tomb, and the author does not know its location. Lorca was murdered by the fascists on 18 Aug. 1936 in Granada. This poem, a sonnet, is reproduced in *ABC*, 18 Feb. 1972, and in Franco (ed.), *Imágenes de Isaac Albéniz*, 48. A reproduction of the original handwritten copy appears in this latter source as well as in José Subirá, *Historia de la música española e hispanoamericana* (Barcelona: Salvat, 1953), 797. '¡Oh dulce muerto de pequeña mano! | ¡Oh música y bondad entretejida! | ¡Oh pupila de azor, corazón sano! | ¡Duerme en olvido de tu vieja vida! | Duerme cielo sin fin, nieve tendida. | Sueña invierno de lumbre, gris verano. | ¡Duerme en olvido de tu vieja vida!'

Appendix I

Father's Side

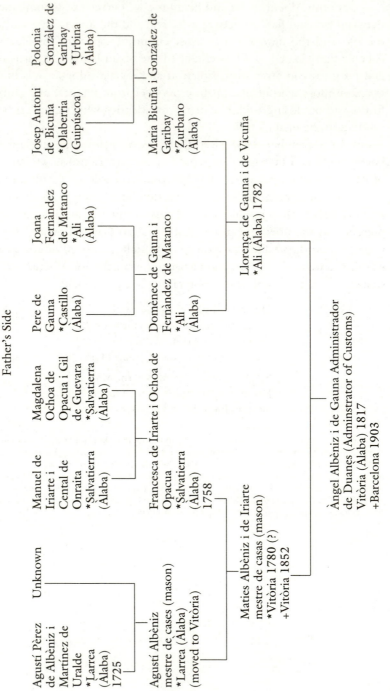

Mother's Side

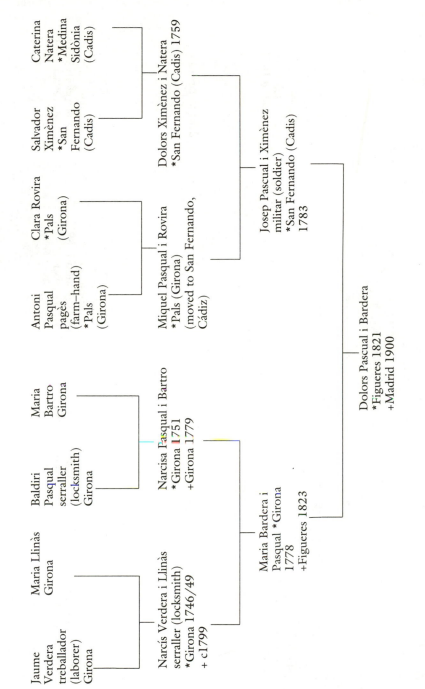

294

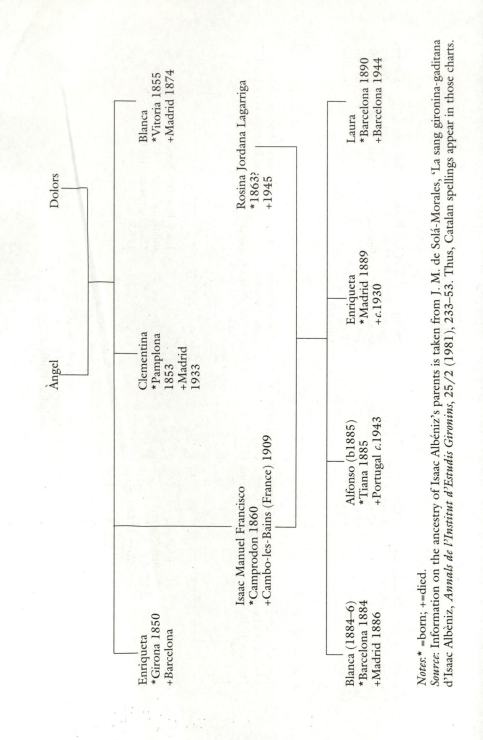

 Àngel

Dolors

Enriqueta
*Girona 1850
+Barcelona

Clementina
*Pamplona
1853
+Madrid
1933

Blanca
*Vitoria 1855
+Madrid 1874

Isaac Manuel Francisco
*Camprodon 1860
+Cambo-les-Bains (France) 1909

Rosina Jordana Lagarriga
*1863?
+1945

Blanca (1884–6)
*Barcelona 1884
+Madrid 1886

Alfonso (b1885)
*Tiana 1885
+Portugal c.1943

Enriqueta
*Madrid 1889
+c.1930

Laura
*Barcelona 1890
+Barcelona 1944

Notes: * =born; +=died.
Source: Information on the ancestry of Isaac Albéniz's parents is taken from J. M. de Solá-Morales, 'La sang gironina-gaditana d'Isaac Albéniz, Annals de l'Institut d'Estudis Gironins, 25/2 (1981), 233–53. Thus, Catalan spellings appear in those charts.

Appendix II
List of Works

The following compilation is greatly indebted to the work of Jacinto Torres Mulas, *MGG* (new edition, Personenteil), s.v. 'Albéniz' (works list), which in turn is based on his *Catálogo sistemático descriptivo de las obras musicales de Isaac Albéniz* (unpublished). The author thanks Prof. Torres for sharing his work in advance of its publication. In addition to the author's own research, the list below borrows from the work of Baytelman, Bevan, Falces Sierra, and Laplane. Opus numbers have little validity and are not used. The works are organized first by medium and then in approximate chronological order by date of composition. Works from the same year are listed alphabetically. Publication information pertains to first editions. Alternate titles from later editions appear after the original title. The location of any manuscripts is given in brackets at the end of the entry.

1. Piano Works

Marcha militar (1869). Madrid: Calcografía de B. Eslava, 1869.

Rapsodia cubana (1881). Madrid: Antonio Romero, 1886.

Pavana-capricho, also called *Pavane espagnole* (1882). Madrid: Benito Zozaya, c.1885.

Serenata napolitana (1882). Lost.

Fantasía sobre motivos de la jota (c.1883). Lost (perhaps an improvisation).

Barcarola, also called *Barcarolle catalane* (c.1884). Barcelona: Valentín de Haas, 1884.

Seis pequeños valses (c.1884). Barcelona: R. Guardia, 1884.

Sonata 1 (c.1884). Barcelona: R. Guardia?, 1884 (only Scherzo extant).

Deseo. Estudio de concierto (c.1885). Madrid: Antonio Romero, 1886.

Dos caprichos andaluces (c.1885). Lost (perhaps used in the first *Suite española*).

Dos grandes estudios de concierto (c.1885). Lost (possibly *Deseo* and *Estudio impromptu*).

Estudio impromptu (c.1885). Madrid: Antonio Romero, 1886.

First Mazurka, Second Mazurka (c.1885). London: Stanley Lucas, Weber & Co., 1890 (same as Nos. 1 and 2 of *Seis mazurkas de salón*).

Marcha nupcial (c.1885). Lost.

Seis mazurkas de salón (c.1885). 1: 'Isabel'. 2: 'Casilda'. 3: 'Aurora'. 4: 'Sofía'. 5: 'Christa'. 6: 'María'. Madrid: Antonio Romero, 1886 (Nos. 1 and 2 same as First and Second Mazurkas).

Serenata árabe (c.1885). Madrid: Antonio Romero, 1886.

Suite ancienne [1] (c.1885). 1: 'Gavota'. 2: 'Minuetto'. Madrid: Antonio Romero, 1886.

Suite morisca (c.1885). 1: 'Marcha de la caravana'. 2: 'La noche'. 3: 'Danza de las esclavas'. 4: 'Zambra'. Lost.

Siete estudios en los tonos naturales mayores (c.1886). Madrid: Antonio Romero, 1886.

Suite española [1] (*c*.1886). 1: 'Granada (Serenata)'. 2: 'Cataluña (Curranda)'. 3: 'Sevilla (Sevillanas)'. 4: 'Cádiz (Saeta, Canción, or Serenata)' [same as *Serenata española*]. 5: 'Asturias (Leyenda)' [same as No. 1 of *Chants d'Espagne*]. 6: 'Aragón (Fantasía)' [same as No. 1 of *Deux Morceaux caractéristiques*]. 7: 'Castilla (Seguidillas)' [same as No. 5 of *Chants d'Espagne*]. 8: 'Cuba (Capricho or Nocturno)'. The original suite consisted of all eight titles but only four scores, for Nos. 1, 2, 3, and 8 (No. 3 composed before 1886, Nos. 1, 2, 8, in 1886). These were published separately in Madrid: Benito Zozaya, 1886 (Nos. 1 and 3) and 1892 (Nos. 2 and 8). The other numbers were later added to the suite by Hofmeister in 1911, and had originally appeared under the titles in brackets. [Mc, Nos. 2 and 8 only]

Angustia: Romanza sin palabras (1886). Madrid: Antonio Romero, 1886.

Balbina valverde (Polka brillante) (1886). Madrid: Antonio Romero, 1886 (under pseud. Príncipe Weisse Vogel).

Diva sin par (Mazurka-capricho) (1886) Madrid: Antonio Romero, 1886 (under pseud. Príncipe Weisse Vogel).

Minuetto 3 (1886). Madrid: Antonio Romero, 1886.

Sonata 2 (1886). Lost.

Suite ancienne 2 (1886). 1: 'Sarabande'. 2: 'Chacona'. Madrid: Antonio Romero, 1886.

Suite ancienne 3 (1886). 1: 'Minuetto'. 2: 'Gavota'. Madrid: Antonio Romero, 1887.

Andalucía (Bolero) (1886–7). London: Joseph Williams, 1899 (same as No. 5 of *Recuerdos de viaje*).

On the Water (Barcarole) (1886–7). London: Stanley Lucas, Weber & Co., *c*.1892 (same as No. 1 of *Recuerdos de viaje*).

Recuerdos de viaje (1886–7). 1: 'En el mar (Barcarola)' [same as *On the Water*]. 2: 'Leyenda (Barcarola)'. 3: 'Alborada'. 4: 'En la Alhambra'. 5: 'Puerta de tierra (Bolero)' [same as *Andalucía (Bolero)*]. 6. 'Rumores de la caleta (Malagueña)'. 7: 'En la playa'. Madrid: Antonio Romero, 1886–7.

Mazurka de salón (*c*.1887). Barcelona: Juan Ayné, 1887.

Menuet (G Minor) (*c*.1887). Paris: Alphonse Leduc, 1922 (in *Dix Pièces en un recueil*).

Rapsodia española (solo-piano version) (*c*.1887). Madrid: Antonio Romero, 1887.

Recuerdos (Mazurka) (*c*.1887). Barcelona: Juan Ayné, 1887.

Cotillón. Album de danzas de salón (1887). 1: 'Champagne (Carte Blanche), vals de salón' [also called *Champagne vals* or *Cotillon valse*]. Madrid: Antonio Romero, 1887.

Pavana fácil para manos pequeñas (1887). Madrid: Antonio Romero, 1887.

Seis danzas españolas (1887). Madrid: Antonio Romero, 1887.

Sonata 3 (1887). 1: Allegretto. 2: Andante. 3: Allegro assai. Madrid: Antonio Romero, 1887.

Sonata 4 (1887). 1: Allegro. 2: 'Scherzino' (Allegro). 3: 'Minuetto' (Andantino). 4: 'Rondó' (Allegro). Madrid: Antonio Romero, 1887.

Sonata 5 (1887). 1: Allegro non troppo. 2: 'Minuetto del gallo' (Allegro assai). 3: 'Rêverie' (Andante). 4: Allegro. Madrid: Antonio Romero, 1887.

Sonata 6 (*c*.1888?). Lost.

Sonata 7 (*c*.1888). Madrid: Unión Musical Española, 1962 (only Minuetto extant).

Dos mazurkas de salón (1888). 1: 'Amalia'. 2: 'Ricordatti'. Madrid: Benito Zozaya, 1892.

Douze Pièces caractéristiques, also called *Doce piezas características* (1888). 1: 'Gavotte'. 2: 'Minuetto a Silvia'. 3: 'Barcarolle (Ciel sans nuages)' ['Barcarola (Cielo sin nubes)']. 4: 'Prière' ['Plegaria']. 5: 'Conchita (Polka)'. 6: 'Pilar (Valse)'. 7: 'Zambra'. 8: 'Pavana'. 9: 'Polonesa'. 10: 'Mazurka'. 11: 'Staccato (Capricho)'. 12: 'Torre Bermeja (Serenata)'. Madrid: Antonio Romero, 1888–9.

La fiesta de aldea (1888). Madrid: Unión Musical Española, 1973 (piano reduction of No. 1 from *Escenas sinfónicas catalanas*). [Lc]

Deux Morceaux caractéristiques, also called *Deux Dances espagnoles, Dos danzas españolas*, and *Spanish National Songs* (*c*.1889). 1: 'Jota aragonesa' [same as No. 6 of first *Suite española*]. 2. 'Tango'. London: Stanley Lucas, Weber & Co., 1889; Paris: Max Eschig, 1889.

Suite española 2, also called *Seconde Suite espagnole* (*c*.1889). 1: 'Zaragoza (Capricho)'. 2: 'Sevilla (Capricho)'. Madrid: Antonio Romero, 1889.

Cádiz-gaditana (*c*.1890). London: Joseph Williams?, 1890?

Serenata española, also called *Célèbre Sérénade espagnole* (*c*.1890). Barcelona: Juan Bautista Pujol y Cía., 1890 (same as No. 4 of first *Suite española*).

España: Six Feuilles d'album, also called *España: Seis hojas de album* (1890). 1. 'Prélude'. 2. 'Tango'. 3. 'Malagueña'. 4. 'Serenata'. 5. 'Capricho catalán'. 6. 'Zortzico'. London: Pitts & Hatzfield, 1890.

L'Automne (Valse) (1890). Barcelona: Juan Bautista Pujol y Cía, 1890.

Mallorca (Barcarola) (1890). London: Stanley Lucas, Weber & Co., 1891.

Rêves, also called *Sueños* (1890–1). 1: 'Berceuse'. 2: 'Scherzino'. 3: 'Chant d'amour' ['Canto de amor']. London: Stanley Lucas, Weber & Co., *c*.1891.

Zambra granadina (Danse orientale) (*c*.1891). London: Carlo Ducci & Co., *c*.1891.

Zortzico (*c*.1891). Paris: Édition Mutuelle, *c*.1911.

Album of Miniatures, also called *Les Saisons* (1892). 1. 'Spring' ['Le Printemps']. 2. 'Summer' ['L'Été']. 3. 'Autumn' ['L'Automne']. 4. 'Winter' ['L'Hiver'] London: Chappell & Co., 1892.

Chants d'Espagne, also called *Cantos de España* (1891–4). 1. 'Prélude' [same as no. 5 of first *Suite española*]. 2. 'Orientale' 3. 'Sous le palmier (Danse espagnole)'. 4. 'Córdoba'. 5. 'Seguidillas' [same as No. 7 of first *Suite española*]. Barcelona: Juan Bautista Pujol y Cía., 1892 (Nos. 1–3) and 1897 (Nos. 4–5).

Espagne: Souvenirs (1896–7). 1: 'Prélude'. 2: 'Asturias'. Barcelona: Universo Musical, 1897.

The Alhambra: Suite pour le piano (1897). 1. 'La Vega'. San Sebastián: A. Díaz y Cía., 1908 (same as MS in Mm entitled *Fantasie espagnole pour le piano* of 1898). [Bc]

Iberia: 12 nouvelles 'impressions' en quatre cahiers (1905–8). 1er Cahier: 'Evocación' ['Prélude']; 'El puerto'; 'Fête-Dieu à Séville' ['El Corpus en Sevilla']. 2me Cahier: 'Rondeña'; 'Almería'; 'Triana'. 3e Cahier: 'El Albaicín'; 'El polo'; 'Lavapiés'. 4^{e}

Cahier: 'Málaga'; 'Jerez'; 'Eritaña'. Paris: Édition Mutuelle, 1906–8. [Bc, Oc, Mm, Lc]

Yvonne en visite! (*c.*1908). 1: 'La Révérence'. 2: 'Joyeuse Rencontre et quelques penibles événements'. Paris: Rouart, Lerolle et Cie, 1909.

Azulejos (1909). 1: 'Preludio'. Paris: Édition Mutuelle, 1911 (posthumous, completed by Enric Granados).

Navarra (1909). Paris: Édition Mutuelle, 1912 (posthumous, completed by Déodat de Séverac).

2. Stage Works

Cuanto más viejo (Sr. Zapino), zarzuela, one act (1881–2; premiered Bilbao, Coliseo, 1882). Lost.

Catalanes de gracia (Leopoldo Palomino de Guzmán), zarzuela, one act (1882; premiered Madrid, Teatro Salón Eslava, 1882). Lost.

El canto de salvación (author?), zarzuela, two acts (1882?). Lost.

Poèmes d'amour (Paul-Armand Sylvestre), incidental music (1892; premiered Barnes, Lyric Club, 1892). [Bc, Mm]

'Oh! Horror! Horror!' (Harry Greenbank), finale of Act II of operetta *Incognita* (original by Charles Lecocq, *Le Cœur et la main*) (1892; premiered London, Lyric Theatre, 1892). Vocal score pub. London: Hopwood & Crew, 1892.

The Magic Opal (Arthur Law), lyric comedy in two acts (1892; premiered London, Lyric Theatre, 1893). Vocal score pub. London: Joseph Williams, 1893. Revised as *The Magic Ring* (London, Prince of Wales's Theatre, 1893) and in Spanish as *La sortija* (Madrid, Teatro de la Zarzuela, 1894). [Bc]

Poor Jonathan (H. Wittmann, J. Bauer, Harry Greenbank), operetta, two acts, 16 (?) additional numbers (original by Karl Millöcker, *Der arme Jonathan*) (1893; premiered London, Prince of Wales's Theatre, 1893). [Bc]

San Antonio de la Florida (Eusebio Sierra), zarzuela, one act (1894; premiered Madrid, Teatro de Apolo, 1894; produced in French as *L'Ermitage fleuri*, Brussels, Théâtre Royal de la Monnaie, 1905). Vocal score pub. Barcelona: Juan Bautista Pujol y Cía., 1894. [Bc, Mm, Oc, Se]

Henry Clifford (Francis B. Money-Coutts), opera in three acts (1893–5; premiered in Italian as *Enrico Clifford*, Barcelona, Liceu, 1895). Vocal score pub. Barcelona: Juan Bautista Pujol y Cía., 1895. [Bc, Mm, Oc]

Pepita Jiménez (Francis B. Money-Coutts, after novel by Juan Valera), lyric comedy in two acts (1895 first version in one act; premiered in Italian, Barcelona, Liceu, 1896; 1896 second version expanded to two acts and produced in German, Prague, Neues Deutsches Landestheater, 1897; reorchestrated 1899–1902 and produced in French, Brussels, Théâtre Royal de la Monnaie, 1905). Vocal and orch. scores pub. Leipzig: Breitkopf und Härtel, 1896 and 1904 [Bc, Mm, Am]. Revised by Pablo Sorozábal as opera in three acts and premiered Madrid, Teatro de la Zarzuela, 1964. [Bn, Se]

Mar y cel (Àngel Guimerà), opera (1897), incomplete. [Bc]

King Arthur (Francis B. Money-Coutts), operatic trilogy: *Merlin*, *Launcelot* (incomplete), *Guenevere* (incomplete). *Merlin*, opera, three acts (1897–1902; premiered in concert version Brussels, 1905, and staged Barcelona, Liceu, 1950). Vocal score pub. Paris: Édition Mutuelle, 1906. [Bc, Mm]

La Sérénade (author?), lyric drama (1899), incomplete. [Bc, Mm]

La real hembra (Cristóbal de Castro), zarzuela in three acts (1902), incomplete. [Bc]

La morena (Alfred Mortier), lyric drama (1905), incomplete. [Bc]

The Song of Songs (Francis B. Money-Coutts), incidental music (1905), incomplete. [Mm]

3. Vocal Works

Solo voice and piano:

Cuatro romanzas para mezzo-soprano (*c.*1886). Lost.

Tres romanzas catalanas (*c.*1886). Lost.

Rimas de Bécquer (Gustavo Adolfo Bécquer, *c.*1886). 1: 'Besa el aura'. 2: 'Del salón en el ángulo oscuro'. 3. 'Me ha herido recatándose en la sombra'. 4: 'Cuando sobre el pecho inclinas'. 5: '¿De dónde vengo?' Madrid: Benito Zozaya, 1892.

Seis baladas (Marquesa de Bolaños, 1887). 1: 'Barcarola'. 2: 'La lontananza'. 3: 'Una rosa in dono'. 4: 'Il tuo sguardo'. 5: 'Moriro!!' 6: 'T'ho riveduto in sogno'. Madrid: Antonio Romero, *c.*1889.

'Il en est de l'amour' (M. Costa de Beauregard, 1892). Paris-Baudoux: T. Cée, n.d.

Deux Morceaux de prose de Pierre Loti (*c.*1895). 1: 'Crépuscule'. 2: 'Tristesse'. San Sebastián: A. Diaz y Cía., 1897.

To Nellie: Six Songs (Francis B. Money-Coutts, 1896). 1: 'Home'. 2: 'Counsel'. 3: 'May-Day Song'. 4: 'To Nellie'. 5: 'A Song of Consolation'. 6. 'A Song'. Paris: Au Ménestrel-Heugel & Cie., 1896?

'Chanson de Barberine' (Alfred de Musset, *c.*1897). Madrid: Unión Musical Española, 1972.

'The Gifts of the Gods' (Francis B. Money-Coutts, *c.*1897). Brussels: Dogilbert, 1897.

Six Songs (Francis B. Money-Coutts, 1897). Only two extant: 2. 'Will you be mine?'. 3. 'Separated'. Madrid: Instituto de Bibliografía Musical, 1997. [Oc]

Conseil tenu par les rats (*c.*1900, only 15 bars). [Bc]

'The Caterpiller' (Francis B. Money-Coutts, 1903). Paris: Édition Mutuelle, 1913 (with 'The Gifts of the Gods', in English and French, trans. Henry Varley, entitled 'La Chenille' and 'Les Dons des dieux').

'Art thou gone for ever, Elaine?' (Francis B. Money-Coutts, 1906). Madrid: Instituto de Bibliografía Musical, 1997. [Ah]

Quatre Mélodies (Francis B. Money-Coutts, 1908, in English and French, trans. M. D. Calvocoressi). 1: 'In Sickness and Health' ('Quand je te vois souffrir'). 2: 'Paradise Regained' ('Le Paradis retrouvé'). 3: 'The Retreat' ('Le Refuge'). 4: 'Amor summa injuria'. Paris: Rouart, Lerolle et Cie., 1909.

Chorus and orchestra:
El Cristo (*c*.1886), oratorio. Lost.
Lo Llacsó (Apel.les Mestres, 1896), symphonic poem for orch., chorus, soloists, incomplete. [Bc]

Chorus alone:
Salmo VI: Oficio de difuntos (1885) for SATB chorus. Madrid: Instituto de Biblio-grafía Musical, 1994. [Mc]

4. *Orchestral Works*

Piano Concerto No. 1 in A minor ('Concierto fantástico') (1886–7). Madrid: Unión Musical Española, *c*.1890 (2 pianos) and 1975 (orch.).
Rapsodia española for piano and orchestra (1886–7). Madrid: Antonio Romero, 1887 (2 pianos) and Instituto de Bibliografía Musical, 1997 (original orchestration reconstructed by Jacinto Torres).
Suite característica (*c*.1887). 1: 'Scherzo'. 2: 'En la Alhambra'. 3: 'Rapsodia cubana'. Lost. Presumably orchestrations of the solo-piano versions.
Escenas sinfónicas catalanas (1888–9). 1: 'Fête villageoise catalane'. 2: 'Idilio'. 3: 'Serenata'. 4: 'Finale: Baile campestre'. [Mm]
L'Automne (*Valse*) (*c*.1890). Orchestration of the solo-piano version. [Oc]
Célèbre Sérénade espagnole (*c*.1891). Barcelona: Juan Bautista Pujol y Cía., n.d.
Piano Concerto No. 2 (1892), incomplete. [Bc]
La Alhambra (1896). 1: 'La vega'. 2: 'Lindaraja'. 3: 'Generalife'. 4: 'Zambra'. 5. '¡Alarme!' 6. No title. Nos. 1 and 3 incomplete, others titles only. [Bc]
Petite Suite (1898): 1: 'Sérénade Lorraine'. [Oc]
Rapsodia Almogávar (1899), incomplete. Initial version of *Catalonia*. [Bc]
Catalonia: Suite populaire pour orchestre en trois parties (1899). Only first number, 'Catalonia', completed. Paris: A. Durand & Fils, 1899. [Bc]
Guajira (*Chant populaire cubain*) (1905), incomplete. [Bc]
El puerto (1907). Orchestration of 'El puerto', *Iberia*. [Bc]

5. *Chamber Works*

Concert Suite for sextet (*c*.1883). 1: 'Scherzo'. 2: 'Serenata morisca'. 3: 'Capricho cubano'. Lost. Probably strongly resembled the later *Suite característica* for orchestra.
Trio in F for piano, violin, and cello (*c*.1885). Lost.
Berceuse (1890) for piano, violin, and cello. London: Stanley Lucas, Weber & Co., *c*.1892. Arrangement of 'Bereuse', *Rêves*.

Bibliography

ABBATE, CAROLYN, and PARKER, ROGER (eds.), *Analyzing Opera* (Berkeley and Los Angeles: University of California Press, 1989).

Admissions to Trinity College Cambridge, v: *1851–1900* (London: Macmillan & Co., 1913).

ALBÉNIZ, ISAAC, *Impresiones y diarios de viaje*, ed. Enrique Franco (Madrid: Fundación Isaac Albéniz, 1990).

ALIÉR, ROGER, 'Musical Life in Barcelona 1888–1936', in *Homage to Barcelona: The City and its Art 1888–1936* (London: The Arts Council of Great Britain, 1985), 277–84.

ALONSO, CELSA, 'Nazionalismo spagnolo e a vanguardia: la presunta praticabilità dell' Impressionismo', *Musica/Realtà* 15/44 (1994), 81–106.

ANDRADE DE SILVA, TOMÁS, 'El piano de Albéniz', *Música* (Revista de los Conservatorios), 2 (Oct.–Dec. 1952), 71–82.

Annuaire du Conservatoire Royal de Musique de Bruxelles, vols. i–iv (1877–80), (Brussels: Librairie Européenne C. Muquardt, 1878–81).

APARICIA, MARÍA PILAR, ' "Pepita Jiménez", correspondencia Valera–Albéniz', *Boletín de la Real Academia Española* (1975); repr. in Enrique Franco (ed.), *Albéniz y su tiempo* (Madrid: Fundación Isaac Albéniz, 1990), 80–100.

ARBÓS, ENRIQUE F., *Arbós* (Madrid: Ediciones Cid, 1963); excerpt entitled 'Santander, 1883' appears in Enrique Franco (ed.), *Albéniz y su tiempo* (Madrid: Fundación Isaac Albéniz, 1990), 63–7.

AVIÑOA, XOSÉ, *Albéniz*, Conocer y Reconocer la Música de (Mexico City: Daimon, 1986).

—— *La música i el modernismo* (Barcelona: Ediciones Curial, 1985).

BARCE, RAMÓN, 'La ópera y la zarzuela en el siglo XIX', in *España en la música de Occidente: Actas del Congreso Internacional celebrado en Salamanca 29 de octubre–5 de noviembre de 1985*, ii (Madrid: Instituto Nacional de las Artes Escénicas y de la Música, 1987), 145–53.

BAYTELMAN POLA, *Isaac Albéniz: Chronological List and Thematic Catalog of his Piano Works*, Detroit Studies in Music Bibliography, 72 (Warren, Mich.: Harmonie Park Press, 1993).

BERGADÀ, MONTSERRAT, 'Les Pianistes catalans à Paris entre 1875 et 1925 (Contribution à l'étude des relations musicales entre la France et l'Espagnole)' (thèse doctorat, Université François Rabelais, Tours, 1997).

BEVAN, CLIFFORD, 'Albéniz, Money-Coutts and "La Parenthèse londonienne" ' (Ph.D. dissertation, University of London, 1994).

BOSQUET, ÉMILE, *La Musique de clavier* (Brussels: Les Amis de la Musique, 1953).

BRETÓN, TOMÁS, *Diario 1881–1888*, 2 vols., ed. Jacinto Torres Mulas (Madrid: Acento Editorial, 1994).

BRETÓN, TOMÁS, 'En la muerte de Albéniz', *ABC* (21 May 1909), 4–5; repr. in Enrique Franco (ed.), *Albéniz y su tiempo* (Madrid: Fundación Isaac Albéniz, 1990), 121–4.

BRODY, ELAINE, *Paris: The Musical Kaleidoscope 1870–1925* (New York: George Braziller, 1987).

Burke's Peerage (London: Burke's Peerage, 1970), s.v. 'Latymer'.

CAMPÉ, R., DUMON, M., and JESPERS, J. J., *Radioscopie de la presse belge* (Verviers: André Gérard, 1975).

CAROL-BÉRARD, M., 'La Souvenir d'Albéniz à Paris', *La Semaine à Paris*, 139 (23–30 Jan. 1925), 35–7.

CARR, RAYMOND, *Spain 1808–1975*, 2nd edn. (Oxford: Clarendon Press, 1982).

CARREIRA, XOAN M., 'Centralismo y periferia en el teatro musical español del siglo XIX', in *España en la música de Occidente: Actas del Congreso Internacional celebrado en Salamanca 29 de octubre–5 de noviembre de 1985*, ii (Madrid: Instituto Nacional de las Artes Escénicas y de la Música, 1987), 155–72.

CASTELLÁ, CONDESA DE, *La Suite Iberia* (Barcelona, n.d.).

CHASE, GILBERT, *The Music of Spain* (New York: Norton, 1941).

CLARK, WALTER AARON, 'Albéniz en Leipzig y Bruselas: Nuevas luces sobre una vieja historia', *Revista de musicología*, 14/1–2 (1991), 213–18.

—— 'Albéniz in Leipzig and Brussels: New Data from Conservatory Records', *Inter-American Music Review*, 11/1 (Fall–Winter, 1990), 113–17.

—— '"Cavalleria Iberica" Reassessed: Critical Reception of Isaac Albéniz's Opera *Pepita Jiménez*', *Actas del XV Congreso de la Sociedad Internacional de Musicología*, in *Revista de musicología* 16/6 (1993), 3255–62.

—— *Isaac Albéniz: A Guide to Research* (New York: Garland Publishing, 1998).

—— 'Isaac Albéniz's Faustian Pact: A Study in Patronage', *Musical Quarterly*, 76/4 (Dec. 1992), 465–87.

—— 'Recent Researches in Spanish Music 1800 to the Present', *Inter-American Music Review* 16/1 (Summer–Fall 1997), 85–94.

—— '"Spanish Music with a Universal Accent": Isaac Albéniz's Opera *Pepita Jiménez*' (Ph.D. dissertation, University of California, Los Angeles, 1992).

COLLET, HENRI, *Albéniz et Granados* (Paris: Librairie Félix Alcan, 1926; rev. edn., Paris: Éditions Le Bon Plaisir, 1948; repr. Paris: Éditions d'Aujourd'hui, 1982); Spanish trans. by P. E. F. Labrousse (Buenos Aires: Tor-SRL, 1948).

—— 'Isaac Albéniz y Joaquín Malats', *Revista musical catalana*, 6/72 (Dec. 1909), 377–9.

—— 'Isaac Albéniz', in *L'Essor de la musique espagnole* (Paris: Éditions Max Eschig, 1929), 50–7.

—— 'La Musique espagnole moderne', *Bulletin français de la Société Internationale de Musique*, 4/3 (15 Mar. 1908), 272–90; 4/9 (15 Sept. 1908), 951–84.

—— 'La Renaissance musicale espagnole', in *Encyclopédie de la musique*, iv (Paris: Librairie Delagrave, 1920 edn.), 2481–2.

CORDA, GIOVANA, *Journaux quotidiens belges de langue française en cours de parution* (Brussels: Commission Belge de Bibliographie, 1986).

CORREDOR, J. M., *Conversations with Casals*, trans. André Mangeot (New York: E. P. Dutton, 1956).

COUTTS, FRANCIS, *Egypt and Other Poems* (London: John Lane, 1912).

—— *Ventures in Thought* (London: John Lane, 1915).

CROW, JOHN A., *Spain: The Root and the Flower*, 3rd edn. (Berkeley and Los Angeles: University of California Press, 1985).

DAHLHAUS, CARL, *Nineteenth-Century Music*, trans. J. Bradford Robinson (Berkeley and Los Angeles: University of California Press, 1989).

Debrett's Peerage & Baronetage (London: Macmillan, 1990), s.v. 'Latymer'.

DEBUSSY, CLAUDE, 'Concerts Colonne: Société des Nouveaux Concerts', *Bulletin français de la Société Internationale de Musique*, 9/12 (1 Dec. 1913), 42–4.

Deutscher Bühnen-Spielplan (Leipzig: Breitkopf und Härtel, 1896–1905).

Dictionary of National Biography (1886 edn.), s.v. 'Burdett, Sir Francis'.

Dictionary of National Biography (1912 edn.), s.v. 'Burdett-Coutts, Angela Georgina'.

Dod's Peerage, Baronetage, Knightage, Etc. (London: Dod's Peerage, 1923), s.v. 'Latymer'.

DOMENECH, ESPAÑOL M., 'Isaac Albéniz', *Revista de música* (Buenos Aires), 2 (1928), 150–5.

ESPERANZA Y SOLA, JOSÉ MARÍA, 'Concierto en el salón Romero de Madrid', *La ilustración musical* (1886); repr. in Enrique Franco (ed.), *Albéniz y su tiempo* (Madrid: Fundación Isaac Albéniz, 1990), 69–72.

ESPINÓS, VÍCTOR, *El maestro Arbós* (Madrid: Espasa-Calpe, 1942).

FALCES SIERRA, MARTA, 'Albéniz en Inglaterra: Una etapa oscura', *Revista de musicología*, 14/1–2 (1991), 214–19.

—— *El Pacto de Fausto: Estudio lingüístico-documental de los lieder ingleses de Albéniz sobre poemas de Francis Money-Coutts* (Granada: Universidad de Granada, 1993).

FALLA, MANUEL DE, *On Music and Musicians*, trans. David Urman and J. M. Thomson (London: Marion Boyars, 1979).

FERNÁNDEZ-CID, ANTONIO, *La música española en el siglo XX* (Madrid: Publicaciones de la Fundación Juan March, 1973).

—— 'Matices diferenciales y nexos afectivo-musicales de Enrique Granados e Isaac Albéniz', *Notas de música* (Boletín de la Fundación Isaac Albéniz), 1 (Dec. 1988), 16–19.

FISHTINE, EDITH, 'Don Juan Valera the Critic' (Ph.D. dissertation, Bryn Mawr College, 1933).

FORNET, EMILIO, *Isaac Albéniz*, Figuras de la Raza, 2/24 (Madrid: A. Marzo, 1927).

FRANCO, ENRIQUE (ed.), *Albéniz y su tiempo* (Madrid: Fundación Isaac Albéniz, 1990).

—— *Imágenes de Isaac Albéniz* (Madrid: Fundación Isaac Albéniz, 1988).

Franco, Enrique, 'La Suite Iberia di Isaac Albéniz', *Nuova rivista musicale italiana*, 7 (1973), 51–74.

Gallego, Antonio, 'Isaac Albéniz y el editor Zozaya', *Notas de música* (Boletín de la Fundación Isaac Albéniz), 2–3 (Apr.–June 1989), 6–14.

Gallego, Julián, 'Albéniz: La España que (acaso) fue', *Notas de música* (Boletín de la Fundación Isaac Albéniz), 1 (Dec. 1988), 27–8.

Gauthier, André, *Albéniz*, trans. from French to Spanish by Felipe Ximénez de Sandoval (Madrid: Espasa-Calpe, 1978).

Gilson, Paul, 'Albéniz à Bruxelles', in *Notes de musique et souvenirs* (Brussels: Collection Voilà, 1924), 11–19; repr. (in Spanish) in Enrique Franco (ed.), *Albéniz y su tiempo* (Madrid: Fundación Isaac Albéniz, 1990), 29–32.

Givanel i Mas, Joan, *Bibliografia catalana premsa*, 3 vols. (Barcelona: Institució Patxot, 1931).

Gómez Amat, Carlos, *Historia de la música española*, v: *Siglo XIX* (Madrid: Alianza Música, 1984).

Goodman, Andrew, *Gilbert and Sullivan's London* (Tunbridge Wells: Spellmount Ltd., 1988).

Grew, Sydney, 'The Music of Albéniz for Piano-forte', *Chesterian*, 6/42 (1924), 43–8.

Grout, Donald J., *A Short History of Opera*, 3rd edn. (New York: Columbia University Press, 1988).

Grunfeld, Frederic V., *The Art and Times of the Guitar* (New York: Macmillan, 1974).

Guerra y Alarcón, Antonio, *Isaac Albéniz: Notas crítico-biográficas de tan eminente pianista* (Madrid: Escuela Tipográfica del Hospicio, 1886); extract in G. Arteaga y Pereira (ed.), *Celebridades musicales* (Barcelona: Centro Editorial Artístico, 1886), 650–2; original repr. Madrid: Fundación Isaac Albéniz, 1990.

Guzmán, Juan Pérez, 'Los Albéniz', *La época* (21 May 1909); repr. in Enrique Franco (ed.), *Albéniz y su tiempo* (Madrid: Fundación Isaac Albéniz, 1990), 23–8.

Healy, Edna, *Coutts & Co. 1692–1992: The Portrait of a Private Bank* (London: Hodder & Stoughton, 1992).

Henken, John, 'Francisco Asenjo Barbieri and the Nineteenth-Century Revival in Spanish National Music (Ph.D. dissertation, University of California, Los Angeles, 1987).

—— 'Ópera española versus Zarzuela: A Nineteenth-Century Grudge Match', *Opera Journal*, 21/1 (1988), 13–22.

Heras, Antonio de las, *Vida de Albéniz* (Barcelona: Ediciones Patria, 1940).

Hess, Carol Ann, *Enrique Granados: A Bio-bibliography* (New York: Greenwood Press, 1991).

—— 'Manuel de Falla's *The Three-Cornered Hat* and the Advent of Modernism in Spain' (Ph.D. dissertation, University of California, Davis, 1994).

Howard, Diana, *London Theatres and Music Halls 1850–1950* (London: Library Association Publishing, Ltd., 1970).

HUGHES, ROBERT, *Barcelona* (New York: Alfred A. Knopf, 1992).

IGLESIAS, ANTONIO, *De la dificultad del gran piano de Isaac Albéniz* (Madrid: Editorial Alpuerto, 1988).

—— *En torno a Isaac Albéniz y su 'Iberia'* (Madrid: Real Academia de Bellas Artes de San Fernando, 1992).

—— 'Isaac Albéniz', in *Enciclopedia Salvat de los grandes compositores*, iv (Pamplona: Salvat SA de Ediciones, 1982), 230–50.

—— *Isaac Albéniz (su obra para piano)*, 2 vols. (Madrid: Editorial Alpuerto, 1987).

—— *La ópera en España: Su problemática. VII Ducena de Música en Toledo 17–26 mayo 1975* (Madrid: Ministerio de Educación y Ciencia, Dirección General del Patrimonio Artístico y Cultural, Comisaria Nacional de la Música, 1976).

ISTEL, EDGAR, 'Isaac Albéniz', trans. Frederick H. Martens, *Musical Quarterly*, 15 (1929), 117–48.

JANKÉLÉVITCH, VLADIMIR, 'Albéniz et l'état de verve', in *Mélanges d'histoire et d'esthétique musicales: Offerts à Paul-Marie Masson*, i (Paris: Bibliothèque d'Études Musicales, 1955), 197–209.

—— *La Présence lointaine: Albéniz, Sévérac, Mompou* (Paris: Éditions du Seuil, 1983).

JEAN-AUBRY, GEORGES, 'Isaac Albéniz (1860–1909)', *Musical Times*, 58 (1917), 535–8.

—— *La Musique et les nations* (London: J. et W. Chester, 1922; Buenos Aires, 1946), 89–112 (reprint of an article dated 1912. Source unidentified).

—— *Les Musiciens célèbres*, ed. Jean Lacroix (Geneva: Éditions Contemporaines, 1946).

—— *Notices sur quelques compositeurs contemporains* (no publisher or date; bears a dedication to Albéniz dated 1910).

KALFA, JACQUELINE, 'Isaac Albéniz à Paris', *Revue internationale de musique française*, 9/26 (June 1988), 19–37.

—— 'Inspiration hispanique et écriture pianistique dans *Iberia* d'Isaac Albéniz' (thèse de 3ᵉ cycle de musicologie, Université de Paris-Sorbonne, 1980).

KIRK, H. L., *Pablo Casals* (New York: Holt, Rinehart & Winston, 1974).

KLEIN, HERMAN, 'Music and Musicians: *Pepita Jiménez*', *Sunday Times* (5 Jan. 1896).

—— *Musicians and Mummers* (New York: Cassell, 1925).

—— 'Albéniz's Opera "Pepita Jiménez"', *Musical Times* (1 Mar. 1918), 116–17.

KRAUSE, WILLIAM CRAIG, 'The Life and works of Federico Moreno Torroba' (Ph.D. dissertation, Washington University, 1993).

LAPLANE, GABRIEL, *Albéniz, sa vie, son œuvre*, preface by Francis Poulenc (Geneva: Éditions du Milieu du Monde, 1956); *Albéniz: Vida y obra de un músico genial*, trans. from French to Spanish by Bernabé Herrero and Alberto de Michelena (Paris: Editorial Noguer, 1958).

LARRAD, MARK, 'The Catalan Theatre Works of Enric Granados' (Ph.D. dissertation, University of Liverpool, 1991).

—— 'The Lyric Dramas of Enrique Granados (1867–1916)', *Revista de musicología*, 14/1–2 (1991), 149–66.

LATYMER, LORD, *Chances and Changes* (Edinburgh: William Blackwood & Sons, 1931).

LEBRUN, VERA, 'A Great Spanish Composer', *Radio Times* (17 Apr. 1936), 11.

LIVERMORE, ANN, *A Short History of Spanish Music* (New York: Vienna House, 1972).

LLONGUERES, JOAN, 'Cómo conocí a Isaac Albéniz', in *Evocaciones y recuerdos* (Barcelona: Dalmau, 1944); repr. in Enrique Franco (ed.), *Albéniz y su tiempo* (Madrid: Fundación Isaac Albéniz, 1990), 111–13.

LLOPIS, ARTURO, 'En el centenario de Isaac Albéniz', *Destino* (13 Feb. 1960), 13–17.

LLORENS CISTERÓ, JOSÉ MARÍA, 'El "Lied" en la obra musical de Isaac Albéniz', *Anuario musical*, 15 (1960), 123–40.

—— 'Isaac Albéniz a través de unas cartas inéditas', *San Jorge*, 38 (Apr. 1960), 26–31.

—— 'Notas inéditas sobre el virtuosismo de Isaac Albéniz y su producción pianística', *Anuario musical*, 14 (1959), 91–113.

LONG, MARGUERITE, *At the Piano with Gabriel Fauré*, trans. Olive Senior-Ellis (London: Kahn & Averill, 1980).

LUCENA, LUIS SECO, 'En la Alhambra', *Cuadernos de la Alhambra* (Granada, 1982); repr. in Enrique Franco (ed.), *Albéniz y su tiempo* (Madrid: Fundación Isaac Albéniz, 1990), 105–9.

Madrid en sus diarios, 5 vols. (Madrid: Instituto de Estudios Madrileños, 1961–72).

MANDER, RAYMOND, and MITCHENSON, JOE, *The Theatres of London* (London: Harvest Books, 1963).

MANOLL, MICHEL, 'Albéniz, virtuose ambulant', in Pierre Hiegel (ed.), *Sur les pas des musiciens* (Paris: Les Éditions de l'Illustration, 1967).

MARCO, TOMÁS, *Historia de la música española*, vi: *Siglo XX* (Madrid: Alianza Música, 1983).

MARLIAVE, JOSEPH DE, *Études musicales* (Paris: Librairie Félix Alcan, 1917), 119–38; repr. in Enrique Franco (ed.), *Albéniz y su tiempo* (Madrid: Fundación Isaac Albéniz, 1990), 33–40.

MARTÍNEZ, JULIA, *Falla. Granados. Albéniz*, [series:] Temas españoles, 6, 2nd edn. (Madrid: Publicaciones Españolas, 1959).

MAST, PAUL BUCK, 'Style and Structure in "Iberia" by Isaac Albéniz' (Ph.D. dissertation, University of Rochester, Eastman School of Music, 1974).

MENÉNDEZ ALEYXANDRE, ARTURO, *Albéniz, primer universalizador de la música española* (Barcelona: Gráf Valero, 1960).

MINOR, MARTHA D., 'Hispanic Influences on the Works of French Composers of the Nineteenth and Twentieth Centuries' (Ph.D. dissertation, University of Kansas, 1983).

MITJANA, RAFAEL, 'Merlín', *Revista musical de Bilbao* (Oct. 1902); repr. in Rafael Mitjana, *¡Para música vamos!* (Valencia: Casa Editorial F. Sempere, 1909), 202–7; repr. in Enrique Franco (ed.), *Albéniz y su tiempo* (Madrid: Fundación Isaac Albéniz, 1990), 77–80.

MONEY-COUTTS, FRANCIS BURDETT, *King Arthur: A Trilogy of Lyrical Dramas Founded on the Morte d'Arthur of Sir Thomas Malory* (London: John Lane, 1897).

MONTERO ALONSO, JOSÉ, *Albéniz: España en 'suite'* (Barcelona: Silex, 1988).

MONTESINOS, JOSÉ F., *Valera o la ficción libre* (Madrid: Editorial Gredos, 1957).

MORAGAS, RAFAEL, 'Epistolario inédito de Isaac Albéniz', *Música*, 1/5 (May–June 1938), 38–45.

MORALES, PEDRO G., 'Notes for an Essay on Albéniz', in Felix Aprahamian (ed.), *Essays on Music* (London: Cassell & Co., 1967), 5–9.

MORPHY, GUILLERMO, 'Porvenir de los compositores españoles', *La correspondencia de España* (30 Dec. 1894).

MOYA, MIGUEL, 'Isaac Albéniz', *El liberal* (25 Jan. 1886).

'Necrologie', *Bulletin français de la Société Internationale de Musique*, 5/7 (15 July 1909), 717.

NECTOUX, JEAN-MICHEL, 'Albéniz et Fauré: Correspondance inédite', *Tilas* (Travaux de l'Institut d'Études Ibériques et Latino-américaines) (Strasbourg, 1977), 159–86.

NEWMAN, ERNEST, 'Albéniz and his "Merlin"', *New Witness*, 10/254 (20 Sept. 1917), 495–6.

NEWMAN, WILLIAM S., *The Sonata since Beethoven* (Chapel Hill: University of North Carolina Press, 1969).

PAHISSA, JAIME, *Sendas y cumbres de la música española* (Buenos Aires: Librería Hachette, 1954).

PASARELL, EMILIO J., *Esculcando el siglo XIX en Puerto Rico* (Barcelona: Ediciones Rumbos, 1967).

PEDRELL, FELIP(E), 'Albéniz: El hombre, el artista, la obra', in *Músicos contemporáneos y de otros tiempos* (Paris: P. Ollendorf, 1910), 375–81; also in *Revista musical catalana*, 6 (May 1909), 180–4 (in Catalan); and in *La vanguardia* (15 June 1909).

—— 'Isaac Albéniz', in *Diccionario biográfico y bibliográfico de músicos y escritores de música*, vol. i (Barcelona: V. Berdós y Feliu, 1894).

—— 'Concierto de Albéniz', *La ilustración musical española*, 1/14 (15 Aug. 1888); repr. in Enrique Franco (ed.), *Albéniz y su tiempo* (Madrid: Fundación Isaac Albéniz, 1990), 63–7.

PENA, JOAQUIM, 'Musichs que fugen', *Joventut*, 3 (1902), 383–5.

PEÑA Y GOÑI, ANTONIO, *España, desde la ópera a la zarzuela*, ed. Eduardo Rincón (Madrid: Alianza Editorial, 1967).

PINSART, GÉRARD, 'Louis Brassin et la vie musicale à Bruxelles de 1860 à 1880', *Annales du XLIIIe Congrès de la Fédération des Cercles d'Archéologie et d'Histoire de Belgique, Sint-Niklaas 1974* (1975), 457–62.

PISTONE, DANIÈLE, 'Paris et la musique, 1890–1900', *Revue internationale de musique française*, 10/28 (Feb. 1989), 7–56.

PLÁ, JOSEP, 'El poeta Moréas y Albéniz', *La vida de Manolo contada por él mismo* (Barcelona: Ediciones Destino, 1947); excerpted in Enrique Franco (ed.), *Imágenes de Isaac Albéniz* (Madrid: Fundación Isaac Albéniz, 1988), 17–19.

POHREN, DONN E., *Lives and Legends of Flamenco* (Madrid: Society of Spanish Studies, 1988).

—— *The Art of Flamenco* (Shaftesbury: Musical New Services Ltd., 1984).

POWELL, LINTON E., *A History of Spanish Piano Music* (Bloomington: Indiana University Press, 1980).

PRECKLER, MERCEDES TRICÁS (ed.), *Cartas de Paul Dukas a Laura Albéniz* (Bellaterra: Universidad Autónoma de Barcelona, 1983).

RAUX DELEDICQUE, MICHEL, *Albéniz, su vida inquieta y ardorosa* (Buenos Aires: Ediciones Peuser, 1950).

REDFORD, JOHN ROBERT, 'The Application of Spanish Folk Music in the Piano Suite "Iberia" by Isaac Albéniz' (DMA document, University of Arizona, 1994).

REIG, RAMÓN, 'Isaac Albéniz', *Revista de Gerona*, 5/6 (primer trimestre de 1959), 55–6.

REVERTER, ARTURO, 'Albéniz–Arbós: Amistad, relación musical, escenarios', *Notas de música* (Boletín de la Fundación Isaac Albéniz), 2–3 (Apr.–June 1989), 23–7.

RODA, CECILIO DE, 'La "Suite" Iberia', *Programas de conciertos, Sociedad Madrileña* (1911–13); repr. in Enrique Franco (ed.), *Albéniz y su tiempo* (Madrid: Fundación Isaac Albéniz, 1990), 73–6.

ROGERS, P. P., and LAPUENTE, F. A., *Diccionario de seudónimos literarios españoles*, (Madrid: Editorial Gredos, 1977).

RUBINSTEIN, ARTHUR, *My Young Years* (New York: Alfred A. Knopf, 1973).

RUIZ ALBÉNIZ, VÍCTOR, *Isaac Albéniz* (Madrid: Comisaría General de Música, 1948).

RUIZ TARAZONA, ANDRÉS, *Isaac Albéniz: España soñada* (Madrid: Real Musical, 1975).

SAGARDÍA, ÁNGEL, *Albéniz*, Gent Nostra, 46 (Barcelona: Editions de Nou Art Thor, 1986).

—— *Isaac Albéniz* [series:] Hijos ilustres de España (Plasencia, Cáceres: Editorial Sanchez Rodrigo, 1951).

SAINT-JEAN, J., 'Isaac Albéniz (1860–1909)', *Revue française de musique*, 10/1 (1912), 3–16, 79–83.

SALAZAR, ADOLFO, 'Isaac Albéniz y los albores del renacimiento musical en España', *Revista de Occidente*, 12/34 (Apr.–June 1926), 99–107.

—— *La música contemporánea en España* (Madrid: Ediciones La Nave, 1930).

—— *Música y músicos de hoy: Ensayos sobre la música actual* (Madrid: Editorial Mundo Latino, 1928).

SALES, JULES, *Théâtre Royal de la Monnaie 1856–1970* (Nivelles: Éditions Havaux, 1971).

SALTER, LIONEL, 'Spain: A Nation in Turbulence', in Jim Samson (ed.), *The Late Romantic Era: From the Mid-19th Century to World War I*, Music and Society (Englewood Cliffs, NJ: Prentice-Hall, 1991), 151–66.

SALVAT, JOAN, 'Epistolari dels nostres músics: Isaac Albéniz a Joaquim Malats', *Revista musical catalana*, 30/357 (Sept. 1933), 364–72; repr. in Enrique Franco (ed.), *Albéniz y su tiempo* (Madrid: Fundación Isaac Albéniz, 1990), 129–36.

SAPERAS, MIQUEL, *Cinc compositors catalans: Nicolau, Vives, Mossèn Romeu, Lamote, Albéniz* (Barcelona: Josep Porter, 1975).

SCHONBERG, HAROLD C., *The Great Pianists* (New York: Simon & Schuster, 1987).

SCHREINER, CLAUS (ed.), *Flamenco: Gypsy Dance and Music from Andalusia*, trans. Mollie Comerford Peters (Portland, Ore.: Amadeus Press, 1990).

SEIFERT, W., 'In Memoriam', *Musica* (German), 13 (June 1959), 402–3.

SELLECK-HARRISON, MARIA B., 'A Pedagogical and Analytical Study of "Granada" ("Serenata"), "Sevilla" ("Sevillanas"), "Asturias" ("Leyenda") and "Castilla" ("Seguidillas") from the *Suite española*, Opus 47 by Isaac Albéniz' (DMA essay, University of Miami, 1992).

'Señor Albéniz at Home', *Pall Mall Gazette* (30 Jan. 1891), 1–2.

SERRA CRESPO, JOSÉ, *Senderos espirituales de Albéniz y Debussy* (Mexico City: Costa Amic, 1944).

SHAW, BERNARD, Shaw's Music: The Complete Musical Criticism in Three Volumes, ed. Dan H. Laurence (New York: Dodd, Mead & Co., 1981).

SMITH, RHEA MARSH, *Spain: A Modern History* (Ann Arbor: University of Michigan Press, 1965).

SOLÀ-MORALES, J. M. de, 'La sang gironina-gaditana d'Isaac Albèniz', *Annals de l'Institut d'Estudis Gironins*, 25/2 (1981), 233–53.

SOPEÑA, FEDERICO, *Dos años de música en Europa* (Madrid: Espasa-Calpe, 1942).

—— 'Gracia y drama en la vida de Isaac Albéniz', *Historia y vida*, 2/12 (Mar. 1969), 122–33.

—— *Historia de la música*, 2nd edn. (Madrid: Ediciones y Publicaciones Españolas SA, 1954).

SOROZÁBAL, PABLO, *Mi vida y mi obra* (Madrid: Fundación Banco Exterior, 1986).

STOKES, VERONICA, *A Bank in Four Centuries* (Derby: Bemrose Security Printing, 1982).

TARIN-IGLESIAS, JOSÉ, *El Palacio de Pedralbes y el Palacete Albéniz* (Madrid: Editorial Patrimonio Nacional, 1974).

TASIS, RAFAEL, and TORRENT, JOAN, *Historia de la premsa catalana* (Barcelona: Editorial Bruguesa, 1966).

TORRES MULAS, JACINTO, 'Catálogo sistemático descriptivo de las obras musicales de Isaac Albéniz' (unpublished).

—— 'Concentración vs. dispersión de fondos documentales. El desdichado caso de Isaac Albéniz', *El patrimonio musical: Los archivos familiares (1898–1936)* (Trujillo, Cáceres: Ediciones de la Coria, 1997).

—— 'El largo sueño de Pepita Jiménez', liner notes for *Pepita Jiménez* (Harmonia Mundi CD HMC 901537, 1995).

—— 'Isaac Albéniz en los infiernos', *Scherzo*, 80 (Dec. 1993), 150–3.

—— 'La inspiración "Clásica" de Isaac Albéniz', liner notes for *Isaac Albéniz: Sonatas para piano no 3, 4, 5/L'Automne* (Harmonia Mundi CD HMI 987007, 1994).

—— 'La metamorfosis de Isaac Albéniz: De intérprete a creador', liner notes for *Albéniz: Klavierwerke* (Koch-Schwann CD 3-1513-2, 1996).

TORRES MULAS, JACINTO, 'La producción escénica de Isaac Albéniz', *Revista de Musicología*, 14/1–2 (1991), 167–212.

—— *Las publicaciones periódicas musicales en España (1812–1990): Estudio crítico-bibliográfico* (Madrid: Instituto de Bibliografía Musical, 1991).

—— Liner notes for *Suite española* No. 1 and *Chants d'Espagne*, arranged for two guitars (Opera Tres CD 1026-ope, 1997).

—— 'Música y masonería en España', in J. A. Ferrer Benimeli (co-ord.), *La masonería española entre Europa y América: VI Symposium Internacional de Historia de la Masonería Española*, 2 vols. (Zaragoza: Gobierno de Aragón, Dept°. de Educación y Cultura, 1995), ii. 769–813.

—— 'Un desconocido "Salmo de difuntos" de Isaac Albéniz', *Revista de musicología*, 13/1 (Jan.–June 1990), 279–93.

TURINA, JOAQUÍN, 'Encuentro en Paris', *Arriba* (14 Jan. 1949); repr. in Enrique Franco (ed.), *Albéniz y su tiempo* (Madrid: Fundación Isaac Albéniz, 1990), 115–16.

VALERA, JUAN, *Pepita Jiménez*, ed. Francisco Muñoz Marquina (Madrid: Editorial Burdeos, 1987).

—— *Pepita Jiménez*, trans. Harriet de Onís (New York: Barron's Educational Series, 1964).

VAN LOO, ESTHER, 'La Vie picaresque d'Isaac Albéniz (1860–1909)', *Musica* (chaix), 67 (Oct. 1959), 35–8.

VAN VECHTEN, CARL, 'Isaac Albéniz', in *Excavations* (New York: Alfred A. Knopf, 1926).

VERASTEGUI, ALEJANDRO DE, 'Isaac Albéniz, oriundo Vitoriano', *Boletín de la Real Sociedad Vascongada de los Amigos del País*, 17/1 (San Sebastían: Museo de San Telmo, 1961), 43–9.

VERONA PAUL, 'The Iberia suite of Isaac Albéniz: performance practice of a problematic masterpiece revealed through the interpolation of flamenco forms with transcedental technique' (DMA thesis, Manhattan School of Music, 1991).

VILLALBA MUÑOZ, P. LUIS, 'Imagen distanciada de un compositor-pianista', *Gaceta de Mallorca* (1909); repr. in Enrique Franco (ed.), *Albéniz y su tiempo* (Madrid: Fundación Isaac Albéniz, 1990), 51–61.

—— *Últimos músicos españoles del siglo XIX* (Madrid: Ildefonso Alier, 1914).

VILLAR, ROGELIO, 'Isaac Albéniz', in *Músicos españoles*, i (Madrid: Ediciones 'Mateu', 1918, 73–9).

VINCENT, MARY, and STRADLING, R. A., *Cultural Atlas of Spain and Portugal* (Abingdon: Andromeda Oxford Ltd., 1995).

WATELET, JEAN, *Presse des spectacles, 1747–1939* (Paris: Bibliothèque Nationale, 1974).

WEARING, J. P., *The London Stage, 1890–1899*, i: *1890–1896* (Metuchen, NJ: The Scarecrow Press, 1976).

ZAMORA LUCAS, FLORENTINO, and CASADO JORGE, MARÍA, *Publicaciones periódicas existentes en la Biblioteca Nacional* (Madrid: Ministerio de Educación Nacional, 1952).

Index of Works

General Index

Teatro Fuencarral, production of *San Antonio de la Florida* at 268
Teatro Lope de Vega, Albéniz's concerts at 28
Thalberg, Sigismond, Albéniz compared to 82
Théâtre Royal de la Monnaie, production of *L'Hermitage fleuri* at 220
production of *Pepita Jiménez* at 220–1
Thibaud, Jacques 264
Thomas, Brandon 95 n.
Toro, Albéniz's concerts in 30
Torres Mulas, Jacinto 7, 70
Torroba, Federico Moreno, influence of Albéniz on 5, 272 n., 284
Toulon, Albéniz's concerts in 56
Tourville, Charles 95
Tragó, José 250
Trio Iberia 252
Turina, Joaquín 227
assistance from Albéniz to 253
influence of Albéniz on 5, 284
performance by of *Iberia* 253

Ubeda, Albéniz's concerts in 28
Unamuno, Miguel de 282, 289
Universal Exposition, *see* Exposición Universal in Barcelona 72
Unspruch, Anton 167
Utrillo, Miquel 207 n.

Valencia, Albéniz's concerts in 27, 51
Valera, Carmen 143, 271
Valera, Juan 136, 211–12
Asclepigenia 142
correspondence of with Albéniz 139–43
El maestro Raimundico 141
Lo mejor del tesoro 141–2

opinion of novel and opera *Carmen* 141
Pepita Jiménez 136–7
Valladolid, Albéniz's concerts in 27, 28 30
Venta Eritaña 64, 247
Verdi, Giuseppe, influence on Albéniz of 129
Vianna da Motta, José 202, 250
Vieuxtemps, Henri 36
Vigo, Albéniz's concerts in 51, 53, 58
Villalba, Albéniz's concerts in 27
Viñes, Ricart 16–17
Vitoria, Albéniz's concerts in 40, 74
Vives, Amadeu 160, 206, 208, 281
Artus 181
Vizconde del Bruch 26
Vogrich, Max, *König Arthur* 181

Wagner, Richard 264
Albéniz's opinion of works of 180–1
Die Götterdämmerung 2, 181
impact in Barcelona of 207–8
importance to Albéniz of 209
influence of in *Henry Clifford* 132
influence of the *Ring* by in *Merlin* 184
works performed by Albéniz 39, 57, 76
Weber, Carl Maria, works performed by Albéniz 32, 83
Widor, Charles-Marie 75
Wright, Frank Lloyd 1

Ysaÿe, Eugène 83

Zamora, Albéniz's concerts in 27
Zapino, Sr. 48
Zaragoza, Albéniz's concerts in 27, 47, 61
zarzuela 114, 288–9
Zozaya, Benito 57, 62
Zuloaga, Ignacio 74, 205